OVY 8 91

12-08
11 ~@ 7-45
20

Analytical Index

to Publications of the

TEXAS
FOLKLORE
SOCIETY

VOLUMES 1-36

JAMES T. BRATCHER

SOUTHERN METHODIST UNIVERSITY PRESS · DALLAS · 1973

Library of Congress Catalog Card No. 72-97597

ISBN *0-87074-135-7*

TYPOGRAPHICAL
ADVISOR

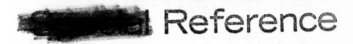

FOR MORRIS COOK AND MABEL MAJOR

J. FRANK DOBIE
Secretary-Editor, 1923-1943

LEONIDAS WARREN PAYNE, JR.
Founder

STITH THOMPSON
First editor for the Society

JOHN AVERY LOMAX
Founder

MODY C. BOATRIGHT
Secretary-Editor, 1943-1963

WILSON M. HUDSON
Secretary-Editor 1964-1971

J. FRANK DOBIE

FRANCIS EDWARD ABERNETHY
Secretary-Editor, 1971-

The Folk-Lore Society of Texas

PRESIDENT

DR. L. W. PAYNE, JR.
The University of Texas, Austin.

VICE-PRESIDENTS

JUDD MORTIMER LEWIS,
The Houston Post, Houston.

HON. EDWARD ROTAN,
Waco.

MRS. LILLIE T. SHAVER,
Southwestern Normal, San Marcos.

SECRETARY

JOHN A. LOMAX,
The Agricultural and Mechanical College of Texas, College Station.

TREASURER

MISS ETHEL HIBBS,
Rosenberg Library, Galveston.

COUNCILLORS

HON. THEO. G. LEMMON, Dallas.

MRS. JOSEPH B. DIBRELL, Seguin.

MRS. C. C. GARRETT, Brenham.

The Texas Folk-Lore Society was organized at Dallas, Texas, December 29, 1909, with a membership of sixty-six, the list of charter members being held open until April 1, 1910. The constitution provides for four kinds of members:

1. **Annual Members,** or those who pay an initiation fee of fifty cents and annual dues of twenty-five cents.

2. **Annual Members with Journal Privileges,** or those who pay, through the Texas Folk-Lore Society, Three Dollars as the annual subscription price of the "Journal of American Folk-Lore," thereby becoming members of the Texas Folk-Lore Society and of the American Folk-Lore Society without the payment of any additional fee.

3. **Life Members,** or those who shall at any one time pay Five Dollars into the treasury of the society.

4. **Patrons,** or those who shall at any one time donate Twenty-Five Dollars to the furtherance of the work of the society.

All members shall have equal voice in the organization. An annual meeting will be held at such time and place as the Executive Board may decide. The official organ of this society will be the "Journal of American Folk-Lore," and, as has been previously mentioned, members of the Texas Folk-Lore Society, by the payment of an additional fee of $2.25, become subscribers to this Journal and also members of the National organization, and can thus keep intelligently informed about the work being done throughout America. The Journal will publish from time to time the results of the work in Texas; particularly, it is expected, the important papers read at the annual meetings will be given a place in its pages.

FOLK-LORE IN TEXAS.

Songs and Ballads.—Many people sing songs learned from their parents or neighbors and that have, as far as known, never been printed. A collec-

TABLE OF
CONTENTS

Part I: *Specialized Indexes*

Part II: *Tale Synopses*

Part III: *Alphabetical Index*

ix

FOREWORD

⟋⟍ THE CAUSE OF FOLKLORE studies should benefit by the appearance of Mr. Bratcher's index to the first thirty-six numbered volumes of our Publications. He has undertaken to prepare his index in order to make the resources of our annuals readily available to folklore scholars all over the world. The Society has assembled a wealth of material which only the analysis and tabulation of an index will reveal in its variety and scope.

When the Texas Folklore Society was organized in 1909, the standard techniques now employed by specialists in folklore had not yet come into use. The editor of the Society's first volume, Stith Thompson, became in time America's foremost scholar in the field of folklore. Among his contributions are his revision and amplification of Aarne's *Types of the Folk-Tale* and his own monumental *Motif-Index of Folk-Literature*. The second editor for the Society, J. Frank Dobie, did not employ numbers for the designation of tale types and motifs after these techniques were taken up by folklorists, nor did Mody Boatright, Dobie's successor, think it necessary to insert numbers in the material which he edited. Numbers did not begin to appear in the Society's Publications until 1951. The result is that much of the Society's early material has been neglected by scholars in search of this or that tale type or motif. Mr. Bratcher has supplied the appropriate numbers for the tales and motifs in our Publications. Ballads he indexes under Child's and Laws' numbers. Part I of his index will make the pursuit of variants in PTFS easy.

The researcher who consults Mr. Bratcher's Tale Synopses (Part II) can tell at a glance whether he needs to read the original in full. The nine headings of this section constitute a classification and summary of the tales in the Society's Publications.

Besides indexing tales, motifs, and ballads and providing synopses of the tales, Mr. Bratcher has prepared an exhaustive alphabetical index (Part III) of all kinds of subjects interesting to folklorists, such as place names, sayings, customs, folk medicine, and folk artifacts. The Publications reflect the view that the study of folklore has to do not only with the imaginative side of folk life but also with traditional ways of making and doing things. Moreover, the Society has long recognized that history and folklore overlap, and its editors have been friendly to contributions from this twilight zone. The vast amount of quasi-historical material in the Society's volumes is made readily available through the alphabetical index. Whatever might be missed in the first two parts of Mr. Bratcher's index can be approached through this third part.

The Society is like a man who has been making regular deposits in a savings account for more than half a century and at last discovers that he has grown rich little by little. Mr. Bratcher's index will reveal a kind of total which even long-time members of the Society are not aware of. To make it easier for students of folklore, and others as well, to find and use our materials is the goal of this index.

— WILSON M. HUDSON
Associate Editor, TFS, 1951-1964
Editor, TFS, 1964-1971

PREFACE

⟍⟋∤ THIS *Analytical Index* has three main parts. The first presents a group of Specialized Indexes, the second an assemblage of Tale Synopses, and the third an Alphabetical Index. A procedural note begins each of the last two divisions. While the concluding segment, the alphabetical index, requires no additional word here, perhaps the earlier two segments do.

Part II arranges and summarizes the approximately two thousand folktales recorded in the Texas Folklore Society Publications, volumes 1-36. The "tales" (not always the precise word for them) range from one-line moron jokes — simple puns — to complex relatings of marvels and adventures. Mere summaries cannot, of course, do justice to the bulk of the texts; but it is hoped that Part II will help the folktale specialist in his search for comparative data, since there is only so much that the fleshless tale-type and motif numbers in use by folklorists can accomplish in reflecting narrative content. Part II, then, supplements Part I as regards the prose-narrative content of the TFS volumes.

As for Part I, the nonfolklorist may well scratch his head at the ticker-tape-like sequences of "tale types," "motifs," and "ballad numbers." These number labels perform much as do item numbers in a commercial catalogue. For the comparative folklorist they identify, "name," such items of folklore as receive scholarly treatment in master catalogues like Stith Thompson's *Motif-Index of Folk-Literature* and Francis J. Child's *English and Scottish Popular Ballads.* Actually, however, the nonfolklorist will not have recourse to the specialized indexes; his possible curiosity will not restrict his use of parts II and III; and if interested in the numerical designations he can consult the references ("master catalogues") that are cited in headnotes to the respective sections of Part I. May his interest compel him to these works.

Grants-in-aid from two sponsoring organizations made this index possible. One came in 1970 from the Texas Folklore Society, which now operates out of Nacogdoches after six decades of maintaining its center in Austin. A second materialized as manna from Galveston in 1972, when the Moody Foundation, which conducts its affairs in that city, provided further aid.

Several individuals assisted; above all, my wife Nancey claims special thanks. For many months now, weekends and weekdays, she

xiii

has checked references, sorted notecards, and proofread demanding typescript and galleys—these exciting tasks in addition to her regular "galley" duties. I hope I appreciate her sufficiently.

Professor Wilson M. Hudson of the University of Texas at Austin repeatedly extended guidance and support. As past Secretary-Editor of the Society (1964-1971), he wished to see the resources of its Publications made easily accessible to working folklorists, students, and other researchers. Another who looked with favor on the project—the late Mody C. Boatright—did not live to see it completed.

With Dr. Hudson, Professors Américo Paredes and W.O.S. Sutherland joined in the initial planning. While they did not subsequently "read," in the usual sense, the product of their formative suggestions, they kindly examined the manuscript.

Throughout its preparation Mrs. Mary Lou Morgan, typist, worked capably and patiently with difficult material. Once the pages were in order and it came time to seek a subsidy beyond the one the Society had provided, Mr. Leroy E. Brown of Galveston proved himself a friend indeed, as did Mr. Joe Graham of Alpine. Finally, with characteristic generosity my fellow neighborhood stroller, Dr. Carl Hertzog of El Paso, lent his renowned hand (twisted arm?) in the typescript-to-book metamorphosis—besides being a good raconteur.

— JAMES T. BRATCHER

HISTORICAL NOTE ON
THE TEXAS FOLKLORE SOCIETY

FRANCIS EDWARD ABERNETHY, *Secretary-Editor*

GEORGE LYMAN KITTREDGE of Harvard planted the seed in 1907. At the end of that semester, as ballad-hunter John A. Lomax prepared to leave Harvard and return to Texas, he asked Kittredge what he could do for him back home. Kittredge—the former student of Francis James Child—suggested that he go back and form a society for the study of Texas folklore as a branch of the American Folklore Society.

Lomax returned to Texas and began teaching at the state Agricultural and Mechanical College. In 1908 he visited Leonidas Warren Payne, a fellow folklorist and a professor at the University of Texas. Payne harbored an interest in folk speech. Lomax passed along Kittredge's suggestion, and they began to discuss the possibilities. In 1909 the thought became action. Lomax and Payne met after the Thanksgiving UT-A&M game, again discussed their common desire backed by Kittredge's proposal, and resolved that the time had come to found a society to gather and study Texas folklore.

The place and date of the founding was a meeting of the Texas State Teachers' Association in Dallas on December 29, 1909. Neither Payne nor Lomax could attend, but their friend Killis Campbell, the Poe scholar, presented the resolution before the body for the formation of the Folklore Society of Texas. Payne was elected the first president because he was on the University of Texas campus where the Society was to be headquartered and because he had drawn up the constitution and drafted the aims and purposes of the Society. Lomax was to be the first secretary. Charter membership began with sixty-six members and closed on April 1, 1910, with ninety-two. The initiation fee was fifty cents; annual dues, a quarter.

The Society issued its first publication in 1910, a circular by Payne which listed the officers, explained the kinds of participation, and stated the purposes of the Society. At that time, the official organ was to be the *Journal of American Folklore.* In the circular Payne went on to define folklore, set up a simple classification system, and give advice about responsible collection.

Annual spring meetings began in 1911 in Austin. Mrs. Bess Brown Lomax was on the program and gave a paper on the now famous "Boll Weevil" song. By 1912 the Society had published its first work, a monograph by W. H. Thomas entitled "Some Current Folk-Songs of the Negro." Kittredge came down for the 1913 meeting and tendered his formal blessing in an encouraging address to the membership. Except for interruptions occasioned by the two world wars, the Society has met annually since 1911.

Publications of the Texas Folklore Society Number One came out in 1916 under the editorship of Stith Thompson. The volume was slim but rich, and it remains a valuable resource book for folklorists. Thompson's own article, "Prehistoric Development of Satire," still can excite interest. In the book, Kittredge again blessed the Society—this time with a preface in which he charged members to go forth and collect, remarking, "Texas is the happy hunting ground of the folk-lorist." In 1935, when J. Frank Dobie brought out a reprint of the 1916 publication as *Round the Levee*, he titled his preface "Upon This Rock," the rock being this first publication on which the Society's later strength of continuation was founded.

Then World War I claimed America's full attention. Stith Thompson left Texas, and the Society lapsed into inactivity. It did not revive until 1922 when Leonidas Payne, J. Frank Dobie, and other Texas folklorists decided to schedule the eighth annual meeting for the spring of 1922.

Frank Dobie's vitality and enthusiasm soon took hold, and his spirit has been the Society's guide from that day till this. The spasms of this second creation were over by 1924 when Dobie brought out the classic PTFS III, *Legends of Texas*. Dobie established the leadership of the Society in the office of Secretary-Editor. In his first years in that office he cut the cord that had bound the Texas group to what he considered to be the academic pedantry of the American Folklore Society.

The Society's early meetings were just as lively and eventful as they are today. Singing, dancing, and performances of all the folk arts by both members and guests were parts of the programs. In 1926 the Society got statewide publicity with its resolution to the Texas Legislature to save the longhorn. It met for a few years, beginning in 1925, with the Texas State Historical Association, until in 1930 it voted to affiliate with the Texas Academy of Sciences. This affiliation was due to the influential membership of scientists, especially John Strecker and H. B. Parks. It was Parks who urged the Society's adoption in 1932 of the *paisano* (Texas roadrunner) as its emblem. Ben C. Mead's *Correr del Paisano* emblem, presently appearing on the Southern Methodist

University Press advertisement sheet for PTFS, was first used on PTFS X (1932). The *paisano* currently gracing the Society's letterhead was drawn by Betty Boatright in the late 'thirties.

In 1937 Dobie called on Mody Boatright for editorial help. Harry Ransom was added as an associate editor the following year. Dobie resigned his secretary-editorship to Boatright in 1943, and Boatright was to be the acting leader for the next twenty years. Like Dobie, he was a deeply-rooted Texas spirit whose guidance remained after his hands had relinquished the reins.

The Society paused again for World War II, but meetings were resumed in 1946 and were well attended with wide participation. Wilson M. Hudson edited *The Healer of Los Olmos and Other Mexican Lore* (PTFS XXIV) in 1951 and later became an associate editor with Boatright. In 1963 Boatright resigned the secretary-editorship to Hudson, who was to hold that office until 1971, when the Society's headquarters were moved to the Stephen F. Austin State University campus in Nacogdoches and Francis Edward Abernethy became Secretary-Editor.

Except for the American Folklore Society, the Texas Folklore Society ranks as the oldest folklore organization in the United States, and it has varied little from its established traditions over the past sixty-three years. It meets annually in the spring on the weekend before Easter. Thursday night is set aside for beer, barbecue, and music. Members read papers in formal sessions on Friday and on Saturday morning. A guest speaker addresses the banquet session on Friday night, and the Society conducts its business at the end of the meeting on noon Saturday. Membership is open to those who are prosperous enough to pay dues of $7.50 a year, which pays for both membership and the annual PTFS.

With few exceptions, the Society has given its members a book a year, the gaps usually being filled by Society-inspired works like Dobie's *Coronado's Children* (1930), Boatright's *Folklore of the Oil Industry* (1963), Abernethy's *Tales from the Big Thicket* (1966), and Martha Emmons' *Deep Like the Rivers* (1969). The Society has also published two specialized series: the five books in the Range Life series which Dobie edited, and the five in the Paisano series edited by Wilson Hudson.

The highest honor the membership can bestow is Fellow of the Texas Folklore Society. This honor, created in 1941, was first accorded to founders Leonidas W. Payne and John A. Lomax. J. Frank Dobie became a Fellow in 1961, Mody C. Boatright in 1968, and Wilson M. Hudson, Jr., in 1972. The philosophy and direction of the Society have been largely the result of the direction of these men.

Our philosophy and direction have never been static. We have honored the folklorist as a collector in the field, and we have honored the academic folklorist, the one who studies his subject as a science. In recent annuals the amount of space devoted to analytical studies has increased. The most and best of the Publications of the Texas Folklore Society were responsibly done and were motivated by a love of the people and the soil from which they came. And if the Society has placed its emphasis on the collection of Texas and Southwestern lore, this emphasis has been the result of geographical availability of materials rather than an isolation in regionalism. Our books and pamphlets reflect the understanding that folklore is of all places and of all times. What the Society has collected is "Texas folklore" only because our state has provided a fertile ground for universal manifestation.

LIST OF

SOCIETY PUBLICATIONS

(REGULAR SERIES)

A LIST OF PUBLICATIONS of the Texas Folklore Society, volumes I—XXXVI, follows. (Roman numerals are replaced by Arabic elsewhere in the *Analytical Index*.) In some few instances, indicated by asterisks, reprint editions have supplied titles for volumes originally untitled in the series. The dates shown are the dates of first issue.

XXVII   *Mesquite and Willow.* Ed. Mody C. Boatright, Wilson M. Hudson and Allen Maxwell. Dallas: Southern Methodist Univ. Press, 1957.

XXVIII   *Madstones and Twisters.* Ed. Mody C. Boatright, Wilson M. Hudson and Allen Maxwell. Dallas: Southern Methodist Univ. Press, 1958.

XXIX   *And Horns on the Toads.* Ed. Mody C. Boatright, Wilson M. Hudson and Allen Maxwell. Dallas: Southern Methodist Univ. Press, 1959.

XXX   *Singers and Storytellers.* Ed. Mody C. Boatright, Wilson M. Hudson and Allen Maxwell. Dallas: Southern Methodist Univ. Press, 1961.

XXXI   *The Golden Log.* Ed. Mody C. Boatright, Wilson M. Hudson and Allen Maxwell. Dallas: Southern Methodist Univ. Press, 1962.

XXXII   *A Good Tale and a Bonnie Tune.* Ed. Mody C. Boatright, Wilson M. Hudson and Allen Maxwell. Dallas: Southern Methodist Univ. Press, 1964.

XXXIII   *The Sunny Slopes of Long Ago.* Ed. Wilson M. Hudson and Allen Maxwell. Dallas: Southern Methodist Univ. Press, 1966.

XXXIV   *Tire Shrinker to Dragster.* Ed. Wilson M. Hudson. Austin: Encino Press, 1967.

XXXV   *Hunters & Healers: Folklore Types & Topics.* Ed. Wilson M. Hudson. Austin: Encino Press, 1971.

XXXVI   *Diamond Bessie & The Shepherds.* Ed. Wilson M. Hudson. Austin: Encino Press, 1972.

ORDERING TFS PUBLICATIONS

As of 1973, Number 23, *Texas Folk Songs*, remains out of print. Other volumes may be secured from publishers:

Volumes 3-5, 13-15: Gale Research Co., Detroit, Mich.

Volumes 1-2, 6-12, 14, 16-33: Southern Methodist Univ. Press, Dallas, Tex.

Volumes 34-36: Encino Press, Austin, Tex.

"A good tale and a bonny tune."

PART ONE
Specialized Indexes

Coyote outwits rattlesnake; see Synopsis 2.29.

PART I: SPECIALIZED INDEXES
Section 1: Tale Types

References: Antti Aarne and Stith Thompson, *The Types of the Folktale*, 2nd rev. ed., FF Communications No. 184 (Helsinki, 1964); Earnest W. Baughman, *Type and Motif Index of the Folktales of England and North America*, Indiana Folklore Series No. 20 (The Hague, 1966).

Baughman utilizes the arrangement and type descriptions of Aarne-Thompson. In the following list, types included by Baughman, and for which he provides detailed references to English and North American occurrences, are designated by a letter "B" placed to the right of (and not a part of) the type number.

In the use of any index of tale types reflecting the Aarne-Thompson classifications, it should be borne in mind that single motifs can constitute tales ("simple tales"), so that in actuality a motif-index affords an extension of a type-index as regards "types" themselves. For example, the "hat-in-mud" tale finds no exact representation in the Aarne-Thompson or Baughman type-indexes; rather, it appears in the Thompson and Baughman motif-indexes as Motif X1655.1, "The man under the hat, which is the only thing seen above the mud." Users of the present *Analytical Index* (Part I) will of course know whether they are approaching a narrative, or a narrative element that can stand alone as a narrative, as a tale type or as a motif.

Type		Volume and Page	Type		Volume and Page
2B		cf. 25:241-242	68		cf. 19:44-49
8		cf. 22:60-61	73		cf. 25:235-238
9		cf. 25:220-224	81	B	18:48-49
9A		cf. 12:16-17; 14:32-34	100		12:215
9B		cf. 9:153-156	101*		cf. 12:104-106
34		12:13-19, 214; 14:80; 22:62-64; 32:49-52	113A	B	11:99-100
			123		cf. 31:27
37		14:121-123	130	B	6:33-37
47A		25:241-242	135B*		cf. 22:67-70
47D		cf. 12:104-106	154		14:8-17
49		12:103-104	155		12:4-7; 14:24-27; 18:191-194
49A		12:17-18; 32:51			
51A		14:27-32	166B₄*		cf. 20:97-98
55		18:172-177	169H*		9:158; 10:37-38
56A*		17:115-116	175		12:13-14; 14:118-120; 25:226-228; 32:49-50
58		cf. 14:135-144			
60		25:8-9			
63		27:109	178A		cf. 12:26-27; 31:37
66B	B	25:230-233; cf. 14:256-259; 19:81; 30:125-126	179B*		17:108; 30:191-192
			183*		18:172-177; 25:224-233
			207A		18:190-191; 25:240-241

Type		Volume and Page	Type		Volume and Page
220		8:92-93	554		32:23-29
231*		6:47-48; 27:114-117	560A*		32:23-29
235B*		cf. 28:156-157	563	B	6:45-46; 8:93-95
235C*		12:19-20	564		6:45-47; 27:87-88
275B*		12:87	569	B	cf. 6:45-47
285B*	B	5:62	592	B	30:228-229
289		cf. 12:19-20	612		32:12-17
293		22:108	650A		12:194-200
300	B	12:194-200; 31:135-140	670	B	15:126-133
301		cf. 12:77-79	671		cf. 15:122-133; 22:76
301A	B	12:77-79	676		31:25-26
302	B	12:79-86, 123-129; 14:241-249; 32:44-49	720	B	6:53; 31:11-12, 161-163
312	B	6:55	726	B	cf. 12:61-62; 32:35
313A	B	7:128-130; 12:61-66	735		cf. 32:33-37
325	B	32:30, 41-42; cf. 12: 61-66	735*		cf. 3:89-91
			737B*		cf. 32:33-37
325*		30:255-256	752C*		cf. 14:239-240
326	B	25:247-249; 33:107; cf. 34:109-110	754***		(see Type 777)
			756B	B	12:61-66; cf. 12:7-10
327B	B	cf. 25:217-219	761*		cf. 30:264-265
328	B	34:201	767		cf. 30:232-233
330 (pt. II)	B	cf. 27:87-88	774K		cf. 10:128-129
330 (pt. IV)	B	cf. 12:10-13	777	B	24:80-81
330D		30:241-242	780A		cf. 31:161-163
331	B	12:68-72	780B		cf. 31:161-163
332	B	12:76-77	782	B	15:134-135; 30:239-240
332B*		9:70-71	824		cf. 12:117-118
333	B	(see Type 2028)	830A		cf. 6:10-11
366	B	6:41-42, 54; 24:77-78; 25:183-194; 31:12-13, 15-16, 163	834		24:128-132
			834A		cf. 32:32-33
			835*		cf. 14:234-236
400	B	12:79-85; 14:241-249; cf. 12:61-66, 123-129; 32:44-49	835A*		cf. 20:14
			882		cf. 32:8-12
			889		12:27-29
403		cf. 14:106-107; 27:89-91	901	B	30:175; 31:21-22
425	B	35:127-128; cf. 8:99-101	910A		30:261
			910B	B	11:13-15; 12:7-10; 30:173-175
444C*		cf. 24:132-136	910F		31:26-27
460B		cf. 32:33-37	921	B	10:21-23; 18:11-48 passim; 30:263-264
480	B	6:42-45; 27:89-91			
505		6:56-64; 28:152-156; 32:17-23	953		34:103-116
			955	B	6:55
510		14:106-107; 27:89-91	956C		cf. 28:118-120
510A	B	14:106-107; 27:89-91	990	B	cf. 19:81
513A	B	11:9-50	1004 (pt. I)		12:49-50
552	B	12:123-129	1009		(see Type 1653A)

Type		Volume and Page	Type		Volume and Page
1030	B	9:153-156	1543		cf. 10:28-29; 21:97-98
1037		13:87	1551	B	cf. 13:91
1062	B	12:53	1558		30:279-280
1063A		10:50-51; cf. 12:52	1563*		cf. 25:3
1085		12:52-53	1575*	B	cf. 10:26-29; 21:97-98
1119	B	25:217-219	1587	B	12:55
1137	B	32:39; 34:114	1587**		14:168
1178**		cf. 7:130-132	1617		12:46-47
1186		cf. 29:142-143	1626	B	cf. 13:98; 21:89-90
1201	B	19:156	1640	B	31:135-140
1229		(see Type 169H*)	1641	B	10:24-25; 22:179-184
1238		18:48-50	1653		6:37-38
1255	B	19:155-156	1653A	B	31:10-11, 14
1262		cf. 22:63-64	1656	B	15:79-80; 32:5-8
1278	B	19:155	1676B	B	28:164; 29:168
1313A*		cf. 29:168-169	1687	B	cf. 6:54
1315*		cf. 25:245	1693		7:72; 14:163-164;
1319	B	20:11			25:243-245
1319B*		32:32	1694		13:104-105
1319J*		cf. 32:32	1698B	B	cf. 15:82-83
1331C*	B	19:159	1698I		cf. 15:82-83
1332*		19:159	1698K	B	9:159-160
1336	B	(see Type 34)	1699	B	10:16-18; 17:57-58;
1336A		10:30-31			32:54
1345*		13:106-110; 19:155-161	1705	B	cf. 25:248-249
1346*		21:93	1710	B	31:22
1352A		cf. 12:21-26	1735C	B	cf. 29:165-166, 169
1358A		30:192-193	1737	B	12:34-36, 54-55;
1377		cf. 32:53			21:73-75
1380	B	10:165-166;	1738	B	10:18-19; cf. 25:5-6
		23:207-209;	1785C		13:103
		cf. 6:223-225	1791	B	10:38-42;
1416	B	9:57			22:207-214;
1430		cf. 24:6			25:245-247;
1430A		cf. 24:6			29:169; 31:17-19
1447		cf. 31:103	1821		30:183
1479*		31:26; cf. 34:105	1832M*	B	(see Type 1694)
1525D	B	10:15-16; 18:177-180;	1833		30:125
		25:233-235	1833A	B	29:165-166
1525M	B	10:12-13	1833E	B	14:161; 21:96-97;
1530		12:16-17; 14:32-34			30:136-139
1535	B	12:29-44, 54-55;	1833J	B	22:204-206;
		21:35-42;			30:191-192;
		24:128-132;			cf. 10:46-48
		28:154-156	1833M	B	30:125
1536B	B	cf. 12:57-60	1835B*		13:102-103; 30:139
1539A	B	12:41-44	1839*		cf. 29:169
1539B	B	12:29-36	1839A		cf. 30:125
1541	B	cf. 31:10-11	1841	B	13:96

Type		Volume and Page
1851		cf. 13:93-94, 97-99; 14:167-168
1860		cf. 18:208-217; 25:5-6
1860A	B	25:5-6
1861		18:206-208
1870		8:121-122; 13:100-101; 14:162; 28:139-140; 30:127-128
1875	B	9:34-37
1875A	B	9:158; 10:37
1878*		cf. 28:131-132
1889A	B	14:264; 20:59-60
1889C	B	32:55
1889J	B	cf. 10:53-54
1889L	B	14:264; 20:95-96; 30:179
1889M	B	8:128; 20:90
1890	B	18:85; 20:11
1890A	B	7:43
1890D	B	18:85
1890E	B	18:85
1895	B	18:85
1910	B	20:97-98
1913	B	7:39-40
1917	B	7:43-44
1920A	B	12:56; 18:79-80; cf. 19:36-41
1920B	B	20:29; 22:78-79
1920C*	B	cf. 20:97; 27:167
1920D	B	12:56; 19:68
1920D*		cf. 30:236-237

Type		Volume and Page
1920E		cf. 10:25-26; 12:55-57; 19:36-41
1920E*		32:54-55
1920F*		18:85-88
1920M	B	19:69
1948		25:13-15
1951	B	13:87-88
1960A		7:56-57; 20:90-91
1960D		14:269; 18:79; 19:67
1960F	B	18:79
1960M$_1$	B	18:79-80; 20:73-74
1960M$_2$	B	20:92
1960Z		7:49-51, 53-54, 58-61; 9:21-24; 20:65-66, 68, 88-89, 93-94
2010		27:138-150; 30:220
2019*		cf. 5:7-48 passim
2023		24:81-84; 30:234-235
2024*		27:114-117
2025	B	6:30-33
2028	B	6:47-48; 24:78-80
2030	B	6:55
2031		18:188-190
2032		(see Type 2034)
2034	B	6:39-41
2040	B	31:16-17
2200	B	30:176-177
2300	B	19:75-79
2301	B	30:15-16
2404		21:94-95
2411		21:85-86

Horned toad "spits" blood.

Section 2: Motifs

References: Stith Thompson, *Motif-Index of Folk-Literature,* rev. ed., 6 vols. (Copenhagen and Bloomington, 1955-1958); Earnest W. Baughman, *Type and Motif Index of the Folktales of England and North America,* Indiana Folklore Series No. 20 (The Hague, 1966).

Except for systematically inserted additions appropriate to English and North American folk narrative, the motifs treated in Baughman derive from Thompson's more inclusive *Motif-Index.* The bibliographical references to occurrences differ, Baughman's and Thompson's works being complementary. Motifs which appear in Baughman are here designated by a letter "B" following the motif number.

A plus mark (+) following the volume-and-page references for a motif indicates that further references may be found immediately below, cited in connection with more particularized forms (if provided for) of the narrative element in question. Thus the references for Motif A2411.2, "Origin of color of bird," conclude with a "+" to signify the presence, immediately below, of references for motifs A2411.2.1.6, "Color of crow," and A2411.2.1.13, "Color of red-bird."

A. MYTHOLOGICAL MOTIFS

Motif	Volume and Page
A21.1	6:109; 14:127-128, 132-134; 29:194-199
A102.17	1:53; 4:78-79
A106	1:52-53
A107	1:52-53
A151.1	3:153-156, 207-208
A151.1.1	3:207-208, 230-233
A162	1:52-53; 30:231
A188	12:159-161
A284.2	cf. 22:33-36
A300	12:143-151; 22:156, 158, 163, 167
A418.1	28:125-126
A511.1.3.3	(see T541.1.1)
A511.4.1	1:40; 6:110; 21:72; 22:46
A515.1.1	14:114-118; 22:30 ff.; 29:194 ff.
A516	34:199
A521	22:30-51 +
A522.1.2	1:47-49; 7:137-138; 9:153-156; 12:103-104; 14:118-120, 135-144; 18:172-180; 21:73-77; 25:220-238, 241-242

Motif		Volume and Page
A522.1.3		(see "Coyote" in Part III of *Analytical Index*)
A524.1.2		34:191-193
A527.3.1.1		14:108-109; 35:131
A531		1:39-40; 6:109-110; 22:20-22, 27-44
A541		14:195-199; 29:198; cf. 13:276-277, 294-296; 21:67-70; 22:22-26
A571	B	3:130-132; 28:116-117
A572		1:40; 6:110; 14:197
A651.2		1:75-76
A661.0.1.2	B	9:160-162; 12:10-13, 156; 19:29-35; 32:5-8
A673		1:75-77
A700		6:109; 14:72, 127-128
A702		6:109; 12:75; 14:127-128
A710		6:109; 14:72, 127; 22:24-25
A714.3		22:22-25
A715.1		6:109
A720		22:22-25 +
A721.1		22:73-74; cf. 22:22-26

Motif		Volume and Page
A736.1		4:77; 29:197
A736.2		22:34-35
A737		24:115; cf. 14:127-128
A750	B	1:52-53; 4:77; 6:109; 7:80; 29:194-200
A751		4:76-77; 22:26; 29:197 ff. +
A751.1.1	B	7:80
A751.8		4:76-77; 22:25-26; 29:194-200
A753		4:77; 29:197
A758		1:52-53
A761		cf. 3:117
A771		9:49; 12:211
A773		22:141
A778		8:91; 9:50; 14:128
A791		4:79
A811		21:65-66; 22:18
A812		21:65-66
A901		14:231
A910	B	3:204-205, 218-219, 296-297; 4:78-79; 22:20-22
A930		13:296-297
A941.5		4:79; 14:198; cf. 13:296-297 +
A941.5.1		3:205; 10:124; 13:69
A960	B	cf. 14:233
A961.1		21:65-66
A968.2	B	cf. 1:50-51; 3:163-167, 169-176, 202-204
A970	B	10:79-81; 22:20, 22, 25, 34 +
A973	B	cf. 14:239
A974		cf. 10:79-81
A977		12:134; 14:114 +
A977.5		22:20, 22; 30:265
A985		(see A968.2)
A1003		3:218-219; 4:78-79; cf. 29:196; 31:3-5
A1010		3:218-219; 4:78-79; 12:87; 14:68; 29:199
A1018		3:218-219; 4:78-79; 22:21-22
A1020		4:78-79
A1111		cf. 13:296-297
A1120		6:109; 14:131-134
A1122		6:45-47
A1131.1		9:48-49

Motif		Volume and Page
A1150		14:73; cf. 6:109
A1151		14:73-74
A1172		6:109; 12:86; 14:127-128
A1200		4:75-77; 14:66-69; 22:18; 29:198 +
A1224.3		32:177; cf. 32:4-5
A1232.3		21:66; 22:22
A1241		14:67-69; 21:66
A1275.1		32:4, 178-180
A1300	B	4:76-77; 22:20-22; 29:194-200; 32:4-5
A1331		31:3-5
A1333		1:92; 21:66; 29:198
A1335		14:68; 22:22
A1344		14:68
A1371.1		32:178
A1411		22:22-26
A1414	B	14:71; cf. 22:22-26
A1415		14:71-73; 22:23-25
A1425		13:294-297
A1429.3		13:296-297
A1446		29:198
A1556.3		29:194-196, 198; cf. 14:70
A1559		22:51
A1600		14:131-134; 21:66; 29:198-199 +
A1614		14:131-134; 29:198-199
A1620		21:66; 29:198
A1640		21:66
A1675		3:218; 14:69
A1700	B	4:76-77; 14:69, 127-134; 22:18-20
A1714.3.1		22:52-53
A1751.1.1		7:80
A1834.1		14:66
A1910		14:197
A2200	B	6:8, 10-11; 8:92-93, 95-96, 98-99; 12:19-20, 86-87; 17:115-117; 19:60-62; 21:79-80; 22:18-22, 53-55, 56; 28:156-157; 32:29-31 +
A2213.1		22:56
A2213.2.1		22:56

Motif		Volume and Page
A2213.3		20:75-78; 22:56
A2213.4.1		22:56
A2218	B	22:60-61 +
A2218.4		14:44
A2221.2.4		24:117
A2230	B	21:79-80 +
A2231	B	6:10-11; 8:92-93; 28:70; 32:31
A2231.7.1(a)	B	cf. 6:69
A2233.1		18:172-177
A2239		28:70
A2241		12:19-20

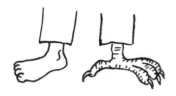

A2275.5.3		cf. 12:20
A2291	B	12:87
A2313		6:10-11; 12:19-20; 19:60-62; 28:156-157
A2317.3		17:115-117
A2317.12		22:20
A2332.5.1		22:56
A2345		22:20
A2345.2		14:89
A2356.3		22:20
A2371.3.1		32:178
A2378.7.1		22:57-59
A2378.7.1		22:57-59
A2378.8		22:19
A2411.1.2.4		22:20
A2411.1.3.2		14:44-45
A2411.2		6:10-11; 12:19-20; 14:44-45; 17:117; 28:156-157 +
A2411.2.1.6		22:53-55
A2411.2.1.13		8:98-99; 14:197
A2412.1		12:86; 22:20 +
A2412.1.3		14:44
A2416.3		7:137-138
A2422		14:70; 29:198
A2423		8:96, 98 f.; 12:215; 14:56-59

Motif		Volume and Page
A2426.2		6:10-11; 12:20; 21:79-80 +
A2426.2.8		6:8; 8:98
A2426.2.17		12:20
A2426.3		8:95-96
A2427.2		29:198
A2433		8:93; 12:20; 28:70-71
A2435.3		12:87
A2435.4		8:93 +
A2435.4.5.1		32:29-31
A2435.4.7		22:53, 55
A2435.6.2.1		9:66
A2442		8:93
A2471	B	12:19-20
A2491.1		cf. 12:19-20
A2491.2		12:19-20
A2493.1		28:71
A2510		22:51-52 +
A2513		14:70-71; 22:38-39
A2521.1		6:8; 8:98
A2542	B	6:69; 8:92-93; 21:79-80; 22:53-55; 32:29-31
A2571		8:92-93; 12:19-20; 14:40-41; 19:60-62; 22:61-62
A2611.0.4.1		3:197, 200-201; 8:101; cf. 22:51
A2615		3:198-200
A2620	B	13:68; cf. 6:9-10, 12-14
A2630		6:9-10, 12-14; 22:51
A2650	B	3:197, 198-201; 6:12-13; 8:99-101; 22:51
A2681		7:79-80
A2730	B	3:197-200; 6:9-10, 12-14; 13:68
A2772		3:197-200; 6:9-10; 13:68
A2817.2	B	cf. 9:53-54
A2851		12:60-61

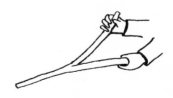

B. ANIMALS

Motif		Volume and Page	Motif		Volume and Page
B11.2.3	B	12:199	B211.1.8	B	7:132-134; 11:98-100;
B11.5	B	21:78			25:248-249;
B11.6.2	B	3:34-35			34:109-110
B11.10		22:102-104	B211.3.4		12:21-26; 27:82-87;
B11.11	B	10:79-81; 12:199;			28:158
		31:140	B211.5		12:126, 247; 32:27
B15	B	22:67-70; 25:23-39	B211.7.1		10:48-50
		passim;	B216		15:127; 18:190-191
		27:105-112 +	B217		15:128
B15.4.2	B	2:46; 12:118; 29:138	B230		8:92-93; 14:27-31 +
B16.5.1		12:199; 15:125-126;	B238		18:172-180
		21:78	B238.1		cf. 8:92-93
B41.2		32:25-28; 34:199	B239.1		cf. 14:27-32
B81	B	10:135, 162-163;	B240	B	5:59; 12:62; 18:76 +
		28:36 +	B241.2.3	B	11:99-100; 25:247-249
B81.13.7	B	10:162	B242		7:37; 8:92; 12:62
B91.3	B	21:68	B243		12:61
B91.5	B	4:60	B244.1		5:59
B91.5.2		22:102-104; 24:132-136	B250	B	6:10-11; 8:98;
B100.2		6:45-47			17:108-110
B120		12:61-63; 15:127-128;	B268.11		34:109-110
		18:188-194 +	B272.2		cf. 18:172-177
B121.1		18:85-88	B280		5:5-48; 23:254-255;
B123.1		15:127-128			24:81-84; 30:234-235
B133.1		cf. 31:38-40	B285		30:234-235
B134.1		14:70; 29:198	B291.1.3		12:66
B147.1.1.4		24:115	B292	B	22:39, 51-52 +
B147.1.2.2		11:97-98; 13:182-184	B292.8	B	3:54, 102-103
B147.2.1.2		34:190, 199	B292.11		cf. 13:68; 34:188, 196
B147.3.2		5:119, 121-122;	B296		6:34-35; 24:84-86
		7:26-37, 62-68,	B297		10:50; 19:162-164
		119-121; 10:55;	B300	B	6:34-37; 12:81-82;
		13:160-161			14:243-244, 250;
B151.1.1		31:38-40			22:83-84; 27:93-95;
B155.1	B	31:38; cf. 25:78-82			32:24-29, 46-47 +
B161		15:127-128	B311		cf. 12:26-27; 27:92-95
B165.1		15:128	B312.2		12:26-27; 27:92-95
B175		12:126 ff., 247;	B314		12:123-129
		32:26-27	B331.2	B	cf. 12:26-27; 31:37
B182		12:72-75	B342(b)	B	11:99-100
B184.1		6:46; 32:24-29	B350		12:79-86, 131-132;
B184.1.6		32:25-28			14:241-249;
B184.1.10		cf. 34:192 f., 199 f.			15:127-129;
B210.1	B	25:248-249;			32:46-47 +
		34:109-110	B391	B	15:129; 22:76;
B210.2	B	10:48-50			32:46-47 +

Motif		Volume and Page
B392		12:81, 131-132; 14:243
B392.1		12:81, 132; 14:243; 22:76
B401		6:46-47; 32:24-29
B421		14:252-254; 25:219
B431.2		12:26-27, 81-82; 14:241-249; 27:91-95
B443.2		14:243
B449.2		cf. 22:51-52
B455.3		12:62-63, 81-82; 14:243-244
B470		12:126; 32:27
B481.1		12:81-83; 14:244
B491		cf. 20:76-78 +
B491.1		15:127-128
B501		12:79-86, 123-133; 14:243-244; 32:46-47 +
B505		8:93-95
B505.1		12:123-133
B512		32:14
B521	B	27:93-95; 31:39-40 +
B521.3		1:53-54
B526		1:53-54
B535	B	13:82-84 +
B535.0.9		13:82-83; 14:120-121
B542	B	32:26-28
B548		20:77-78 +
B548.2.1		32:27
B549.1	B	12:26-27
B551.4		21:68
B552	B	32:29
B557.5		27:94-95; 34:188
B560		27:93-95
B563		12:62
B571		20:76-78, 98 +
B571.1		12:82-83, 128-129, 133; 14:248-249; 32:48-49
B576.2	B	3:34-37, 46-47; 6:19-20; 24:100 +
B576.2.1*	B	3:54, 102-103
B576.2.4*	B	9:58
B581		27:93-95
B582.1.1		27:94-95
B582.2		12:79-86, 123-133; 14:241-249; 22:82-85; 27:91-95; 32:23-29; 34:44-49

Motif		Volume and Page
B600		22:47-51 +
B601.1.1		12:77; 30:9; 31:28
B602.1		12:159-161
B604.1		22:100-101; cf. 24:132-136
B604.4		12:123-125, 133-134
B610		13:83 +
B611.1		12:77-79; 30:9 f.; 31:28
B611.3		22:97-100
B613.1		24:134-135; cf. 29:195-196
B614		12:159-161
B623		12:159-161
B631.9		12:77-79; 30:9; 31:28
B632		13:85
B635.1		12:77-79; 30:9 f.; 31:28
B640		12:123-134; cf. 22:97-100
B651		22:97-100
B720		7:39-41; 14:252-254; 20:58-59, 96
B730	B	12:190-193
B733	B	29:226-227
B750	B	9:67-68; 16:396-402 +
B751.1	B	5:66-67; 21:43-64; 25:35-37
B765.1(ab)	B	8:127-128
B765.4	B	4:45
B765.4.1		9:66
B765.7	B	4:46; 5:74; 8:124-126
B765.7.2		4:46; 5:74; 8:124-126
B765.10	B	5:60, 73-74; 8:94-95; 12:88 +
B765.10(a)	B	4:50-51; 8:94-95; 12:99-100
B765.11		4:46-47; 8:128
B765.13	B	4:49
B765.14	B	14:34-35
B765.16	B	4:47
B765.18.2		5:68-69; 6:86-87; 13:51-52
B765.20	B	4:49
B765.22	B	5:67
B765.23	B	4:49
B765.24.1	B	5:57-58
B766.1		11:95
B766.2		11:95

Motif		Volume and Page
B776.3.2	B	4:52
B784.1.7	B	5:65; cf. 5:105
B784.1.8	B	5:62-63
B784.2.1	B	5:62; cf. 20:94
B784.2.4	B	30:250
B802		(see "Horse" in Part III of *Analytical Index*)

Motif		Volume and Page
B871.1.1.1	B	7:56-70
B871.1.1.2		3:119-122, 128; 19:46-49
B875.1	B	5:59; 12:199; 15:125-128; 20:75-76; 21:78
B871.1	B	20:90-91 +
B871.1.1.1	B	7:56-57

C. TABOO

Motif		Volume and Page
C10		12:66; 30:255-256; 31:29 +
C12.5	B	3:124-126; 8:103; 29:143 +
C12.5.3(a)	B	18:81-82
C12.5.7	B	8:103; cf. 29:142-143
C30		22:100-101
C51		1:53 +
C51.3		1:86
C58		7:80
C94	B	12:118-119, 166-168; 14:239-240 +
C94.5		34:189, 196-197
C120		12:66
C200	B	34:105 +
C211	B	12:63
C220.1		12:119-120
C260	B	34:105
C300	B	22:34, 72 +
C311.1	B	29:140-141
C313.1		35:131
C321	B	9:57
C331		9:149; 13:139, 141; 30:69-75
C400	B	9:159-160; cf. 21:86-87 +
C410		12:8
C411		12:9
C425		15:128-133
C430	B	1:86-87
C432.1	B	1:87
C480.1	B	13:160, 239
C483		13:160, 239
C499.1		cf. 25:11-13
C500		21:69
C530		1:84
C573		3:157-159
C631		7:80

Motif		Volume and Page
C687		12:21-26
C726		2:84; 13:155, 173; 24:115 +
C726.1		1:84; 25:196
C735.1		12:80 +
C735.2		12:63
C735.2.8		34:105
C757		12:2
C761.3		14:107
C771.1		21:66; 24:84-86; 29:198-200
C811		22:34-35
C841	B	5:75; 13:155, 159; 24:117 +
C841.10.1	B	4:60-61
C915	B	9:57; 12:70
C920	B	3:157-159; 12:76-77; 29:139-141

D. MAGIC

Motif		Volume and Page
D838.2	B	34:111-112
D861	B	32:28; 34:111-112 +
D861.1	B	6:45-47; 8:93-95
D881.2		cf. 6:47
D905		3:125-128; 8:146-147, 149
D932		3:153-156; 6:103; 12:246-249; 28:106-127 passim; cf. 22:71
D950	B	22:107-108; 25:219; 30:241-242
D958		8:99-101
D965	B	6:13-14; 12:32, 76-77, 143 ff.; 22:155 ff.; 32:14-17
D992.1		15:134-135; 30:239-240
D1011		21:73
D1013		13:139; 17:113; 22:64
D1021		12:127, 129, 132-134; 14:243-244, 247; 32:47-48
D1024		9:58; 12:79-86; 32:49
D1030.1		6:46-47; 12:119-120; 32:48
D1050.1		12:84-85; 14:106-107; 27:89-91
D1067.2	B	12:42-44, 125-129; 14:250
D1073		22:57-59; cf. 22:20-22
D1076		34:114-115
D1081		34:111; cf. 12:125-126
D1094		6:46-47
D1131.1		27:95
D1171.7		12:79-86
D1192		8:93-95
D1209.1		12:64
D1222		22:80-82
D1233		12:79; 30:228-229
D1240	B	6:13-14; 7:129; 32:14, 28; 34:188, 195-196 +

Motif		Volume and Page
D1241	B	2:82-84; 5:124-125; 8:14, 21, 45, 50 f., 58, 60-62, 65-72 passim, 79-82; 30:251-252; 34:163-173 passim; 35:12-16 passim
D1242.2		24:116
D1254		12:125-126; cf. 8:93-95
D1266		30:255-256; 32:41
D1273	B	8:94-95; 12:80; 22:42-44; 24:116; 27:88; 30:42, 255-256; 31:28 +
D1273.1.1	B	5:122; 30:251; 32:28
D1273.1.2		(see "Four" in Part III of Analytical Index)
D1273.1.3	B	1:94; 13:144; 22:109; 34:188
D1273.1.3.1		1:85
D1273.1.6	B	5:122; 9:116; 34:201
D1273.3		8:31, 79; 13:176-181; 14:268; 30:251; 34:165 f., 168-171; 35:15
D1274		2:32, 89; 8:11, 13 f., 51, 58, 60-61, 65 f., 69 ff., 80-81; 9:151-152; 13:137-145 passim, 174; 17:113; 30:183-184; 31:108 ff.; 35:14-15
D1311.14		30:255-256
D1313.1		25:218-219
D1314	B	9:45-46 +
D1314.2	B	3:45, 91, 100 f.; 6:5; 9:132
D1314.2.2	B	13:176 ff., 233; 28:162
D1316.5		15:135-136; 30:239-240
D1318.5	B	31:162-163
D1335.1.2		34:194
D1338.1.1	B	32:27-28
D1346.5		12:32 ff.; 32:14
D1355	B	32:14-15 +

Motif		Volume and Page
D1355.3	B	13:141; 24:116; 31:108 ff.
D1361	B	17:114 +
D1361.14		12:125-128
D1386	B	13:140
D1401	B	6:47 +
D1401.3		8:95
D1412.1		27:87-88
D1413.1		30:241-242
D1415.2.5		30:228-229
D1426.1		22:80-81
D1427.1	B	22:80-81
D1430		25:218-219
D1442.1		12:64
D1451		8:93-95
D1454	B	6:44; 24:131; 28:156
D1454.1.1	B	6:42-45
D1454.2		6:42-45
D1472.18	B	6:45-47
D1472.1.22		cf. 6:46
D1473.1		cf. 14:106-107; 27:89-91
D1475		12:79
D1500.1.4		32:12-17
D1500.1.23	B	8:80-81; 13:166-167; 14:192-194, 268; 27:193-195; 30:252; 34:164-174; 35:14
D1500.1.23.2*	B	8:58; 35:14
D1500.1.33.1.2		34:188
D1500.1.37		8:33, 42, 45, 56, 65
D1502.2.2	B	8:66
D1503.10		6:13-14
D1504.1	B	8:31, 51, 60-61, 79; 30:251; 34:166; 35:15
D1515.4.2		28:4-5, 7, 14-16; 29:147
D1515.5	B	17:73 +
D1515.5.1	B	8:24, 66; 28:3-17; 29:147-152; 31:37
D1521.1		12:125-126
D1551	B	3:211, 213, 217; 22:104-105
D1552		22:33
D1565.1.1		cf. 22:107; 25:219
D1567.6		3:204-205; 4:78-79; 10:124-126; 13:69

Motif		Volume and Page
D1601.10.1	B	cf. 14:50-51; 22:76-77
D1602	B	12:165-166; 22:73-74
D1602.1(b)	B	cf. 22:73-74
D1610.2		22:107
D1611	B	22:31, 106 +
D1611.5		12:65
D1611.7		22:105-108
D1622.3		30:232-233
D1645.4		34:111
D1653.1.1		34:111; cf. 12:125-129
D1654	B	cf. 12:165-166; 22:73-74 +
D1654.3.1		27:182-183, 185; 35:100
D1654.5	B	cf. 27:173-174, 176-177
D1678		cf. 30:255
D1711	B	9:53-57, 151-152; 10:63, 67, 82-98; 11:26; 12:115-117, 119-120; 13:139-141, 144; 14:110-114; 17:73, 113-114; 18:222; 19:21 ff.; 24:9-70; 25:195-199; 29:14-44; 31:108-113, 117; 32:41-42, 44-49
D1711.0.1		32:41-42; cf. 30:255-256
D1712.3		13:142-144
*D1713		3:204-205, 211-217; 6:102-106; 10:124-126; 12:118-121, 165-169, 175-183; 13:68-69; 14:198, 239-240; 22:104-105; 24:102-106; 25:207-211; 27:172-178; 30:232-233; 32:32-33

Motif		Volume and Page	Motif		Volume and Page
D2064.4	B	1:86, 88; 2:82-83; 4:92; 8:59-60; 10:84-85; 13:162; 17:73; 18:69, 139; 24:107-109; 25:198; 27:187-188; 35:11-12	D2136.2		13:185-189
			*D2140.1		24:102-103
			D2143.1	B	3:198-200; 6:9-10; 12:120-121; 19:88-93
			D2143.2		14:237
			D2151.2	B	21:77; 22:57-59 +
			D2151.2.1.1		3:211 ff.; 22:105; cf. 14:198
D2065		3:135-137; 9:138-140			
D2071.1		1:88; 2:82-83; 4:92; 10:84-85; 18:139; 24:107-109; 27:187-188	D2151.2.5	B	3:204-205; 13:69, 74; 14:198, 297; 22:57-59
			D2161	B	8:69, 79-80; 12:66-72, 76-77; 27:4 +
D2072.0.2	B	14:35; cf. 27:173-174, 176-177	D2161.1		5:124-125; 8:14, 21, 30, 70-72, 80-81; 14:192-194, 268; 24:114; 27:194-200 passim; 30:205-211, 251-252; 34:164-165, 167-171; 35:11 +
D2072.0.5	B	21:78			
D2074.2.2		12:81-82, 127, 129			
D2084.2 (dd)					
	B	14:194			
D2098	B	3:146, 149			
D2100		6:44, 46; 8:94-95; 12:80, 83-85; 24:131-132; 27:159-160; 31:3; 32:33 ff.	D2161.2.2	B	8:31, 51, 60-61, 79; 30:251; 34:166; 35:15
			D2161.4.1	B	8:13, 50, 65
D2105		6:46-47; 12:119-120; 22:49-50, 75-76; 32:48	D2161.4.3	B	8:11
			D2161.5.3		6:13-14
			D2161.5.6(a)		
D2120	B	3:115-118, 132-135; 9:52; 10:64, 68; 12:80, 120, 125-128, 249; 13:188; 27:90, 93; 30:220-223; 32:25-29, 48		B	8:69
			D2161.5.7	B	cf. 8:69, 79-80; 27:4
			D2174	B	30:228-229
			D2176.3	B	8:105; 12:118; 14:236; 25:209-210; 29:143; 31:160
D2135.0.1	B	3:115-118, 132-135; 14:197-198	D2177.1		12:69
			D2178.5		12:79

E. THE DEAD

E37.1		12:2-4	E222	B	7:123
E79		12:125-128; 25:219	E231.5(b)	B	cf. 12:207-210
E80		7:129; 32:27	E232.1	B	12:207-210
E105	B	12:32 ff., 76-77; 32:14, 17	E232.2(a)	B	18:142
			E233*(a)	B	3:135-137; cf. 9:138-140
E162		12:2-4			
E168		30:238-239	E234.2	B	3:111
E181		32:14	E234.3		3:135-137; 18:142; 28:117, 120
E215	B	31:32			
E221.1.4.2*			E235	B	24:94-95 +
	B	cf. 30:229-231	E235.1	B	24:115

Motif		Volume and Page
E235.2	B	18:140-141
E235.4	B	24:77-78; 31:12-13, 163-164 +
E235.4.1		25:183-194; cf. 6:41-42
E236	B	9:138-140
E238	B	12:8-9
E266	B	7:123; 13:122
E272	B	6:19-20; 7:121-122; 28:125-126, 163-165 +
E272(a)	B	9:50
E275	B	6:87-89; 28:164-165
E279.3	B	9:51-52; 13:121
E281	B	2:46; 6:14-18, 87-89; 7:121-123, 126-127, 135-136; 9:51-52; 10:58; 13:128-129, 14:178-179; 18:141-142; 24:91-92, 94-96; 27:180-186; 29:219-222, 226-227
E283	B	24:97
E291	B	28:114-116, 125-127 +
E291.1	B	3:101-102; 28:125; cf. 3:183; 24:98
E291.2.1	B	3:56-59; 6:19-20
E291.2.2	B	3:35, 46-47, 54-55, 102-103; 6:19-20; 24:100
E292	B	cf. 3:143
E293.2(a)	B	13:186-187
E299	B	9:50; 18:142
E300	B	13:189; 24:93 f. +
E310	B	3:168
E320		24:93-94
E321	B	9:52; 18:141-142 +
E321.3	B	7:125-126
E321.5	B	13:135
E323.5	B	9:54; 13:121; 24:74
E328*(a)	B	10:59
E332.3.3.1	B	18:137-139, 146-147
E332.3.3.1(c)		
	B	18:146-147
E332.3.3.1(h)		
	B	18:136-139
E332.3.3.1(i)		
	B	18:137-139

Motif		Volume and Page
E332.3.3.1(j)		
	B	18:138-139
E333(c)	B	6:88-89
E334	B	3:143-149; 7:124; 9:50-51; 18:140-141; 24:95-96; 28:116-117; 30:118-120 +
E334(d)	B	18:145-146; 24:74
E334(f)	B	cf. 28:164-165
E334.2(a)	B	29:219-222
E334.2.3	B	3:157-159 +
E334.2.3(ab)		
	B	9:51
E334.2.3(cc)		
	B	13:185-189
E334.2.3(cd)		
	B	3:201
E334.2.3(ce)		
	B	3:143
E336.1	B	30:265
E337	B	18:146 +
E337.1	B	30:119; 35:100 +
E337.1.1(h)		
	B	3:55-56
E337.1.1(k)		
	B	6:17
E337.1.1(m)		
	B	7:126
E337.1.1(ob)		
	B	18:146
E337.1.4	B	7:125
E337.2(d)	B	6:88-89
E338(b)	B	7:123; 13:126-127; 29:161-162
E338(d)	B	7:136; 27:180-186
E338.1(ac)	B	7:123
E338.1(f)	B	9:52; 10:58; 13:121-122, 125, 127, 129; 24:91-92, 94; 29:161-162
E338.1(hf)	B	13:128
E338.1(hg)		
	B	35:100

Motif		Volume and Page
E338.1(i)	B	6:17, 88-89; 14:179; 29:219-222
E338.6*	B	18:143
E338.10*	B	35:100
E341	B	6:56-65; 28:154-156; 32:17-23
E341.1	B	6:56-65; 32:17-23
E363.3(e)	B	24:90-91; 28:165
E363.4	B	13:130-136
E371	B	13:122-123; 28:155 +
E371.4*	B	3:54, 188-189; 13:125-128; 28:127
E371.5*	B	3:90; 13:127; 29:161-162
E378.4*	B	7:135
E401	B	3:167-168
E402	B	3:54-56, 141-142; 18:141; 24:94, 96-99 +
E402.1.1	B	24:95-96 +
E402.1.1.1	B	3:157-159
E402.1.1.2	B	7:123
E402.1.1.3	B	7:124; 24:76, 96; 28:116-120
E402.1.1.4	B	3:137-141
E402.1.1.8*	B	7:135-136
E402.1.2	B	27:180-186; 29:226-227
E402.1.3(a)	B	3:137-138; 18:141-142
E402.1.4	B	13:123-126
E402.1.5(a)	B	18:141
E402.1.8	B	9:50-51 +
E402.1.8(a)	B	7:127
E402.1.8(l)	B	28:109; 30:119
E402.2	B	13:182-184 +
E402.2.3	B	3:54-56; 6:87-89; 24:99
E402.3(a)	B	3:141-142; 28:124-125
E402.4	B	3:137-142
E410	B	6:14-18; 7:126-127, 135-136; 10:58; 18:141-142; 24:91-92 +
E411	B	24:74 +
E411.0.3	B	24:88
E411.1	B	12:169-173; 13:120-121; 24:74; 28:116

Motif		Volume and Page
E413	B	6:87-89; 9:51-52; 24:95-96; 27:180-186; 29:226-227; 30:119-120
E414	B	14:178-179; 18:145-147
E415.4	B	6:56 ff.; 28:155; 32:17-23
E419.7	B	6:41-42; 24:77-78; 25:183; 31:12-13, 15-16, 163 +
E419.7.1*	B	18:141
E419.8	B	10:57-59
E421.1	B	9:51 +
E421.1.1	B	24:90-91
E421.2	B	9:50-51
E421.3	B	18:144-145; 28:163
E422	B	12:114; 24:95 +
E422.1.1(b)		
	B	3:136-137; 9:51-52; 10:100; 18:140-141; 28:164-165
E422.1.1.3	B	9:52; 10:100; 18:141 +
E422.1.1.3.1		
	B	3:136-137; 28:164-165
E422.1.1.5*(f)		
	B	3:136-137
E422.1.11.3	B	12:207-210
E422.1.11.4	B	3:56
E422.4.4(a)	B	3:58, 143; 6:19; 13:126-127; 29:219-222; 31:158
E422.4.4(ea)		
	B	18:136-139
E423	B	3:35-36, 47; 7:123; 29:138-141 +
E423(b)	B	13:137-145
E423.1.1.1(a)		
	B	3:102-103; 7:122, 125; 13:126; 15:119-121; 24:89-90; 30:265
E423.1.1.1(c)		
	B	3:54; 7:124; 12:207-210; 13:142
E423.1.2	B	2:46; 11:98-99; 13:182-184

Motif		Volume and Page
E423.1.8	B	3:102, 115; 13:126
E423.2.6	B	7:122
E423.2.7	B	7:62-68
E423.3	B	1:53-54; 6:20, 53; 8:103; 13:121; 14:197; 30:264-265; 31:12
E425.1	B	3:115-118; 6:19-20; 24:76 +
E425.1.1	B	3:143
E425.1.4	B	6:88; 29:219-222
E425.2.2	B	cf. 24:76; 30:230
E425.2.3	B	10:77-78
E434.3	B	18:83
E434.8	B	13:122-123
E451.3	B	24:91-92
E334	B	3:143-149; 7:14;
E338.1(ac)	B	7:123
E461		3:130-132
E467		6:14-18
E471		13:128-129
E474		22:93-97
E474.1		22:93-97
E491	B	cf. 16:354-355
E500	B	3:111-115; 30:118-119 +
E502	B	3:131
E510	B	3:148-149 +
E511	B	4:61-62
E520	B	3:111-115; 24:100 +
**E522		15:119-121
E530.1	B	3:46-47, 145; 28:107-108, 124-125, 163-164; 30:117 +
E530.1.0.1*	B	7:124; 9:53-54; 24:89
E530.1.1	B	18:145-146
E530.1.2	B	18:144
E530.1.3	B	18:144-145
E530.1.6	B	17:118-119
E535.1	B	24:101-102 +
E535.1(b)	B	3:55; cf. 30:119
E535.3	B	3:148-149; 4:61-62 +
E535.3(h)	B	3:191-193
E539	B	13:162; 18:141-146
E541	B	18:130-131
E542.1	B	12:207-210
E545.2	B	24:91

Motif		Volume and Page
E545.3	B	24:90-91
E554	B	3:138-141
E556	B	7:127
E574(bc)	B	6:17
E574(i)	B	29:139-141
E574(ia)	B	12:207-210
E575	B	24:90-91; 28:165; 30:118
E579*	B	7:136
E581.2	B	9:151; 28:164-165; 30:119-120
E581.8*	B	18:137-139, 146-147
E599.7	B	18:144-146
E599.8	B	18:137-139, 146-147
E610.1.1	B	6:53; 31:12
E613	B	6:8 +
E613.0.1		6:63; 31:11-12
E631	B	3:197, 200-201; 7:79-80; cf. 31:162 +
E631.0.1		10:134, 146-149; 23:53; 25:63, 67, 92 f.
*E631.0.5		24:106
E696.1		31:11-12
E710		1:83-84; 12:82-83, 128-129, 133; 14:248-249; 22:27-28; 32:47-49
E711.1		1:84; 12:82-83, 129, 133; 14:247-248; 32:49
E713		12:82-83, 128-129, 133; 14:247-248; 32:48-49
E722.1.4	B	8:103
E723	B	24:90-91; 30:118
E730	B	3:54, 102-103; 7:124-125; 12:207-210; 24:89-90; 30:265
E732		8:103
E732.1		8:103; cf. 12:66
E741.1.1		13:161
E742.2	B	9:53-54
E745.4		3:200-201
E752.2		8:103
E752.5		1:75-77

F. MARVELS

Motif		Volume and Page	Motif		Volume and Page
F511.2.2		15:134-135; 30:239-240	F641		32:55
F521.1		3:244-253	F681		11:19-47; 14:187-189
F521.1.1		13:79-85	F715		19:37; 21:68, 77
F531	B	3:118-129; 6:109-110; 7:49-51; 8:142-147; 10:79-81, 127-130; 11:17-47; 12:52-54, 78-79, 126 ff., 133-134, 194-200; 14:114-118; 20:68; 32:37-40; 34:112-115	F721.1		3:237-238; 12:249
			F721.2	B	3:130-132, 153-157, 207-208, 230-233
			F721.5		3:230-233; 12:246-248; 13:189
			F750		3:238-241; 12:173-174
			F771		3:231-233; 12:173-174, 246-249; 13:187-189; 20:89; 27:94 f.; 32:48
F531.3.2	B	11:22, 24, 43			
F531.5.3		32:37-38			
F535.1.1		32:37-40	F771.1.9		cf. 12:8-9; 34:189
F545.2.2		9:55; 21:72			
F565.2		18:61-78			
F567		3:244-253; 14:120-121; 18:92-93	F772.1		21:66; 24:84-86; 29:194-200
			F802	B	22:71-73
F567.1	B	3:242-253; 13:82-85; 18:92-93	F810	B	12:76-77; 14:269; 19:67; 28:61-62; 32:14, 16-17 +
F571.2		12:61-62; 32:35			
F577.2		14:114-118; 22:35; 29:194	F811		22:38, 107; 25:219; 30:241-242; 32:56
F601		11:17-47; 12:78-79	F815.1	B	18:83-84; 20:87
F601.1		11:22-47	F821.1.3.1		22:38
F601.2		11:41-47	F833		34:111
F610		3:118-129; 7:49-51; 8:142-147; 11:17-46; 12:77-79, 194-200; 19:53-54; 20:68; 34:187-200	F910	B	19:46
			F913		6:47-48; 24:78-80
			F932		3:211-219; 14:198; 21:77; 22:104-105
			F933.1		3:204-205; 4:79; 10:124-126; 13:69-70
F610.4		12:194-200			
F611.1.1		12:77-79; 30:9; 31:28	F933.5		3:204
F611.2.1		14:120-121	F941.1		13:189
F611.3.2		34:187-200	F950	B	5:124-125; 6:13-14; 8:11, 13 f., 21, 30 f., 50-51, 60-61, 65, 69-72, 79-81; 12:66-72, 76-77; 14:192-193, 268; 24:114; 27:4, 194-200 passim; 30:205-211, 223, 251-252; 34:164-171; 35:11, 15
F613		12:195			
F614.1		cf. 7:44; 19:53-54			
F614.10		34:191			
F615.2.1		34:188, 196			
F621		cf. 11:17			
F622		11:19 ff.			
F628.1.1.1		34:196			
F632		12:194-200			
F633		12:194-200			
F636		11:43-44			
F636.3		7:128-129; cf. 13:297	F959.3		6:13-14

G. OGRES

Motif		Volume and Page
G295*(e)	B	cf. 24:90
G296*(e)	B	12:119
G297*	B	31:28-29 +
G297*(b)	B	cf. 30:255-256
G299.5*	B	cf. 13:184
G303.3.1	B	12:66; 24:87-88; 25:206-210; 29:144 +
G303.3.1.2		18:81-82; 24:86; 29:144-145
G303.3.1.6		3:126-128
G303.3.2.3	B	3:126-127; 8:147; 25:213
G303.3.3.1.1	B	12:201 ff.; 24:86, 89-90
G303.3.3.1.2	B	8:147
G303.3.3.1.3	B	12:61-62
G303.3.3.1.4	B	3:121-122, 128; 8:144, 146 f.; 12:119
G303.3.3.1.5	B	24:86, 90; 25:213
G303.3.3.2.3	B	6:103
G303.3.3.2.7		3:129-130; 8:148
G303.3.3.2.11*	B	6:103
G303.3.3.2.13*	B	14:235-236
G303.3.3.6.1	B	24:132-136
G303.3.3.7.1	B	14:234-236
G303.3.4.2.1		24:88-89
G303.3.4.4.1		8:103-106
G303.3.5.1		3:126-129; 8:147
G303.4.1.2.2	B	3:125-126; 8:146; 24:87; 25:213-214; 31:28, 159
G303.4.1.6	B	3:126; 8:105, 146 +
G303.4.1.6.2	B	9:55
G303.4.1.7.1		14:236

Motif		Volume and Page
G303.4.5	B	3:126; 8:105, 146; 24:86-87; 29:144-145; 31:159 +
G303.4.5.3.1	B	18:81-82
G303.4.6		3:126-129; 8:105, 146-148; 14:236
G303.4.8.1	B	3:127; 8:103, 147; 18:81-82; 24:86; 29:138-139; cf. 31:160
G303.4.8.14*	B	cf. 9:50-51
G303.6.1.2	B	3:124-126; 8:103, 147; 18:81-82; 29:143
G303.6.1.3		cf. 3:124-126; 8:103; 18:81-82; 29:143
G303.6.2.1	B	18:81-82; 24:86-87; 25:207; 29:144-145
G303.6.3.4	B	3:127; 8:103, 147; 18:81-82; 24:86; 29:138-139
G303.7.1	B	3:129; 8:146, 148
G303.8.1.2		cf. 30:231; 32:178
G303.9.6.1		3:118-130; 6:102-106; 25:205-215
G303.9.6.2	B	cf. 30:231; 32:178
G303.9.9.16	B	cf. 29:145-146; 30:229-231
G303.10.4		24:86-87; 25:205-215 +
G303.10.4.1	B	18:82; 29:144
G303.10.4.4	B	18:81-82; 24:86-87; 25:207; 29:144
G303.10.17(a)	B	7:26, 30
G303.11.2		9:54-56
G303.11.5		7:128-130; 12:61-66
G303.12.5	B	7:128 +
G303.12.5.2	B	12:66-72
G303.12.6	B	cf. 24:76; 29:145-146; 30:229-231
G303.16	B	12:68-71; 24:89; 31:29, 160 +

Motif		Volume and Page	Motif		Volume and Page
G303.16.2	B	29:143	G500	B	21:77; 34:112 +
G303.16.3	B	6:105; 25:207-212 +	G501		12:52-55; 21:75-77
G303.16.3.4		8:105; 24:87; 29:145	G511	B	34:114
G303.16.8	B	24:86	G512	B	1:40; 6:110; 12:54,
G303.16.14	B	2:84; 9:57; 12:71;			129, 134;
		14:194; 18:135			14:113-117; 22:20,
G303.16.19.3					22, 28, 34, 40, 43;
	B	7:130-132			32:39; cf. 32:22,
G303.17.2.8		3:127; 8:103, 147;			49 +
		24:86; 29:138-139	G512.3		21:79
G303.18		12:71	G512.3.1		31:140; 34:201
G303.20.6	B	cf. 29:140-141	G514.1	B	cf. 12:69; 25:209-213;
G303.21.2	B	cf. 24:131; 28:156			27:87-88
G303.25.21.2*			G526		34:201
	B	9:55-56	G530.1	B	12:128-129, 133;
G308.2		22:102-104;			14:246-247; 32:49;
		24:132-136			34:113
G346		8:99-101; 10:79-81	G530.2		7:128-130; 12:61-66;
G350		14:70-71; 22:27-29;			34:201
		38-40, 44 +	G532	B	34:113
G354.1		12:199-200; 21:78;	G550		12:129, 134; 14:248;
		22:101-104;			22:107; 25:219;
		24:132-136; 31:140			32:49
G361.1.4		12:199-200	G572		12:49-55
G461		cf. 12:7-10, 63-65	G610.3	B	34:201
G465		12:62-66; 14:110-114;	G613		1:83-84; cf. 34:111-112
		27:93-95; 32:27-29	G661		34:111

H. TESTS

Motif		Volume and Page	Motif	Volume and Page
H12		12:13	H312.2	12:66-72
H36.1		27:90-91	H316	cf. 34:193, 200, 202
H50	B	32:8-12; 34:115	H317.1	7:128-130
H83		12:198-200; 31:140	H331	3:201-203; 8:101-102;
H105.1		12:198-200; 31:140		22:46-47 +
H105.1.1		12:199-200; cf. 31:140	H331.5.1	34:200, 202
H120		12:25	H331.5.1.1	34:193, 200, 202
H152.2		cf. 32:16	H335	3:202-203; 11:35-46;
H210	B	24:102, 106; 30:265		12:63-64, 126-129,
H248.2.1		cf. 14:256-259; 19:81;		199; 22:46-47,
		25:230-233;		83-84; 27:93-95;
		30:125-126		31:138-140; 32:25-29
H251.3.2	B	cf. 13:176-181	H335.0.1	12:63-64, 128-129
H301		11:35-46; 22:85-89;	H335.3.1	cf. 12:198-200; 31:140
		31:139-140	H380	31:26 +
H310	B	11:35-46; 22:46-47;	H386	22:90-93; 30:175;
		32:21-22		31:21-22;
				cf. 32:22-23

Motif		Volume and Page	Motif		Volume and Page
H473	B	(see also H386)	H1154.12		34:188, 195-196
		12:21-26; cf. 9:57	H1194		10:14-15
H500		10:24-25; 17:115-117;	H1211		32:24-28; 34:105, 188
		22:180-184;	H1212		34:188, 196, 199
		27:78-82;	H1219.1		34:105
		32:21-22 +	H1233.6.1		32:25-29
H530		27:79-82; 30:42	H1236.2		21:67-70
H561	B	27:79-82; 30:42	H1242		32:23-29
H921.1		cf. 31:26-27	H1247		34:105
H931		11:36-44; 27:94-95;	H1250		13:276-277, 294-296;
		31:139-140; 34:105			21:67-70;
H942		34:105			30:238-239
H945		12:125, 131; 14:242;			
		21:67; 22:83;	H1270		12:61-66
		30:238; 32:46	H1281		32:33-37
H961		27:78-82	H1284.1		21:67
H971.1		14:110-114	H1301.1.2		32:26-27
H972		32:17-23	H1320		32:28
H982		6:34-37; 12:79-86,	H1321.1		32:28
		123-133; 14:241-249;	H1324		32:27-28; 34:188,
		27:91-96; 32:23-29,			195-196
		44-49	H1360		34:188 ff., 196, 198 f.
H1010		11:35-44; 12:62-66;	H1361.1		34:188, 196
		14:110-114;	H1385		12:123-134; 22:82-85;
		27:93-95;			32:44-49 +
		32:27-29 +	H1385.3		14:241-249; 32:8-17
H1023.3		22:48; cf. 27:93-94	H1400	B	22:120-122;
H1024.4		27:78-82			34:109-110 +
H1101		11:41-44; 12:64	H1411	B	cf. 6:37-38; 31:13-14
H1103		12:64	H1416		28:164; 29:168
H1132.1.1		32:27	H1554.1	B	9:57
H1135		cf. 27:94-95; 31:137-138;	H1555.1		12:27-29
		34:190-191	H1557.4	B	cf. 9:57
H1151.13.3		34:105-109	H1567		35:131
H1154.3.1		12:64	H1578	B	cf. 22:44

J. THE WISE AND THE FOOLISH

J21	B	11:13-15; 12:7-10;	J217.0.1.1	B	10:31-32; cf. 14:164;
		30:173-175			22:206; 30:191-192
J21.2		12:8	J320		10:28-29; 18:39;
J21.5	B	11:14; 12:8			21:97-98
J21.6		12:7-10	J461.1		22:108
J21.23		30:261	J486		9:70-71; 12:76
J120	B	13:91-92	J514		12:6-7; 18:194
J151.4		cf. 6:10-11	J581.1		12:215
J163.4		(see J21)	J620		20:61-62
J191.1		12:2-4; 18:190-191;	J811.2		14:29-32
		32:42-44	J911		13:91-92

Motif		Volume and Page
J955.2		35:131
J1021		31:26-27, 31
J1074		10:48-50
J1113		13:94; 14:108-109; 19:69; 22:49-50; 30:129, 263-264; cf. 13:91-92
J1115.7		14:163
J1117		1:47-49; 7:137-138; 9:153-156; 12:4-7, 13-19, 50-51, 103-106, 214-215; 14:8-17, 21-34, 118-124, 135-144; 17:108-109; 18:172-180, 190-194; 21:73-75; 22:57-67, 71-74, 76-79; 25:8-9, 220-238, 240-242; 27:114-117; 32:49-52
J1117.2		(see "Coyote" in Part III of *Analytical Index*)
J1130		13:111-119; 18:208-212; 21:100-101
J1146.1		cf. 12:13-14; 14:118-119; 25:226-228; 32:49-50
J1172.2		36:125-133
J1155.1.1*(a)	B	10:20-21
J1155.1.1*(b)	B	21:102-104
J1169	B	18:208-212; 21:100-101; 30:281
J1172.3		12:4-7; 14:24-27; 18:191-194
J1189		21:98-99
J1250	B	2:50; 10:11-12, 14-15, 19-23, 33-36; 13:94, 101-102; 14:168; 18:205-206; 19:69, 131-132; 21:81-83, 85-88, 92-94, 98-99; 25:3, 242-243, 251-252; 29:166-168; 30:139, 263-264; 31:103-104 +

Motif		Volume and Page
J1251		13:88-89, 98, 101-102; 21:89-90
J1260	B	10:28-29, 33-34, 36-37; 13:96, 98-99, 101, 103; 17:4; 21:97-100; 24:104-105; 25:9-10; 30:125-127, 139, 263
J1261.1	B	10:28; 13:96; 30:128
J1262	B	13:98-101; 14:160-164; 21:96-97; 28:139-140; 30:127-128, 136-139
J1309.6*	B	13:90
J1341.11	B	cf. 7:139
J1350	B	7:72; 10:14-15, 18-19; 13:87-89, 94, 101-102; 14:160-161; 15:81-84; 18:11-60 passim, 205-206; 19:69; 25:3-4; 29:164-165; 30:126-127, 129, 136-139, 263-264, 279-280; 31:104-106 +
J1369.3	B	25:3
J1369.6*	B	cf. 15:83-84
J1390	B	14:168; 17:70-71; 21:83, 87-88, 93-94; 25:242-243 +
J1391.3.1	B	10:20; 21:85-86
J1400		13:99-100
J1440	B	2:50; 7:72; 10:23-24, 35-37, 50-52; 13:93-94; 15:99-100; 19:68-69; 21:90-92; 25:243-245; 29:166; 32:53
J1455(a)	B	cf. 21:89
J1495	B	10:38-42; 17:20-24; 25:245-247; 29:168-169; 31:17-19 +
J1495.1	B	25:247-249
J1495.3*	B	18:82-83
J1495.4*	B	18:82-83
J1499.3*	B	cf. 29:168-169
J1499.7*(a)	B	25:11-13

Motif		Volume and Page
J1499.10*	B	9:182; 17:3
J1499.11*(a)		
	B	13:88-89
J1499.11*(b)		
	B	7:58
J1499.13*	B	12:57; 18:84; 19:68; 27:167; 28:16; 32:54-55
J1510	B	12:36-41, 46-47
J1540		30:134-135 +
J1545.9	B	cf. 10:165-166; 23:207-208
J1549*(a)	B	13:92-93
J1549*(e)	B	13:87
J1561.3		30:279-280
J1565		25:8-9
J1579.7*	B	7:71
J1617		10:26-28, 31-32
J1649*(c)	B	5:78
J1649*(e)	B	18:13, 15, 20, 24, 27, 39
J1649*(g)	B	7:56
J1649*(i)	B	15:76-77
J1730	B	6:54, 80; 9:159-160, 163-164; 10:16-18, 107; 13:87, 103-104, 106-110; 15:82-83, 105; 17:57-58; 19:155-161; 20:11; 27:167; 31:10-11; 32:54 +
J1732(b)	B	32:32
J1738	B	14:160-163; 21:96-97; 30:136-139 +
J1738(a)	B	14:160
J1738.3	B	14:161; 30:137
J1738.4	B	14:161, 166; cf. 30:136
J1738.5	B	14:162
J1738.6	B	14:162-163; 21:96-97
J1742	B	10:44; 13:236; 25:245; 28:145-148; 29:56-57, 163; 30:183; 31:22 +
J1742.5.1	B	7:71
J1742.7*	B	7:69-70
J1750	B	13:87
J1761	B	17:20; 32:32
J1762		25:252-253
J1771		5:73-74; 12:13-15; 14:119

Motif		Volume and Page
J1772	B	7:69-71; 12:16-19, 214; 22:64; 32:49-52 +
J1772.1	B	20:11
J1780	B	10:39-40 +
J1781.1		cf. 25:245
J1782	B	17:19-22 +
J1782.4	B	9:43-44
J1782.6	B	10:40-42
J1791.3	B	12:16, 214; 14:80; 32:52
J1791.5		22:64
J1791.7	B	cf. 10:30-31
J1793		12:39; cf. 14:108-109
J1795.3*	B	10:30-31
J1803		10:107; 13:87, 183; 14:160-163; 30:139; cf. 10:16-18; 17:57-58; 32:54
J1805.1		32:54
J1811.1.1	B	13:98
J1811.5*(b)		
	B	cf. 10:48-50
J1813.8	B	7:72; 25:243-245
J1819	B	10:43-44; 12:47; 13:107-110 passim; 15:105; 19:155-161 passim; 29:56-57, 163; 31:22
**J1820		9:163-164; 15:105 +
J1823.1		12:44-46
J1880	B	20:90
J1881.2.2	B	12:29-36
J1900	B	6:87 +
J1902.1		12:47
J1911		12:47
J1919.2	B	18:11-60 passim; 19:161
J1922.1	B	19:155
J1930	B	7:53, 57-58; 10:53-54; 14:264; 15:105; 18:69; 20:60, 64-65; 27:167 +
J1934	B	19:155-156
J1935	B	31:22
J2012	B	10:31
J2030		10:44-46; 21:83-84
J2040(a)	B	19:159
J2060.1		cf. 24:6
J2061.1.1		cf. 24:6

K. DECEPTIONS

Motif		Volume and Page
K1771.2	cf. 25:3	
K1776		21:94-95
K1811		9:70-71; 12:168-169; 14:239-240; 27:87-88, 172-174, 175 +
K1811.1		24:105-106
K1812.17		30:263-264
K1815.2		14:108-109; cf. 22:49-50, 81
K1816	B	32:15-16; 34:190, 197-198
K1833		10:31-32
K1847		33:110-117
K1860	B	12:32-33; 14:259; 18:177-180; 19:81; 25:230-235 +
K1867		1:47-49
K1875	B	12:32-33; 34:104
K1916		6:55; cf. 28:118-120
K1923.1		33:116 f.

Motif		Volume and Page
K1932		12:198-200
K1951.1		31:135-140
K1951.3		31:135-140
K1956		10:24-25; 22:179-184
K1969.3		35:131
K1971	B	10:26-29, 46-48
K1984.5		22:67-70
K2011	cf. 6:42	
K2030		27:113-117
K2112.1		32:11
K2116.1		30:120-122
K2212.1		14:106-107; 27:89-91
K2213.4		12:128-129
K2217		34:192
K2241		6:45-47; 8:93-95
K2320		17:111-112
K2322		12:57-60
K2371.1(a) B		9:160-162; 19:29 +
K2371.1(ac)		
	B	12:152-158
K2371.1.1		12:11

L. REVERSAL OF FORTUNE

"After a while I returned to the girl and asked her if she'd dance the next cotillion with me.— 'No,' she replied, 'not looking as you do.' [The cowboy narrator explains that his hair had been trimmed by a companion just before the dance. The result was not good.] Thinking to retaliate, I said: 'Thank you . . . and please remember that there are as good fish in the sea as were ever caught out of it.'—'Yes, sir, I'm familiar with that old saw,' she fired back, 'but unfortunately for you those wise fish have stopped biting at toads.'" Branch Isbell, PTFS 5:105.

Motif		Volume and Page
L10	B	6:45-47; 11:9-47; 32:23-29 +
L10.1.1		34:201; cf. 12:194; 32:39
L50	B	14:105-107; 27:89-91
L54		27:89-91
L55	B	14:106-107; 27:89-91
L100	B	12:194-200; 19:60-62; 31:135-140 +
L101	B	12:79-85
L102	B	14:105-107; 27:89-91
L111.1		34:199
L111.3		11:9-47
L112.4		14:108-109; 22:45-50, 81-89
L114.3		12:77-79, 194-200
L142.2		32:42

Motif		Volume and Page
L143		12:29-44; 21:35-42; 24:128-132
L144	B	13:91-92, 94; 30:263-264
L160	B	(see L100, L102, L112.4, L161)
L161	B	11:47; 12:200; 14:108-109; 22:47, 85; 27:95; 32:22-23, 28
L162	B	27:91
L165		11:47; 32:28-29; cf. 12:76, 129; 22:81-82, 85
L310		14:79-80
L400	B	12:118; 13:94; 30:263-264; 32:42-44

M. ORDAINING THE FUTURE

N. CHANCE AND FATE

Motif		Volume and Page
N400	B	9:34-37; 10:24-25; 22:180-181; 25:78-84; 33:118-125
N465		15:134-135; 30:239-240
N467		30:263-264
N511	B	3:28-185 passim; 6:18; 8:118-121; 9:136-141; 12:173; 13:258-269; 14:259-261 +
N511.1		3:12-215 passim; 6:19; 9:142-144; 10:119-121; 14:175-176, 259-261; 24:99-100; 28:106-122 +
N511.1.6		3:185-189
N511.1.7		3:31-33, 51-52, 78-84; 6:18
N511.1.8	B	3:49-51, 84-89; 8:119-120; 9:133-141; 14:259-262; 28:143-145
N511.1.9	B	3:51, 81-84; 9:130-132; 10:120
N511.1.10	B	3:89-91
N511.1.12	B	9:142-144; 28:143-145
N511.2		3:12-27, 37-38, 60-75, 77-78, 80-81; 9:131, 133; 10:71-75; 12:173-174; 22:150-153; 30:60-62, 266-272; 32:60-61
N512	B	3:34-37, 45, 233-236; 9:133-141; 10:75-77
N513	B	3:33-34, 95-97, 103-104; 34:37-49
N513.3	B	3:31
N513.4	B	3:33-35, 85-89, 103-104
N513.5	B	3:191-193
N517	B	28:165-166 +
N517.1	B	3:185
N525	B	3:49
N531	B	3:89-91, 189-191

Motif		Volume and Page
N532	B	3:46-47; 10:77-78; 24:100-101; 31:28-29, 32
N534		3:20-23, 28-43, 62-63, 80-81, 97-99; 8:120-121
N534.1		3:80-81
N536		28:126
**N537		15:129
N551		3:53-54
N553	B	31:28-29, 32
N556		3:182-184; 24:99
N558		13:122-123; cf. 3:53-54; 28:154-156
N563	B	3:31-33, 54-56, 100-101, 190
N564	B	cf. 3:183; 24:99
N570	B	3:43-49, 52-57, 179-185; 10:77-78 +
N571.2*	B	3:34-37, 46-47; 6:19-20; 9:58-59; 24:100 +
N571.2*(b)	B	24:99
N571.2*(d)	B	3:54, 102-103
N571.2*(g)	B	9:58
N572.1	B	3:57-59; 13:126-128
N576	B	3:56-57, 99-103; 13:123-126 +
N576.2	B	3:58-59, 101-102
N576.3		3:101-102; 12:169
N591		3:78-80 22:81-82; 85
N595		3:51-52
N596	B	3:12-22, 24-27, 37-38, 60-78; 9:131, 133; 10:71-75; 22:150-153; 30:60-62, 266-272; 32:60-61
N597	B	9:45-47; 25:78-84 +
N597.1	B	20:51-52
N611	B	22:181-184
N620	B	7:43; 18:85 +
N621	B	10:25-26; 19:40-41
N688	B	10:25; cf. 22:180-181
N711.2		32:21-22

P. SOCIETY

Q. REWARDS AND PUNISHMENTS

Motif		Volume and Page
Q91		10:15-16; 27:78-82
Q94		32:17
Q172.1		cf. 30:232-233
Q172.3		12:120-121
Q210	B	18:142
Q211.4		3:136-137; 6:53; 12:205-210; 24:77-78; 31:12
Q212	B	9:138-140; 19:29-35; 31:15-16; 32:32-33
Q212.2	B	6:41-42; 25:183; 31:12-13, 163
Q220	B	10:119; 12:118-119; 14:239-240; 28:62-63
Q221.9*	B	29:142-143
Q222	B	12:166-168; 27:178
Q223	B	12:118-119
Q223.3		24:103
Q223.6.1*(b)	B	7:80
Q223.6.3*	B	28:60
Q251		24:114
Q261		14:227-233; 32:12-17
Q267		34:196-197
Q271.1		28:154; 32:17
Q272		13:128-129; 28:155-156

Motif		Volume and Page
Q275		3:145
Q280		3:206; 6:42-45; 27:90
Q291		3:144; 12:5-6; 14:24-27; 18:193-194; 28:61
Q305		3:218-219
Q331		6:10-11; 8:92-93, 95-96; 14:92; 28:156-157
Q380	B	30:73
Q386.1	B	18:81-82; 24:86-87; 25:207; 29:144
Q411		3:144
Q412		6:53; 31:12
Q414.1		12:15
Q416.2	B	32:29
Q502.1	B	24:80-81; cf. 9:81-83
Q520	B	9:81-83
Q550.1	B	30:222-223
Q551.3.4	B	30:265
Q551.6.8*	B	9:83
Q552.3.5		cf. 20:72
Q555		9:138-140
Q556	B	1:91-94; 9:127-128; 10:119
Q565	B	cf. 8:106-109; 19:29-35
Q581		34:194

R. CAPTIVES AND FUGITIVES

Motif		Volume and Page
R11	B	14:114-118; 22:103-104 +
R11.1		8:99-101; 12:77, 123-129; 14:110-114, 241-249; 32:44-49
R11.3		14:114-118
R13.1.5		13:79-85; 14:120-121 +
R13.1.6		12:77-79
R45.3		12:77; 25:238-240; 32:48
R100	B	14:117; 20:92 +
R110		22:83-84 +
R111		3:156; 18:8; 22:80-81 +
R111.1.3		12:198-200; 14:241-249; 32:22-29, 44-49

Motif		Volume and Page
R131		14:120-121
R151.1		14:241-249; 32:12-17
R153.3.2		25:238-240
R153.3.3		34:103-116
R161.4	B	23:45-47; 30:42
R163		6:63; cf. 32:17
R165		24:103-104
R181		12:70
R200	B	3:159-161, 171-176; 6:51-53; 19:45-47; 14:176-177; 22:110-120, 130-133; 24:100 +
R210		(see R200)
R211.3		3:237-238; 12:249; 22:188; 29:201-202
R215		12:49, 55

Motif	Volume and Page	Motif	Volume and Page
R220	3:32-34, 50-52, 79-80, 86-87, 95-97, 103-104, 211-213, 216-218, 251-252; 6:18; 7:128-130; 14:187-189, 265; 19:44-49; 21:78; 22:105-108; 25:217-219; 28:149-151; 32:41-42 +	R225.2	3:161-163
		R231	7:128-130; 12:65-66; 19:129-130; 31:29-30; 34:202
		R243	7:129; 14:113; 22:82-85; 25:219
		R260	(see R200)
		R261.1	29:196
		R300	19:42-56 +
		R311	22:107; 25:219, 235-238
R221	14:107		
R225	1:51; 3:147, 174-175; 7:124 +	R315	14:176-177 +
		R315.1	3:161-163

S. UNNATURAL CRUELTY

Motif	Volume and Page	Motif		Volume and Page
S11	3:146 +	S211		9:53-54
S11.3	8:103; 9:54-56; 12:169-173; 19:18	S221.1		12:123-133
		S261		2:8-13; 14:153
S12	6:53-54; 13:120-121; 24:74; 31:161-163	S263		1:67; 2:8-13; 3:155-156, 197; 22:156
S22.3	7:130; 12:61			
S31	6:42-45, 53-54; 14:106-107; 27:89-91; 31:11-12, 161-163	S264	B	cf. 22:101-104; 24:132-136
		S300		3:205-206; 6:53-54; 14:114-118; 28:117-118; 25:217-219; 29:202; 31:11-12, 161-163 +
S62	14:109-114			
S123.2	1:67; 32:13, 40			
S139.2	28:164-165			
S141	32:15; 34:190, 197	S301		31:27, 32
S142	6:62	S352		13:79-85; 14:120-121
S143	32:11	S400		6:42-45; 14:106-107; 27:89-91 +
S210	12:80, 123-125, 131; cf. 6:63 +	S432		cf. 32:15

T. SEX

Motif	Volume and Page	Motif		Volume and Page
T11.2	32:13-15; cf. 12:25	T70	B	3:175-176 +
T11.2.1	12:25	T71		18:9-10
T11.4	12:25 +	T80		3:168 +
T11.4.2	27:90-91	T81		1:50-51; 3:158, 164, 167-168, 171, 175-176, 200-202 +
T50.1.2	12:64-65; 32:44			
T56.1.1	22:81-82			
T66.1	6:59-65; 32:17-23	T81.6		3:163-167, 169-174, 202-204
T68	3:203; 11:9-47; 12:199-200; 27:91-95; 31:138-140	T86		3:202
		T91	B	3:200-201 +

Motif		Volume and Page
T91.3		12:159-161
T91.4		3:147
T91.6.4		14:108-109; 22:47-51, 81-89
T230		9:171; 13:92-93; 29:194-200; 32:53
T251		30:176 +
T251.1.1		10:164-165; 23:54-56; 27:72-73
T251.2		22:90-93 +
T251.2.3		30:175; 31:21-22
T300	B	28:118-120; 32:42-44 +
T311.1		3:175-176
T320		3:203

Motif		Volume and Page
T332	B	24:76; 29:145-146; 30:229-231
T400	B	12:117-118
T465	B	12:159-161; 13:85; 22:46, 97-100; cf. 29:202
T510	B	(see T540, T541.1.1)
T540		4:76-77; 6:109 +
T541.1.1		1:40; 6:110; 22:46
T550	B	9:54-56 +
T551.2	cf.	12:57
T554		13:85
T580	B	19:21-28
T615		1:39-40; 6:109-110; 21:72-73; 22:46
T685.1		22:30-44; 29:194-200

U. THE NATURE OF LIFE

U30		2:50-51; 12:4-7; 14:24-27; 18:191-194
U60	B	9:70-71; 12:29-44; 21:35-42; 24:128-132; 31:25-26

V. RELIGION

V22	B	24:74
V50		10:26-34, 36-37; 13:97-99; 14:164-165; 17:4; 21:97-98; 30:128 +
V52		12:176-177; 14:236; 19:19-20; 24:103-104 +
V52.4		13:101-102
V61.6	B	18:144-145
V72	B	2:71; 5:107-111; 8:90; 9:76-77; 10:55; 13:166, 171; 14:207-224; 18:115; 32:157-158, 168-175
V80		13:102-103; 14:155-169; 19:9-20; 29:165-166, 169; 30:139, 185-192; 34:51-62; 35:19-33
V86		8:105-106; 10:63-64; 12:24; 13:187; 14:237; 17:73; 30:252

V115	B	28:124-125
V120		12:165-169; 24:102-103; 27:172-178; 30:232-233
V132		24:115
V200	B	3:132-135; 9:70-71; 11:48-89; 13:97; 14:239-240; 17:126-140; 24:105-106; 27:175; 32:29-31 +
V220	B	12:44-46, 118-119, 165-169; 24:102-104; 32:32-33
V221		6:13-14
V236	B	30:231; 32:178
V250	B	3:165-166; 6:9-10, 12-13; 24:104-105; 27:175; 30:228 +
V256		6:13-14
V310		8:121-122; 13:100-101; 14:162; 28:139-140; 30:127-128

Motif		Volume and Page	Motif		Volume and Page
V340		14:239-240	V511.1		1:75-76; 10:18-19
V412		30:232-233			

W. TRAITS OF CHARACTER

W10		(see Q40, Q41, Q42, **Q51)	W152.14.2(h)	B	cf. 9:158-159
W37	B	12:27-29 +	W154	B	13:87-88; 29:163-164; 30:265 +
W37.1	B	20:62-63	W154.2.1		12:4-7; 14:24-27; 18:191-194
W111	B	17:115-117 +			
W111.5.10.1	B	13:87-88	W155	B	3:206, 218-219; 25:4; 27:114-117; 30:265
W111.5.12	B	cf. 21:85-86	W157	B	7:43, 78; 14:163, 180-184, 251-252; 18:149-150; 19:166; 22:185-193; 29:201-208; 30:265
W111.5.15*	B	18:61			
W115	B	14:180-184; 15:99-100			
W125		14:121-124			
W137	B	9:57; 12:7			
W150	B	3:118-130; 8:129-151; 10:129-130; 19:175-199; 22:195-199 +	W158		18:11-60 passim; 31:13-14
			W167	B	18:190-191; 25:240-241
W151		7:76; 27:114-117; 29:163-164; 31:3-5	W181.6		35:131
			W183*	B	12:7-8; 19:53-54
W152	B	29:163-164 +	W196	B	12:2-4
			W211.1		21:85-86
			W225.1	B	19:161; 25:13-15

X. HUMOR

X111	B	15:82-83 +	X410	B	13:96, 98, 101-103; 17:108-109; 21:99-100; 29:165-166, 169; 30:138-139, 191-102; 36:78 +
X111.11	B	cf. 9:159-160			
X111.15	B	19:158			
X137		31:104 +			
X137(c)	B	7:60			
X143.1	B	10:38-39; 25:245-247; 31:17-19	X411.3		13:103
X215*	B	14:251-252	X424	B	10:38-42; 22:207-214; 25:245-247; 29:169; 31:17-19
X310	B	18:208-217; 20:54; 25:5-6			
X312.1*	B	25:5-6	X434.2		13:96
X330	B	13:114-119; 14:254-256; 18:206-207; cf. 13:96-97	X435.1	B	29:165-166
			X435.2		13:96
			X438		10:18-19; cf. 25:5-6
			X441		cf. 10:32-33; 13:104-105
X350		9:162	X455*	B	(see J1738)
			X459(d)	B	(see X312.1*)
			X459.1.1	B	13:99-100
			X459.2*	B	21:99-100; 30:138 +

Motif		Volume and Page
X459.2*(a)	B	13:100-101
X583	B	18:11-60 +
X583(a)	B	13:94
X584	B	9:37-43; 18:84-85; 19:42-56; 20:4-5; 25:252-253 +
X584.1	B	9:39-40; 10:35-36
X584.2*	B	10:51-52; 21:91-92
X597*	B	12:153-158 +
X597.1*(b)	B	15:79-80
X599.1*	B	13:96-97; 15:83-84; 30:278
X610	B	14:162 +
X611	B	32:5-8
X621*	B	18:83
X641*	B	13:88-89
X680	B	8:121-122; 27:166
X691*	B	12:10-13
X700	B	13:92-94; 19:96, 156; 30:134-135; 32:53
X750	B	13:97-98 +
X753		31:26; cf. 34:105
X800	B	3:208-209; 12:57, 60; 13:90-91; 17:19-22; 19:155-161; 29:168-169
X811		17:19-22
X828*	B	29:168-169
X904.2(a)	B	19:68
X905.4		20:29; 22:78-79
X907.1	B	10:25-26; 12:55-57; 18:79-80; 19:36-41
X908		19:37
X911	B	9:36-37
X916	B	7:53 +
X916(ba)	B	18:69
X916(ga)	B	18:78
X916(hb)	B	18:61
X916(he)	B	18:70
X920	B	4:7-8; 7:45-54; 12:194-200; 14:263-264; 20:68
X921	B	20:68
X921(g)	B	7:60
X921(ga)	B	7:60
X921(p)	B	20:68
X923(b)	B	18:61
X923(ba)	B	18:61
X924(c)	B	18:61
X924(h)	B	18:61
X929*(f)	B	20:68
X931	B	7:56; 14:189-191 +
X931(b)	B	12:195-196
X931(c)	B	12:194
X932(a)	B	12:195
X933(a)	B	7:50
X934(a)	B	18:71
X936(b)	B	cf. 32:55
X937(a)	B	15:77; 29:51 +
X937(aa)	B	18:75
X937(b)	B	18:75
X941(j)	B	20:71
X943	B	11:43 +
X943(cc)	B	cf. 19:53-54
X945(a)	B	3:121; 10:129; 34:198
X945(b)	B	10:128
X945(c)	B	10:129
X945(d)	B	7:49
X955(ac)	B	18:68
X955(c)	B	18:64
X957*	B	7:61
X957*(a)	B	7:54
X958(ga)	B	7:61
X958(gf)	B	7:61
X958(hd)	B	cf. 20:83-85
X958(m)	B	7:61
X959.2(c)	B	32:55
X967(a)	B	18:68
X972(a)	B	3:118 ff.; 10:127 ff.; 18:61 ff. +
X972(bb)	B	20:99-100
X972(c)	B	18:73
X973(a)	B	29:202
X980	B	3:236-237; 20:62-63, 85-88
X981*	B	(see also X1121[a] ff.) 9:1-14 +
X981*(af)	B	9:7
X981*(ca)	B	9:5
X981*(cb)	B	9:8
X981*(cc)	B	9:9
X981*(cd)	B	9:10-11
X981*(ce)	B	9:13
X981*(cf)	B	9:9
X981*(cg)	B	9:9
X981*(ch)	B	9:7
X981*(ck)	B	9:4
X986(i)	B	12:198

Motif		Volume and Page	Motif		Volume and Page
X1084.2*(d)			X1086.1*(e)		
	B	7:51, 58-59		B	7:60-61
X1084.3*(a)			X1092.1*	B	14:269; 19:67
	B	20:63	X1110	B	18:84-85; 19:42-56;
X1084.3*(b)					20:94-95 +
	B	7:58	X1112	B	18:85
X1084.3*(c)			X1113*	B	(see X1124.1[a])
	B	20:70	X1119	B	20:94-95 +
X1084.4*(aa)			X1119.1	B	19:68; 20:95
	B	7:60	X1121(a)	B	20:95
X1084.4*(ab)			X1121.1.2*	B	20:94-95
	B	20:79	X1121.2*(b)		
X1084.4*(ba)				B	20:95
	B	7:53	X1121.4*(c)		
X1084.4*(bb)				B	20:95
	B	7:60	X1121.6*	B	20:94-95
X1084.4*(bc)			X1122.1(b)	B	20:95
	B	20:71	X1122.2	B	18:85; 20:95
X1084.4*(d)			X1122.3.2*	B	18:85
	B	20:75	X1122.4*(a)		
X1084.4*(e)				B	9:8
	B	20:66-67	X1124	B	18:85-88 +
X1084.4*(f)			X1124.1(a)	B	14:264; 20:59-60
	B	20:69	X1124.2	B	cf. 18:67
X1084.4*(g)			X1124.3	B	18:85; 20:11 +
	B	20:67-68	X1124.3.1	B	7:43
X1084.4*(i)			X1130	B	6:48-51; 14:252-254 +
	B	20:72	X1130.2	B	32:55
X1084.5*(a)			X1132.1(a)	B	18:67
	B	7:52	X1133	B	14:252-254 +
X1084.5*(b)			X1133.3	B	9:34-37
	B	7:51-52; 20:60-62	X1133.3.2(a)		
X1084.5*(c)				B	9:158; 10:37-38
	B	20:69	X1153	B	7:40-41; 22:201
X1084.6*(a)			X1156(b)	B	cf. 22:201
	B	7:51; 20:83	X1201	B	7:56-70; 19:36-41;
X1084.6*(b)					20:90-91
	B	20:72	X1202.1(c)	B	20:58-59
X1085.1*(b)			X1203(f)	B	9:17; 30:178-179
	B	20:72	X1205.1(ba)		
X1085.1*(c)				B	8:128
	B	7:59	X1205.2*(a)		
X1085.2*(a)				B	20:90
	B	20:78	X1206(bb)	B	9:24-25
X1085.3*(c)			X1207*(e)	B	7:60-61
	B	7:56	X1215	B	12:72-75 +
X1085.3*(d)			X1215.7(a)	B	20:97
	B	20:72-73			

Motif		Volume and Page
X1215.8(ac)		
	B	18:85-88
X1215.9	B	15:95; 18:85-88; 20:97
X1215.11(b)		
	B	14:264; 20:95-96; 30:179
X1216.1	B	20:97-98
X1221	B	9:37-43; 18:76; 20:97-98; 31:106 +
X1221(bb)	B	9:40-43
X1221(d)	B	18:71-72, 77
X1233	B	7:60-61; 9:17-26; 14:264; 15:80-81; 20:58-60; 30:178-179
X1233(bc)	B	9:18-20
X1233(db)	B	18:83
X1233(gb)	B	9:20-21
X1233(gc)	B	9:23
X1233(gd)	B	9:23
X1233(gg)	B	9:25-26
X1233(gi)	B	29:165
X1233.1	B	9:21-24
X1233.2.1	B	15:80
X1233.3.2*	B	19:66
X1235	B	22:201 +
X1235(eb)	B	20:88
X1237	B	7:56-57
X1237(ba)	B	19:44
X1237.2.3*(eh)		
	B	7:56-57
X1237.2.9*(b)		
	B	cf. 22:202-204
X1237.2.11*(a)		
	B	cf. 7:53
X1241	B	14:265; 16:342, 396-402, 406-407; 19:54-56; 20:90-92; 32:55 +
X1241.1(ac)		
	B	20:91
X1241.1(ba)		
	B	20:90-91
X1241.1(cc)		
	B	7:58
X1241.1(cd)		
	B	16:294
X1241.1(fc)		
	B	20:91

Motif		Volume and Page
X1241.2.1	B	19:55-56
X1242	B	20:86; 22:202-204; 28:59, 135-138
X1242(b)	B	28:59, 135-138
X1242(da)	B	cf. 29:51
X1243.1	B	5:157-158; 23:230; 25:102
X1250	B	18:84
X1252	B	19:68
X1266*(aa)		
	B	15:163
X1266*(ab)		
	B	15:167
X1266*(ac)		
	B	14:34-35; 15:167
X1266*(ad)		
	B	15:166-167
X1266*(b)	B	15:154
X1266*(d)	B	15:172
X1266*(e)	B	15:172
X1280	B	20:90 +
X1280.1	B	20:41-42
X1286.1.4.1*		
	B	18:79-80; 20:73-74
X1286.1.5(e)		
	B	29:92
X1288.1*(c)		
	B	20:29
X1301.5*(c)		
	B	20:98-99
X1303	B	20:98-99 +
X1303.1	B	9:157-158
X1305*(c)	B	22:201
X1321	B	12:89-100; 19:162-164; 20:76-77 +
X1321.1.1(b)		
	B	5:59
X1321.1.1(i)		
	B	20:75-76
X1321.2(bb)		
	B	5:68
X1321.2(bc)		
	B	8:126-127
X1321.3	B	12:89-100 +
X1321.3.1	B	8:127-128
X1321.3.1.1*(b)		
	B	5:59-60
X1321.3.1.2*		
	B	8:127-128

Z. MISCELLANEOUS GROUPS OF MOTIFS

WJ '30

Section 3: Ballad Numbers (Child and Laws Listings)

References: Francis James Child, *The English and Scottish Popular Ballads*, 5 vols. (Boston: Houghton, Mifflin and Co., 1882-1898); G. Malcom Laws, *Native American Balladry*, rev. ed. (Philadelphia: The American Folklore So., 1964).

Of course Child's "English and Scottish" and Laws' "native American" ballads constitute but a small portion of popular song. For alphabetized titles or first lines of all songs and ballads (including a number in Spanish) either appearing or cited in the Texas Folklore Society Publications, volumes 1-36, see Part III of the *Analytical Index*.

A. BRITISH BALLADS

Child No.	Volume and Page	Child No.	Volume and Page
2	10:137-138; cited, 27:24 (foldout), 29, 42 ff., 65, 74	43	cited 27:44
		44	cited 27:44
		46	cited 27:24 (foldout), 74
3	cited 27:24 (foldout), 74	49	cited 27:24 (foldout), 29, 35 ff., 58 f., 74
4	10:138-140; 23:34-36; cited, 27:24 (foldout), 28 f., 39-40, 44, 47	51	cited 27:35
7	cited 27:24 (foldout), 29, 60, 74	53	cited 27:24 (foldout), 29, 55, 74 f.
8	cited 27:24 (foldout), 74	54	cited 27:24 (foldout), 74
10	10:141-143; cited, 25:93, 102; 27:24 (foldout), 29, 44, 48, 54, 59, 66 f., 74; 30:31	58	35:65-72; cited, 27:132; 30:41, 43
		59	cited 27:44
		63	cited 27:24 (foldout), 74
12	cited 20:10; 25:63; 27:24 (foldout), 29, 67, 74; 30:36	68	10:143; 23:44; cited, 10:133; 27:24 (foldout), 29, 39, 60, 62, 74
13	23:59-63; 26:137-138 (reprint); cited, 25:63; 27:24 (foldout), 29, 35, 74; 30:31	72	23:71; cited, 10:156
		73	10:144-146; 23:39-42; cited, 27:24 (foldout), 28 f., 31, 55, 60 f., 70, 74
16	cited 27:35	74	cited 10:134, 146; 25:67, 92 f.; 27:24 (foldout), 29, 44, 50 f., 55 f., 62, 70 f., 75; 30:43
18	cited 27:24 (foldout), 29, 68, 74		
20	cited 27:24 (foldout), 74		
26	7:110; 14:280-283; 23:42-43; cited, 25:91, 99 f.; 27:24 (foldout), 29, 64, 69, 74; 30:34	75	cited 27:24 (foldout), 28 f., 75
		76	23:58-59; cited, 27:24 (foldout), 29, 71, 75
29	cited 27:44		
34	cited 27:44	77	cited 27:44
35	cited 27:44	78	cited 27:44
37	cited 27:135	79	23:32-34; cited, 27:24 (foldout), 29, 44, 49, 57, 75
39	cited 27:44		
40	cited 27:44		
42	cited 27:44	81	cited 27:24 (foldout), 40, 57, 75

Child No.	Volume and Page
84	7:111-112; 10:146-149; 23:49-51; 25:51-57, 61-62, 65-67; cited, 10:131, 134; 27:24 (foldout), 28 f., 56, 71, 75 f.; 28:35; 30:31; 32:245
85	cited 27:24 (foldout), 29, 75
93	cited 27:24 (foldout), 75
95	23:45-47; cited, 27:24 (foldout), 29, 61, 75
105	cited 27:24 (foldout), 75
112	cited 27:24 (foldout), 75
155	cited 27:24 (foldout), 29, 38 f., 57 f., 63, 72, 75
157	cited 27:134
162	cited 27:29
173	23:63-65; cited, 27:24 (foldout), 75
181	cited 27:29
200	23:47-49; cited, 27:24 (foldout), 29, 41, 75
209	cited 27:24 (foldout), 29, 75
214	cited 27:44
215	cited 27:24 (foldout), 75
218	cited 27:24 (foldout), 75
225	cited 27:29
226	cited 27:24 (foldout), 74 f.

Child No.	Volume and Page
236	cited 27:24 (foldout), 75
243	10:159-162; 23:56-58; cited, 10:135; 27:24 (foldout), 28 f., 61, 63 f., 75
250	cited 27:24 (foldout), 29, 75
255	cited 27:44
265	cited 27:44
272	cited 27:24 (foldout), 44, 74 f.
274	23:65-66; cited, 27:24 (foldout), 29, 75
277	23:66-68; cited, 27:24 (foldout), 29, 75 f.
278	10:164-165; 23:54-56; cited, 10:131, 136; 27:24 (foldout), 29, 34, 44, 72 f., 75
279	cited 27:24 (foldout), 75
286	cited 27:24 (foldout), 29, 75
287	cited 27:24 (foldout), 75
289	10:162-163; cited, 27:24 (foldout), 29, 75
295	23:37-38; cited, 27:24 (foldout), 75
296	cited 27:29
299	cited 10:134; 27:24 (foldout), 75

B. NATIVE AMERICAN BALLADS

Laws No.	Volume and Page
A8	cf. 6:152-153; 32:188-198; cited, 7:167
A10	6:143-144
A11	6:143-144
A14	6:150; 7:167
A15	6:144
A17	6:132-134; 23:120
B1	4:53
B1.0	2:45; 6:201; 18:2-6; 32:172-173
B2	6:173 ff.; 7:147; 9:183-184; 29:88-92; cited, 6:158
B3	6:143
B4	6:184; 26:131 (reprint)
B5	cited 6:158, 184; 26:131
B7	6:190; 26:136 (reprint)
B13	14:273-279

Laws No.	Volume and Page
B15	7:170-172
B16	6:184; 16:295-296; 26:131 (reprint)
B18	16:295
B20	6:185; 26:132-133 (reprint)
B23	6:187; 26:134-135 (reprint)
C25	7:176
E4	23:122-124; 26:138-140 (reprint); cited, 4:53; 6:158, 202
E11	23:118
E15	6:186-187; 26:133-134 (reprint)
F1	23:100-102
F14	23:125
G1	29:122
G16	6:210; 23:257-259

Laws No.		Volume and Page
G17		6:215; 23:98
G19		23:155-157
G22	cited	32:229-230
G31		23:128-131; 26:141-142
		(reprint); cited, 28:66
H1		5:108; 14:162, 187;
		18:11-60
H3		2:40-41
H4		23:183
H6		23:110-111
H8		23:102-104; 26:137
		(reprint)
H13		23:219-221

Laws No.		Volume and Page
I1	cited	29:173-174; 30:31, 34
I2		7:115
I3		25:99, 113
I4		23:179-180; cited, 30:93
I17		1:5; 5:173-175; 7:87;
		26:165-167 (reprint)
I19		23:212
dB28		7:161-162; 10:110-114,
		122-123
dB35		6:216
dB39		10:155
dB42		6:207
dE33	cited	6:198

"There were three crows sat on a tree . . . ."

Priest sprinkles holy water on Devil snake; see Synopsis 5.26.

PART TWO
Tale Synopses

Phantom steers on Stampede Mesa; see Synopsis 8.39.

PART II: TALE SYNOPSES
Note on Procedure

Locating tales. Synopses appear under nine headings as outlined in the Table of Contents. As an aid to locating tales and motifs, a "Guide to the Section" begins each division. In addition, the Alphabetical Index (Part III) identifies many tales by subject, theme, or traditional label— for example, "Forts, legended," "Dividing waters theme," "Stupid's Cries tale." Finally, should a user of the *Analytical Index* come equipped with a tale-type or motif number from the Aarne-Thompson, Thompson, or Baughman indexes (see the headnotes to sections 1 and 2 of Part I), the specialized indexes in Part I provide for yet a third mode of approach. Note: Not all of the narrative material in the Texas Folklore Society volumes answers to catalogued tale types and motifs.

Numbering of synopses. As a means of referring to them in the introductory guides and in cross-reference where needed, synopses carry identifying numbers. Thus the number 1.1 designates the first synopsis in Section 1 below, and 9.151 the last synopsis (it happens) in Section 9. These numbers bear no relation to tale-type or motif numbers.

Provenience. Whereas many synopses indicate the ethnic provenience of tales, others do not. When no indication is given, the tale is of "Anglo" provenience so far as could be determined. Otherwise, either the spelled-out name of an Indian tribe or race, noted in parentheses, or one of the following abbreviations will precede a synopsis:

    (I) = Indian (affiliation not clear)
    (N) = Negro
    (M) = Mexican or Mexican-American

Duplicated tales. Usually a single synopsis, providing multiple references, serves for tales that occur more than once in the Society's volumes. Occasionally, however, narrative variation has seemed to warrant separate treatment. In most such instances variants of tales have been grouped. When not grouped (see the next paragraph), similar or cognate tales have been linked by cross-references.

Problems of classification. The perfect system of classifying folktales has yet to evolve. Among the difficulties, the spirit in which a tale is told — humorous, didactic, awe-provoking, etc. — can determine its character and hence affect its narrative classification, so that what now seems a comic anecdote, for example, may emerge elsewhere as a "scare" story. Observe these occurrences of Type 1676B, "Clothing Caught in Graveyard," as found in the Society's volumes:

> (N) A Negro is to go into a graveyard at night and prove he is not afraid of ghosts by sticking a knife into a grave. After accidentally sticking the knife through his coat-tail, he thinks he is being held and collapses from fright. 29:168.

> On a dare, a young girl visits a cemetery at night. Next morning she is discovered dead beside a grave, her face frozen in an expression of horror. As part of the dare, she was to have stuck a knife into a grave. When the girl is found, her dress is pinned to the grave by a knife. (The cause of the pinned clothing, whether the girl's inadvertence or a hand from the grave, remains unspecified.) 28:164.

Although manifestations of the same basic tale, these variants belong to different narrative categories despite their kinship and the fact that the type number assigned to them indiscriminately places both in the Aarne-Thompson category "Jokes and Ancedotes." In the following pages, accordingly, they appear as estranged entities under the headings "Realistic-Minded Tales of Humor" and "Tales of the Supernatural," respectively. This and similar problems of classification are mitigated through the use of cross-references—the only practicable recourse.

Section 1: Myths and Explanatory Tales

GUIDE TO THE SECTION

MYTHIC BEINGS, THEMES: Amerind prime-movers, demigods, culture heroes, 1.1—1.13; good and evil spirits vie, 1.14; theft of fire, 1.15, cf. 1.21; paradise lost, 1.16, cf. 1.3; deluge, 1.17, cf. 1.6, 8.3; journey to otherworld, 1.18—1.19; god-mortal intercourse (eagle as girl's lover), 1.20; man (woman) in the moon, 1.21—1.22, cf. 1.3, 1.6; evil enters the world, 1.23. (Tower of Babel, 1.5—1.6; preternatural power over animals, 1.53.) SPECIFIC ORIGINS: petrified wood, 1.24; rain, 1.25; water in streams, 1.26, cf. 1.12, 1.17; buffalo, 1.27; pecan tree, 1.28. See also 1.7, 1.11—1.12 (flint), 1.15, 1.21 (light), 1.17 (rainbow), 1.46—1.48 (desert plants). CHARACTERISTICS EXPLAINED: coyote and wildcat, 1.29; beasts of prey, 1.30; rabbit, 1.31; crow, 1.32; *pájaro cu* and owl, 1.33; *tengo frío* bird, 1.34; peacock, 1.35; mockingbird, 1.36; dove, 1.37— 1.38; whippoorwill, 1.39; roadrunner, 1.40, cf. 1.33; buzzard, 1.41— 1.42; cardinal, 1.43; cicada, 1.44; butterfly (and thundercloud), 1.45; *el cardo santo* (thistle-like shrub), 1.46; *cenizo* (ash) shrub, 1.47; *Guadalupana* vine, 1.48; wine, 1.49; woman, 1.50. See also 1.6 (why dog howls at the moon), 1.11—1.12 (animal and human traits and life-patterns established through forfeits and otherwise), 5.53 (why turkeys exist in wild state), 8.28—8.29 (bluebonnet flower). OTHER: how Apaches got horses, 1.51; archangel Michael fights Lucifer, 1.52; divine-ly-favored hero subdues lion, uses as pack animal, 1.53.

1.1 (Tejas) Old Man and Old Woman make heaven by placing timbers in a circle. Old Woman sprang from an acorn; daily gives birth to the sun, moon, weather phenomena, corn. 6:109.

1.2 (Navajo) First Man creates heaven; coyote causes the first eclipse; Fire Boy makes the Milky Way. First Woman and helper Bego-chidi create first the Navajos, then other Indians, the white man, and domestic animals—all of wind and mist. 14:127-134.

1.3 (Chibcha: Columbia) Creator Chiminigagua populates the earth; humans are to have dominion. Breathes on lake to produce the nymph Bachue, whose son Chibchacum "lay down with the puma." Following discord among created beings, Chibchacum is appointed lawgiver. Bachue, in her old age, is recalled by the creator, who rejuvenates her as the moon. 4:76-77.

1.4 (Alabama-Coushatta) Earth diver. Water covers all; a few ani-mals float on a raft. Crayfish dives to build a mud chimney, then earth. Buzzard forms hills and valleys by fanning the soft earth (cf. 1.11) with its wings. 21:65-66.

1.5 (Alabama-Coushatta) Indians are made from clay (cf. 1.11) deep in a cave. They emerge only at night until tricked by the white man (who furnishes whiskey) into staying out in the daytime. Tower of Babel. 21:66.

1.6 (Piegan-Blackfoot) First Man and Woman have twin boys to help make the world—one clever, the other stupid. Boys witness their mother's adultery with a white man, who appears as a snake with a horn in its head. Father kills the rival, severs his wife's head; the rolling head pursues father and sons. Mother takes up residence in the moon, father in the sun. Clever boy creates the white man, bestows tools; stupid boy creates Indians, divides into tribes. Tower of Babel; deluge. Explanatory element: why dog howls at woman in the moon. 29:194-200.

1.7 (Kiowa-Apache) Indian family, including Lucky Boy, is destroyed by the stone monster Nistcre, except for a daughter who marries Thunderman, gives birth to twin boys. (Thunderman shatters Nistcre with hurled lightning: origin of flint.) Fire Boy and Water Boy render deer, horses, and buffalo useful to man. Play game with a witch, whom they kill; elude old couple who would eat them; struggle with cyclone, which carries them off but cannot harm them because of the feather covering they wear. 22:30-44.

1.8   (Tejas) Acorn Man is born from a blood clot after his mother is
       eaten by giant (drop of blood falls on acorn). Following miracu-
       lously speedy growth, he avenges his mother, withdraws to the sky
       to govern earth.   1:39-40; 6:109-110.

1.9   (Alabama-Coushatta) Baby found by the Alabama Indians grows
       to adulthood in three nights. He has horns, is called Horned Man.
       Puts the head of a vicious wolf on a stake; the head turns to mark
       the direction of approaching enemies.   21:72-73.

1.10   (Kiowa-Apache) Boy born from a blood clot is raised by a
       sorceress mother. Miraculous growth. Because ungainly and un-
       clean, is called Poor Boy. Is tricked by coyote in a wooing contest;
       nevertheless wins the chief's daughter by performing miracles
       (gathers plums in winter, mesmerizes buffalo herd) that coyote
       attempts only to make a fool of himself. Boy becomes a comely
       young man, then a yucca plant. Explanatory element: why
       Indians have two wives.   22:45-51.

1.11   (Kiowa-Apache) The earth is soft and in semi-darkness. Humans
       are shaped from mud (cf. 1.5). Stone monster Nistcre plays a hand-
       game with the animals; physical characteristics and habits of ani-
       mals are established through forfeits and otherwise. Nistcre loses
       the final game, is pushed off a cliff in the Texas Panhandle, where
       the monster's shattered remains form big rocks.   22:18-20.

1.12   (Kiowa-Apache) Herb-eating animals play a hand-game with
       Nistcre (here multiple monsters). Nistcre lose; animals push them
       over a cliff but Nistcre have rosin on their feet, bounce back. Coyote
       gets turtle's necklace which, when pressed, causes huge streams of
       water to inundate Nistcre. (People now sharpen knives on the
       stone remains.) Peeved at its own ugliness, crow says there shall
       be death in the world; coyote stipulates resurrection after death.
       22:20-22.

1.13   (Kiowa-Apache) External soul. Coyote sees Nistcre hide it heart;
       spears the heart as it jumps away, thus killing Nistcre. Coyote
       later roasts fat people.   22:27-29.

1.14   Dark Spirit defeats White Spirit, steals the moon. With the beat-
       ing of tom-toms Indians revive the good spirit, release the moon.
       1:52-53.

1.15   (Kiowa-Apache) Cave people (cf. 1.5) possess daylight and fire.
       By trickery coyote steals fire, which is passed from animal to ani-
       mal until turtle hides it within its shell. Coyote uses fire to make
       the sun and flintstones. (Cf.1.21.)   22:22-25; cf. 14:71-72.

1.16   In East Texas a golden log spans a creek and links villagers with
       a sawmill (where they work) and its commissary. The village

women chip splinters from the log for unnecessary purchases; a vain young bride, wanting new clothes, chips until the log breaks. Villagers are thus separated from sources of sustenance; bad luck follows.   31:3-5.

1.17   (Chibcha: Columbia) People become wicked; the creator, Chiminigagua, destroys them by flood. A few "chosen" are saved. Rainbow appears; water flows from struck rock (cf. 8.5).   4:78-79.

1.18   (Alabama-Coushatta) As a panther, wolf, and wildcat, three men reach the otherworld after passing obstacles: a river, a war in progress, a mass of snakes. They receive seeds for vegetables, return to their kinsmen.   13:276-277, 294-296; 21:67-70.

1.19   (N) A Negro in the woods suddenly finds himself in hell. Hell hounds chase him into different levels of hell, then into heaven.   1:75-77.

1.20   (Aztec) Eagle lover. Unsuccessful suitor sees an eagle descend from heaven, make love to a princess. He shoots an arrow into the lovers. (Enmity between two knightly orders among Aztecs thus established.)   12:159-161.

1.21   (Kiowa-Apache) Ant steals daylight from a house where it is kept by two women. One woman helps ant. Daylight is passed from animal to animal (cf. 1.15); the women become the two women in the moon.   22:25-26.

1.22   Farmer who burns brush on Sunday is translated to the moon to burn brush forever.   7:80.

1.23   (Chichimecs: Mexico) First king, Xolotl, accepts a flaming flower from the god of lost souls, Mictlantecentli. The flower brings power, then sorrow. The god refuses to take it back. Explanatory elements: evil qualities in men; how brother came to hate brother.   12:143-151.

1.24   Petrified wood represents the burned parts of a monster that defied the sun until natural forces destroyed it.   10:79-81.

1.25   (M) God observes the parched earth and is saddened. Weeps, causing rain.   9:48-49.

1.26   (Alabama-Coushatta) In a dice game, an Indian loses all the water in the land. He prays for forgiveness. God tells him to break large pieces of cane, from which water flows to replenish the streams.   13:296-297.

1.27   (Kiowa-Apache) Coyote changes into a puppy, tricks crow into revealing a cave where crow has hidden the buffalo.   22:52-53.

1.28   (Kiowa) Green plant springs from the grave of a fallen leader, becomes a tree yielding edible nuts (pecan).   7:79-80.

1.29   (Kiowa-Apache) Coyote and wildcat are both handsome but make each other ugly by playing tricks. Their physical characteristics are thus established.   22:56.

1.30   (Kickapoo: Mexico) Flood brings animals together on a hilltop. Here lions, bears, wolves, and wildcats learn to eat other animals.   12:87.

1.31   (Kickapoo: Mexico) Bear wants the world to stay dark; rabbit wants light. Rabbit wins the argument. Bear scratches him, leaving marks near his eyes and tail.   12:86.

1.32   (Kiowa-Apache) Crow is white; but because he warns animals when the Indians are hunting, Indians punish him by smearing him with charcoal, condemning him to a carrion diet.   22:53-55.

1.33   (M) At the creation, one bird, the *Pájaro Cu*, is left without feathers. Other birds contribute feathers. Impressed with its new appearance, *Pájaro Cu* flies to heaven without making payment. Owl, who has acted as surety for the feathers, now must hide from the other birds. Owl seeks *Pájaro Cu* at night, crying *cu cu cu*. Roadrunner searches in the daytime.   12:19-20.

1.34   (M) *Tengo frío* (I am cold) bird of northern Mexico was beautifully feathered, but gave plumage to an Indian chief. Was left naked and cold, hence its cry. Other birds contributed their dullest feathers, hence its appearance.   19:60-62; cf. 6:8.

1.35   (M) Peacock has attractive red and yellow feathers; is boastful, ridicules crow. Crow daubs mud on peacock. Other birds take pity and design new plumage. Today peacock is modest as well as beautiful.   28:156-157.

1.36   (M) Animals speak a common language. Mockingbird has the sweetest song but is boastful, denies receiving aid from God. Hawk seizes mockingbird. It prays for aid and is saved, but its wings are so tattered that dove donates three white feathers for mending. Mockingbird now sings *"con el favor de Dios."*   6:10-11.

1.37   (M) Dove not told of the Saviour's birth; mourns because it was the only creature not to worship at the manger.   8:98.

1.38   (M) Turtle dove is the reincarnation of an Indian girl who loved a faithless shepherd. Its cry is to the shepherd.   6:8.

1.39   (Alabama-Coushatta) Although Indians have been friendly to all wildlife, whippoorwill steals thread from a squaw. Is sentenced to cry "I stole it."   21:79-80.

1.40 (M) Roadrunner, a distant cousin of the pheasant, presumes on the relationship, addresses the truly noble birds as *"paisano"* ("countryman" or, loosely, "kinsman"). Eagle is outraged; condemns roadrunner to lose the power of flight, subsist on carrion, be called *paisano* in mockery. 8:92-93.

1.41 Burro and lion agree that whichever can catch buzzard alive is the cleverer animal. Burro succeeds by feigning death, thus luring buzzard to stick its head in burro's mouth. Today buzzard has featherless red neck (embarrassment). 17:115-117.

1.42 (Kickapoo: Mexico) Buzzard takes Christ to the sky to get blue paint for Christ's face. Leaves Christ hanging on the tip of the moon (cf. 9.102—9.103). Christ becomes a leaf, floats to earth; then a fox, feigns death. Buzzard descends to feast on the fox. Christ grabs him; will reduce buzzard from preeminence among the sky people to a lowly state. 32:29-31.

1.43 (M) Male cardinal is dull colored, consequently sad. Female cardinal asks Spirit of the Plains to give her mate beauty and song. When made beautiful, cardinal becomes proud and overbearing. Good Spirit pities the female, bestows gift of song. 8:96-98.

1.44 (M) Cicada, formerly of gay appearance, abandons its wife to consort with butterflies and hummingbirds. Wife asks eagle for help. Eagle makes the cicada ugly; now it stays home, complains all day. 8:95-96.

1.45 (Kickapoo: Mexico) Butterfly and thundercloud run a race to the sea to decide who owns the flowers. Butterfly is aided by the wind; now owns the flowers. Thundercloud roars in anger. 12:87.

1.46 (M) The Virgin appears to a dreaming *vaquero* who has complained of the thorniness of desert shrubs. She exhibits lavender and pink flowers that resemble thistles but are not. Next morning the *vaquero* discovers a desert plant bearing the same flowers (*el cardo santo*). 6:12-13.

1.47 (M) In time of drouth ranchers pray to the Virgin. Rain comes, and with it the *cenizo* (ash) shrub. The day is Ash Wednesday. 6:9-10.

1.48 (M) A *vaquero*, injured by a fall from his horse, is cured when the Virgin appears to his companion and bestows the small red fruit of the *Guadalupana* vine for placing in the wound. *Guadalupana* seed bears the image of the Virgin. 6:13-14.

1.49 (M) Satan helps God plant grapes. Sets characteristics of wine by sprinkling the ground with the blood of the mockingbird, lion, and hog. 12:60-61.

1.50   (M) At the creation, woman was fashioned from a wildcat's tail. Wildcat had grabbed Adam's rib; God grabbed wildcat's tail as it ran.   32:4-5.

1.51   (Kiowa-Apache) Apaches, being without horses at first, ask the mole for help in capturing them. Mole changes ripples in a pond to a rope that settles around a lead mare's neck as she drinks. 22:51-52.

1.52   (M) Following Lucifer's revolt, the archangel Michael catches him doing a particularly evil deed on earth; kicks him. Michael's toes are broken and his foot burned.   30:231; cf. 32:178 (Michael fights Satan, the latter in serpent form).

1.53   (M) Hero's pack animal is killed by a lion or tiger; the predator made to carry the baggage the animal had carried.   13:68; 34:188, 196.

Section 2: Animal Tales

GUIDE TO THE SECTION

DECEPTION EMPHASIZED; ATTEMPTS TO IMITATE: feigning death, 2.1—2.3, cf. 1.41—1.42; wolf thinks sleeping colt dead, ties tail to colt's, 2.4; tarbaby, 2.5—2.6; mistaking reflection of moon on water for giant cheese, 2.7—2.8, cf. 2.5; holding up the world (fool's task), 2.9; partnership in raising vegetables, 2.10—2.11; duping into taking one's place in basket about to be thrown into sea, 2.12; fox eats bear cubs, replaces heads in cradles, 2.13; fat and lean sheep race toward coyote, 2.14; Uriah letter, illicit intercourse, wife cooks child as father's meal, 2.15—2.16; coyote covets another's wife, 2.17; coyote tricks white man, 2.18—2.19; clever animal (rabbit) invites animals to house, offers first visitor (cockroach) to second (hen), etc., 2.20; clever escape from entrapment (rabbit), 2.21—2.22; rabbit causes coyote to dig in ant bed, 2.23, cf. 2.5; coyote foiled in attempt to masquerade as dog or to imitate bird's handsome dress, jackrabbit's ability to remove its eyes, lion's spring onto colt's back, Indian's use of meatscraper, 2.24—2.28; repaying good with evil (snake trapped under stone), 2.29; trickster tricked in payment (alligator evens score with rabbit, beaver with coyote), 2.30—2.31; fox and heron (Aesop), 2.32. OTHER: beavers furnish coyote new hide, 2.33; quail scares coyote, 2.34; coyote cannot steal medicine bag which is the sun, 2.35; coyote addresses parts of its body, 2.36; rabbit hypnotized by snake, roadrunner saves, 2.37; ox refuses to work, 2.38; animals assemble (various motives), 2.39—2.42; "Sister Fox," 2.43; animal calls man's dogs to pursue animal foe, 2.44, cf. 2.36. See also 3.16

(goose in courtroom of foxes) and, for animals in explanatory tales and formula tales, sections 1 and 4 of Part II.

2.1   (N) Rabbit, seeing a wolf walking home with string of fish, twice feigns death by the roadside. When wolf sees what he thinks is a second dead rabbit, he leaves the fish to go back for the first. Rabbit steals fish.   25:233-235; 18:177-180 (opossum the animal deceived).

2.2   (N) Helping an aging raccoon to catch frogs, rabbit has him feign death by the riverbank. Rabbit then advises frogs to dig dirt from under the "corpse" to bury it securely. When the pit is too deep for the frogs' escape, raccoon "revives," captures them.   1:47-49.

2.3   (N) Wolf feigns death to attract rabbit. Rabbit draws near, remarks that dead creatures usually kick up their legs and say "Baaa-Baaa." Wolf does this, gives self away.   25:230-233.

2.4   (N) Wolf and rabbit see a sleeping colt—apparently dead. Wolf allows rabbit to tie wolf's tail to the colt's to drag the "corpse" to the wolf's lair. When the colt bolts, rabbit cries "Hold! Hold!" (Cf. 2.27.) 25:241-242.

2.5   (M) Thieving Fox is caught by a sticky wax (or gum) scarecrow. Persuades coyote to hold the figure while he pulls loose; coyote is himself stuck. Coyote is next made to believe that the reflection of the moon on water in a creek is a giant cheese; jumps into cold water to retrieve the "cheese." When coyote locates fox to take revenge, fox is asleep in a small cave under large boulders, lying on his back with his feet in the air. Fox convinces coyote that the world is falling; he is "holding up the world" (cf. 2.9). Dupes coyote into assuming the task while fox escapes. Other motifs include convincing coyote that hornets trapped in a hole are a cache of tamales (coyote reaches in; cf. 2.23).   12:13-19; 32:49-52.

2.6   (N) Rabbit and wolf raise peas in partnership (cf. 2.10—2.11). Rabbit steals peas; wolf traps him with tarbaby.   25:224-233; 14:118-120 (Pueblo variant: rabbit steals water; coyote traps with tarbaby).

2.7   (M) Raccoon shows coyote "golden cheese" (cf. 2.5); coyote drowns. 12:214.

2.8   (Kiowa-Apache) Porcupine tricks buffalo into carrying porcupine in his mouth. Shoots quill into buffalo's heart. Coyote wants part of the meat; pretends to be crippled, suggests a jumping contest with porcupine (cf. 6.192). Porcupine is in tree cooking the meat, but convinces coyote that his fire is beneath the water of a creek beside the tree (reflection of fire on water). Coyote jumps in, cannot reach fire. Weights self with a stone in a second attempt; drowns.   22:62-64.

2.9   (M) "Holding up world" as in 2.5.   14:32-34.

2.10   (N) Rabbit and bear form a partnership (cf. 2.6) to raise potatoes, oats, and corn. Rabbit says his part will be the roots of the potatoes, the tops of the oats, the middle parts of the cornstalks. 9:153-156.

2.11   (N) In a farming partnership with other animals, rabbit does none of the work, eats a crop of peas (cf. 2.6, 2.12). Manages to have bear punished for the theft.   25:220-224.

2.12   (Alabama-Coushatta) As punishment for stealing his peas (cf. 2.6, 2.11) a farmer places a rabbit in a basket, which he says he will throw into the sea. En route, the farmer leaves the basket unattended for a moment. Rabbit tells a passing traveler he is being taken to marry a chief's daughter, dupes the traveler into taking his place in the basket (cf. 5.39, 6.97). Later rabbit appears to the farmer (who thinks him drowned) and convinces him that it is lucky to be thrown in the sea. Farmer allows himself to be thrown into sea.   21:73-75.

2.13   (Pueblo) Fox tricks bear into leaving cubs in fox's care. Eats cubs, replaces heads in cradles. When fox eats all the artichokes in a field, leaving none for seed, they swell in his stomach; fox bursts. 14:121-124.

2.14   (M) Coyote meets fat and lean sheep, which he says he will eat. Pretending to race toward him to see which is to be eaten first, the sheep butt coyote, escape.   14:21-24.

2.15   (Kiowa-Apache) Turkey, caught by coyote and charged with bearing a message to coyote's home, ordering its own death, has intercourse with coyote's wife, then causes her to kill her youngest child to serve as a meal to coyote.   22:65-67.

2.16   (Kiowa-Apache) Coyote, herding sheep, eats them and convinces the shepherd that the sheep sank in quicksand. Coyote then seduces the shepherd's wives by bringing false orders from shepherd.   22:77-78.

2.17   (Kiowa-Apache) Coyote covets the wife of another coyote. Tricks husband into climbing a rock for eaglets; magically causes the rock to grow tall so that the husband is stranded.   22:71-73.

2.18   (Kiowa-Apache) White man dares coyote to trick him. Coyote says he cannot because he is without his medicine bag. Thus tricks

the man. (Cf. 6.130, liar who says he does not have time to lie.)
22:78-79.

2.19   (Kiowa-Apache) Coyote sells white man a bucket that supposedly cooks without fire.   22:76-77; 12:50-51 (Mexican version:
picaro puts dirt on the coals beneath a pot and sells "magic" pot).

2.20   (M) Rabbit invites cockroach, hen, fox, and man to his house
under pretext of selling corn. As the guests arrive, rabbit offers
cockroach to the hen, hen to the fox, fox to the man (cf. 4.4). Man
leaves with the corn; rabbit has the money the others had brought
for purchasing corn.   27:114-117.

2.21   (N) Bear asks a frog to guard a rabbit trapped in a hollow tree.
Rabbit gains his freedom by pretending to help the frog keep the
"thing" in the tree. (Makes "sushing" sound while backing away
from the hollow in the tree.)   25:235-238.

2.22   (N) Rabbit tricks a man into releasing it from a trap, saying that
a big black "cat" with a stripe down its back is responsible for
stealing the man's shallots. When the man grabs a skunk and
skunk retaliates, rabbit calls out saying the "cat" has bad breath
from eating shallots.   7:137-138.

2.23   (M) Rabbit convinces coyote that an ant bed conceals honey.
Coyote digs and is stung. (Cf. 2.5.) 12:103-104.

2.24   (M) Coyote masquerades as a dog in order to enjoy a ranch
fiesta. Gives self away by starting to "sing" (yap) after drinking
spilled tequila.   12:215.

2.25   (Kiowa-Apache) Coyote attempts to acquire the pretty red markings of the yellowhammer by setting fire to himself.   22:60-61.

2.26   (Kiowa-Apache) Coyote learns to remove his eyes, juggle them,
and then replace them—in imitation of the jackrabbit. Performs
the feat in a thicket and is blinded.   22:67-70.

2.27   (M) Lion convinces coyote that coyote can catch food as the lion
does. Coyote springs on a colt's back; lion shouts "Ride him! Ride
him!" (Cf. 2.4.)   12:104-106.

2.28   (Kiowa-Apache) As the guest of a man and his wife, coyote spies
as the wife scrapes meat from the man's back for the evening
meal. Coyote later attempts this feat, having his own wife apply
a meatscraper to his back—with painful results.   22:74-76.

2.29   (M) Man releases a snake trapped under stone. Snake is about
to bite the man when coyote intervenes, tricks snake into entrapment again. Man takes his benefactor home, feeds him until

ravenous coyote becomes burdensome. Man releases his dogs to chase coyote away. "The way of the world is to repay good with evil." 12:4-7; 14:24-27; 18:191-194.

2.30   (N) Rabbit sets fire to a canebrake, causing alligator to be scorched. Alligator later offers to ferry rabbit across a bayou. Alligator sinks progressively lower in the water; rabbit is forced to perch on his jaws.   14:135-144.

2.31   (Kiowa-Apache) Beaver, sleeping on a creek bank, is carried far from the water by coyote prankster. Later beaver magically causes a flood to engulf coyote.   22:57-59 (two versions).

2.32   Heron asks coyote to dinner; serves fishes in a long-necked bottle. 25:8-9.

2.33   (Kiowa-Apache) Coyote and beavers play a game in which the animals bet their hides. When coyote loses, beavers furnish him a new hide.   22:59-60.

2.34   (Kiowa-Apache) Coyote scoffs when quail observes that the quail's name is "scare-the-people," but is frightened when quail suddenly takes flight (abrupt whirring sound).   22:61-62.

2.35   (Kiowa-Apache) While visiting in a man's teepee, coyote steals his medicine bundle. Coyote flees but finds himself returned to the man's teepee in the morning. Man tells him that the bundle is the sun; he will never succeed in stealing it.   22:73-74.

2.36   (M) Dove calls a rancher's dogs to pursue coyote (cf. 2.44). Coyote escapes into a cave, where he addresses the parts of his body, asking of their contribution to the escape. Tail says that it showed dogs the way. Coyote orders tail out of the cave as a betrayer. Coyote thus backs out himself, is caught by dogs. 14:8-17.

2.37   (M) Rabbit is hypnotized by rattlesnake's gaze. Roadrunner saves rabbit by placing a thorn between snake's open jaws.   14:34-35.

2.38   (M) When his ox refuses to work, a farmer consults Solomon. On Solomon's advice he mentions a butcher within his horse's hearing. Horse reports to ox; ox resumes work.   18:190-191; 25:240-241 (Negro version involving a mule).

2.39   (M) Lion calls the animals together to settle a dispute over which animal's nose stinks the worst. After disaster meets those animals who cast a vote, fox says that he has a bad cold and cannot smell.   14:27-32.

2.40   (N) During a drouth, the animals assemble to dig a spring. Deer does none of the work but drinks from the spring. Animals capture deer, who escapes by beguiling them with singing and dancing. 18:172-177 (cf. 25:229-230 for mode of escape).

2.41   (N) Animals conspire to scare a trapper out of the woods at night.   17:11-12.

2.42   (N) Opossum preaches to the other animals. After inspiring the "congregation," opossum naps while the animals cavort in religious ecstasy. Later he pretends he has preached all night.   17:108-109.

2.43   (N) "Sister Fox" (animals conceived of as belonging to a religious congregation) asks Brother Rabbit, the storekeeper, for red flannel "protractions" instead of for underwear.   17:110.

2.44   (N) When raccoon steals opossum's grapes, opossum calls man's dogs to chase the thief.   (Cf. 2.36.)   9:165-166.

Section 3: Tales With a Pointed Moral
GUIDE TO THE SECTION

Solomon, 3.1—3.2; Christ and disciples, 3.3; Death the only friend of the poor, 3.4; Wandering Jew, 3.5; Midas ("king has ass's ears"), 3.6; "Don't tell all you see" ("tongue put us here"), 3.7; bundle of sticks, 3.8; man's arms argue with him, 3.9; fox and hen, 3.10; "Rise early, see a white sparrow," 3.11; "Don't forget the best," 3.12; foolish consistency (folk doctor's patient dies, *huisache* tree dies), 3.13; wise man learns from slave boy, 3.14; ferryman knows settlers will find good land or bad, 3.15; goose in courtroom of foxes, 3.16. See also 2.29 (repaying good with evil), 6.203 (man "feeds" his clothes); 6.277 (miller and the Devil).

3.1   (M) Before dying, Solomon tells his servant how he may be resuscitated. Servant yields to the urgings of impatient subjects and unwraps the body too soon. Solomon is lost to his people forever. 12:2-4.

3.2   (M) Solomon tricks his own mother into licentious conduct. "We need God's help to keep us from evil."   32:42-44.

3.3   When the disciples comment on a dead dog by the roadside, Christ admonishes them to notice that its teeth are like pearls.   13:97.

3.4   (M) Christ appears to a laborer and requests part of his lunch. The laborer refuses. When Death appears, the laborer offers all his food. "Death is the only friend of the poor."   9:70-71.

3.5   (M) A prince is granted his wish to be immortal; he lives un-happily ever after. 24:80-81.

3.6   (M) Horns grow on a king's head. Although his hair covers them, the king's barber cannot contain the secret and shouts "The king has horns!" into a hole. A tree grows from the hole; it bears leaves on which the gossip is inscribed. 15:134-135; 30:239-240.

3.7   (N) A slave who insists that a frog has spoken to him is whipped for lying after the frog fails to speak before others. Later the frog tells the slave that he did not offer proof because the slave talks too much. (Two variants; in the second it is a turtle who sings, plays the banjo, and admonishes "Live in peace; don't tell all you see.") 10:48-50.

3.8   Man gives his sons a bundle of sticks and tells them to break the bundle. They cannot. He shows how the bundle can be broken stick by stick. (Informant understood the moral to be: large tasks are accomplished bit by bit.) 31:26-27.

3.9   (Kiowa-Apache) Man's arms argue with him about which of them is the more valuable to him. His right arm grabs the man's knife, stabs him. 22:108.

3.10   A fox is unsuccessful in flattering a hen so that she will descend from the roost—approaching farmer causes the fox to flee. "The flatter seldom gains his ends;/The wise are never without friends." 6:65-66.

3.11   A friend tells a lazy farmer to rise early, he will see a white sparrow. The sparrow is not seen but the farmer catches his em-ployees stealing from him and becomes more prosperous as a result of rising early. 30:261.

3.12   Man shows his young friend through a cave of riches. The young man can have anything he wants if he "doesn't forget the best." When they leave, the door locks. The young man has forgotten "the best"—the key. 31:25-26.

3.13   (M) Folk doctor believes that the *huisache* tree will cure any-thing. On successive days he gives a patient the leaves, twigs, and bark of the tree; but the patient gets worse. On the fourth day, the patient is given wood from the heart of the tree. He dies; the tree dies. 28:158-159.

3.14   A wise man, ready to die because he thinks he knows everything, realizes that a slave boy knows more than he because the boy has cleverly carried a live coal, without using a shovel, to light the man's pipe. The wise man had never learned this trick. 13:91-92.

3.15   A ferryman knows that the settlers he transports will find exactly what they seek in a new land—good land or bad, according to the kind of people they are.   13:89-90.

3.16   (N) A goose, attempting to settle its dispute with a fox, finds no justice in a courtroom filled exclusively with foxes. "The Negro cannot expect justice in a white man's court."   2:50-51.

Section 4: Formula Tales

GUIDE TO THE SECTION

CHAINS: ant finds a penny, 4.1; animals on a ladder, 4.2; stronger and strongest, 4.3; devoured creatures escape, 4.4—4.5; fleeing pancake (johnny-cake), 4.6; mouse regains its tail, 4.7; climax of horrors, 4.8. See also 2.20 (cockroach fed to hen, hen to fox, etc.). OTHER: catch tale (scare conclusion), 4.9; unfinished tale (digression), 4.10; endless tale, 4.11; onomatopoeia as device, 4.12; fingers as actors, 4.13.

4.1   (M) Ant finds a penny and buys new clothes. After several proposals of marriage from animals whose voices frighten her, she marries a mouse (wee voice). "Ratoncito Pérez" later drowns in a bowl of soup.   24:81-84; 30:234-235 (cockroach instead of ant).

4.2   (M) A little old woman who finds a coin buys a ladder and starts climbing to heaven. Animals join her, each asking the last animal on the ladder whither they are bound. Ladder breaks; all fall to earth.   24:84-86.

4.3   (M) After ant's foot is broken on frozen snow, attempt is made to determine the strongest force on earth. Sun stronger than snow; cloud stronger than sun; etc. Strongest force is God.   18:188-190.

4.4   Cricket is eaten by a lizard, lizard by a frog, frog by a snake, snake by an eagle. Man shoots the eagle; creatures escape.   (Cf. 2.20.)   6:47-48.

4.5   (M) In turn, members of a family go to buy food. En route, each is eaten by a "fat man." Family's pet monkey, the only survivor, cuts open the ogre's stomach when accosted; persons escape.   24:78-80.

4.6   A johnny-cake comes to life, runs away. It meets various people whom it .taunts; finally is eaten by a wolf that lures it nearer by feigning deafness.   6:31-33.

4.7   Cat bites off a mouse's tail; mouse must bring it a saucer of milk to regain tail. After dealing with many animals in quest of a chain of required items for barter, the mouse returns with milk, regains its tail. 6: 39-41.

4.8 In climactic order, a slave informs his master of tragedies befallen the household during the master's absence. Dog died of eating too much burned horseflesh; horse died when the barn burned; barn caught fire from candles placed on the mother-in-law's coffin; etc. 31: 16-17.

4.9 The first *paisano* bird (roadrunner) was very small. (Teller proceeds to emphasize smallness of the bird, the voice becoming increasingly soft and low.) "Do you know what the first word of the baby paisano was?—MAMA!" 30: 176-177.

4.10 Yarn-spinner sets out to relate a thrilling story about a fight with Indians; keeps digressing; the tale never told. (Like Mark Twain's story about a goat.) 19: 75-79.

4.11 (M) For eight years a planter hoards all the corn he raises on a large plantation. A locust enters the planter's giant corncrib through a small hole. It carries off a single grain; then another locust enters, carries off a single grain . . . and so on. (Like Mark Twain's bluejay yarn.) 30: 15-16.

4.12 (N) Negro searches for work on a plantation where he will be fed well. At each plantation he listens at the kitchen window to learn by the "pot sound" whether the food is thick or thin, good or poor. (Imitative sounds: "Z-z-z-z-z-z," "Flippity-flop," "Kerplop.") 7: 139.

4.13 (Accompanied by dialogue, fingers enact the roles of a friar and a maid. Like "Katherine Nipsy.") 6: 27-28.

Section 5: Tales of Magic, Marvels, Adventure, Intrigue

GUIDE TO THE SECTION

DEATH, DESTINY PERSONIFIED: Death sticks to a tree, 5.1; Death grants man the power of healing except when Death by sickbed, 5.2; luckless man seeks Destiny, 5.3. (Death the only friend of the poor, 3.4.) MAGIC OBJECTS, ANIMAL HELPERS, EXTRAORDINARY COMPANIONS: flute beguiles auditors, 5.4—5.5; violin causes auditors to dance (Jew among thorns), 5.6; wishing into a sack, 5.7; marvelous purse, colt, napkin lost to innkeeper, 5.8—5.9; animals aid youth in quest, 5.10—5.17; boulder-hurling giant, mighty blower aid youth, 5.18, cf. 5.31. (External soul motif, 5.10—5.12; magic vase, 5.13; extraordinary hearer, 9.32.) FLIGHTS: speaking moccasin, magic tree aid in flight, 5.19; witch's magic ball pursues children, tree assists them (ogre kills own children),

5.20; obstacle flight with the Devil's daughter (transforming objects), 5.21—5.22; Satan and his pupil, 5.23. BEAUTIFUL AND UGLY: monster bridegroom, 5.24; ugly youth transforms after girl's consent to marriage, 5.25. CREATURES (NOT HELPERS IN A QUEST) AND HUMANS, VARIOUS RELATIONSHIPS: serpents and water monsters, 5.26—5.29; woman marries a stallion, 5.30; John the Bear, 5.31; dogs save master from poopampareno (fabulous beast) as result of life token, 5.32; monster lizard (dragon?) that paralyzes, 5.33; wolf (hunger?) at little girl's door, 5.34. FAR-FLUNG ADVENTURE: Gulliver-in-Brobdingnag, Odysseus-and-Polyphemus themes, 5.35, cf. 5.46; abducted wife regained by huband who crosses ocean in a barrel, 5.36; Arabic hero tale following expulsion-return formula, 5.37. See also 5.46 (robber who tells adventures). OGRE OR THE DEVIL OUTWITTED: rabbit-trickster takes man-eater on journey, 5.38; picaro dupes and kills ogre, 5.39; man poses tasks the Devil afraid to perform, 5.40; woman changes Satan into a wasp, seals in a jug, 5.41. See also 5.10—5.12, 5.25, 5.43, 5.54—5.55. (For an additional stupid-ogre tale, see "Thirteen" in Part III of *Analytical Index*.) LUCKY ACCIDENTS (SHAM HERO IN KING'S SERVICE): Dr. Know-All (charlatan poses as seer), 5.42, cf. 6.276; the brave tailor ("seven with one stroke"), 5.43. WAGER ABOUT MAN'S WIFE: reported mole on thigh, 5.44; frame tale: wagerer assumes form of parrot storyteller, 5.45. OTHER: robber tells three adventures to gain freedom (frame tale of "Black Thief"), 5.46; grateful dead man, 5.47—5.48; three wise counsels, 5.49—5.50; dragon-slayer ("Catorce") exhibits fangs, proves deed against another's claim, 5.51, cf. 5.43; good gal and bad gal, Cinderella, 5.52—5.54; Bluebeard-like ogre, 5.55; ogre eats twins who kill him from within, 5.56; faithful servant, 5.57. (Oldest animal motif, 5.3, 5.22; swan maiden, 5.22.)

5.1 (M) Man has a tree that grows grapes as big as oranges. People climb the tree for fruit but refuse to pay. Man appeals to the gods, receives power to keep anyone up the tree until he permits descent. When Death comes for the man, he traps Death in the tree. Death promises not to take him if he releases Death. Later the man wishes Death would take him, to no avail. 30:241-242.

5.2 (M) To her "godson," a woman who is actually Death gives a flower with which he can cure ills and become a famous healer. He is, however, forbidden to use the flower when he sees her standing by a sickbed. After disobeying twice, to save a king and the king's beautiful daughter, the man forfeits his power and is himself taken by Death. (Cf. 5.41.) 12:76-77.

5.3 (M) A poor man meets a beautiful old woman who identifies herself as his rich brother's fate. He then meets an ugly, destitute old woman who identifies herself as his own luck. He seeks out Destiny (oldest animal motif), who tells him to marry the sister of his brother's wife. He does so and fares well; however, he can never claim anything of his own (his wheat field catches fire when he says it is his own) but has to say that his property is his wife's.   32:33-37.

5.4   (Kiowa-Apache) When the pretty girls of a village disappear, a youth discovers that an otter with a magic flute has been charming them, carrying them underwater.   27:80-81.

5.5   (Kiowa-Apache) An orphan boy finds a magic flute with which he attracts the chief's daughter, who consents to marry him. 22:81-82.

5.6   (M) The Virgin gives a boy a magic violin that causes all who hear it to dance. His grandmother, who constantly beats the boy, is made to dance until dead. Sentenced to hanging by the villagers, the boy plays until they free him.   30:228-229.

5.7   (M) Man gives his last piece of bread to a stranger, who is God. God bestows a magic sack; anything the man wishes to enter the sack will enter it. In a haunted house he meets devils, wishes them into the sack.   27:87-88.

5.8   (M) After thoughtlessly losing to an innkeeper a magic purse that a woodpecker has given him, a man is given a magic whip. When he says "Whip," the whip becomes a whipsnake that punishes him for his stupidity.   8:93-95.

5.9   To keep boy from plugging the hole through which it blows down apple trees, the Northwest Wind bestows a magic colt, magic napkin, and magic pot. When the boy loses the colt and napkin to an innkeeper, the pot enables him to recover them.   6:45-47.

5.10   (M) Old man sells his three daughters to three lizards (shapeshifters). The mother bears a son who will retrieve the girls. The boy tricks the Four Sons of the Air, gains magic objects: seven league boots, hat that makes wearer invisible, stick that kills and resuscitates. The lizards have changed into other animals; they set tests for the youth and bestow magic talismans (fish's scales, bull's hairs, eagle's feathers). The youth kills a giant who has an external soul and faithless wife. He regains the abductors' sister and, in payment, his own sisters. (Two versions, the second of Pueblo Indian provenience.)   12:123-133.

5.11   (M) Young man whose bride is stolen on their wedding night sets out to find her and other brides similarly stolen. With the aid of a lion, eagle, antelope, and ant, he reaches the stronghold of the ogre responsible, slays him. External soul motif.   14:241-249.

Ant buys new clothes; see Synopsis 4.1.

5.12   (M) Although locked behind seven doors with seven locks, a princess is spirited away by a magician. Her sweetheart, searching for her, befriends an ant, hawk, and lion; they aid him in rescuing the princess. External soul motif: magician's soul an egg in a dove in a room guarded by a bear. Through transformations, the young man gains the egg, breaks it, causing the magician's death. 32:44-49.

5.13 (M) A fisherman and his wife give their son to a fairy in exchange for a vase that fills with money on command. When the boy, who loses his fairy escort, meets a lion, eagle, and ant in the desert, he divides food among them. They give him talismans that will enable him to call on them for aid (lion's hair, eagle's feather, ant's foot). He finds the fairy again, eventually returns to his home. 12:79-86.

5.14 (M) A flying horse of seven colors, a fish, and a bird help a poor boy to win a princess and kill the king who wanted to marry her. The boy's brothers, who have been mean to him, are dragged to death by mules. Fish finds princess's lost ring; bird brings "water of life"; horse finds the "*Pájaro Cu.*" 32:23-29.

5.15 Boy who seeks his fortune takes with him a rooster, gander, ram, bull, cat, and dog. When they stop at a house for the night, each animal undertakes to guard a particular part of the premises, according to its special abilities. So fiercely do they attack a man who appears, he hurries away. Next morning the boy searches the house and finds treasure, which he shares with the animals. 6:34-37.

5.16 (M) A prodigious youth has an enchanted lion (a prince) as a helper. He wins a princess, foils plots on his life, conquers Moors. The lion is released from enchantment; the boy gains the kingdom. 27:91-95.

5.17 (Kiowa-Apache) With the aid of a spider, an orphan boy rescues a chief's son and wins the boy's sister. 22:82-85.

5.18 (Mayo) An orphan, *Totolegoji* (Spur-of-the-Cock), sets out to marry Montezuma's daughter. An oracle provides counsels: do not scorn help, stick to the highway, be careful of your dress, fear nothing (cf. 5.49—5.50). The boy encounters extraordinary helpers, one a giant who can hurl huge stones, the other a man who can blow people down. Montezuma poses three tasks: kill a jaguar, scale a cliff, level an island. The youth accomplishes the tasks with the aid of his helpers, wins the princess. 11:9-47.

5.19 (Kiowa-Apache) When an Indian flees his cannibalistic companion, he is aided by his moccasin, which imitates the man's voice (cf. 5.22). The moccasin delays the pursuer until the man can escape into a magic tree (cf. 5.20) which speaks and traps the pursuer. 22:105-108.

5.20 (N) Boy saves himself and his sister from stabbing by a witch with whom they spend the night. Boy substitutes a dark bedsheet for the light-colored one the witch puts over them at bedtime. The witch stabs her own children instead (sheets exchanged). Boy and girl are pursued by the witch's magical ball, but are helped by a magic tree. They are saved by the boy's twelve dogs. 25:217-219.

5.21 Youth who desires to marry the Devil's pretty daughter works seven years for her. At the end of this time he is told he must marry the girl's sister. He and the pretty daughter flee, taking with them a bottle of water, a stone, a piece of shrubbery, the Bible. The Devil's chickens sound alarm. Each time the Devil draws near, the girl throws down one of the magic objects, which serves as a temporary obstacle. At last the Bible so frightens the Devil that he backs into a stream and is drowned. 7:128-130.

5.22 (M) Man who has sold his soul to the Devil visits the other-world to fulfill his contract. (Oldest animal, swan maiden motifs.) With the help of the Devil's youngest daughter he performs tasks, escapes with the girl. (Person's spittle speaks to deceive enemy; obstacle flight.) 12:61-66.

5.23 (M) Satan hires a boy who reads his books and learns black magic. Boy escapes and is pursued (flight involving transformations). When Satan becomes a grain of rice, the boy becomes a rooster, eats the grain. 32:41-42.

5.24 (Aztec) A black shapeless beast that is sent to punish the Indians can only cease to be evil when a maiden with "hair like the rays of the sun, eyes like the royal emerald, and a face like a magnolia blossom" will allow him to kiss her. When a princess is born who fulfills these requirements, her father hides her in a house surrounded by a wall of cactus. She cannot avoid her destiny and falls prey to the wooing of the beast. When she feels his burning kiss, she pricks her finger with a cactus thorn a witch-nurse has given her. Immediately she becomes a pale yellow blossom on the cactus. Kissing the blossom, the beast feels something born within him—a good heart. 8:99-101.

5.25 (Pueblo) When a beautiful girl offers to marry an ugly boy, he tells his grandmother—a magician. She removes a mask from the boy's face, revealing him as, in truth, a handsome youth. She had not wanted a bad girl to marry him simply for his looks. 14:108-109.

5.26 (M) A fisherman who is down on his luck curses and casts his net. He draws in a small snake of many colors (the Devil). He becomes enamored of the snake, sleeps with it. His wife informs a priest, who casts holy water on the man and snake. In a searing flash they disappear. Drownings become frequent in the river where the man and the snake take up underwater habitation. 24:132-136.

5.27   (Kiowa-Apache) Man who insists on eating some eggs he has found by a lake turns into a snake-like water monster. He instructs his friend to capture four children and throw them into the lake, which the friend does.   22:101-104.

5.28   (M) A shepherd who aids a serpent is rewarded with a knowledge of animal language. Forbidden to reveal his understanding, he has difficulty explaining to his wife a treasure revealed to him by crows.   15:122-133.

5.29   (Kiowa-Apache) Two boys kill a snake in their grandmother's teepee. She tells them that they have killed their grandfather. 22:100-101.

5.30   (Kiowa-Apache) A newly-married woman who sees some bones and wishes they would turn into a handsome abductor is subsequently lured from her husband by a young man who transforms into a stallion. The woman becomes a wild thing, lives with horses.   22:97-100.

5.31   (M) Young girl, stolen by a bear, gives birth to a son who is called Juan Oso. He grows into an uncontrollable young man. In the mountains, he falls in with two very strong men (extraordinary companions); the three join together to rob and plunder. 12:77-79.

5.32   Hunter meets a poopampareno, a creature that is vulnerable only under its chin. His dogs are at home, much upset because the milk in their bowls has turned to blood (life token). They leap the fence, reach their master barely in time to save him from the beast. (Accompanying rhyme—a call to the dogs.)   14:252-254.

5.33   (Alabama-Coushatta) Six men, hunting a bear, encounter instead a horrible monster lizard that lives in a hollow tree. They are magically paralyzed. One escapes to bring help. The monster is trapped, burned to death.   21:77-79.

5.34   Small girl, left alone by her parents, calls into the night: "Who is going to stay with me." Voice answers: "I am." It is a wolf, from which the girl barely escapes.   31:27.

5.35   (M) A youth has adventures like those of Gulliver in Brobdingnag. The pet of giant's daughter, he is kept in a cage; an eagle flies off with the cage. Later he performs as does Odysseus in the escape from Polyphemus. At another place he becomes a saddler. 32:37-40.

5.36   (M) Man places himself in the crypt with his dead wife. He sees a mouse that bears a small flower. After accidentally killing it, he resuscitates the mouse by passing the flower under its nose. Man thus resuscitates his wife. Soon a foreign king who has seen the wife's picture abducts her. The husband places himself in a barrel, crosses the ocean, gets work in the king's kitchen. His wife recognizes him and the king, also learning his identity, orders his execution. The man is restored to life by a friend. He then restores the life of the emperor's dead daughter. The emperor orders the king's death; husband and wife are reunited. 32:12-17.

5.37 An Arabic romance that follows the expulsion-return formula, the life-pattern of the hero. A youth shows signs of greatness; attempts are made on his life. He is secreted in a waterproof coffin which is set adrift. The coffin touches shore at a foreign land, where the youth enters the service of the king, defends the country against attack, and is rewarded. He returns to his homeland. With the aid of his sister, an Amazon, he overthrows the wicked oppressor who has thought him dead, his uncle. 34:187-194.

5.38 (Alabama-Coushatta) Rabbit offers to rid the Indians of monsters who live on human flesh. He tricks a man-eater into taking a trip with him and makes the creature uncomfortable, causing him to burn himself with hot ashes, to sleep under a tree that is about to fall. At the end of the trip, he causes the creek beyond which the man-eaters live to widen into an ocean. 21:75-77.

5.39 (M) A series of anecdotes in which a trickster gets the better of several dupes, including an ogre. He sticks hogs' tails in mud and sells his "herd" of bogged hogs. He gets a pot of beans to boiling, then covers the fire and sells the pot as a magic pot (cf. 2.19). He fixes coins to a tree and sells the tree as a money-bearing tree. He meets a giant and through cunning impostures (throwing rock, knocking hole in tree) convinces the giant that he, the trickster, is the more powerful of the two. About to be drowned in a barrel (cf. 2.12), he convinces a man to take his place in the barrel ("they are trying to compel me to marry the king's daughter"). He is condemned to hanging but gets to choose the tree; chooses a sunflower plant. 12:49-55; cf. 34:201 (stupid-ogre tale in which trickster is named "Thirteen").

5.40 (N) A man (Jolly Baker) has sold his soul to the Devil. Each time the Devil comes for him he tricks the Devil into granting a reprieve (asking the Devil to card wool, sharpen a double-edged axe). 7:130-132.

5.41 (M) Vain girl says she will marry none but a man with a golden tooth. Such a one appears and they are married. His actions are queer and the girl's mother, after consulting a priest, realizes that he is the Devil. She learns how to get rid of him by magic, finally reducing him to a wasp. When she hires the village drunkard to bury the jug in which she has trapped the wasp, the Devil bribes the drunkard for his release, bestowing the magic power of healing (cf. 5.2, 5.45), which the drunkard eventually loses. 12:66-72.

5.42 (M) Dr. Know-All. When a king's daughter loses her ring, a poor farmer poses as a seer. He accidentally passes tests the king poses and causes thieves who stole the ring, palace servants, to confess. 22:179-184.

5.43 (M) A peasant is taken for a brave man because, referring to flies, he is overheard to remark: "I killed seven with one blow." Through luck he routs an army of Moors, causes giants to fight and exterminate themselves, kills a dragon. 31:135-140.

5.44 (M) Man bets another that his (the second's) wife is unfaithful. He hires an old woman to trick the wife into undressing. The old woman sees a mole on the wife's thigh. The first man reports this private knowledge to the second; the wife is banished. Later the second man learns the truth, searches out his wife. 32:8-12.

5.45 (M) Frame tale. A bet between a student and a merchant about the dutifulness of women, in particular the merchant's wife, provides the frame. The student has himself magically transformed into a parrot. He becomes the wife's pet and beguiles her with stories about a princess of Spain. (The princess, possessing marvelous powers of healing, releases a king's daughter from enchantment; replaces speech to a girl who, refusing to marry a Turk, had had her tongue locked with a golden key. The princess is herself married to a prince who chances on her beautiful doll and says he must have the girl who owns it.) As a result of the stories, the merchant's wife forgets to perform duties her husband has instructed her in; the student wins the bet. 12:21-26.

5.46 Frame tale. Four robbers are captured in their attempt to steal a giant's horses. To free himself and the three sons of the King of Ireland (his accomplices), the oldest robber tells three adventures, each more thrilling than the last. They involve an encounter with ghost-like cats, the theft of a sword of light from witches, the blinding of a giant (like Odysseus vs. Polyphemus), and the substituting of a corpse for a child about to be cooked for a giant's supper. The rescued child turns out to be the robbers' present captor. 34:103-116.

5.47 (M) Ghost of a man whose corpse is buried by an orphan leads the youth to an enchanted city, where the ghost helps him to break the enchantment and gain the king's daughter. (The youth presents the sorcerer's head to the daughter. So that daughter will be faithful to the youth, the ghost tells him to whip her into a lagoon, then whip a mare and dove into the lagoon with her. Thus the wife will not be giddy and wild, will not go about sighing.) 32:17-23.

5.48 (M) Ghost bestows a fortune on two men who are to pay the debts of the ghost. One of the men takes his share of the money but does not keep the bargain. He dies. His part of the treasure turns to mud; there is mud on his mouth when he is found. 28:154-156.

5.49 (M) An oracle sells a youth three counsels: to never leave the highway, never ask about things that are not one's business, never lose one's temper (cf. 5.18). The Devil tempts the youth three times, exhibiting, as one test, a severed head — about which the youth asks nothing (cf. *Peredur*). Having followed the counsels, the youth becomes a successful merchant. 12:7-10; cf. 11:13-15 (the "purchased counsels" motif only).

5.50 Three men mine gold and gain one bag apiece. They meet an oracle who gives advice: to never travel at night, never try to cross a flooded river, never confide in a woman. The third man follows the first two injunctions and succeeds until he disregards the last. 30:173-175.

5.51 (M) A giant is named *"Catorce"* because he always does things by fourteens (eats every 14 days, drinks 14 gallons of coffee, etc.). Working for a rich man, he performs prodigious feats (eating 14 oxen, chopping huge quantities of wood). A giant blacksmith makes him a giant axe. He kills a giant serpent with seven heads. Another man claims the deed but Catorce exhibits the fangs. He marries the king's daughter. 12:194-200; cf. 32:39.

5.52 Poor girl who is kind to "little things" she meets at a spring is rewarded by beauty and wealth (combing gold and silver from her hair, spitting out diamonds) while her rude sister becomes ugly and is plagued with lice and toads after ill-tempered treatment of the same creatures. 6:42-45.

5.53 (Pueblo) Turkey Girl tends fowl belonging to her two stepsisters, the corn maidens. She wants to attend the corn dance but has no new clothes; contemplates suicide. The turkeys provide her with clothes, caution her that she must return by sundown. She overstays; her clothes turn into a deer, snake, and green scum. The turkeys scatter; this is why they are found wild throughout the country. 14:106-107.

5.54 (M) A combination of "The Good Gal and the Bad Gal" and "Cinderella." The good girl is helped by a fairy woman after pleasantly performing the tasks of soothing a crying baby and setting overturned waterjars upright. A star affixes itself to her forehead. (Magic wand, elegant clothes, coach and horses, handsome prince, lost slipper.) 27:89-91.

5.55   (Pueblo) A giant marries pretty girls, then finds excuses to shut
them in a cave and marry another. He marries Flower Petal, tires
of her, sets impossible tasks (shelling corn, drawing water from a
distant lake). Spider Woman helps the girl to perform the tasks.
Later Spider Woman stings the giant, who dies.   14:110-114.

5.56   (Pueblo) An ogre eats the children of a village. Supernatural
twins are called on for help. They allow the ogre to eat them;
once inside him, they seek out his heart and, with magic bows and
arrows, kill him.   14:114-118.

5.57   (M) A rancher bets a fellow rancher that an old herder,
renowned for his veracity, will not lie under any circumstances.
The daughter of the second rancher tricks the herder into killing a
valuable bull, but, when questioned, the herder admits to the
deed.   12:27-29.

Section 6: Realistic-Minded Tales of Humor
GUIDE TO THE SECTION

RELIGION; HEAVEN AND HELL: the saints, 6.1—6.3; preachers, 6.4—
6.15; praying, 6.16—6.27; Gabriel's call, 6.28—6.30; perverse understanding of religious texts, phrases, terminology, 6.31—6.39; sects
6.40—6.44; other religious ancedotes, 6.45—6.51; jests about heaven
and hell, 6.52—6.58 (entering, being ejected from), 6.59—6.61 (other).
CLEVERNESS AND DECEPTION: theft, 6.62—6.75; clever remarks not involving theft, 6.76—6.79 (quips by boys), 6.80—6.95 (other); clever
behavior not involving theft, 6.96—6.98 (poor man dupes rich),
6.99—6.100 (old woman dupes thief, prankster), 6.101—6.105 (trickster extricates self from immediate difficulty), 6.106—6.107 (runaway
slave captured), 6.108—6.109 (boy tricks priest, drunkard tricked into
disposing of priests' bodies), 6.110—6.114 (other tricksters); attempted
deception backfires, 6.115—6.122; abrupt reversal of attitude, feigning
sick or dead person recovers, 6.123—6.127; liars, 6.128—6.133; practical jokes, "Fool Killer" hoax, 6.134—6.143. See also 5.38—5.39
(stupid ogre outwitted) and "Thirteen" in Part III of Analytical Index.
IGNORANCE, FOOLISH CONDUCT, ABSURDITY: slaves, 6.144—6.151; Indians enter wrong teepees, 6.152; backwoodsmen and tenderfeet,
6.153—6.166, cf. 6.134—6.135, 6.176, 6.220—6.221, 6.223, 6.230—
6.233, 6.272, 9.146; the foolish boy, 6.167 (eats frog thinking it is a
fig), 6.168 (sent to the mill: Stupid's Cries), 6.169—6.170 (other);
words misunderstood (see also under "Religion" above), 6.171 (deaf
man), 6.172 ("Hard Times"), 6.173—6.175 (ignorance of Spanish),
6.176—6.180 (other); Little Audrey, Little Moron jokes, 6.181—6.182.

COMIC FRIGHTS, COWARDICE: graveyard the scene, 6.183—6.188; deserted house or mill the scene, 6.189—6.192; other, 6.193—6.198. See also 6.20—6.21, 6.27—6.30, 6.36, 6.72, 6.106, 6.114, 6.140, 6.172, 6.180, 6.270. ECCENTRIC BEHAVIOR; ANECDOTES OF CHARACTER: rich or newly-rich behave humbly, 6.199—6.201; newly-rich Negro, 6.202; *ranchero* "feeds" clothes or stands on head to gain his point, 6.203—6.204; fathers whip sons, 6.205—6.206; breaking news of death gently, 6.207; man's death might have been worse, 6.208; judges, lawyers, politicians, 6.209—6.217; other, 6.218—6.230. SOCIAL EMBARRASSMENT: food or eating, 6.231—6.234; other, 6.235—6.238. COURTSHIP; HUSBANDS AND WIVES: "Johnny in the mornin'," 6:239; princess like a cactus, 6.240; taming the shrew, 6.241—6.242; shrewish wife dies twice, 6.243; "briars" were rosebushes, 6.244; wife saves money received from every kiss, 6.245. See also 6.34—6.35. OTHER: railroads, 6.246—6.250; jokes against Arkansas, Texas, 6.251—6.252; finicky eaters, 6.253—6.254; oil, 6.255—6.256; snuff, beans, whiskey, 6.257—6.265, cf. 6.125, 6.209, 8.186, 9.98; parrots, 6.266—6.268; mules, 6.269—6.270, cf. 6.271, 9.31; loud shouters, 6.271—6.272; revered guns, 6.273—6.274; contradictory dreams, 6.275; lucky accident: "You got de ole coon dis time," 6.276; miller and the Devil, 6.277.

6.1   (M) Woman tells a saleslady that she needs blue satin to dress her child in, so as to keep a promise to the Virgin. The saleslady suggests another blue material that is in stock—the Virgin will not know the difference. "No, that Virgin is very devilish [cunning]."   24:104-105.

6.2   (M) Juan borrows Tomás's image of St. Anthony and the Christ child and pretends that St. Anthony has told him that Tomás has stolen an ox. In revenge, Tomás breaks the figure of St. Anthony and threatens that of the Christ child lest it, too, grow up and be a traitor.   12:44-46.

6.3   (M) Young man scoffs at his fiancée's faith in St. Anthony, but in jest wishes for a new pair of pants. He is a mail carrier and subsequently a dog tears his pants.   24:104.

6.4   Preacher's son pastes pages of the preacher's Bible together. When the preacher reads to his congregation concerning the measurements of the ark, and turns the page, the measurements appear to be those of Noah's wife.   13:102-103.

6.5   Young men paste the leaves of a preacher's Bible together. During a sermon he reads: "And there was a green bay [turns the page] horse!"   30:139.

6.6   Wasps build a nest in a preacher's pants while he is on vacation. When he returns, he addresses his congregation saying: "The spirit of the Lord is in my mouth." Then: "And the Devil is in the seat of my breeches!"   13:103.

6.7   (N) Preacher has arranged for a boy to drop a ham through the church window when he asks the Lord for ham, but is caught in his deception when he asks for a third ham. "The hog only had two hams."   29:169.

6.8   (N) Preacher sends a boy to get him whiskey from one Moses, a moonshiner. Later, in church, when the preacher asks, "What did Moses say?" the boy blurts out that Moses had said he would send no more whiskey until the preacher had paid for the last jug.   29:165-166.

6.9   When a preacher's son is asked what his father says at table (the expected answer being "grace"), he replies: "Gol dern these biscuits; they are heavy as lead!"   13:96.

6.10   Preacher staying at a house in the country is told by a boy to get out of bed—his mother wants the sheet for a tablecloth.   30: 138.

6.11   (N) Preacher eats all the chicken and tells his host's young sons to "eat gravy—gravy's good." At the next meal the boys eat the chicken beforehand. When the preacher comes to the table and wants to know where the chicken is, they say, "Eat gravy—gravy's good."   21:99-100.

6.12   Congregation arrives at a camp-meeting, but the preacher is absent. The box that is to serve as the pulpit starts to move; the preacher has been asleep under the box.   30:191-192.

6.13   When a preacher asks an old Negro woman "for a little information," she says she is too old for that sort of thing.   30:139.

6.14   Although a Baptist preacher believes in predestination, he takes his gun on a trip "just in case it is an Indian's time to go."   13:98.

6.15   Preacher who has been called to a larger church prays for guidance in making the decision—while packing his books.   13:101.

6.16   Woman who wants a mountain removed from in front of her cabin is told that if she prays and has enough faith, it will be removed. The mountain does not move. "Just as I expected."   13: 98-99; 14:165.

6.17   An old maid, praying for a man, answers an owl's hoot with "Anybody, O Lord!"   13:97-98.

6.18   An old man always ends the blessing thus: "For-Christ-sake-Amen-Paralee-pass-the-potatoes."   17:4.

6.19   Rancher does not believe that prayer will bring rain as long as the wind is in the east.   14:165.

6.20   When a prayer is made for the Day of Judgement to come, and suddenly a strange noise is heard, the praying person changes his mind.   14:164.

6.21   (N) Man meeting a bear in his path tells his comrade, who kneels and prays, that prayers should be used at a prayer meeting, not a bear meeting.   10:36-37.

6.22   (N) Caught at a secret prayer meeting forbidden by the plantation owner, a slave points out that he had invoked his "Master," not his "Massa."   10:33-34.

6.23   (N) A slave rewords his prayer for a turkey in order to justify his stealing one.   10:29-30.

6.24   Negro who prays for food includes a barrel of pepper in his petition, then cancels the order. "Naw, Lord, that's too damn much pepper."   30:128.

6.25   (N) A slave who prays, beneath a tree, for $20.00 with which to buy his freedom, refuses to give up the $15.00 that his master (in the tree) has tossed down, to risk receiving $20.00 in exchange.   10:28-29; 21:97-98.

6.26   (N) A slave prays, beneath a tree, for God to kill the whites and save the Negroes. He is shocked when he believes that God is throwing rocks at him, a Negro. (The thrower is his master, who is in the tree.)   10:26-28.

6.27   (N) A praying slave who says he will readily go whenever God calls, hides under the bed when pranksters at his window identify themselves as God and call for him.   10:31-32.

6.28   Preacher hires a Negro boy named Gabriel to blow a horn outside the church on the preacher's cue. "Gabriel, blow your horn." The congregation scatters.   30:191-192.

6.29   Hunters who overhear a Negro preacher's boast that he is ready to answer Gabriel's call, blow on a fox-horn. The preacher and congregation vanish.   22:204-206.

6.30   (N) By listening every night to his master's talk with his wife, a slave is able to prophesy what is to happen the next day. When he hears that he is to be whipped, he arranges for a friend to hide in a tree with a lantern and trumpet and pretend to be Gabriel. The master is properly frightened by "Gabriel," but the latter reveals himself when the first slave refuses an offer of freedom for all the slaves.   10:46-48.

6.31   Anecdotes about backwoodsmen's ignorance of religion. Twists on "Ye must be born again," "laborer for the Lord," "Jesus died for you," to "know Christ," the words "faith" and "crucified." On foreign missions: "You can be a heathen anywhere." On a preacher's preaching: "We didn't know what sin was till you came amongst us." Man catechizes a woman and is given off-the-point answers: "Sister, don't you know who died for you?"—"Ole Dyce Jacobs died [dyed] for me up until last fall." Woman does not know heaven from Arkansas nor the religious meaning of "in the dark." Woman thinks that a Presbyterian must be a varmint of some kind. (And so on.)   14:160-163; 21:96-97; 30:136-139.

6.32   Cowboy "stands up for Jesus" when no one else in the congregation rises to the preacher's exhortation. "I'll stand up for any man who hasn't any more friends than he has."   14:161-162.

6.33   Misapplication of scripture. A clerk insists that he has followed the teaching of the Bible in cheating a woman. "She was a stranger and I took her in." A preacher says that each man must "take up his cross." A member of the congregation hefts his wife.   14:163.

6.34   When a preacher tells a woman to heap coals of fire on the head of her irreligious husband, she pours hot water on him, thinking it would be as effective.   14:163-164.

6.35   During a drouth, a woman pledges $2.00 to the church. Her husband reproves her but she says that she has prayed and "the Lord will provide." When their cow dies, the woman says that the Lord has provided—the hide will bring $2.00.   14:167-168.

6.36   A barber, wishing to prosyletize the man he is about to shave, says "Prepare to meet thy God" as he approaches with the razor. 14:165-166.

6.37   A reformed man interprets a "vision" of the letters G.P.C. as "Go Preach Christ." A man who doubts his vision interprets the letters as "Go Pick Cotton."   13:99-100.

6.38   When a preacher repeats the question, "How can a sinner get to Heaven?" a man who has been sleeping and dreaming of baseball awakes and yells "Slide! Slide!"   30:125.

6.39   Leader of a prayer meeting says he will read from "One-Eyed John" (*I John,* or "John with the Big I").   30:133.

6.40 Woman is advised by her husband, who is to be away on business, about how to entertain an evangelist who is to spend the night. If a Presbyterian, she is to put a Bible by the bed. If a Baptist, whiskey. If a Methodist, wire the husband to return home immediately. 13:100-101.

6.41 Boy says kittens that were Methodists are now Baptists. Their eyes have opened and they have "seen the light." 30:127-128.

6.42 The men of Archer City, Tex., are frightened and vow to build a church. Denomination of the church is decided by votes costing $25.00 each. (Baptists, Methodists, Campbellites vie.) 8:121-122.

6.43 Rival religious factions (Baptist and Methodist) quarrel over whether John the Baptist ate grasshoppers or wild locust beans in the wilderness when he lived on "honey and wild locust." 28:139-140.

6.44 Cowboy attends his first sermon and the next day knocks down a Jew as a Christ-killer. The Jew observes that that happened 1,800 years ago. "Yes, but I only heard about it yesterday." 14:162.

6.45 A congregation repeats the minister's words exactly, though he is trying to tell them it is so dark he cannot read the words in his hymnbook. (Cf. 6.117.) 13:104-105.

6.46 When a deacon, who is a freighter, needs to swear, he lays aside his hat (symbol of office). 13:96.

6.47 A respected old lady shocks the congregation with her dictum on "necking." "If there were more of it done and less talk about it, the world would be better off." 13:93-94.

6.48 (N) A slave preacher vainly expects to be beaten because St. Paul had been. 10:34-35.

6.49 (N) A Negro, seeing his reflection in a mirror for the first time, thinks he is seeing God. He had not realized that God was a Negro or would have *made* God give him his freedom, instead of merely praying for it. 10:30-31.

6.50 White preacher advises an old Negro who wants to join his congregation to ask the Lord for guidance (stalling). Negro does and reports that the Lord said that He also had been trying to get into that preacher's congregation. 30:126-127.

6.51 Comic definition of an "anthem" involving a straightforward sentence recast in very emotional and redundant form (pulpit manner). 25:9-10.

6.52   Negro allows a white politician to ride him so that both can enter heaven. St. Peter says that the horse must stay outside.   9: 160-162.

6.53   (N) Big Sam is unable to persuade St. Peter to let him enter heaven. He tries to redeem himself when his newly deceased mule appears. The mule is needed to pull the golden chariot, since the heavenly horses have foundered. Big Sam drives the chariot to convey a Negro minister to paradise. The minister insists on trying to convert the Devil, and both he and Sam are lost.   19: 29-35.

6.54   (M) Although no Mexicans are allowed in heaven, Juan de Toluca gets in by throwing his hat in and pretending it has blown in. St. Peter lets him pass to retrieve it. He is safely lost in the throng until he starts to steal things. When a Texan, borrowed from hell, says that *"La Cucaracha"* is a weakness of all Mexicans, the Lord arranges for it to be played. Juan reveals himself.   12: 10-13.

6.55   (M) When Pedro de Urdemañas reaches hell, he is so self-assured that the Devil undertakes to put him in his place. Pedro tells the Devil of Texas, which the Devil then visits. He is so discomfited there, he returns to hell and ejects Pedro.   8: 106-109.

6.56   (M) After saving twenty people during the Monterrey flood, Juan García becames famous and vain. On going to heaven he introduces himself to Napoleon, Hannibal, and others as the hero of the Monterrey flood. Noah spurns him.   12: 153-158.

6.57   When an oil speculator finds heaven crowded, he spreads the rumor of an oil discovery in hell. So many exit that the speculator thinks there may be something in the rumor, goes himself.   15: 79-80.

6.58   (M) St. Peter admits prospectors to heaven, but they dig up the streets. He circulates a rumor of a gold strike in hell; the prospectors leave.   32: 5-8.

6.59   (N) Master and slave tell their dreams of the Negro and white heaven. The slave admits that the white man's paradise was lovely, but he did not see a soul in sight.   10: 18-19.

6.60   (M) Man learns that angels are stealing his corn—they descend a rope from heaven. When the man climbs the rope, the Lord apologizes for the theft, saying that there was a shortage of corn in heaven.   30: 236-237.

6.61   Man burned in an oil fire thinks he is burning in hell.   20: 14.

6.62   (N) Slave who has hidden a stolen pig in a cradle exists hastily when his master insists on looking at the "sick baby."   10: 12-13.

6.63 (M) A slave swears to his master that he has put a possum in his cooking pot, not chickens, and will throw out any chickens the master might find there. If the possum has turned to chicken, it is bewitched.   10:11-12; 21:81-83; 25:251-252.

6.64 (N) A slave, discovered in his attempted clubbing of a sheep for food, pretends that he is carrying the club as protection. "Ah ain't gonna let no daw-gone sheep butt me to death."   10:19-20; 21:85.

6.65 (N) At night, a slave jumps on a pile of white ashes under which coals still glow, thinking the ashes are sheep (attempted theft). After being rescued by his master, he insists he was trying to rescue sheep from the coal-bed.   25:242-243; cf. 22:130.

6.66 (N) By calling out "Change yo' tone," a slave boy's father warns him not to reveal, in talking to the master, that the father has just stolen the master's calf.   10:21-23.

6.67 (N) Master has forbidden his slaves to catch catfish in his lake. When he discovers a clever slave with a large catfish on his stringer, the slaves says that the fish had been bothering his string of perch; he had merely tied it up.   21:87-88.

6.68 (N) When a clever slave is caught coming from his master's watermelon patch and is asked what direction he is coming from, he replies: "What's direction got to do with an honest man?" 21:83.

6.69 (N) On a wager, by stealing his master's best suit while both the master and his wife are guarding it, a slave gains his freedom. 10:15-16.

6.70 A trickster bets a baker he cannot face the clock and swing his arms like the pendulum for half an hour. He steals bread while the baker's back it turned.   30:261-262.

6.71 Judge give a man permission to sell a stray horse, not knowing that the horse is not his. When he learns of the fraud and questions the man, the man tells him he knew he did not need permission to sell his own horse.   17:70-71.

6.72 Hog thief on trial whispers to each juror, "Now is the time for all hog thieves to hang together." He is acquitted.   13:95-96.

6.73 A dying man's partner insists that he is losing his mind when, in the presence of neighbors, he begins confessing their theft of cattle.   14:168.

6.74 (M) When a herder responds to the whistle of his employer, who is hidden on a hillside, he condemns himself as the accomplice of cattle thieves.   12:214.

6.75   (N) When a man who has dropped his lunch on the road returns
to find that his friend has found and eaten it, the friend says that a
dog could have eaten the lunch.   21:93-94.

6.76   Traveler calls a boy a fool when he cannot tell him the way to
the city. The boy says that he may be a fool, but at least he knows
he is not lost.   13:94.

6.77   Frederick the Great goes about the land disguised. He asks a boy
what he is doing out of school. "You want to be emperor and don't
know there is no school on Saturday?"   30:263-264.

6.78   A teacher asks a boy, a new pupil, if he can spell his name for
her. "Hell no! This is my first day in school!"   30:129.

6.79   On hearing his sisters tell of the earliest thing they remember, a
small boy says that he remembers crying in the womb for fear he
would be a girl.   19:69.

6.80   The Scottish physicist Lord Kelvin is hard to follow in his lectures. During his absence a Mr. Day lectures in his place. The
students can follow him. When it is learned that Kelvin is to
return, a student says, "Work . . . while it is day."   15:75-76.

6.81   On a cold night an Indian tells a white man that he is not cold
because he is "all face."   13:90.

6.82   (N) Interrupted during a forbidden dance, slaves escape to
their cabins. One man does not reach his cabin in time and parries
the master's questions about his being abroad after dark by repeating how lucky he has been, dropping a biscuit with the buttered
side turned up.   10:19.

6.83   (N) When his master catches a slave off the coach seat, where
he is supposed to be watching the horses, the slave says he is catching rats. "How many have you caught?" The slave says that when
he gets the one he is after and one more, he will have two.
21:85-86.

6.84   (N) Clever whip-handler, a slave, pops horse flies but will not
attack hornets because "they're organized."   10:23-24.

6.85   (N) A slave brags about his cursing the master out. When his
friend tries it and is punished, the first slave admits that the master
had not heard him when he did it.   21:94-95.

6.86   (N) Two Negroes wager on whether a decapitated turtle is dead.
The one says the turtle is "dead but don't know it" (is still crawl-
ing).   2:50.

6.87 (N) Man tells a judge that he was not violating the judge's warning about the next time he caught him winning money in games of chance. When caught this time, he was losing. 21:98-99.

6.88 Man declines a challenge to a duel, saying he does not fight "downhill." 25:3.

6.89 Man comes face to face with his opponent on a boardwalk and says he never steps aside for scoundrels. The other says that he does, and steps aside. 25:3.

6.90 Man says that he will shoot anyone uglier than he is. Another man says, "If I was uglier than you I would shoot myself." 31:104.

6.91 Man will not throw a drunk out of a saloon because "he is an old schoolmate." Another man tries but is beaten. "Why didn't you throw him out?"—"Found out he was an old schoolmate of mine, too." 31:103-104.

6.92 (N) Man assures others that he is not fleeing from a bear (panther), he is leading it home. 10:35-36; 21:92-93; 29:166-168; 19:131-132 (Anglo version about a cowboy who ropes a bear).

6.93 In reply to a priest who requests a horse to visit churches on, Frederick the Great says that the Bible tells priests to go and preach to all nations, but says nothing about riding. 30:263.

6.94 When a man asks another, who owes him money, when he is going to pay, the debtor replies that he is no prophet. 18:205-206.

6.95 When a suitor asks a Texas girl why she is so sweet, she says her father is a sugar planter. 19:69.

6.96 (M) When an industrious man tries to cheat a lazy man out of a treasure hoard, the lazy man is vindicated in literal terms of the maxim he is accustomed to cite: "To whom God wishes to give He will give, even if He has to put it in through the window." The treasure turns to mud when stolen (cf. 5.48) and back into coins when, as mud, it is returned through the lazy man's window. 24:128-132.

6.97 (M) After selling his rich neighbor a rabbit that is supposed to carry mail and a flower that is supposed to revive the dead, a poor man tricks the dupe into being drowned. (Cf. 2.12.) 12:29-36.

6.98 (M) A poor man who is tricked into killing his one cow to make rawhide, avenges himself on his rich neighbor by making him believe that the sale of the rawhide was very profitable. 12:36-44;

21:35-42 (three versions, the second involving a cap that supposedly pays one's bills; the third, the sale of tamales made of cow
chips).

6.99 A robber climbs down an old woman's fireplace. She sees him
and, scolding her cat, which is on the hearth, makes him think she
is going to throw coals on the cat. Instead she blinds him.
31:20-21.

6.100 When the village wag drops bread through a poor widow's
chimney and then calls down a jibe at her prayerful thanks, she
answers that the Lord can use even the Devil for his good works.
13:101-102.

6.101 (N) Stranded in town, a clever slave cannot afford the $10.00
rental on a horse and buggy. He gets the doctor to make a house
call at his cabin for a $5.00 fee; rides with the doctor.   21:101-102.

6.102 (N) Two men compete in a slingshot contest. When the first's
rock does not come down after ten minutes, the second starts
waving his hand; says he is warning the angels to get out of the
way.   (Cf. 5.39.)   10:50-51.

6.103 (N) When a mule gets sick, a slave is made to plow with a
good horse. He rides the horse to a dance that night. The horse
dies suddenly and the slave hauls it back to the plantation. Next
morning, being questioned by the master, he attributes the death to
plowing with the horse the day before.   21:88-89.

6.104 (M) Locked out by his wife, a man returning from saloons
tricks her into admitting him by saying he has been "cut."   32:53.

6.105 (M) In answer to a neck-riddle, a man has to tell the king how
long it will take to teach a donkey to read and then prove his cal-
culation. On the advice of a friend, he says one year. He and his
friend make a book that has boards for leaves. They teach a donkey
to turn the pages and bray.   27:78-82.

6.106 (N) A slave who could not be caught to whip is caught when he
is enticed to dance by a fire in the woods at night. He is so
frightened when surprised that he throws the master onto the fire.
10:13-14.

6.107 (N) Capture of an escaped slave is effected when a reward is
offered and another slave, after seeing the man and asking him to
shake hands over the fence, holds tight.   10:52-53.

6.108 (M) Juan Pelón is a rascal and practical joker who tricks several people (chiefly a priest) before he is jailed. He places prickly
pear at the bottom of a sack and grapes on top—the priest gets

thorns. The priest tells him to watch eggs boil. The priest passes wind and says, "Eat this egg." Juan eats all the eggs. In jail, he discovers a treasure buried in his cell, kills three men in order to escape.   12:47-49.

6.109   (M) Drunk man is tricked into disposing of the bodies of three murdered priests under the impression that there is only one body.   12:57-60.

6.110   (N) Dividing apples, a slave cheats his friend by saying "One for me, one for you [one apple apiece]; two for you, two for me [the counter gives himself two apples more]."   21:95-96.

6.111   (M) Pedro de Maulas swears that all women are curious and proves it by placing a bird in a box and asking a woman to keep the box for him but not to open it.   9:57.

6.112   (M) A rogue hurriedly informs his wife that they are leaving town "on the railroad." Excitedly believing that they are to catch a train, she readies herself swiftly. Instead, he leads her down the tracks.   32:53-54.

6.113   (Kiowa-Apache) A girl will not marry until her eight-year-old brother has killed his first enemy. A suitor, Orphan Boy, trains the youth and makes it appear that he has counted coup.   22:85-89.

6.114   Preacher stays overnight in a house. When his hostess's drunk husband comes home, the woman's lover hides in a barrel under cotton lint. She insists that there is no one in the spare room but the preacher. The husband, outside the door of the room, says he has heard that this particular preacher can raise the Devil. The preacher, inside, tells the husband to wait at the door with a stick. He then sets fire to the cotton. The husband thinks it is the burning Devil that runs by him and gives the lover a whack.   (Jest told of Lorenzo Dow.)   30:192-193.

6.115   In a game where grains of yellow corn are chips, Jim Baker ("Pie Biter") seeks to replenish his supply by going outside and shelling an ear of corn in the dark. When he gambles with some of the grains, he finds that the ear he had shelled had red kernels.   14:186-187.

6.116   (M) A banker who tries to keep a man's deposits unfairly is deceived into delivering them when the dupe's father pretends that he is to deposit money and has the son come in to retrieve his own money at that very time.   12:46-47.

6.117   (N) A slave who cannot read but who is coached by his master (hiding outside a window) betrays his ignorance by repeating exactly what his master says. "Hold the book up higher, John." (Cf. 6.45.)   10:32-33.

6.118   Man caught with an illegal still claims that the mash is slop for his hogs. The "slop" is fed to the hogs; they get drunk.   29:165.

6.119   (Kiowa-Apache) Indian sneaking into an Apache camp makes a noise like a frog. Boy throws a rock at the "frog," hit the thief in the head and kill him.   22:122.

6.120   (N) Turkey hunter shoots an Indian who is imitating a turkey's call in trying to lure the hunter to his death.   25:250-251.

6.121   Cowboys finally shoot a scrawny calf that they keep finding on the range. It is an Indian in disguise who has been driving off cattle.   25:249-250.

6.122   (N) A Negro, in court on a charge of stealing, hears a white thief say that he has owned a disputed horse since it was a colt. The case is dismissed. The Negro then claims that he has owned the wagon he is accused of stealing since it was a wheelbarrow.   21:100-101.

6.123   (N) By changing his words slightly, a slave makes his initially contrary sentiments agree with his master's and hides his dislike for work. ("More rain, more rest" becomes "More rain, more grass.")   10:22-23.

6.124   (N) After claiming part of the credit for his hunting companion's excellent shooting all day, a slave hastily denies any part in the killing of the master's mule when a shot goes astray. "What do you mean, 'we'?"   10:52; 21:90-92; 29:166.

6.125   Man who pretends fainting spells so that his wife will give him whiskey rises from his "faint" when his wife bemoans not having any more whiskey on hand.   30:125-126.

6.126   When wounded by Indians, a man plays dead until Indians are to cut off his finger for the ring he wears. He forgets himself and pulls the ring off for them.   19:81.

6.127   Man who thinks he has killed another with a poker, and is desperately trying to find signs of life, says he will give six sections of land if only a toe will wiggle. The toe wiggles.   14:256-259.

6.128   (M) Two liars agree to work their way through the countryside, the second corroborating the lies of the first. They tell of a river that burns, a bird so huge that its shadow darkens an entire valley, a lucky shot through the foot and ear of a deer. (Deer was scratching its ear with its hind foot.)   19:36-41; 10:25-26 (Negro version, master and slave).

6.129   (M) Two liars join forces to earn their living by lying. The second is more modest than the first. When the first tells of seeing a baby with seven heads, the second verifies the marvel half-heartedly. (He did see, hanging on a clothesline, a little white shirt with seven collars.) 12:55-57.

6.130 Notorious liar, seen walking, is asked to stop and tell a lie. He says he does not have time to—he is on his way to the scene of an accident where his brother has just been killed (a lie). 20:29-30; cf. 22:78-79.

6.131 (N) By making his master laugh, a slave wins his freedom. The slave says that the master is good-looking. The master says that he cannot say as much for the slave. The slave says that if he were as big a liar he could. 10:14-15.

6.132 (N) After inadvertently admitting having killed a deer out of season (or having stolen chickens), a slave introduces himself as the biggest liar in the South. 10:20-21; 21:102-104.

6.133 When a disbeliever questions a man's claim to having seen a flight of crows 25 miles long, the liar agrees to pare half a mile "from the thinnest point." 19:68.

6.134 Tenderfoot is dissuaded from sharing a bed with another man when the man cautions him about his frenzied dreams of hand-to-hand combat with Indians. 19:70.

6.135 An Indiana lawyer, setting up practice in Texas, is appalled by a cowboy's (mock) plan to bait a rival for his girl's affections into a gunfight. The lawyer leaves Texas. 22:222-224.

6.136 During the night, a prankster gives his wife a glass of water with false teeth in it. 29:64.

6.137 A dirty diaper is sewn to pillow ticking and placed underneath the upholstery of a buggy. 29:64-66.

6.138 At a dance, cowboys exchange the wraps and pallet positions of babies that have been put to bed in a spare room. 22:229-230; 33:110-117.

6.139 Cowboys exchange cowchips for candy in a gift box that a fellow cowboy presents to a girl. 22:221.

6.140 Whites who set out to frighten Negro trespassers with a hanging skeleton are themselves made the butt of a "scare." 17:23-25.

6.141 Practical jokers change the animal in a Negro's sack from a puppy to a pig, and then to a puppy again, until he believes the animal to be enchanted. 13:91.

6.142   (M) *Vaqueros* chain a sheepherder's delapidated old saddle to a tree, claiming that such a thing would surely eat chickens if not chained.   9:65.

6.143   Newspapers reputedly once hired a Jesse Holmes as a "Fool Killer." He carried a club and beat out the brains of fools. Editors saw much work for him in their respective communities.   8:152-154; 14:169-173.

6.144   (N) A slave who can count to 50 finds an old watch and pretends to keep time for participants at a prayer meeting. He is found out when he tells them the time is "39."   10:46.

6.145   (N) A slave pretends he can count hogs: "dis one and dat one and dis one."   21:83-84.

6.146   (N) A slave who can count to ten is made overseer but loses his job when his master bets on his ability and learns of his limitation. Instead of "eleven" he says, "an' annuder One."   10:44-46.

6.147   (N) A slave tells another he will give him "both chickens" if the other can guess how many are in the sack he carries.   21:93.

6.148   (N) Rowing his master, a slave falls asleep. The boat turns 180 degrees. When the slave wakes, he tells the master that he has already oared past the guiding star.   10:43-44.

6.149   (N) At night, a slave goes to sleep in an unmoored boat, thinking the tide will rise and carry him to New England and freedom. When in the morning a friend wakes him by calling his name, he asks who it is that knows him so soon in New England.   10:42-43.

6.150   (N) A Negro teamster, driving oxen, thinks that a distance marker gives notice of the minimum speed limit. He cannot go that fast.   10:44.

6.151   (N) Negro who has never seen a deer goes hunting. A buck appears but the hunter does not shoot, thinking it to be a man "with a big rocking chair on his head."   25:252-253.

6.152   (Kiowa-Apache) At night, Apache hunters return to the wrong camp and enter teepees they think are theirs but which are inhabited by strangers.   22:122-123.

6.153   Ignorant farm woman thinks her husband intends to send a bale of cotton to town *via* the telephone wire.   31:22.

6.154   (N) Man does not understand the principle of the telephone; does not dial, shouts over the phone.   29:163.

6.155   Man is asked to speak into a tape recorder and voice his feelings to the President. He says, "Mr. President," then waits for an answer.   29:56-57.

6.156   A backwoods boy is whipped for lying when he returns from the circus and tells his family of having seen a two-wheeled vehicle called a bicycle.   13:236.

6.157   Wife of a newly-elected constable corrects her misapprehending children. "You ain't constables—just me and yer father."   13:87.

6.158   A rural doctor, asked to name the girl-child of ignorant parents, names her Placenta.   30:183.

6.159   In a horse trade, a sharpster pays an old man, a pioneer not used to paper money, with an advertisement for "Mustang Liniment."   28:145-148.

6.160   Boy visits well-to-do neighbors. He side-steps a woven rug, believing it to be fine piece of cloth. (Woven rugs were rare on the frontier; hides served as rugs.)   7:71.

6.161   (N) Two backwoodsmen who have never seen a train make camp near a railroad track. When in the night a train passes and another approaches, the men wake in a fright. One tells the other that "Hell done moved one load [of sinners] and it's going to move the other one."   25:245.

6.162   A backwoodsman eats all of a "pound cake," referring to it as "yaller bread" and refusing bread made with white flour. "No ma'am, this here yaller bread is good enough for me."   7:69-70.

6.163   Having learned his lesson from the unexpectedly great distance to a mountain that he had thought was near, a tenderfoot strips to swim a two-foot-wide creek.   15:105.

6.164   Tenderfoot working on a sheep ranch is told to shear every animal in the field. He shears a pig as well as the sheep; claims he got more noise than wool.   13:87.

6.165   When a drummer in a western saloon complains to the bartender that a cowboy's horse has stepped on his foot, the bartender says, "What are you doing in here afoot, anyway?"   31:105-106.

6.166   Farmer sells pumpkins to a city dweller as "mule eggs."   20:11.

6.167   (M) Backward boy eats figs that boys in a fig tree throw down to him. Presently he asks, "How many legs has a fig?"   32:32.

6.168   Boy is sent to the mill for a peck and a half of meal. After misadventures, he is thrown into the mill-hopper by the miller, whom his foolish words have angered (cf. 6.171), and is ground into meal. (The boy is sent for "sheep's head and pluck" in English variants: "Stupid's Cries").   6:54.

6.169   Mentally defective boy thinks he can make a man. He makes a clay figure that is stolen before completed. A one-armed preacher moves into the community and the boy asks: "Why did you run away?"   13:103-104.

6.170   (N) Negro boy, a fool, is taught to keep his mouth shut so as to conceal his stupidity. He refuses to answer when a merchant wants to buy a wagonload of wood; the merchant calls him a fool. When his father returns to the wagon, the boy says: "Pappy, dey's done found hit out."   9:159-160.

6.171   A deaf man sees a traveler approaching and guesses at what the traveler will ask him. His replies to the traveler's questions turn out to be *non sequiturs* that makes a fool of the man.   15:82-83.

6.172   An old man tells his wife he is hoarding his money for "Hard Times." A thief identifies himself as "Hard Times" and the wife gives him the money. Later, husband and wife pursue the thief. The woman takes the door of their house with them because the husband has always told her to "mind the door." That night they tie the door in a tree and sleep on it. Robbers gather under the tree to gamble. The door falls, frightening the robbers away. (Cf. 6.192.)   31:10-11.

6.173   (M) Mexican rogue who has been to Texas tries to pass himself off as a Texan. With an unlit cigarette in his mouth, he says to a Mexican freighter, "You gottie maeches [matches, understood as *machos*, mules]?" "*No, señor, son puros burros* [just burros]." 32:54.

6.174   (N) Pretending to know Spanish, a slave makes a trip to Mexico as his master's interpreter. His ignorance is made clear when he attempts to purchase a horse.   10:16-18.

6.175   A misunderstanding of the Spanish word *frijoles* leads a man to believe that a restaurant does not charge for food.   17:57-58.

6.176   (M) When asked if his band plays by note, a rural bandleader says that they play for chickens, corn, etc.—do not require notes. 10:107.

6.177   Man asks a station agent for a round-trip ticket. "Where to?" "Back here, of course."   27:167.

6.178   By "buffalo chips" a naive woman understands a man to mean buffalo bones.   6:80.

6.179 (M) Robbers who try to steal an old man's "treasure" are chagrined to learn that it is only a nanny-goat the priest has just blessed. 14:238-239.

6.180 (N) Juror tries to run away when the court recesses, because he has heard that this was going to be a "hung jury." Negro jurors have searched all over but cannot "find" a verdict against an ex-Confederate. 9:163-164.

6.181 A series of "Little Audrey" jokes of the 1930's. Typically they involve puns and usually the phrase, "Little Audrey just laughed and laughed." Example: "When an oak tree fell on her mother Little Audrey just laughed and laughed because she knew her mother couldn't *carioca* [a dance]." (See the following entry.) 13:106-110.

6.182 A series of "Little Moron" jokes involving puns or a *non-sequitur*, and sometimes cruelty.—Paints arrow on a boat to mark a spot in the lake.—Sleeps with his head on the curb to keep his mind out of the gutter.—Does not pay because his name is Crime. —Gets into a barber's chair; when the barber asks what he will have, orders a cup of coffee.—Takes cream and sugar to the movie because he has heard there was going to be a serial.—Cuts his elbow to see if there is any beer in the joint.—Hits himself on the head because it feels good when he quits.—Tells a man that the man's car can make it across a swollen river because a duck just went across and the water only came up to "here" on the duck. —Two morons utter two contradictory sentences in five hours; a third says he is going home if they do not stop quibbling (cf. 6.220).—When asked if he can hold his liquor, moron grabs his tongue.—When told that a suit is virgin wool, says he is not interested in its morals.—Says he bit himself on the cheek; when asked how he managed that, says he stood in a chair.—Says the streetcar has already gone by because he sees its tracks.—Learns how to tell the black horse from the white; the black an inch taller.—Kills his parents so he can attend the Orphans' Picnic.—Buys roundtrip ticket to go to a distant town where he has left his car.—Does not know what is in a letter he has written to himself; has not received it yet.—Refuses to wager he cannot climb up a flashlight beam; says the other man would turn off the light when he is halfway up.—Writes a letter to his girlfriend slowly because she cannot read very fast.—Takes whiskey to bed so he can sleep tight.— Takes a bale of hay to bed to feed the nightmare.—Receives beer in his hat and turns the hat over so the bartender can give him more beer.—When his friend is dismembered by a train, tells him to pull himself together.—Wants to be a vitamin because he has seen a sign that says "Vitamin B_1." 19:155-161.

6.183 Thieves plan to steal sheep and meet in a graveyard. An old sick man, being carried on a boy's back, comes by the graveyard.

One of the thieves thinks it is his partner returning with sheep and asks in dark, "Is he fat or lean?"—"Fat or lean . . . you can have him!" The boy throws the old man down, but the man beats the boy home. 10:38-39; 25:245-247; 31:17-19. (Four instances, two of Negro provenience and all involving a crippled man. The version given is that of 31:17-19. See also the following two entries.)

6.184   (N) Three Negroes steal watermelons and agree to eat them in a graveyard. The third man is slow in coming. When his white shirt and eyeballs appear, his companions flee, thinking him a ghost. His words, "I'm one o'yaw-ll," are misunderstood to mean, "I want one o'yaw." 10:40-42.

6.185   (N) Two slaves divide stolen sweet potatoes. They are mistaken by eavesdroppers for God and the Devil in the act of dividing souls. The eavesdroppers flee when they hear, "You take those two over by the fence." 10:39-40; 29:169.

6.186   (N) A Negro is to go into a graveyard at night and prove he is not afraid of ghosts by sticking a knife into a grave. After accidentally sticking the knife through his coat-tail, he thinks he is being held and collapses from fright. (Cf. 7.78.) 29:168.

6.187   (N) Drunk man falls into an open grave and cannot get out. When another drunk falls into the grave, the first taps him on the shoulder and tells him he cannot get out. The man gets out. 29:168-169.

6.188   At night, drunk men are frightened by what they think are "galloping" tombstones—a herd of white goats. 17:19-22.

6.189   (N) Traveler enters an empty mansion, where a large yellow cat appears and speaks to him. Though the man runs as fast as he can, the cat keeps up with him. The cat remarks that they have had a good race. The man assures the cat that the race is not over; he outruns the cat. 25:247-249; cf. 34:109-110.

6.190   Man sleeps in a deserted house. Two ghosts enter and the man outruns partridges, a rabbit, and deer. When he crosses a stream of running water he knows he is safe because ghosts cannot cross running water. 18:82-83.

6.191   Cowboy, sleeping in an abandoned shack, wakes in the night to see white objects jumping through the windows. He knifes 18 sheep, thinking they are ghosts. 9:44.

6.192   An orphan, seeking his fortune, tries to spend the night in the house of a girl who tricks him, in a jumping match (cf. 2.8), into jumping outside the house. The girl slams the door. Jack spends the night in a deserted mill. When he is awakened by voices and unintentionally knocks over the hopper in which he is hidden, the men (robbers) flee, abandoning their loot. (Cf. 6.168, 6.172.) 6:37-38; 31:14 (two men sleep on a door in a tree, which falls and frightens robbers).

6.193   (N) When a Negro hunter who is inside a hollow tree, where he has followed a bear cub, wants to know who is darkening the hole, his companion, who is holding the mother bear's tail, tells him that if the tail-hold slips he will find out soon enough. 9:158; 10:37-38.

6.194   Men are trying to load a huge log onto a flatcar. Man with his false teeth in his hip pocket backs into an object. The teeth bite him and he loads the log single-handedly.   30:179.

6.195   A Negro knows that he has been shot at, for he heard the bullet twice—when it passed him, and again when he passed it.   9:162-163.

6.196   (Kiowa-Apache) Man who is thought to be a coward deceives and frightens supposedly brave men, who try to bribe him not to tell on them.   22:120-122.

6.197   Pat the Irishman goes into the army as the clock is striking one and leaves while it is striking the same "one."   18:83.

6.198   Pat the Irishman enters hell with his pipe filled. He does not stay long enough to light it.   18:83.

6.199   Man who comes to buy rams from a wealthy sheep rancher does not recognize the rancher because he dresses in tattered clothing (cf. 6.203). When he tosses the rancher a coin for holding his horse, the rancher keeps it.   15:100.

6.200   Wealthy sheep rancher dresses in common work clothes. When asked why he does not dress like the rich man he is, he says he does not need to: everyone who knows him knows he is wealthy. When asked same question while in St. Louis, he reasons that no one there knows who he is.   15:99-100.

6.201   Elderly farm woman, newly rich as a result of oil strikes on her land, asks only for a new axe with which to chop wood.   25:75-78.

6.202   (N) Negro who leaves a plantation in Mississippi and does well in Texas is to send a telegram to his former master and mistress. When asked if he wants to send the telegram to Mississippi, he says, " 'Missi' nothin'—jes' 'sippi'!"   29:164-165.

6.203   (M) A rich *ranchero* is to be invited to a *fiesta* in a town distant from where he lives. Because he is not dressed in fine clothes when men come to extend the invitation, they do not recognize him (cf. 6.199) and invite an employee, who is well dressed, by mistake. The rich man attends the *fiesta* dressed in fine clothes. He smears food on the clothes, saying he "feeds" the clothes because it was the clothes that were invited.   30:279-280.

6.204   (M) In a dispute involving branded cattle, a *ranchero* stands on his head. He is the same man whether he stands on his head or not; therefore his brand is his own whether put on upside down or not.   30:281.

6.205   (M) When discovered beating his son, a peasant says that he had been dreaming of getting rich and buying a beautiful blue bowl out of which his two sons would drink together, and that the son he is beating has refused to drink out of the bowl with his brother.   24:6.

6.206   In the boy's father's absence, a Chinese grandfather whips the boy. When the father returns, he is angered; and in presence of *his* father he whips himself.   15:76.

6.207   Widow of a recently killed man is informed "gently" of her husband's death. "Does Joe Toole live here?"—"Yes."—"Bet he don't."   25:11-13 (two versions).

6.208   (N) In lamenting the accidental death of a young man whose riding mule fell on him, a woman observes that the situation might have been worse: the saddle might have been broken.   9:158-159.

6.209   Judge who is against prohibition dismisses a grand jury that has attempted to indict a Negro for making corn whiskey.   18:206-208.

6.210   In arguing against legislation to do away with hanging, a Texas lawyer inadvertently says, "Hanging was good enough for my father and it's good enough for me."   18:214-217.

6.211   Man enters a room and likens it to hell because all the lawyers (or preachers) are closest to the fire.   25:5-6.

6.212   Young lawyer's first client is a man who complains of his neighbor's turkey eating his garden. The young lawyer speaks with great gravity for a while, but soon he and his client see the humor of the situation.   18:212-214.

6.213   Smart lawyer wins his case by reminding the jury that if they find against his client, he, the lawyer, will receive more money in handling the appeals.   18:208-212.

6.214 Senator who has bet his fellow senator that the other cannot repeat the Lord's Prayer admits defeat when the other begins, "Now I lay me . . . ." 13:96-97.

6.215 When Stephen F. Austin accuses an early Texas settler of having served time in prison, the man admits this but begs Austin to suppress the rumor that he has also served two terms in the Kentucky legislature. 30:278.

6.216 When a political orator wishes for a "window in his breast that his constituency might read his heart," a heckler asks if a pain in the stomach would not do. 15:83-84.

6.217 When a legislator who gambles approaches a colleague for a loan and is asked if he is not drawing his *per diem*, the legislator answers yes, but not his *per noctem*. 15:83.

6.218 For excitement on a Saturday night a man orders his darky to set fire to the man's own corn crib. 30:278-279.

6.219 A lazy man about to be hanged would rather be hanged than shell a gift of corn for his family. "Is it shelled?" 13:87-88.

6.220 Old-timer used to solitude departs (or, if a guide, overcharges) when companions "talk too much." (Cf. 6.182.) 25:13-15.

6.221 When a panther screams at night, a bachelor cowboy says, "Igod, I hope it ain't a woman!" 31:101.

6.222 Drunk cowboy tries to rope a train. 31:101.

6.223 A saloonkeeper tries to cash $1,300 worth of sawmill checks at the company commissary. When told that there is not that much cash on hand, he says he will take $1,300 worth of Star chewing tobacco. (Cf. 9:25.) 30:181.

6.224 Ex-Confederate general Jubal Early gives $10.00 to an old G.A.R. veteran who is an amputee. When commended for his brotherly love he says, "Hell . . . that's the only example I've seen of a Yankee carved up enough to suit me." 25:4.

6.225 Texas pioneer is land hungry. When questioned about his greed he says he does not want all the land in the world — just what belongs to him and everything joining it. 7:76.

6.226 Cowboy who has met a girl at a dance returns her overshoe the next day. When she says that she had left two overshoes, he says he knows, and will bring the other one the next day. "Miss Anne, I just wish you was a centipede." 22:220-221.

6.227   A slave causes his master to lose a wager by butting in on a conversation when it turns to food.   21:86-87.

6.228   (N) Negro applicant for the position of school principal says that he can teach geography by either the flat or the round method.   9:162.

6.229   Negro couple find money hidden in a tree. They tell their white boss and are given a "reward" of 25¢ each.   29:163-164.

6.230   After making camp, a frontiersman hands a tenderfoot a stick of wood for a pillow, warning him that the following night they will be out on the prairie and he will have to "rough it." (Two versions: one about Bigfoot Wallace, the other about a Scots youth on a border raid. When the youth forms a snowball as a pillow, his father kicks it away. "No effeminacy, my son!")   25:4-5.

6.231   Frontiersman spits out unexpectedly hot food (rice pudding) that is strange to him. "A damn fool would have swallowed that!" (Told of Sam Houston.)   25:2.

6.232   A boy, left to watch the pot boil while his mother visits neighbors, embarrasses his mother by running to tell her that the pot is boiling over. He thus reveals the poor fare they are having for supper. "Ram's head buttin' the cabbage out of the pot."   7:72; 25:243-245 (Negro version).

6.233   By referring to "flour biscuits" a boy causes embarrassment at a dinner party designed to impress his sister's suitor. (Bread made of white flour was rare on the frontier.)   7:70-71.

6.234   Guest at dinner says the wrong thing. In attempting to make amends he adds to his embarrassment. "There's plenty, such as it is." "It's fine, what there is of it." "I must be the biggest fool around, present company excepted."   15:81-82.

6.235   Man who wants to be a lithe dancer rubs panther fat on his limbs. At a dance, his body warms and he begins to stink. (Cf. 8.60.)   19:130-131.

6.236   When a lady asks a bashful cowboy the name of the horse she is riding ("Old Guts"), he finally answers, "Old Bowels."   16:241-242.

6.237   Elderly sheepherder always wears his hat, even during sleep. A *vaquero* tricks him into removing his hat, revealing his baldness.   8:88-91.

6.238   Farmer whose corn is being stolen sets a steel trap in the crib, near a crack in the wall. Next morning the thief, a neighbor, is seen standing outside the crib with his hand in the crack. The farmer merely bids his neighbor good morning; no more corn is missed. 7:78.

6.239 Boy tells a girl he will marry her if she will spend the night on a housetop. She does and freezes to death. "O-ooooh, I'm gonna marry Johnny in the mornin'." 31:26; cf. 34:105.

6.240 (Aztec) A princess says she will marry the warrior who brings her the gift that most resembles her. Suitors are rejected until an Aztec warrior brings her a *pitahaya* cactus in bloom, saying that she is fair like the flowers but sharp and forbidding like the thorns that surround them. 8:101-102.

6.241 A farmer owns a magnificent white stallion that he is proud of. On his wedding day he and his bride leave the church in a buggy pulled by the stallion. Along the way the horse repeatedly stumbles until finally the man shoots it. ("That's once" . . . "that's twice" . . . "that's the last time.") When the bride scolds him for the rash act, he says, "That's once." 30:175; 31:21-22.

6.242 (Kiowa-Apache) A young wife is frightened into obedience by her husband and his friend, who make it appear that a supernatural power is advising the husband to kill her. 22:90-93.

6.243 A rancher's wife — a scold — dies. The "bump gate" on his ranch, when struck by the auto carrying the coffin, jars her heart to life. Ten years later she again dies. This time the rancher opens the gate by hand. 30:176.

6.244 When at a prayer meeting a man thanks the Lord for the night he "courted" his wife in the briars, the wife hastily interrupts to say that the "briars" were rosebushes. 30:134-135.

6.245 When a husband learns that his wife has saved and invested the ten-dollar bills he has given her each time he kissed her, he regrets not having done all his kissing at home. 13:92-93.

6.246 Railroad conductor announces San Angelo, Tex., as a town with 23 churches "all working to beat the Devil." 27:166.

6.247 When a rancher writes complaining that his calf was killed by a train, the railroad claims agent replies in such a way that the rancher offers to pay the railroad for trespassing on the right-of-way. 27:168.

6.248 A railroad conductor, when reminded by a passenger that he was to have put the passenger off at a certain stop, says "My gosh, who *was* that we put off!" 27:166.

6.249   Train is so slow that when a mother, who had got on with a babe in arms, misses the child somewhere in Texas, she finds him in the baggage car shooting craps with a safety razor as stakes. 27:169.

6.250   Train is so slow that a passenger suggests placing a cowcatcher at the rear to keep cows from walking into a car and injuring the occupants.   27:168.

6.251   Pioneer East Texan swears he is only 64 years old. He does not count the 21 years he was waterbound in Arkansas while immigrating.   17:3.

6.252   A newcomer to Texas, when told that only newcomers and fools predict the weather there, says that all Texans must be weather prophets.   13:88-89.

6.253   On the frontier, when fussy eaters complain of the common fare, they are urged to help themselves to the mustard.   7:72.

6.254   Anglo businessman who is finicky about food refuses to eat in Mexican cafés. But to help close a leasing arrangement with an old Mexican whose land contains oil, he visits the man and partakes of delicious *cabrito* stew. On the back porch he sees the hides of many goats. He comments on the fact that his host has slaughtered a number of goats recently. "Me no kill goats—they get seek and die." The man throws up.   28:131-132.

6.255   Man notices that a particular bush grows where there are producing oil wells. He searches for the bush on his own land. One day he slips on a weed and breaks his back. "At last I have found the oil-berry bush."   9:47.

6.256   Young man, a novice at oil-field work, drops a large wrench down a drilled hole. Much time and expense are wasted in "fishing" for the wrench. When the wrench is retrieved, the boss tells the worker he is fired. "What for?"—"You know what for."—"You mean this?" The young man tosses the wrench over his shoulder; it again goes down the hole.   28:128-131.

6.257   Rural doctor holds a bottle of snuff under the nose of a woman having trouble in childbirth. The child is delivered.   30:183.

6.258   When a chuckwagon bogs down in a canyon just below a Mexican settlement, cowboys hurry to get it out of the stream before the beans, rice, prunes, and dried apples get wet, dam the canyon, and drown the Mexicans out.   17:57.

6.259   At the end of a cattle drive a cowboy enters a restaurant in St. Louis and tells the waiter to bring him everything on the French menu that is not beans.   17:55.

6.260   When a dying man is refused beans, he sneaks into the kitchen for them. He recovers.   17:55.

6.261   A party-line user breaks up a lengthy telephone conversation between women by telling one of them that he smells her beans burning.   17:55.

6.262   Men in a saloon mock a man who carries home groceries when probably there is no whiskey in his house.   13:90-91.

6.263   When an intoxicating beverage is placed in milk, the supposedly unsuspecting drinker, an old lady, commends the cow.   25:15-16.

6.264   Man searches for a rattlesnake to bite him so that he can take whiskey as a remedy.   31:103.

6.265   Men mix medicine with whiskey. One is caught taking a dose of "medicine" without first shaking the bottle.   8:85.

6.266   (M) Man knocks at a door to seek shelter from rain. A pet crow within keeps saying, "Who is it? What do you want?" 28:157-158.

6.267   (M) A parrot answers a wood vendor's call with "two loads." When the vendor attempts to collect from the master, the parrot is found out and whipped.   27:82-84.

6.268   (M) When a parrot's cursing becomes offensive, its owner places it on a hen's roost so that it will have to stay awake in fear of a marauding owl and thus will sleep in the daytime. When an owl lights on the roost and attempts to push the parrot off, the parrot curses him for a *gringo.*   27:84-87.

6.269   When Indians pursue mustang hunters and shoot arrows into a lagging mule, the mule outruns fast horses.   28:135-138.

6.270   Tornado lifts a mule and returns it to earth, its owner still on its back. The mule lands running faster than anyone thought possible.   28:59.

6.271   Man who hollers "Whoa!" to his mules stops every mule-drawn streetcar in town.   29:51.

6.272   When asked why his door has three cat holes in it, a backwoods-man says that when he says *scat* he means *scat.*   15:77.

6.273   Shotgun is revered because of its ability to get daughters married off.   25:6-7.

6.274   Even though all the parts on his rifle are replacements, a back-woods boy assures a stranger that his gun is the same one his grandfather carried in the Revolutionary War.   14:166-167.

6.275   When a man tells his preacher he has dreamed that the Lord intends for him to take the preacher's corn, the preacher replies that he has had a later dream, canceling the first.   13:98; 21:89-90 (Negro version, master and slave).

6.276   (N) A slave who pretends to be a seer is tested. A raccoon is placed under a washpot. The slave's exclamation of self-pity accidentally answers the question put to him. "You got dis ole coon [Negro] dis time!"   10:24-25; cf. 22:180-181.

6.277   A miller who follows the Devil's directions cheats the rich, average, and poor alike. (The poor get poorer; it is a sin to be poor.)   14:251-252.

Section 7: Tales of the Supernatural

GUIDE TO THE SECTION

GHOSTS; TREASURE-GUARDING SPIRITS OR CREATURES: ghostly warning of death, 7.1—7.2; ghost of deceased appears to friend at time of death, 7.3—7.4; beckoning apparition appears to prodigal son as result of mother's prayers, 7.5; ghost of husband appears to wife, 7.6—7.7; vengeful ghost causes death or insanity, 7.8—7.11, cf. 7.46; corpse speaks or sits upright in coffin, 7.12—7.13; ghost attempts to lead person to treasure, 7.14—7.19; ghost carries lantern, 7.20—7.21; ghostly (vanishing) hitchhiker, 7.22—7.23; the weeping woman (*La Llorona*), 7.24—7.28; the juniper tree ("My mommy cooked me and my daddy ate me"), 7.29—7.30; "I want my golden arm [silver toe, *tripas*]," 7.31—7.36; haunted houses, 7.37—7.54; haunted sites, 7.55—7.68; ghosts, spirits, creatures guard treasure, 7.69—7.77; girl found dead in cemetery, her dress pinned to grave by knife, 7.78; train of ghostly knights, Godmother Death, 7.79; other ghosts, 7.80—7.82. WITCHES AND WIZARDS: witches or supernatural agents as cats, 7.83—7.85 (man severs paws, head), 7.86 (king of the cats), 7.87—7.90 (other); witches exchange eyes with cats, 7.91—7.93; witches fly as owls, 7.94—7.98; witch casts spell, 7.99—7.102; witches identified, 7.103—7.105; wizards, 7.106—7.109. THE DEVIL: mysterious Spaniard and, 7.110—7.112; wishing someone to, 7.113; bartering with, 7.114—7.117; appears at a dance, 7.118—7.122; other, 7.123—7.127. SPIRITS IN ANIMAL FORM; DEMONS: white or spotted dog, 7.128—7.135; wolf, 7.136; panther, 7.137; rooster, 7.138; sow and pigs, 7.139; crow, 7.140; demon-seductress with face of horse, claw-like fingernails, 7.141—7.143. MYSTERIOUS LIGHTS, OTHER PHENOMENA: lights, 7.144—7.148; music, bells, 7.149—7.151; padre's beacon, 7.152; clock, 7.153; hall tree, 7.154; footprints, 7.155;

crows gather as boys read from the Seventh Book of Moses, 7.156. For certain other narratives of a supernatural (eerie) cast, see Section 8 of Part II, "Legends."

Demon seductress of Mexican lore; see Synopsis 7.143.

7.1   (N) Travelers meet a ghost on the road. It tries to speak but cannot. Soon afterward, a relative dies in an accident.   28:165.

7.2   (M) Clammy hand of a ghost brushes a woman's neck, forewarns
her of her father's death.   24:90-91.

7.3   (M) Young man, just returned from military service, visits his best
friend. Later he is told that his friend's funeral was in progress at
the time of the visit.   24:92-93.

7.4   Apparition of a man wearing a bloody shirt appears to the man's
friend, who is 120 miles away on the night the man is murdered.
30:118.

7.5   (M) Prodigal son hears his mother calling to him, sees the figure
of his dead grandmother by his bed, beckoning. On returning home,
he learns that his mother had called out to him while praying for
his return.   24:93-94.

7.6   (N) Woman's dead husband appears to her, asks her to make
coffee for him. When the woman returns from the kitchen, the
ghost is gone.   7:125-126.

7.7   Old man who had always worn two pairs of undershorts is buried
with one pair on. His ghosts haunts his wife until provided with a
second pair.   10:59.

7.8   Oil-field worker falls from the top of a derrick, is killed. Red
handkerchief like the one carried by the man's dead enemy is found
attached to the derrick.   18:142.

7.9   In Germany a "mountain spirit" gives money to a poor miner on
the condition he bring him penny loaves of bread and penny
candles and not reveal his good fortune. After a while, the miner
gets drunk and tells. Next day he is found dead in the mine, his
corpse surrounded by burning penny candles.   30:265.

7.10   Two partners quarrel about selling their property. One strikes
the other with a axe, decapitating him. Haunted by the headless
ghost of his partner, the murderer becomes insane, hangs himself.
3:135-137.

7.11   (M) With two chests of gold that his dying twin has entrusted
to him, a priest intends to build a bigger church instead of sending
the gold to Mexico, as his brother had instructed. Ghost of the
brother haunts the priest until he becomes insane.   9:138-140.

7.12   (M) Cowboys who disrespectfully play cards by a corpse in a
coffin are reprimanded by the corpse.   24:94-95.

7.13 (M) When a house containing a corpse and coffin catches fire, the burning corpse sits upright in the coffin, appears to be burning in hell's fires. (Cf. 6.61.) 12:113-114.

7.14 (M) Cowboy, searching for lost horses in the mountains, encounters a spirit that asks what he is seeking. Ghost offers to show the man treasure, but he flees. 28:125-126.

7.15 (M) While picking mulberries in the mountains, a man hears a woman's voice, sees an angel on a bluff beckoning to him. He flees. 28:126.

7.16 Ghost of Jean Laffite appears to those who sleep in an abandoned house on the Texas coast. Ghost attempts to reveal where treasure is concealed. 3:185-189.

7.17 (N) Ghost of an old woman appears to a sleeping woman and tries to lead her to treasure. Woman refuses to follow. 29:161-162.

7.18 (M) Woman dressed in white appears to a young couple, scoops up handfuls of gold and deposits gold behind a mirror (cf. 7.50). Ghost lures them outside the house, then backs into an irrigation ditch. 13:126-128.

7.19 (M) To keep a ghost from dragging her infant from bed every night, a mother assumes the position of the Cross, asks the ghost what it wants. Ghost reveals the location of treasure, but the mother faints, forgets the location. Later a man finds two earthen pots near the house; they contain only charcoal. 13:122-123.

7.20 (N) Woman who has murdered her husband is haunted by his ghost, which walks down railroad tracks carrying a lighted lantern. 18:144.

7.21 Crazed by the loss of his crops in a flood, a farmer drowns himself in a river, leaving his lantern on the bank. During storms, a light is seen swinging up and down the riverbank. 18:145-146.

7.22 (M) Driver gives a ride to a nun standing by the side of the road. Later he learns that a nun of the name the hitchhiker gave him has been dead for eight years. (Three versions; in the other two the nun prophesies the end of the World War II during the ride; is later identified by a photograph.) 18:137-139.

7.23 Girl approaches a man and his wife who are parked by a lake. She asks that they take her home; she has been in a boating accident. When the address given them is reached, the couple find that the girl has disappeared, though there are pools of water in the back seat of the car. Parents of the girl tell the couple that their daughter drowned recently.   18:146-147.

7.24   Widow drowns her two children at a mill-dam when the man who is courting her says he will not support them. When the woman dies, she haunts the site as a bird, calls to her children. 13:120-121.

7.25   (M) Woman who neglects her children and is glad to see them die is doomed to haunt a neighborhood.   24:74.

7.26   (M) Woman who drowns her two children and does not repent haunts a riverbank.   24:74.

7.27   (M) Missionary and his daughter, traveling at night, hear frightful screams, see a shadow flit by. They think they have seen *La Llorona*, the Weeping Woman.   24:76.

7.28   (M) Man who has mistakenly killed his wife and daughter hangs himself. He haunts a valley every year on the night of the murder, wailing (*El Llorón*).   12:169-173.

7.29   (M) Mother buries, alive, her small son who has eaten figs intended for the father's supper. Red grass grows on the grave; the boy's voice issues from the earth, accusing the mother.   31:161-163; cf. 6:54.

7.30   Stepmother cooks stepchild, feeds it to the father. Child's toenails and fingernails are buried in the garden. Later a bird appears, cries "My mamma cooked me and my daddy ate me." After luring the woman outside the house, the bird drops a large stone on her; transforms into the murdered child.   31:11-12; cf. 6:53-54.

7.31   Grave robber unearths the corpse of a man who had a golden arm, steals the arm. Ghost of the man pursues him.   25:183.

7.32   Before burying her husband's corpse, an old woman cuts off his big toe and uses it to season turnip greens. That night a voice issues form the grave: "I want my big toe!" Ghost enters the woman's room.   31:12-13.

7.33   Old woman digs up the silver toe of a corpse, hides it under her pillow. That night a voice at her door demands the toe. When the woman opens door to defy the creature, she sees a horrible sight. (Ending is like "Little Red Ridinghood.")   6:41-42.

7.34   Boys find two bear toes in a trap, cook and eat them. That night a bear comes after the boys: "I want my two big toes!"   31:15-16.

7.35 (M) Boy buys candy with the money his mother has given him for the purchase of tripe for the family meal. Returning home, he sees a corpse in a coffin, awaiting burial. He removes the entrails, takes them home in place of the tripe. Family unknowingly eats the entrails. That night a ghost appears, cries "I want my *tripas!*" 31:163.

7.36 (M) Woman kills her husband and serves his flesh to friends at a dinner party. Husband's ghost appears, demands its entrails. 24:77-78.

7.37 (N) House is haunted by the spirit of a woman who died in torment, believing that snakes surrounded her bed. She had wanted to leave the bed but was restrained. 10:58.

7.38 (N) House is haunted by a woman who died leaving a small son. When relatives move into the house to care for the child, they hear strange noises. One night they see a ghost take the child. 7:123.

7.39 (N) Boys set fire to a house, the source of a mysterious light. The light persists; one of the boys dies soon after. 7:121-122.

7.40 (N) House is haunted because so many persons who were not ready to die, died there. 7:126-127.

7.41 (N) Plantation house is haunted by the restless spirits of brothers who had led troubled lives in the house because of quarrels. 7:135-136.

7.42 (M) Old house is haunted by its Spanish builders, who refight an ancient duel and seek the gold they buried. 6:14-18.

7.43 (N) Two women take refuge in an empty house during a storm. A light lures them to the third floor, where they see ghosts sitting around a coffin. Ghosts pursue the women. 2:46.

7.44 (N) Dying man, shot by a policeman, begs for milk. His friends are afraid to interfere. People who afterward live in the man's house notice that the milk pans are visited each night. 7:127.

7.45 House is haunted by a young bride who may have been murdered, and by her husband, killed while serving in the Confederate Army. 18:141-142.

7.46 House on an army post is haunted by the ghost of Negro cook who was beaten to death by a drunken colonel. Footsteps are heard in the house; a dog is driven out of its senses by the presence of the ghost. 29:226-227.

7.47   Elaborate ranch house is suddenly abandoned. A young girl, drowned in a cistern, haunts the site.   14:178-179.

7.48   House is haunted by the ghost of a murdered man whose footsteps are heard on the porch, who rattles the door, enters the house, goes to the second floor.   27:180-186.

7.49   In the 1870's Indians murdered women and children at a particular ranch house. Years later, coon hunters spending the night in the house hear a ghostly rider outside, see the ghost of a young girl hovering over a grave.   6:87-89.

7.50   (M) Young couple move into a haunted house where, after investigating a beckoning hand that appears in the mirror in their bedroom, they receive a box of jewels from the ghost of a woman whose husband was killed before their first child was born. Jewels are for first girl-child born in the house.   (Cf. 7.18.)   24:91-92.

7.51   (M) Strange noises come from a house thought to be built over a cave used by Indians for hiding booty.   24:94.

7.52   (M) House haunted by the ghost of its builder. Ghost reveals a treasure to a family, but when they keep all for themselves, a member of the family dies. When an elderly couple move into the house, the ghost gets into bed with the woman, caresses her. 13:128-129.

7.53   (M) Headless ghost of a man pulls the bedclothes off anyone who sleeps in a deserted ranch house, to see if the sleeper is his wife. 9:51-52.

7.54   (M) House has been built over the grave of infant who is heard crying at midday. Ghost of a woman in a ragged white dress, holding an infant, is seen.   29:219-222.

7.55   (N) At the place where bandits roped a man and drug him until he died, people hear, at night, the sound of a wagon rumbling past, horses galloping, something being dragged over the ground. 3:54-56.

7.56   (M) Ghostly wagon of Spaniards who were killed by bandits is heard in the sky near where the massacre occurred.   30:119.

7.57   Headless horseman haunts the site of an Indian massacre during which victims were dismembered.   28:164-165.

7.58   Ghost of a murdered man, riding a gray horse and wearing *charro* clothes, haunts a hill.   30:119-120.

7.59   (M) Ghost of a girl who was thrown into a well to die disturbs all who stay near the well.   24:95-96.

7.60   (M) In a motte of oak brush by an abandoned well, the ghost of the digger of the well can be heard chopping. Ghost has been seen in the daytime; is recognized as a ghost because it casts no shadow. 9:50-51.

7.61   (M) A young man once swung his bride in a particular wooden hammock. She became ill and died; he died soon after. Now his ghost swings the hammock each night.   9:51.

7.62   (M) Pasture gate will not stay shut even when locked. Ghost is thought to be responsible.   9:50.

7.63   When an old graveyard is moved, a number of loose bones are reburied in a single coffin. Headless ghost haunts the spot, seeking its head.   18:140-141.

7.64   (M) Ghosts of Texas frontiersmen and Mexican soldiers are seen fighting above a cemetery at night.   30:118-119.

7.65   Cove is haunted by a ghost ship believed to have been wrecked by supernatural means.   3:148-149.

7.66   Salt marshes are haunted by the ghost of a fisherman's wife. The wife lost her husband during a storm; now she is seen and heard during storms.   3:143.

7.67   Alsate, once chief of the Chisos Apaches, has a cave in the Chisos Mountains, haunts the mountains. His likeness appears, as if carved, on a mountainside. Moccasin tracks are seen in the area.   28:116-117.

7.68   (N) Married woman leaves home with another man. Her husband meets the lovers on the road, kills them. Road is haunted by the ghost of the woman, who is heard screaming.   7:124.

7.69   (M) Ghostly hoofbeats, which grow louder and louder, frighten treasure-seekers.   24:99.

7.70   (N) Ghost—a woman in white with a lighted torch and a rod—guards treasure hidden by Spaniards before they were killed by Indians.   3:57-59.

7.71   (M) Treasure-guarding ghosts in the form of a woman and a huge turkey attempt to overpower a lone traveler.   6:19-20.

7.72   (M) A bear-like animal appears and vanishes several times in the vicinity of a clump of cactus. Later a box of money is plowed up near the cactus.   24:100.

7.73   (M) Tunnel where a rancher buried his wealth is marked by mysterious lights; guarded by a white lion.   3:46-47.

7.74   (N) Huge skeleton guards treasure in a well.   3:56-57.

7.75   Unnamed horror that severely affects treasure-seekers protects pirate booty.   3:182-184.

7.76   (M) Dragon guards treasure-trove in a cave.   3:34-37.

7.77   (N) Buried coins become bumblebees when a man for whom the treasure is not intended attempts to unearth them.   3:53-54.

7.78   On a dare, a young girl visits a cemetery at night. Next morning she is discovered dead beside a grave, her face frozen in an expression of horror. As part of the dare, she was to have stuck a knife into a grave. When the girl is found, her dress is pinned to the grave by a knife.   (Cf. 6.186.)   28:164.

7.79   (M) Man sees a ghostly train of twelve mounted knights, led by woman in white (Godmother Death) who has stolen the man's horse.   16:353-354.

7.80   (M) Black-caped figure enters a shepherd's hut. When asked to take off his hat and cape, the visitor takes off his head.   10:100-101.

7.81   (M) Man whom a murdered robber last looked upon (not the murderer) is haunted by a black panther with blazing eyes. There is a nauseating odor. The man faints; next day he finds large scars—claw marks—on his body.   29:136-139.

7.82   (N) A deer, wounded by hunters at night, runs in a circle, rises heavenward. The following night a ghostly deer and pack of dogs do the same.   7:122.

7.83   (N) On Christmas Eve a plantation overseer is visited by three cats, one larger than the others. They speak to him. Having protected himself by reading the Bible, he severs the forepaws of the largest cat. These immediately become a lady's hands, bearing rings. The cats flee. Next morning the plantation owner recognizes the rings as his wife's. His wife and daughters are discovered in bed, his wife without hands, his daughters decapitated.   7:132-134.

7.84   (N) Gin-owner whose bookkeepers die mysteriously decides to do the books himself. On the first night of work a white cat enters his office; the man decapitates the cat. When he goes home, he finds his wife in pool of blood, her head missing.   11:95-96.

7.85   (N) When a black cat with two white forepaws enters the room of a wizard who is a guest in a woman's house, the wizard severs its forepaws, wraps them in his handkerchief. Next morning he sees that his hostess has no hands. The paws in his handkerchief have become hands.   11:96.

7.86 (N) Man tells his wife he has seen nine cats burying another cat. The couple's big yellow cat leaves the room hurriedly. Cat speaks, saying it must attend the funeral. 11:99-100.

7.87 (N) Huge black cat appears at the bedside of a man, seizes him by the throat and shakes him. Man takes this as a sign he is to repent from a godless life, reforms. 11:97-98.

7.88 (N) Village that has a local ghost in form of a cat with two heads and eight legs experiences disaster after a girl disobeys the cat's order to release a caged dove. Girl dies. 11:98-99.

7.89 (N) A woman is haunted, first by a golden trunk with black cat-heads as knobs, then by a large black cat. 2:46.

7.90 Plantation workers often disappear just before payday. A family is given a warning by a black cat that leads the man to a field exhibiting newly-dug graves. 13:182-184.

7.91 (M) Two sisters become witches at night. One night a man enters their house and sees two pairs of eyeballs near the fire, as if left to warm. He throws them into the fire; the eyes dance until charred. Two lean cats enter the room. They have no eyes and run about crying. Next day the man visits the sisters, who now have cats' eyes and cannot see by day. 10:68-70.

7.92 (M) Man's mother-in-law, a witch, has owls as helpers. She exchanges eyes with a cat before flying about as an owl at night. When her own eyes are destroyed, she tries to steal her daughter's eyes to take the place of the cat's eyes she is still using. 30:223-224.

7.93 (M) Mother and daughter, both witches, drink blood, exchange eyes with cats before flying as owls at night. 30:221.

7.94 (M) Man who vomits blood on Thursdays and Fridays has been bewitched by two owls (witches). For a cure, he ties 12 knots in a horsehair rope, saying prayers (the "twelve truths") while doing so; and burns his clothes. 30:218-220.

7.95 (M) Witch who flies as an owl is "prayed" down. She begs for mercy, which is granted. However, her son comes to practice witchcraft. 30:220-221.

7.96 (M) An owl thought to be a witch is shot through the eye. When men go to a suspected woman's home, they learn that she has been found dead, a bullet hole through her eye. 10:64-65.

7.97 (M) Wife of a respectable man is seen flying on "devil's wings" at night, carrying a lantern. A witch, she is journeying to get poison with which to kill a man against whom she has a grudge.

To see this witch in flight is to be warned of some calamity. To deceive people, she makes noises like screech owl's.   9:52-53.

7.98   (M) Thief captures an owl that turns into a woman, a witch, who promises the thief he will never be caught if he releases her. 30:222.

7.99   Boys steal an old woman's morphine. A witch, she tears off a bush, tells boys that by the time bush is wilted, they will wilt. Boys sink to the ground.   31:19.

7.100   Girl steals cabbage from a witch's garden. Witch tells her she will wilt as does the cabbage leaf. Girl wilts.   31:19-20.

7.101   (M) Witch gives a girl three grains of rice to eat. Girl becomes sick; witch is made to remove the spell. Girl vomits three mice. 10:66.

7.102   (M) A woman is bewitched by a neighbor; her face starts rotting away. An Indian cures her; places the same spell on the witch, who dies in three days.   10:67.

7.103   (M) Man who is wasting away because of a witch identifies her, goes to her home and burns her rag dolls. Witch loses powers. 12:115-117.

7.104   (Alabama-Coushatta) Indians capture a witch, an old woman, by following her footsteps from the grave of her victim. She is found washing in the earth from the grave to atone for sins. 21:70-72.

7.105   (M) Woman suspected of being a witch cannot cross two iron needles in the form of a cross.   10:63-64.

7.106   (N) Negro, a "voodoo man," boils a black cat, tests bones to see which makes him invisible.   17:113.

7.107   (M) When men on an overland journey wish for a home-cooked meal, one of their number offers to provide. He goes into the brush, removes his clothing, vanishes. Presently he returns with freshly-cooked food which some of the men refuse because obtained by sorcery.   12:119-120.

7.108   (M) Wealthy woman consults a wizard to learn what her husband does while away from home. In a lighted cave she is attacked by a billy goat and snake (sexual emblems). When she invokes the saints, the scene disappears amid an explosion.   12:117-118.

7.109   (M) Wizard casts a spell on treasure in a cave so that no one will discover it.   28:114-116.

7.110 Old Spaniard, an ex-pirate with Jean Lafitte, comes to Central Texas, says he will show a man where treasure is buried on Galveston Island. While the Spaniard sleeps, his host sees terrible scars on his body; believes he is the Devil. Owl hoots, wolves howl, stars fall, confirming the suspicion. The Spaniard later dies, leaving a map. 28:143-145.

7.111 (M) Stranger who appears to be a Spaniard visits a ranch to buy cattle. He is snatched up by a hurricane, then half-buried in a cave that the Devil is thought to inhabit. His host saves him by making the sign of the Cross. 8:103-106.

7.112 (M) Body of a Spaniard who has been digging for treasure is found half-buried in a hole. His ghost haunts a family until the woman asks what it wants. Ghost reveals the site of the treasure, asks that the family spend part of it for prayers for 30 souls in purgatory. Woman faints while the ghost speaks; treasure not recovered. 13:123-126.

7.113 (M) Girl who is unkind to her sick grandmother says she wishes the Devil would take her. Girl later sees the Devil under her own bed. The grandmother dies; girl repents of her unkindness. 29:142-143.

7.114 A man has sold his soul to the Devil. He tries to invoke the Devil so the Devil will show him where treasure is. Next morning the man's family finds a boot sticking out of the ground, where the Devil has drawn the man into hell. Wife says her husband did not have the courage to look the Devil in the face, or the Devil would have shown him where treasure is buried. 31:28-29.

7.115 (M) Man's wife dies. He exhumes the corpse, tries to preserve it by covering it with wax. A foul odor issues from the closet where the corpse is kept; mysterious things happen. The Devil visits the man's daughters, gives them presents which turn into a snake, a skull, a bottle of evil-smelling liquid. When the corpse is reburied, all returns to normal. 31:156-160.

7.116 (M) Old woman with twin daughters who are starving sells them to the Devil, who promises to care for them until they are sixteen. After the Devil carries them away, the mother searches for them, becomes a ball of fire that wanders over the prairies (*la luz del llano*). 9:53-54.

7.117 (M) A *vaquero* is thought to have made a pact with the Devil because he can throw his quirt down and make it appear to be a rattlesnake. 9:56-57.

7.118   (M) The Devil devastates a community. He appears at a dance, corrupts a young girl. A priest chases the Devil into a cave; villagers imprison him in the cave with a cross and a fence. 25:205-215.

7.119   (M) Handsome stranger appears at a dance and captivates everyone, especially a young girl. However, when asked what is wrong with his feet (like claws) he disappears in a cloud of sulphurous smoke. Girl's face is scratched.   24:86-87 (two versions).

7.120   (M) The Devil appears at a dance as a handsome stranger in a black suit. He has a foot like a rooster's claw; claws dancers to death.   29:144-145.

7.121   (M) At a dance, a monkey enters the room and touches the dress of girl who is disobedient at home. Later a handsome stranger dances with the girl, carries her off. It was noticed that the stranger had the legs and feet of a monkey.   29:144.

7.122   Woman at a dance boasts that no one can outdance her. The lights dim; a man dressed in black appears. He dances her to exhaustion and bears her off, presumably to hell.   18:81-82.

7.123   (M) When a poor man with many children starves the newest born, his wife puts a curse on him. That night a sulphurous whirlwind sweeps him away. A white dove hovers over the corpse of the child.   8:103.

7.124   (M) Infant son of an evil man has a forked tail, horns on his head. When left alone with visitors the infant prophesies many horrors before the father disposes of him.   9:54-56.

7.125   (M) Horses refuse to pull a hearse bearing the corpse of a bandit. Later, claw marks are found around the place of burial; bandit was the Devil.   24:87-88.

7.126   (M) Young boy is pursued by ball of fire that emerges from the explosion of a Judas effigy during Holy Week.   24:88-89.

7.127   (M) A drunkard is attacked by the Devil in the form of a gray lizard. He prays to the Virgin; is kept from harm; stops drinking. 14:234-236.

7.128   In order to marry a woman, a man kills her father and fiancé. Not suspecting his guilt, the woman agrees to marry him. Before they can be married, the man is harassed by a small white dog and pair of detached hands; confesses the crime.   12:201-210.

7.129   (M) Small spotted dog gets people to follow him, only to disappear at a certain place. Is thought to be either the Devil or a spirit attempting to show where treasure is buried (where dog disappears). 24:89-90.

7.130 (M) Small, gopher-like dog—reared by a ewe—herds sheep. The dog steals sheep but cannot be apprehended by shepherds. Later it mates and gives rise to line of famous sheep dogs in the Devil's River area of Texas. 15:119-121.

7.131 (N) Girl sees a white puppy she knows is a spirit. 7:124.

7.132 (N) Mexican woman is buried in an eerie spot. One night boys see her ghost, in the form of a dog, leap from her grave. Boys shoot at the dog, hit it, but to no avail. 7:125.

7.133 In Germany a mine official is doomed to haunt a mine in the form of an ugly dog because of his unfaithfulness in life. 30:265.

7.134 (N) When two men dig for treasure, a white bulldog rises from the ground to frighten them away. 3:54.

7.135 Ghost of a murdered man, in the form of a dog, haunts scene of the murder, where the man's treasure supposedly is buried. 3:102-103.

7.136 It is bad luck to hunt the white wolf that haunts Bolivar's Peninsula on the Texas coast. Merely to see *le loup blanc* foretells hard times. 7:62-68.

7.137 (M) Herder sees a panther at close range. That night he is told that if he has seen a panther within 20 yards of him he has seen death (Mexican belief). However, he takes the flock out next morning, skeptical and unheeding. Later he is found dead, mangled, with look of frozen terror on his face. The panther a demon. 29:139-141.

7.138 In Germany, a girl's suitor murders her when she refuses his offer of marriage. As her coffin passes his house, a red rooster comes from his yard and perches on the coffin, thus disclosing his guilt. 30:264-265.

7.139 (M) The Devil appears to a drunk man as a sow with pigs, which disappear into a small hole. 24:90.

7.140 (Waco) A crow, as a familiar spirit, warns an Indian of attack by a snake and an approaching prairie fire. 1:53-54.

7.141 (M) Young man, riding horseback, picks up an abandoned baby. The child turns into a shapely young woman. When the young man starts to kiss her, he sees that she has the face of a horse. (*El Nagual*, a monster, attacks young women who stay out

late; while its counterpart, *La Segua,* frightens young men.)
30:229-231.

7.142   The Devil in the form of a shapely girl with long fingernails
appears to a young man who ventures to attend a dance the night
before his wedding. When the young man lights the girl's cigarette,
he sees the hideous face. Girl (Devil) claws the man's back.
29:145-146.

7.143   (M) Two young men follow an enticing woman at night. When
she turns and faces them, they see that she has a horse's head and
shiny tin fingernails.   24:76.

7.144   (M) Mysterious light that appears at a water crossing and follows travelers is said to be a warning of death.   17:118-119.

7.145   Two men, dressed in white and headless, are seen by deer hunters on a moonlit night. Later a mysterious light hovers where the
ghosts were sighted.   30:116-117.

7.146   A spring issues from the place where an Indian chief was
killed. Mysterious light haunts the spot.   28:162-163.

7.147   Ball of fire rises from the grave of a man who was buried, standing, with his gun, lantern, and whiskey flask.   18:144-145.

7.148   Phosphorus causes mysterious lighting phenomena at night. On
one occasion a man sees an entire valley light up. Lights may be
the torch of an Indian spirit who guides kinsmen to paradise.
28:107-108.

7.149   Mysterious violin music is heard at the bend of a river, where
a musician once lived.   3:137-141.

7.150   (N) Tolling of a ship's bell is heard every evening at a point on
a river where a slave-smuggling vessel sank with 300 slaves im-
prisoned below deck.   3:141-142.

7.151   In mountains, bells are heard chiming although no church is
near. Green and red flares are seen. Phenomena are thought to be
petitions of the spirits of men who were murdered and buried with
treasure.   28:124-125.

7.152   On stormy nights a ghostly beacon is intermittently seen at the
mouth of a river.   3:145.

7.153   Hotel clock has failed to keep correct time since the night of a
man's murder. Hotel-keeper and his wife are known to have
robbed and killed lodgers, whose bodies they threw into an abandoned oil well.   18:143.

7.154 Hall tree makes a popping sound every afternoon at one o'clock. Carpenter who made the tree is believed to have secreted a diamond ring in it, intended as an anniversary gift to his wife, who was found to be faithless on the day of their anniversary. 18:141.

7.155 Strange footprints, apparently of a man followed by a woman, repeatedly appear at campsites in a wilderness region. 3:242.

7.156 During their teacher's absence, schoolboys enter his room and read from the Seventh Book of Moses. Crows fly into the room as they read. When the teacher sees crows flocking in the street, he makes for his room and immediately begins reading the book backwards. The crows depart in the order in which they had come. 30:255-256.

Section 8: Legends

GUIDE TO THE SECTION

MIRACLES INDICATING DIVINE FAVOR, DISFAVOR; TORNADOES: rivers and springs, 8.1—8.7; images (santos), Christ, the saints, the Holy Ghost, 8.8—8.23; priest pens Satan in a cave, 8.24; hanged man sends rain, 8.25; woman stops ruinous rain, 8.26; sour fruit turns sweet, 8.27; bluebonnet flower originated, 8.28—8.29; tornadoes act in providential manner, 8.30. See also 1.17 (water from struck rock), 1.22 (man translated to the moon as punishment), 1.26 (water in streams), 1.46—1.48 (origin of desert shrubs), 1.53 (divinely-favored person makes pack animal of lion), 8.82—8.83 (the saints), 8.185—8.186 (wrong-doers miraculously punished, cf. 1.22, 8.9, 8.19, 8.21, 8.30). HIDDEN VALLEYS, ENCHANTED SITES: lost herd of buffalo, 8.31; valley of gold nuggets ("Orange Grove"), 8.32; enchanted city, castle, 8.33—8.34; cave of horn worshipers, 8.35; beings dwell within mountain or mound, 8.36—8.38; Stampede Mesa, 8.39; cursed point on seacoast, 8.40. LOVERS: choose to die for love, 8.41—8.46; other, 8.47—8.49. See also 8.38. SUICIDE (NOT LOVERS): captured girl drowns self to preserve honor, 8.50; defeated warriors jump from cliff, 8.51. CHILD CAST FROM CLIFF: in Texas Big Bend, 8.52; in Texas Panhandle, 8.53. HISTORICAL PERSONS; INFAMOUS FAMILIES: person named, 8.54—8.68; person not named, 8.69—8.72; families, 8.73—8.75. See also 7.67 (Alsate), 8.4—8.5 (Father Margil), 8.24 (Father Urbán), 8.36 (Cheetwah). MYSTERIOUS WOMAN APPEARS: to Indians, 8.76; to Texas Rangers, 8.77. WILD WOMAN; ANIMALS REAR CHILDREN: "wild woman" found to be runaway slave, 8.78; girl runs with wolves, 8.79; coyotes rear child, 8.80; bear steals baby, 8.81. PERSONS WRONGFULLY EXECUTED: saints prove innocence, 8.82—8.83; other, 8.84. CLOSE CALLS; ESCAPES FROM BEASTS, INDIANS: person saved from a bullet, 8.85; panther on the roof, 8.86;

wild animal pursues travelers, 8.87—8.89; Indians escape Indians, 8.90—8.91; whites escape Indians, 8.92—8.94. UNDERGROUND PASSAGE-WAY: used by Santa Anna, 8.95; at Monte Albán, 8.96. See also 8.74—8.75. ANIMALS: giant catfish, bullfrog, 8.97—8.98; dog protects child from mad dog, pet panther rescues girl, 8.99—8.100; mustangs and other horses, 8.101—8.107. OIL: well produced through chance, 8.108—8.110; other, 8.111—8.112. TREASURE: religious vessels, 8.113—8.114; jewels, 8.115; revealed in a dream, 8.116—8.117; discovered through chance, 8.118—8.120; buried by rancher who is killed by bandits, 8.121—8.123; fleeing persons or groups bury, 8.124—8.133; sinks in quicksand or mud, 8.134—8.137; hidden in cave, 8.138—8.140; rock pen marks site of, 8.141; palm trees mark site of, 8.142—8.143; copper boxes contain charts revealing, 8.144; ebony tablet reveals, 8.145; at Ft. Belknap, 8.146; at Painted Bluff, 8.147; Mustang Gray and, 8.148; Jean Lafitte and, 8.149, cf. 8.117; the Snively gang and, 8.150—8.151, cf. 8.129; mysterious Spaniard (Moro) and, 8.152, cf. 7.110—7.112; other, 8.153—8.160. LOST MINERAL DEPOSITS, MINES: paint, 8.161; lead, 8.162—8.164; mercury, 8.165; gold, 8.166—8.169 (Nigger, Padre, Sub-lett mines, other); silver, 8.170—8.174 (San Saba or Bowie Mine, others), gold and silver in Llano River area, 8.175. TRIBAL PSUEDO-HISTORY: Alabama Indians migrate southward, 8.176; Natchitoches and Nacogdoches, 8.177; Tehuanas cross the ocean, join with the Zapotecs, 8.178; Tlaxcalans dope Aztec queen, 8.179. See also 1.2—1.3, 1.5, 1.9, 1.17—1.18, 1.20, 1.23, 1.28, 1.51, 8.51, 8.90, 8.96. OTHER: Kit Carson uses cannon against Indians, 8.180; swordsmen sever heads of running Indians, 8.181; some plains Indians travel to the Pacific, 8.182; boy shares food with animals, 8.183; pioneers follow crows to find game, 8.184; blackguards are crushed under boat they are building, 8.185; whiskey drinker who scoffs at religion is punished, 8.186; mysterious graves explained, 8.187; taco vendor uses cat meat, 8.188; mountain spirit turns man's heart into boulder, 8.189; princely buyers at a depart-ment store (Neiman Marcus), 8.190; last herd of longhorns, 8.191.

8.1   (M) To escape pursuing Indians a priest (or a priest and Chris-tianized Indians) cross a river (the Brazos or Colorado) which miraculously opens in their path. When pursuers attempt to cross, the waters close upon them. (Five accounts; see also 8.2. The priest may be "miraculously borne across"; the river may simply sweep the pursuers away, without mention of the dividing waters theme.) 3:211-217; 14:198.

8.2   (Kiowa-Apache) Indians returning from a raid elude pursuers when their medicine man causes the waters of a river to divide in their path but to engulf pursuers. 22:104-105.

8.3 (I) As punishment for their warlike nature, the Ripas Indians are destroyed by a flood. The one great river, the Caney, becomes a small stream while two new rivers, the Brazos and the Colorado, appear. 3:218-219.

8.4 (M) When Father Margil falls and clutches at a grapevine, uprooting it, the San Antonio River issues from the resulting hole. 3:204; 13:70.

8.5 (M) When Father Margil and co-workers run out of water near Nacogdoches, Tex., the priest strikes a rock with his staff and a stream of good water flows. (Cf. 1.17, 8.71.) 3:204-205; 13:69.

8.6 (M) Drought causes a group of Spaniards to leave mines on the San Saba River. When they reach the Brazos River, it flows despite lack of rain. 3:214-215.

8.7 (M) When a ship in need of fresh water sails into a river's mouth, the crew names the river *Los Brazos de Dios* (the Arms of God). 3:213-214.

8.8 (M) A sister of Don Cristobal de Oñate thrice removes a doll from a mesquite tree, only to have it mysteriously return to the tree. Concluding that the doll is a saint, she has a shrine built. When the first stone is laid, a spring issues from ground; later the Virgin appears at the site. 12:165-166.

8.9 (M) A saint, *El Señor de los Guerreros* (Lord of the Warriors), lives in mesquite tree, where his shrine is. Disbelievers conceal dynamite sticks in candles and ask a priest to light these at the shrine. A voice issues from the tree and warns the priest. Disbelievers meet their death the following day. 12:166-168.

8.10 (M) Image of St. Lorenzo disappears from its shrine when placed in the fields to bring rain. It is believed to have removed itself. 24:102-103.

8.11 (M) Image of *El Niño Perdido*, the lost (Christ) child, disappears from its niche and appears to believers in scattered parts of the world. During World War II, mothers made promises to the image in hope of their sons' safe return. The Christ child appeared to their sons. 24:103.

8.12 (M) Mysterious strangers leave a box at a residence. The mistress of the house loses a scarf; a fragrance issues from the box and the scarf is mysteriously returned. When opened, the box is found to contain an image of Christ. 12:168-169.

8.13 (M) Woman who gives lodging to a stranger finds an image of Christ in the room the following day. A priest attempts to take the image (interpreted as a sign) to Chihuahua City to convince the bishop that money is needed for a new church (cf. 7.11). Mules refuse to transport the image from Ojinaga, Mex. 27:172-174, 176-177 (three versions).

8.14 (M) A kind young stranger who lives among the people of Ojinaga, Mex., transforms as the *Cristo* in the church there. 27:175.

8.15 (M) The *Cristo* in the church at Ojinaga, Mex., grows hair and fingernails. During a drought, it leaves the church to walk the fields and bring rain. After rain, the vestments of the image are wet and muddy. 27:178.

8.16 (M) A waif is chased by a policeman. It is Christmas Eve. He enters a church and, having no gift for the infant Jesus, plays his violin before the image. The statue's foot moves forward and drops a golden sandal into the boy's hand. The miracle is repeated when the policeman arrives and thinks the waif has stolen the sandal. 30:232-233.

8.17 (M) An old couple share what food they have with a traveler, who then shows them a valuable gold mine. He is Christ. 24:105-106.

8.18 (M) Old man who has replied rudely to a stranger's questions about his garden finds it full of rocks. When the stranger returns, the man realizes that he is Christ, and kneels. His garden grows handsomely. 14:239-240.

8.19 (M) St. Isidore gives a shepherd a golden snake, which the shepherd pawns. When later the pawnbroker pretends that the snake has been stolen, the saint causes it to become a real snake. 32:32-33.

8.20 (M) When St. Isidore prays to her spirit, a dead girl reveals the whereabouts of a ring she had borrowed before her death. 32:32.

8.21 (M) When a priest asks a wealthy woman to provide wine for the feast of St. Isidore, and she refuses, her house crumbles in smoking ruins. 12:118-119.

8.22 (M) When seven young men, all of them drunk, go to the plaza, only six are picked up by the police. The seventh has prayed to the saints for aid; he is made invisible. 24:103-104.

8.23 (M) In New Mexico, Don Juan Oñate and a servant hide in a cave to escape Indians. The servant performs a brave deed and the Holy Ghost rewards him by frightening the Indians away. Thus did the Holy Ghost admonish Oñate to heed the merit of the poor and meek. 12:175-183.

8.24 (M) The Devil has made the country a wasteland. He is seen dancing gleefully on a rope between two mountains, one on either side of the Río Grande. A devout priest (Father Urbán) attacks the Devil with a wooden cross and finally pens him in a cave, where he places the cross. Thus the towns of Ojinaga, Mex., and Presidio, Tex., are freed. 6:102-106; 25:207-211.

8.25 (M) Condemned murderer who prays often is asked to petition God for rain once he is hanged. Immediately following his execution, there is rain. (Cf. 8.83.) 12:120-121.

8.26 (M) Woman stops a long and ruinous rain by making the sign of the Cross, with salt, on the kitchen table. She prophesies an ensuing drought. 14:236-237.

8.27 (M) The fruit on trees where owls (witches) nest is sour until people burn the nesting grounds. The fruit turns sweet, provides a marvelous cure for stomach ache. 30:222-223.

8.28 Origin of the bluebonnet flower. When the Comanches are afflicted by a great drought, the Great Spirit demands the sacrifice of the most valuable thing in camp. A little girl hears the decision and determines to sacrifice her doll. She burns it and scatters the ashes. Next morning the hillside is covered with flowers the color of the bluejay feathers which had formed the doll's headdress. 3:198-200.

8.29 When a living sacrifice is needed to free the Aztecs from a plague, a maiden offers herself. As she approaches the altar, her bonnet slips off. Next morning there are blue flowers all about; on each is a red spot like a splash of her blood. 3:197.

8.30 Uncanny happenings wrought by tornadoes. Tornadoes have been known to preserve infants and children; when striking a school, to spare children but injure teachers; to leave flowers unscathed; to pluck chickens clean; to set a player piano playing "Nearer My God to Thee"; to pick up a train and reverse it on the track; to deliver catfish to the door of a Negro who has refused to fish on Sunday; to tar and feather an unscrupulous landlord; to deliver a letter to its proper recipient; to distribute heirlooms to members of a family spread over 50 miles; to place a wagon-wheel rim around the trunk of a large cottonwood tree; to turn a cast-iron washpot inside out; to roll up a mile of barbed wire fence and place the roll at a rancher's front door; to complete construction work on a house; to remodel a brick wall by removing every sixth brick; to leave a signed check made out to "cash" undisturbed on a table while blowing the house away; to pick up a trough of water without spilling a drop; to remove a baby's diaper without injuring the baby; to pick up a setting hen and her eggs and return them to the ground enfolded in a matress; to pull the bodies of 24 milk cows (in stanchions) from the heads; to remove a watch from a man's pocket and place it in another's pocket. When a man in a store, during a tornado, reaches for a broom flying past, a hacksaw severs his thumb. (Do not argue with a tornado.) Once a priest attacked a tornado and reduced it to a thin white streak (cf. 8.24). When a building destroyed by a tornado is rebuilt, another tornado tears it down.   28:55-65; 29:49-51.

8.31   Although supposedly there were no buffalo west of the Pecos River in Texas, a hidden canyon in the Big Bend region contains a fine herd.   3:238-241.

8.32   (M) In the state of Durango, Mex., there exists a hidden valley which, because of the size of gold nuggets present there, is called "the Orange Grove." The valley may contain an enchanted city, perhaps in a subterranean cavern. Powerful bells have been heard. 12:173-174.

8.33   (Zapotec) Each year on the 16th of June, during a certain hour of the night, an enchanted city beneath Monte Albán (Oaxaca, Mex.) comes to life. The city lies beneath mounds at the foot of the mountain. There are three ways of breaking the enchantment: (1) Atop the mountain is a spring that runs only at dawn, and intermittently. In the center of the stream a golden jar contains a silver fish that surfaces to renew its colors in the morning. If one catches the fish, it will reveal the secret of enchantment. (2) A vanishing dog with four puppies roams the vicinity. Should one of the pups be captured, the secret will be revealed. (3) The gods will place a gold disc with the secret written thereon in the path of someone they choose.   12:246-248.

8.34   Haunted house stands on the site of an enchanted castle. With its ghostly inhabitants, the castle was brought to Texas from Ireland by fairies after everyone in it was murdered by a jealous Englishman on the night the daughter of the house was betrothed. Because the fairies promised God that mortal eyes should never again look on the castle, it sank into the earth as the Irish began to move into Texas. It revives every May Eve.   13:185-189.

8.35   (I) Home of the Ruler of All the World is a cave in the Davis Mountains. There his people once gathered every year to bring him gifts of horns. Those who brought the longest horns were rewarded; those who wilfully refused to bring horns were made slaves. Eventually a great bird killed the cave-dwellers and the ruler died of grief. People of today are descended from one of the slaves, who had been doomed to work for his living.   3:230-233.

8.36   (I) Near El Paso, Tex., the Indian Cheetwah and his warriors defeat a band of Spaniards. Following the battle, Cheetwah and his followers vanish into Mount Franklin, to hold the pass forever. 3:130-132.

8.37 When a medicine man's daughter falls ill, he mixes his medicines on one of three mounds near Quanah, Tex., where a good spirit dwells. His daughter is cured; he always returns to the site to mix his potions. 3:207-208.

8.38 The Comanches regarded a mountain of granite near Fredericksburg, Tex., as the home of the gods. A Spaniard once saved his Indian lover from being burned, as a human sacrifice, on the mountain. 3:153-157.

8.39 Herds of cattle held overnight on Stampede Mesa, in West Texas, will stampede. The mesa is haunted by the ghost of a nester who stampeded a herd in 1889, was captured and driven over the cliff on a blindfolded horse. 3:111-115.

8.40 An angry father, his daughter stolen by a boatman, places a curse on Baffle Point on the Texas coast. Confused by shifting dunes and phantom trees, sailors often are drowned in the area. 3:146.

8.41 (Waco) Indian lovers from tribes hostile to each other flee from the girl's people. When discovered, they leap from a cliff. 1:50-51; 3:174-175.

8.42 Girl (Indian or Spanish) leaps to her death after learning that her lover has been killed. 3:163-167, 169-174, 202-204.

8.43 Indian girl, in love with a white man, leaps to her death rather than wed the warrior her father has chosen for her. 3:175-176.

8.44 An Indian princess loves a warrior who is beneath her in rank. As punishment, her father imprisons her and causes the warrior to be slain. She breaks her bonds, rushes to her lover's body at the riverside, and there dies. Next morning a white water lily grows where she fell. 3:200-201.

8.45 Woman's ghost lingers near the bank of the San Gabriel River, where the woman was buried after seeing her lover drowned at the spot. 3:167-168.

8.46 An old and a young Indian brave contend for the hand of the chief's daughter. When she sees the old brave win by trickery, she throws herself into a lake. 3:202.

8.47 An Indian girl in love with an elderly Spaniard is stolen away by a younger man. The sandy peninsula on which the girl and Spaniard had lived gradually disintegrates. 3:147.

8.48 Indian lovers who flee from their tribe find sanctuary in a cave to which they must swim. Their pursuers almost catch them but are warned from the cave by medicine men. 3:161-163.

8.49 (M) When a student priest falls in love with a young girl, his uncle refuses to bless them and turns them out in a storm. They disappear; the youth's ghost calls to his love on stormy nights. 3:157-159.

8.50 (M) Girl is captured by bandits. In the Chisos Mountains she requests permission to bathe and drowns herself rather than submit to the bandits. The screams of her ghost may be heard. 28:118-120.

8.51 (Michis) Rather than be beaten by Spaniards under Don Francisco Ibarra, the remnant of an army of Indians hurl themselves from a precipice now known as Sacrifice Mountain. 12:162-164.

8.52 Indian baby is born in light of the full moon—a bad omen. To save it from an ill fate and herself from shame, the mother drops the child from Agua Fría cliff in the Chisos Mountains. At night the child's cries are heard. 28:117-118.

8.53 In retaliation for an injury done him, an old Indian takes the small daughter of a white man and jumps off a cliff with her. (Texas Panhandle.) 3:205-206.

8.54 Clay Allison, the gunfighter, shoots an adversary in a hotel dining room when the adversary attempts to put him at a disadvantage by asking him to pass a dish of food. He pitches a deputy's hat in the air and shoots two holes in it so that the deputy can say he has been "under fire." He refuses to be disarmed in court, rides away unmolested. 9:27-31.

8.55 A ship that is wrecked at the mouth of the San Bernard River carries one survivor, a woman supposed to be Theodosia Burr Allston, daughter of Aaron Burr. 3:191-193.

8.56 Sam Bass, an Indian boy who comes to Texas and turns bank and train robber, performs Robinhood-like deeds. 3:226-230.

8.57 Roy Bean, "law west of the Pecos," is indignant at the waste of time when horse thieves and rustlers are brought before him instead of being hanged directly. He uses court sessions as a means of increasing business in his saloon. He bribes juries; uses his office as a judge to drive competitive saloons out of business; collects $10 for a bottle of beer; sobers drunks by chaining them just within reach of his pet bear. When there is a bridge-collapsing accident on the Pecos River, he pronounces three badly injured—but still living—men dead so that he will not have to return and perform the inquest again. 13:114-119; 14:254-255.

8.58 Strap Buckner, a Texas ruffian, likes to knock people down. He fights a wild bull, *Noche,* and crushes an ox's skull with his fist. When he attempts to knock down Bruno, a huge Negro, he injures his hand. He knocks down a bee tree and must fight off the bees; he knocks down the side of a cliff where the bees had hived. He boasts of his prowess and challenges the Devil. The Devil fights him and Strap disappears in the heavens astride a huge gray horse, presumably as the Devil's captive.   3:118-130; 8:129-151; 10:127-130.

8.59   (M) Gregorio Cortez, Mexican bandit, outwits Texas sheriffs and rangers. He shoots several lawmen in self defense. He deceives pursuers through strategems: talking so as to make them think he is a band of men; leaping from a cliff onto his horse; gaining water for himself and his horse at a guarded tank by gathering a herd of wild cattle and appearing to be a *vaquero* (rangers assist him). He has his Judas who betrays him. American courts cannot convict him because he has always acted in self-defense. When finally he is sentenced for horse-stealing, Abe Lincoln's daughter falls in love with him and gets him a pardon. Enemies have bribed his jailor, who administers a slow poison before he leaves jail. 27:3-22.

8.60   Mose Evans, "wild man" of the Texas frontier, makes comic blunders and entertaining remarks as a soldier. A plot to cut off his red beard is foiled. Because his rattlesnake vest smells "snakish," he puts thick oil of cinnamon on his head before attending a dance. When his body warms, the oil melts and burns his skin. He possesses a suit made of the skins of wild beasts, in which he plans to attend the 1854 World's Fair in New York. He carries on a newspaper correspondence with the "wild woman of the Navidad" (cf. 8.78).   8:90-95.

8.61   Mustang Gray (cf. 8.148) and confederates masquerade as Indians in order to steal Mexicans' horses. On another occasion, having lost his horse, Gray shoots a buffalo, makes a rope of its hide, captures and tames a wild horse which he rides to the settlements. In Goliad, Tex., he and confederates make a priest dance to "pistol music." The town is cursed by its priest because it harbors ruffians like Gray.   10:115-119.

8.62   A hunter, Uncle Billy Moore of Indiana, is pinned to a tree by the horns of large buck. His dog Tige pulls the buck away, holds it till the hunter can cut its throat.   6:48-51.

8.63   Legends concerning Jack Potter, frontier preacher. How as an unreformed gambler he got even with the town of San Antonio, Tex. How he held church with his sixguns on the pulpit. How he quieted a drunk in the congregation. How he started the first church in San Angelo. How he died in the pulpit, preaching. 30:188-190.

8.64   A Texas Panhandle cowboy, Georgie Sennit, "The Irish Lad," and Will Rogers have a horse race. Accounts of "the Lad's" fondness for liquor, dancing.   30:169-172.

8.65   Belle Starr, woman outlaw, interrupts the making of biscuits to outshoot men conducting a shooting contest in her backyard. She has biscuit flour on her hands.   30:156-158.

8.66   Bigfoot Wallace visits New York and engages in a series of comic verbal misunderstandings concerning a marble statue of an Indian. Bigfoot is to demonstrate how to scalp an Indian; he frightens New Yorkers.   22:195-199.

8.67   Outlaws Wild Bill Hickok, Billy the Kid, King Fisher, Bat Masterson, Wyatt Earp, and Ben Thompson perform marvelous feats of shooting.   9:6-14.

8.68   (Waco) A dying Indian—Placido—cuts off the left hand of a dead adversary and sends it as a proof of his own valiant death. 1:51-52.

8.69   (Kiowa-Apache) A medicine man, wounded internally, shoots himself and is buried. When a blind man visits his grave, the dead man advises him how he may regain his eyesight.   22:108-110.

8.70   Man who does not look like he is able to ride a bronc rides an outlaw horse in expert manner.   16:269-303 (three instances).

8.71   (M)Italian of profligate ways repents and comes to Las Vegas, N. M., to live as a hermit. Performs the miracle of causing water to flow from a rock (cf. 1.17, 8.5). When the railroad reaches Las Vegas, the hermit disappears into Mexico, where he is thought to have been killed by Indians.   10:124-125.

8.72   A peg-legged ex-sailor travels through the South before the Civil War, helping slaves to escape to Canada. Origin of the Negro song, "Follow the Drinking Gourd [Big Dipper, i.e. North Star]." 7:81-84.

8.73 A group of stories concerning the infamous Kilpatrick family who lived near Paint Rock, Tex. Uncleanliness emphasized; the sons became outlaws. 14:180-184.

8.74 Family of lawbreakers near Springtown, Tex., finally incurs the wrath of the community. A vigilante group shoots or hangs all members, including the mother and three daughters. Motifs include: trap door for escaping outlaws; woman wrestles a hog; hanging tree. 29:201-208.

8.75 Stories about the Barber family of Florence, Tex. One of the sons, an outlaw, disguises himself as a woman and eludes lawmen. Escape-tunnel motif. 22:185-193.

8.76 (M) The Jumano Indians tell of a woman in blue robes who appeared to them and urged them to seek aid of the missionaries. (Legend associated with Maria de Agreda.) 3:132-135.

8.77 Following an Indian defeat at the hands of Texas Rangers, a beautiful Indian woman, "Woman of the Western Star," appears to rangers and begs for peace. 3:115-118.

8.78 An unknown creature which leaves very small footprints causes much excitement in southeastern Texas. The creature takes food from settlers' houses at night (has a quieting effect on dogs) but never does harm. Finally a Negro who has escaped from a slave ship is captured; he is thought to have been the "wild woman." 3:244-253.

8.79 An orphaned girl-child disappears and is later seen running with wolves in the Devil's River area of Texas. Although captured once, she is freed by wolves. Some time later, a woman is seen nursing two wolf cubs; again she disappears. 13:79-85.

8.80 Coyotes raise an abandoned Indian child. Later the child is captured and tamed by Indians; becomes a chief who knows secrets learned of the animals. 14:120-121.

8.81 (N) Bear steals a male baby and hides it in a cave, where it is finally discovered by cowboys. 25:238-240.

8.82 (M) Young man, arrested for trying to abduct his sweetheart, is wrongfully murdered just before his release. Where he is buried, a beautiful small tree grows and blooms. Thus the saints proved his innocence. 24:106.

8.83 (M) Young man who is wrongfully executed predicts that there will be rain at the time he dies. There is rain, and everyone believes that St. Joseph has proved the man's innocence. (Cf. 8.25.) 24:102.

8.84 Ghost of an innocent Mexican woman, hanged by townsmen for the murder of a man for his money, is heard crying by the river. Actually the woman's illegitimate son, who had recognized her, was the killer. 30:120-122.

8.85 Accounts of being "saved from a bullet." An object such as a shirt-pocket testament or a belt buckle deters the bullet. 33:118-125.

8.86 A pioneer woman and her baby are left alone in a wilderness cabin at night. The child's crying attracts a panther, which is heard pacing on the roof. The chimney affords an entrance, and the woman nearly exhausts the firewood before morning brings the return of her husband. 28:151-153.

8.87 A woman and baby are chased by a bear in the forest. She throws items of the baby's apparel to the bear to detain it, reaches her father's farm in time. 31:29-30.

8.88 A panther pursuing a wagon is kept at a distance by throwing ears of corn at it. 19:129-130.

8.89 Wild stallion pursues a woman and child who travel in a buggy being pulled by a mare. Narrow escape. 28:149-151.

8.90 (Kiowa-Apache) An Apache medicine man, who beats a white man in a contest of tricks, is killed by Indian foes; his blind wife and boy escape, later are restored to their people with the help of Pawnee Indians. This is how the Apaches and Pawnees came to be friends. 22:110-120.

8.91 (Kiowa-Apache) During a raid in which Osages cut off the heads of fleeing Kiowas, an Apache woman, married to a Kiowa, is stolen by Osages. She escapes and after many hardships makes her way back to the Apaches and Kiowas. 22:130-133.

8.92 Indians steal a South Carolina girl named Huffman. She escapes and finds her way back to a settlement on the Wateree River. She subsists on the drumstick of a crane until brought to safety. 6:51-53.

8.93 A man named Rich Coffee is supposed to have escaped from Indians by slipping through a crack at the back of a shallow cave near Paint Rock, Tex., into another cave. 14:176-177.

8.94 A white man named Lover escapes Indians by hiding among boulders near Palo Pinto, Tex. 3:159-161.

8.95 (M) Santa Anna gets his men into the Alamo on the last day of the siege through an underground passage connecting the Alamo with San Pedro Springs. 3:237-238.

8.96 (Zapotec) While besieged by Montezuma, the Zapotec army would disappear from one hill during the night and reappear on another in the morning. Excavation around Monte Albán, the Zapotec stronghold, confirms the legend; there are underground tunnels connecting one hill with another. 12:249.

8.97 (N) Giant catfish, "Old Joe," is thought to be responsible for fishing accidents on the Brazos River. It chases fishermen's boats. 9:157-158.

8.98 Giant bullfrog, "Hugo," is said to have lived in a lake near Sulphur Springs, Tex., since the 1890's. His skin is so tough a gig will not pierce it. When he starts to croak, other frogs hush. 14:262-263.

8.99 Child's dog protects it from a mad dog. 31:37.

8.100 (M) Pet lion (panther) rescues a girl from kidnappers. Her father had thought the lion responsible for the girl's disappearance. 12:26-27.

8.101 A white mustang in West Texas is called "Ghost of the Llano Estacado" because of its color, speed, and elusiveness. On being chased to exhaustion, it jumps from a bluff into an alkali bog and sinks from sight. 16:84-95.

8.102 A white mustang stallion in Texas, a pacer, outdistances his pursuers and refuses grass and water after his eventual capture. The stallion dies once made a captive. 16:173-179.

8.103 Montana ghost horse, a mustang stallion, is a killer who cannot be held in captivity. He has nocturnal habits, is iron-gray, and has a mane that gives off a phosphorescent glow in the moonlight. 16:155-157.

8.104 Black Kettle, a legended mustang in Kansas, is noted for his long mane and tail, and elusiveness. Is finally captured and ends life as a draft horse. 16:102-142.

8.105 (Apache) Wild horses in New Mexico are said to be descended from a particular Indian warhorse, Diablo, who was incensed by the smell of chili (i.e., of Mexicans). 12:190-193.

8.106 Morzillo, Cortez's black warhorse, is treated as a god by the Itza Indians, who make an idol in its form. 16:218-221.

8.107 A Comanche-trailing horse leads men up a wrong canyon so that they will not be ambushed by the Indians they pursue. 31:38-40.

8.108   Lightning strikes the ground at Bayou Rouge Prairie, La., and oil comes to the surface.   9:46.

8.109   Member of an oil-drilling crew gets drunk and fails to carry out orders to halt drilling. The resulting well is a producer.   25:82-84.

8.110   Oil well is drilled at the point where transportation for the drilling equipment breaks down, and is a producer. The hole dug at the site originally intended is dry.   25:78-82.

8.111   In North Central Texas the story is told that about 1900 the government made a geographical map that included every oil deposit in the nation. There are one or two areas on the map that have not yet been drilled. The storyteller usually owns property in one of these areas.   9:47.

8.112   The oil promoter as trickster. Accounts of "salting" wells, using misleading titles as names of companies, gaining control of oil journals, writing misleading solicitations.   30:80-90.

8.113   (M) When the San Gabriel Mission is abandoned, the people bury the religious vessels somewhere near the church, with the priest's body.   3:99-101.

8.114   Spanish exploring party buries its religious vessels on a high bluff above the Red River when attacked by Indians.   3:81-84.

8.115   Woman hides her jewels from approaching Union soldiers. She dies soon after and the treasure remains unrecovered.   28:165-166.

8.116   Twice a woman appears to a farmer in dreams and tells him to seek treasure in a certain spot on his farm in Leon County, Tex. When he fails to find it, he sells his farm to his brother-in-law, who is more successful.   3:89-91.

8.117   The site of buried treasure is revealed to a woman in a dream, but she never finds it. The pirate Lafitte sails his ships across Galveston Island during a storm.   (Cf. 7.16.)   3:189-191.

8.118   A farmer in Wichita County, Tex., who digs a trench around his fields to keep the buffalo from eating his crops, discovers buried gold.   8:120-121.

8.119   Buried treasure is discovered by accident as post holes are being dug.   3:41-43.

8.120   A trader escaping from Indians finds gold nuggets in a post hole but later is unable to locate the spot.   3:80-81.

8.121   (M) Bandits torture a Mexican rancher until he reveals his treasure. They in turn are slain by a second group of bandits, who are wiped out by Texas Rangers. 3:47-49.

8.122 (M) A Mexican rancher sells a large herd of cattle and buries
the proceeds (silver dollars) in an iron pot. He dies, or is murdered,
and his four-year-old grandson, who was with him at his death, is
unable to repeat what had happened. 9:134-138.

8.123 A rancher buries his gold during the Reconstruction period and
is murdered soon after, having presumably dug up part of the gold
before setting out for Decatur, Tex., to pay his taxes. 14:259-261.

8.124 Raiding Comanches dump a wagonload of silver into Clear Fork
Creek when they are hotly pursued. 3:103-104.

8.125 Seven cartloads of Mexican Army pay money are buried on the
battlefield of Palo Alto, in a trench, and all but one of the soldiers
who helped to dig the trench are shot. 3:51-52.

8.126 (M) An iron chest of money falls from a cart into a stream as
Santa Anna's army is retreating. The place is marked and the
army hurries on. 3:33-34.

8.127 (M) Money buried by Santa Anna's retreating troops apparently is discovered. 3:31-33.

8.128 (M) A Spanish family, fleeing Mexican revolutionaries, buries
its gold in Starr County, Tex., and goes to New Orleans. On the
return trip their guides kill them but cannot locate the gold. 6:18.

8.129 Because of their fear of the Snively gang, members of a Mexican
wagon train bury their gold near the Red River and flee. 3:95-97.

8.130 Spanish miners, endangered by Indians, bury both the copper
they have mined and the gold that they have with them. 3:72-77.

8.131 (M) Spanish raiders steal gold from the Indians but are forced
to bury it and flee. The sole survivor of the party will not guide
anyone to the treasure because he feels it is cursed. 3:78-80.

8.132 (M) A chest of gold is buried on the Nueces River by Spaniards
who are killed by Indians. 3:49-51.

8.133 (M) Smugglers hide their loot when surrounded by federal
troops. They escape, but the loot has never been found. 24:99-100.

8.134 Mexicans, fleeing after the battle of San Jacinto, are said to have
stuffed gold into a cannon dropped into the Neches River near
Boone's Ferry. 3:84-89.

8.135 Stories of silver ingots deposited in Hendricks Lake in East
Texas. 34:37-48.

8.136　Spanish treasure is buried near Bowie Creek in Liberty County, Tex. A copper box contains 12 jackloads of gold. Spanish soldiers on their way to pay troops in East Texas were attacked by Indians and buried the gold on a high spot near the creek. The copper box sank in quicksand. 29:209-213.

8.137　(M) When a blue light on a hillside is investigated, the spectre of a priest, carrying a light, is seen. Three men dig there and find a metal box which keeps sinking into the ground. 10:77-78.

8.138　Bandits hide their loot in a cave near the ruins of a fort in Live Oak County, Tex. 3:44-46.

8.139　(M) After Montezuma's death, his gold is hidden in a cave in the Sonora Mountains, where it is guarded first by the Aztecs, then by the Yaquis. 3:233-236.

8.140　Chief Victorio's daughter falls in love with a white captive and tells him where treasure is, in a cave. It cannot be located after the man's death. 10:75-77.

8.141　Bandits hide their loot in a hastily constructed rock pen when attacked by Indians. 3:28-31.

8.142　(M) A Mexican general's silver plates and chest of money are buried at Resaca de la Palma, in the center of a triangle formed by three tall palms. 3:52.

8.143　(M) A white stagecoach which disappears by two palms marks the spot where once a stagecoach was robbed and the loot buried. 14:101-102.

8.144　Mexicans and Americans buried 15 jackloads of silver near Epley Spring in Mills County, Tex. A priest made four charts showing the location of the treasure, placed them in three copper boxes which he buried some distance from the silver. Two of the boxes have been found, but the treasure has not. 13:259-269.

8.145　(M) Two boys find an ebony tablet, with ciphers, at the foot of a tree. It may be that Indians, after murdering a band of soldiers, buried the money the soldiers were guarding. 6:19.

8.146　A dying bank robber tells a man who helps him where loot is buried near old Ft. Belknap in Young County, Tex. Part is recovered, but not the bulk of the treasure. 8:118-120.

8.147　Silver bullion is supposed to have been buried at the foot of Painted Bluff in Concho County, Tex. 14:175-176.

8.148　Mustang Gray and Billy Richards steal a *morral* containing $16,000 in gold from Mexicans, bury it on the Nueces River. Gray soon dies and his partner fails to relocate the treasure. 10:119-121.

8.149 Lafitte and a group of his men go up a creek carrying full sacks and return empty-handed. 3:184.

8.150 A man named Snively is killed by some Mexicans and buried along with nine jackloads of stolen gold. His ghost now protects the hoard. 3:101-102.

8.151 The Snively gang breaks up near the Río Grande and three of the men stumble onto two cart-loads of silver in Apache Canyon. 3:97-99.

8.152 A Mexican named Moro, who appears to be a Spaniard and dresses like a gentleman, comes to the plantation of Buena Vista and is seen hunting around the grounds. It is believed that he has come to find money he has buried there. 3:104-108.

8.153 On his way to St. Louis from Mexico, an adventurer buries his wealth in Texas. He sends a map to his sweetheart, but the money is never found. 3:91-95.

8.154 (M) An American shoots three Mexicans who have located a hoard of Spanish silver. He buys a large ranch with the silver. 3:49.

8.155 (M) A treasure marked by the bones of Mexicans who were massacred by Indians is never found. (South Texas.) 3:38-39.

8.156 Buried bullion is marked by a sign on a tree and a line of rocks. (South Texas.) 3:39-40.

8.157 Two almost-parallel lines from opposite corners of a boulder are supposed to intersect at the site of buried treasure. (South Texas.) 3:49-41.

8.158 (M) A white light in an abandoned house near Estancias, Mex., indicates the location of treasure. 24:100-101.

8.159 (M) Treasure is sought, and found, beneath the floor before the altar of a church, by a man using an electrical apparatus. Skeletons, possibly of man and wife, are found above the treasure. 24:96-99.

8.160 A chest, unearthed after much searching near Ft. Sam Houston in San Antonio, Tex., contains only Civil War ammunition. 9:140-141.

8.161 Near Bandera, Tex., are paint deposits that were in use by a local artist in the early 1920's. Among the Oklahoma Kiowas and Comanches was a legend about a "valley of paint" to the south, where a chief met his death. 18:126-128.

8.162 A man named Hoffman works a lead mine on his ranch near Sabinal, Tex., but its location is lost before it can be exploited by others. 3:63.

8.163 A horse-dealer, sheltering from rain, finds a deposit of lead somewhere near the Brazos River. 3:77-78.

8.164 A rich lead and silver mine is worked for some time near Packsaddle Mountain in Central Texas, but is then hidden and never rediscovered. 3:24-26.

8.165 Texas Rangers camped near Sabinal, Tex., find quicksilver (mercury) in a ground squirrel's hole, but lose the location. 3:62-63.

8.166 Legend of the Lost Nigger Mine. A Negro working for the Reagan brothers in the Big Bend region of Texas discovers rich gold deposits in Reagan Canyon. His employers take no heed of his claim to having found a "brass mine" until ore samples are examined following the Negro's disappearance. A prospector, "the Dutchman," relocates the deposits but dies before revealing the location. 3:64-67; 30:266-272.

8.167 (M) The Padre Mine. Apaches carry off a padre of the Ysleta Mission, along with gold from a mine he oversaw, and which he had filled in when Indians threatened. Two chiseled arrows on an overhanging rock point to the mine and a spring nearby. 10:71-75.

8.168 Ben Sublett finds a gold mine, once worked by the Mescalero Apaches, in the Guadalupe Mountains. The mine is entered through a deep shaft which is all but impossible to detect. Sublett made periodic trips to the mine, always returning with quantities of nuggets. The secret of its location died with him. 3:67-72.

8.169 A stream with goldflakes scattered over its bottom is discovered and then lost by Texas Rangers. 3:20-22.

8.170 Bowie or San Saba Mine. The Lipan Indians are believed to have had a hoard of silver and a silver mine near the old San Saba Mission. Jim Bowie makes a successful effort to learn the location, but is never able to recover the treasure. An old man, however, once confessed that the story of the mine is a fraud. In Gillespie County, Tex., a large egg-shaped rock supposedly marks the site of the mine. In Bexar County a landslide has covered a cave, near an ore-grinding mill, where silver ore from the mine was stored for processing. 3:12-20, 26-27; 9:131-134.

8.171 An Apache, Quick Killer, wears silver *conchas* in his hair and is believed to have shown John C. Cremony silver deposits in the Guadalupe Mountains. 22:150-152.

8.172 (M) A ledge of silver near the headwaters of the Frío River is known to Indians. It is sought, but never found, by Mexicans from San Antonio. 30:60-62.

8.173 There is believed to have been a Spanish-operated silver mine in the Las Chuzas Mountains in southwestern Texas. Indians relocated the mine. 3:37-38.

8.174 A "blue egg of silver" is discovered in the Sierra Madre. 32:60-61; cf. 9:131.

8.175 A furnace on the Little Llano River marks the location of an early gold and silver mine. Indians showed a man named Reece Butler, who lived near San Marcos, Tex., gold and silver deposits in the Llano River country. Butler smelted ore in his blacksmith shop and sold metals to an Austin jeweler. 22:152-153.

8.176 (Alabama) Alabama Indians live in the north but wish to migrate to better land in the south. Abba Mingo, "Chief of the Sky," guides them by making their totem pole point in the right direction every morning. 13:298-299.

8.177 (Caddo or Tejas) The two sons of a Caddo chief—Natchitoches and Nacogodoches—found separate lands. The town of Nacogdoches, Tex., is founded by the one. A descendant, Red Feather, teaches his people the arts of agriculture and, after his death, watches over them in the form of a redbird. 14:195-199.

8.178 (I) How the Tehuana Indians came to be related to the Zapotecs. 12:137-142.

8.179 (Aztec) When the Tlaxcalan Indians are about to be defeated by the Aztecs, their leader tricks the Aztec queen into taking a heavy potion of marihuana so that she will go mad and thus cause the Aztec general, her husband, to lose the war in his sorrow. The Tlaxcalan leader is caught after doping the queen, and is burned on sulphur pits below volcanoes. 14:227-233.

8.180 (Kiowa-Apache) Kit Carson and U.S. troops skirmish with with Kiowas and Apaches in the Texas Panhandle in 1864. Howitzers are used against the Indians (historical). 22:133-136.

8.181 (Kiowa-Apache) Osages armed with swords attack a Kiowa camp in 1833. Heads are severed, and "the headless body would run a few steps farther before it fell down." 22:130-131.

8.182 (Kiowa-Apache) A group of Oklahoma Apaches cross the Rocky Mountains to visit the Pacific. Then encounter what are, to them, strange marvels along the way, which they tell of on their return after an absence of almost two years. 22:124-129.

8.183 (Kiowa-Apache) As a reward for having shared his food with a wolf and coyotes, a boy is given the ability to find game no matter how poor the hunting might be.   22:76.

8.184 During a time of drouth, with no game in the land, Texas pioneers follow a flock of crows to see where the crows are feeding on mast. Here they find game and send meat back to the settlement. 18:133-135.

8.185 Two blackguards who have insulted a young girl are crushed under the boat they are building after she has prayed that it may never sail.   3:144.

8.186 Whiskey drinker who scoffs at inspired seizures during a religious revival, having himself taken the "jerks," vows he will drink them to death. When he drinks, his "jerks" become so violent that he breaks his neck; his bottle breaks against a sapling. 35:24.

8.187 On the road between Carrizo Springs and Eagle Pass, Tex., are five unmarked graves. Legend explains the graves in various ways: travelers were found dead after eating armadillo meat or spoiled venison; they died of scarlet fever; the graves are of Indians killed by Mexican bandits.   31:53-57.

8.188 (M) In South Texas a taco vendor is suspected of capturing stray cats and making his tacos of cat meat.   12:212.

8.189 In Germany a mine owner promises to share his wealth with the miner who first finds silver. When a poor employee discovers a rich vein, the owner kills him. The "mountain spirit" turns the owner's heart into a boulder in the Schwarzwasser River.   30:265.

8.190 Urban legends connected with the Neiman Marcus Department Store in Dallas, Tex. Foremost motif is that of the princely buyer, who may be a Middle Eastern potentate or a West Texas cotton farmer.   25:161-169.

8.191 For selfish reasons a dishonest rancher and associates cause the drowning of the last herd of longhorn cattle in the Brazos River about 1890. 18:149-150.

Section 9: Tall Tales

Guide to the Section

EXAGGERATED SIZE: boilers on oil-drilling rig, 9.1; corn stalks and kernels, 9.2—9.3; gusher, 9.4; griddle, 9.5; hatchet, 9.6; hogs, 9.7; horse, 9.8; man, 9.9; and mosquitos, 9.10, cf. 9.21; oil derrick, 9.11—9.15; oil tank, 9.16; oil well, 9.17, cf. 9.150; playing cards, 9.18; steer, 9.19; tape-

worm, 9.20; turnip (kettle, mosquitos), 9.21; wooden leg, 9.22—9.23, cf.
9.150. Lake Michigan dug to mix concrete in, 9.24. EXAGGERATED QUALI-
TIES: appetite, 9.25—9.26 (tobacco), 9.27 (pie), 9.28 (beef); faithful-
ness, 9.29 (employee), 9.30 (sheep dog); flatulence, 9.31; hearing ability,
9.32; hilliness of terrain, 9.33—9.40, cf. 9.107, 9.123; narrowness of
trail, 9.41; pluck in fighting, 9:42, cf. 9.146; roping skill, 9.43; shrink-
age, 9.44 (alum), 9.45 (rawhide); soil conditions, 9.46 (rich soil), 9.47—
9.48, cf. 9.79 (mud and sand); strength, 9.49—9.53; swiftness, 9.54—
9.55, cf. 9.103; thief's inclination to steal, 9.56; weather extremes,
9.57—9.58 (cold), 9.59 (fog), 9.60 (rain), 9.61—9.64, cf. 9.48, 9.79
(sandstorm and wind). OIL DRILLING YIELDS CREAM, RUM, RUBBER,
BLOOD, ETC.: substance ruined, 9.65—9.66; other, 9.67—9.71. INGENUI-
TY: drilling oil well, 9.72—9.77; selling "dry" holes as post holes,
9.78—9.80; hunting, 9.81—9.86, cf. 9.119; leading blind hogs, 9.87;
using lightning to touch off cannon, light cigarette, 9.88—9.89; "pipe-
lining" cattle, buttermilk, 9.90—9.91; other activities or circumstances,
9.92—9.98. See also 9.5, 9.45, 9.97, 9.123, 9.142, 9.151. CROSS-FERTILI-
ZATION: deer's antlers yield peaches, 9.99; pecans have peach flavor,
9.100. See also 9.104. FAR TRAVELERS: fencing a Texas pasture, 9.101;
horse hitched to tip of the moon, 9.102—9.103. ANIMALS: imaginary
species, 9.104—9.109; fat, 9.110—9.111; intelligent or gifted, 9.112—
9.113 (bear), 9.114—9.118 (horse), 9.119 (bird dog), 9.120—9.121
(snake), 9.122 (fish); hogs, 9.123—9.129, cf. 9.7, 9.40, 9.87, 9.93; animals think it is winter (night) when not, 9.130—9.131; poisonous bites,
stings, 9.132—9.134. MISHAPS: men, 9.135—9.137; "split" dogs, 9.138—
9.139. See also 9.55, 9.68, 9.71. LUCKY ACCIDENTS, NARROW ESCAPES: lost
valuables miraculously recovered, 9.140; bears pull sleigh, 9.141; boy on
wolf's tail, 9.142; escape from Indians, 9.143—9.144. See also 9.97.
OTHER: backwoods beauty, 9.145—9.146; petrified gravity, 9.147; roping frogs, 9.148; Paul Bunyan's one arm, 9.149; Paul visits hell, 9.150;
Gib Morgan uses coconuts as boiler fuel, 9.151.

9.1   Boilers on Paul Bunyan's oil rig are so big that anyone near the
       injectors is in danger of being sucked in.   7:51.

9.2   Cornstalk is so high that a boy is sent to the top to see how much
       corn is on it. He goes out of sight; so far has thrown down three
       bushels of cobs and shucks (has subsisted on the corn).   14:269.

9.3   Farmer builds a "stone fence" of the huge kernels of corn he har-
       vested.   19:67.

9.4   Paul Bunyan's gusher is so high it has to be roofed to keep it from
       blowing a hole in the sky.   7:58.

9.5   Gib Morgan sells so many pancakes in his boarding house that he uses the bottoms of oil tanks for griddles. He straps sides of bacon to the feet of Negroes who grease the griddles by skating.   20:88-89.

9.6   Paul Bunyan's hatchet weighs eight pounds; he drives any nail to the head with a single blow.   7:49.

9.7   Trying to sell bottom land (subject to flooding) to a newcomer, a promoter tells him the mud streaks high on the trees are made by local razorbacks.   9:21-24.

9.8   Gib Morgan's horse Torpedo weighs 20 tons, is as big as a train. Gib does not turn him around but "puts him in reverse."   20:90-91.

9.9   Gib Morgan hires a giant tool dresser who measures 28 inches between the eyes.   20:68.

9.10   When giant mosquitos attack an oil tank sheltering Gib Morgan and his crew, puncturing the top with their bills, Gib orders the crew to brad the bills with hammers. Their bills bradded, the mosquitos fly off with the tank.   20:74.

9.11   Gib Morgan builds an oil derrick covering an acre. His tool dresser spends 14 days climbing to the top; thirty are men hired so as to keep one always at the top.   20:65-66.

9.12   Paul Bunyan's derrick is so high that alternate crews are kept constantly in motion going up and down; sleeping quarters are installed midway.   7:58.

9.13   Paul Bunyan's derrick is so high that his helpers come down only twice a month, on paydays.   7:50.

9.14   Paul Bunyan's derrick is so high that he and his crew live in heaven while completing it.   7:50.

9.15   Paul Bunyan's derrick is so high it is hinged like a drawbridge to allow the stars to pass.   7:58.

9.16   Paul Bunyan's oil tank is so high that a hammer dropped from the top wears out two handles coming down.   7:53-54.

9.17   Paul Bunyan digs an oil well to China.   7:50, 59.

9.18   In a poker game, Paul Bunyan uses cards so big that five days are required to walk around one.   7:61.

9.19   Paul Bunyan has a giant steer.   7:56-57.

9.20   Gib Morgan has a tapeworm that, when emitted, winds 40 times around an oil tank.   20:93-94.

9.21   Frame tale. Three liars seek lodging. Host will give lodging to the biggest liar. First liar raised a turnip so big that he pastured hogs and cattle on it all winter. Second liar made a giant kettle to cook the turnip in. Third liar was working on the kettle when giant mosquitos attacked (like 9.10). Host lodges all three. 18:79.

9.22   Paul Bunyan has a wooden leg 90 feet long.   (Cf. 9.150.)   7:60.

9.23   Paul Bunyan's wife has a wooden leg requiring six months to paint.   7:60.

9.24   Paul Bunyan digs Lake Michigan to mix concrete in while building the Rocky Mountains.   7:61.

9.25   Paul Bunyan makes a million dollars in the oil business but spends all on tobacco.   (Cf. 6.223.)   7:50.

9.26   Paul Bunyan soaks a million dollars worth of tobacco in corn whiskey to sell for a vast profit; chews all himself.   7:50.

9.27   Jim Baker, "Pie Biter," announces he will eat five sweet-potato pies at once. Someone leaves the pie-tins in place; Jim cannot bite through the stack.   14:189-191.

9.28   In a restaurant, a ravenously hungry man tells the waiter to "cripple a steer and run him through here."   7:56.

9.29   Gib Morgan leaves the country in a hurry, without telling his driller. Years later he finds him still at work on the same drilling operation.   20:62-63.

9.30   Faithful sheep dog, thrown out of a "machine" traveling to the moon, is later seen following alongside—on air.   15:95.

9.31   Bloated mule is given soda through a hunting horn inserted in its throat. Mule bolts. With each bound, it blows a blast that summons every hound in Arkansas.   22:202-204.

9.32   (M) Boy tells hunting companions that there is game in the vicinity, a doe and fawn. No game is in sight, but the boy says he hears the fawn nursing its mother.   32:54-55.

9.33   Paul Bunyan drills on a mountainside, drills through the mountain.   7:51-52.

9.34   Gib Morgan steals a drilling bit that emerges from a mountainside and is digging along the creek near his camp.   20:61-62.

9.35　In hilly country, Gib Morgan sees what he thinks is an abandoned bit. It is suddenly "fished" out of his hands by an oil rig on top of the hill.　20:60-61.

9.36　In hilly country, a farmer falls out of a field when the hoe he uses as a walking-stock snaps.　20:60.

9.37　Land so hilly that one can look up the chimney and watch the cows come home.　20:58.

9.38　Land so hilly that to grease a wagon one must tie it to a stump. 20:58.

Gib Morgan's pet boa constrictor helps in drilling oil well; see Synopsis 9.73.

9.39　Land so hilly that a man riding a mule down a mountainside gets manure on his neck.　20:64.

9.40　In hilly country, pigs' tails are weighted to keep the pigs from flying over the fence when rooting.　9:18-20.

9.41　(M) Trail so narrow that a dead mosquito blocks it.　32:54.

9.42　Gib Morgan and a Negro fight at the bottom of the Ohio River. They cut each other till a truce is called for resharpening knives. 20:99-100.

9.43　(M) Man ropes flying mockingbird.　19:50-52.

9.44　Paul Bunyan (also Gib Morgan) drills in an alum bed; the hole shrinks tight.　7:53, 60; 20:70-71.

9.45　Heavy shower causes rawhide to stretch. When the sun comes out, traces shrink with sufficient force to draw a barrel of water up a hill.　7:43-44.

9.46 Land so fertile that when a man plants cucumbers, the vines entrap him before he can escape. 18:83-84; 20:87.

9.47 Rider starts to pick up a hat lying in a muddy (or sandy) road. Sees that there is a head beneath the hat. Bogged man says he is standing on his horse. 7:75-76; 25:7-8; 33:100-107.

9.48 In sandy country a Negro ties his donkey to a tree. Sandstorm rises and the donkey is left hanging 70 feet in the air. 7:61.

9.49 Paul Bunyan drives a 16-pound hammer into the ground with such force that oil comes to the surface. 7:49.

9.50 Paul Bunyan catches a falling derrick. 7:49.

9.51 Paul Bunyan is on a derrick when a windstorm carries him out to sea astride a board. He kills a whale and, using it as a boat, paddles ashore using the board as an oar. 7:50-51.

9.52 Paul Bunyan jumps astride a "blown" boiler and rides it to earth. 7:51.

9.53 (M) In great anger a man breaks the horn off an anvil, throws it at his adversary. 19:53-54.

9.54 Greyhound is so swift that when its owner leads it while riding in a train going 150 miles per hour, the dog runs on three legs while urinating on the wheel of the train. 20:97.

9.55 Boaster admits he was worried "for a moment" when he accidentally dropped a lighted match into a powder keg—afraid he would not be able to get away from the explosion in time. 27:167.

9.56 Man dives to the bottom of a stream to recover his companion's dropped powder horn. Companion thinks he has drowned and dives to look for him. He finds him on the bottom, transferring powder from the companion's horn to his own. 7:43.

9.57 (M) In cold weather a woman makes fire with "sticks" that turn out to be frozen snakes. 17:70.

9.58 Horseman is barely able to stay ahead of a norther. When he reaches the stable, the front half of his horse is lathered while the back half is frozen. Horse dies of pneumonia. (Cf. 9.60.) 7:75.

9.59 In England, Gib Morgan's crew shingle the roof of a "band-wheel" house; learn that they have been shingling fog. 20:85.

9.60 Horseman barely outruns a rainstorm. On reaching home, he notices that his horse is soaked from the saddle back. (Cf. 9.58.) 7:42-43.

9.61   In a sandstorm, sand pours through the keyhole.   14:266-267.

9.62   In a sandstorm, sand wears a rain barrel to the size of a pickle keg.   14:266-267.

9.63   High wind leaves an oat field covered with barley. The oats are discovered five miles away; owner of the barley could not be found.   14:266-267.

9.64   Wind blows a man's hat five miles away; then changes, returns the hat to his yard.   8:122.

9.65   Gib Morgan invests in an ice-cream plant when his oil drilling strikes cream. He loses his investment when the cream sours. 20:69.

Gib Morgan in Civil War uniform.

9.66   Gib Morgan strikes bay rum instead of oil. When greedy production men order him to drill just one more turn, the well is ruined when it goes too deep and penetrates horse urine.   20:71-72.

9.67   Paul Bunyan's oil drill strikes the root of a rubber tree.   7:60.

9.68   While drilling in Mexico (India) Paul Bunyan (also Gib Morgan) strikes rubber, which covers the oil rig. The rubber hardens. A workman falls from the top of the derrick and bounces for three days and nights. Finally Paul (or Gib) has to shoot him to keep him from starving to death.   7:52; 20:79-82.

9.69   In South America Gib Morgan strikes quinine and whiskey. 20:75.

9.70   Gib Morgan is sent to the Fiji Islands to drill for essence of peppermint. He strikes buttermilk instead, later champagne.   20:66-68.

9.71   In the Fiji Islands, when a monkey falls into Gib Morgan's well and other monkeys form a chain to rescue it, Gib unwittingly drills and kills the monkeys. On seeing blood, he thinks he has struck the jugular vein of the earth.   20:69-70.

9.72   To avoid having to join sections of well casing, Paul Bunyan winds steel pipe around a drum and feeds it into the well as if rope.   7:51, 58-59.

9.73   In South America, when Gib Morgan runs out of cable he uses a giant boa constricter, Strickie, as cable.   20:75-76.

9.74   Gib Morgan uses his pet snake Strickie as a "bailer" and "fishing" tool.   20:76-78.

9.75   While drilling on Pike's Peak, Gib Morgan runs a huge leather pulley-belt from the derrick to the engine at the foot of the mountain. In going back and forth, he puts a saddle on the belt and rides.   20:63-64.

9.76   Gib Morgan strikes granite. The jarring of the drilling bit on the granite causes the drilling site to rise 75 feet in the air. Gib runs 40 barrels of arnica salve into the well, thus lowering the site. 20:83-85.

9.77   Gib Morgan digs a deep well, using a progressively smaller bit and cable until he completes the job with a needle and thread.   20:66.

9.78   Paul Bunyan (also Gib Morgan) cuts dry holes into sections, sells them as post holes. He paints the post holes and wraps them in waxed paper to keep them from rusting.   7:57; 14:264; 20:64-65.

9.79   Paul Bunyan drills on a high hill. When a windstorm blows the hill from around the well, Paul cuts the well into sections to sell as post holes.   7:53.

9.80   Paul Bunyan tries to sell dry holes in Europe, where they may bring in producing wells. However, the holes are warped by the motion of the boat on the way over.   7:53.

9.81   Hunter shoots at the limb on which partridges roost, splits it. When the halves of the limb snap together, the partridges are caught.   7:43.

9.82   Gib Morgan makes long-distance shots and salts his bullets so that the game will not spoil before he can reach it.   20:94-95.

9.83   When Gib Morgan shoots his 24-barrel shotgun, he is buried in passenger pigeons.   20:94-95.

9.84 Hunter uses so many bullets that he uses a bed tick for a shot pouch. 18:84.

9.85 Hunter makes a marvelous single shot that kills ducks, geese, rattlesnake. A chain of lucky accidents nets fish when a button pops off his shirt, quail when the falling ducks land on a covey of quail. 18:85.

9.86 Hunter quickly bends the barrel of his rifle so as to kill a deer that is running out of sight around a mountain. The bullet circles the mountain three times, hitting the deer each time. 18:85.

9.87 Blind hogs are led to water by forming a mouth-to-tail chain behind an old sow with sight. Man cuts the sow's tail and leads the hogs to market (or his own farm). 14:264; 20:59-60.

9.88 Sal Fink, wife of Mike, fights a duel with a thunderbolt. She fragments it and gives the pieces to soldiers to touch off their cannon with. 18:69.

9.89 (M) Horseman in a rainstorm has no match with which to light his cigarette. His horse watches a thundercloud and at the right moment jumps so that the rider can light his cigarette on lightning. 32:55.

9.90 Paul Bunyan runs a giant pipeline for cattle into Chicago. 7:56.

9.91 Paul Bunyan, who likes buttermilk, pipes it from Pennsylvania to the California oil fields. 7:59.

9.92 Paul Bunyan discovers perpetual motion. 7:60.

9.93 In Arkansas, Paul Bunyan trains razorbacks to root in a straight line, thus inventing the first ditching machine. 7:60-61.

9.94 As oilmen use nitroglycerin to make wells produce more, Gib Morgan uses it on a poorly producing milk cow. 20:87-88.

9.95 Gib Morgan buys timber rights on cut-over land (only stumps) and sets his crew to making shoe pegs. When the market for pegs collapses, he has his men sharpen the other end of the pegs and sells the pegs as oats. 20:85-86.

9.96 Jim Baker, "Pie Biter," having no wood to cook cowboys' supper with, sets the prairie afire and moves his utensils as the fire moves. When supper is ready, he is eight miles from camp. 14:189.

9.97 (M) Man escapes from Indians by diving down the gullet of a large bull. He builds a fire inside; cuts steaks off the bull's sides, thus surviving while hiding for three days. 19:44-49.

9.98 Gib Morgan builds a hotel that revolves so that all rooms face southeast. Rooms are equipped with running whiskey as well as hot and cold water. 20:89.

9.99 (M) Man shoots at a buck, using a peach seed for a bullet. The animal escapes. Three years later, in the same meadow, the same man climbs a peach tree that moves as he climbs. The tree turns out to be peach-bearing antlers of the deer the man had shot. 32:55.

9.100 Tornado uproots a peach tree, sets a pecan tree down in its place. Tree now produces pecans with peach flavor. 28:61-62.

9.101 In Texas a man works all day stringing barbed wire. At sundown he starts back to the ranch house, but the pasture is so big that he walks two days getting back. 20:65.

9.102 (M) Man sets out to see where the sun rises. After traveling far, he hitches his horse to a "hook" he finds, and stuffs his hat into what seems to be a hole in a huge wall. Later he learns he has hitched his horse to the tip of the moon (cf. 1.42) and has stopped up the hole where the sun comes out (cf. 5.9). 30:238-239.

9.103 (M) Very swift dog, ridden by a man in a race, outruns horses and then disappears. Dog stops at blue wall, where the jockey hangs his bridle and spurs on a golden hook (like 9.102). 12:72-75.

9.104 Gib Morgan describes "whickles" as a cross between a canary and a bumblebee. They drink crude petroleum. 20:41-42.

9.105 Club-tailed glyptodont bats large rocks to the top of a mountain with its tail, to see the rocks roll back. 7:41.

9.106 Whiffle-poofle fish is tempted only by the "squidge" as bait. To catch them, a hole is bored in the center of a frozen circular lake. The squidge is held over hole and the whiffle-poofle is lured through the hole. When swallowed, the squidge swells in its stomach; the whiffle-poofle cannot return through the hole. 7:40-41.

9.107 Mountain stem-winder has legs shorter on one side than on the other. It grazes in a circular motion around the sides of conical hills in Central Texas. 7:39-40.

9.108 The jointsnake, when broken into pieces, rejoins the segments. Its tail acts as a signalman while the head picks up the pieces as a switch-engine picks up freight cars. 8:125-128.

9.109 The hoopsnake puts its tail in its mouth and rolls like a wheel. 8:125-128.

9.110 (M) Calves become so fat that cowboys must ride around and help them to their feet. 19:44.

9.111   Watt Turner's hogs are so fat that at slaughtering time he has to make them squeal to know which end to knock in the head.   18:83.

9.112   Bear chases a hunter up a tree, picks up his abandoned rifle and motions for him to throw down cartridges.   9:40-43.

9.113   When a cowboy ropes a bear, the bear chases him out of the saddle, mounts his horse and "builds a loop" so as to rope him. 31:106.

9.114   (M) Tequila-drinking horse, used in smuggling liquor, can smell Texas Rangers; is able to warn its owner of their presence. After becoming the property of a priest it stops drinking. 16:396-402.

9.115   Smart "cutting" horse can read brands, sort cattle without a rider.   16:406-407.

9.116   Horse of Gregorio Cortez, Mexican bandit, gallops backwards so that Gregorio can shoot at the posse chasing him.   16:342.

9.117   (M) Horse that brings in a herd of cattle alone taps its foot three times to tell its master that three cows are missing.   19:54-56.

9.118   (M) Horse "single-foots" so rapidly that the sound of its back feet hitting the ground has to catch up with the sound of its front feet.   32:55.

9.119   A bird dog runs in ever smaller circles so as to "herd" a covey of quail into a rabbit hole. It then lets the quail out one at a time for hunter to shoot.   18:85-88.

9.120   When a lonely rancher plays his harmonica, a rattlesnake appears and beats time to the music with its tail. Later the snake is discovered leading a band of 28 rattlers in "Stars and Stripes Forever."   19:162-164.

9.121   (M) Man trains a whipsnake to whip boys who steal his fruit. Boys place chili, garlic, and gunpowder in the snake's food. The snake thinks its master has done this, whips the master (cf. 5.8). 12:89-100.

9.122   When cows give no milk, it is discovered that fish have been milking them as they stand in a creek.   22:201.

9.123   In hilly country, all the hogs have a hole in one ear. When they come to the house, they put a hind foot through the hole and slide down the hill.   20:58-59.

9.124   When a razorback hog swallows dynamite and is kicked by a mule, the mule is killed, the barn wrecked, the razorback made sick.   15:80-81.

9.125   Hog at a lumbercamp swallows dynamite, which explodes. The lumberjacks find two smoked hams, fried pork chops, barbecued ribs.   30:178.

9.126   Hogs feed on pine cones (or sprouts). When butchered they yield little lard but ample turpentine.   9:17; 30:178-179.

9.127   Hogs escape a field through a hollow log under the fence. When the farmer turns the log so that it parallels the fence, a hog goes through the log and comes out in the same field. It becomes confused and runs wildly, wringing its own neck.   9:20-21.

9.128   Hogs mistake a woodpecker's tapping for the sound of corn being broken against a wagon. They run themselves poor following the bird.   9:24.

9.129   Iowa farmer tells a stranger that the circular bare spots to be seen in a field are where hogs have become immobilized from the huge mud balls that cling to their tails. Hogs could root outward just so far; they cleaned the spots bare.   9:25-26.

9.130   Gib Morgan raises popcorn and stores it in a barn. On a hot day the crop explodes. Gib's mule thinks the popped grains are snowflakes and freezes to death.   20:86.

9.131   Flock of passenger pigeons is so large and dense it blots out the sun. Cows come home to be milked.   20:95.

9.132   Rattlesnake bites an old woman's nose. She survives; the snake dies of snuff poisoning.   19:64.

9.133   The hoopsnake has a poisonous spike on its tail. One chases a man, strikes the tree he climbs, then a hoe handle. The leaves on the tree wither; the hoe handle swells and breaks.   8:128.

9.134   A hornet stings the cable of an oil rig. Gib Morgan applies a poultice to the swelling.   20:90.

9.135   A Negro slave falls from a high ladder. He is saved when his son warns him that he is about to fall on "ol' Missus." Immediately he starts to fall upward, lands at the top of the ladder.   10:53-54.

9.136   Cowboy's horse bucks him off. He lands astride a barbed wire fence and is split upward to his Adam's apple. He lengthens his stirrups and continues on his way.   30:176.

9.137   From the Fiji Islands Gib Morgan lays a pipeline to Los Angeles, then to St. Louis, where the pipeline forks—one branch going to Chicago, the other to New York. Gib's helper, Big Toolie, is sent home through the pipeline. Having forgotten about the fork, Gib loses his helper, who is "halved" at St. Louis.   20:72-73.

9.138   A dog, caught in circular saw, is cut into three pieces. Sewn back together in haste, it now chases its nose with its tail.   30:179.

9.139   When a fast dog splits itself on a stump, the owner quickly joins the two halves, but carelessly. Nevertheless the dog now runs faster than ever; it rotates like a cartwheel—one side can "spell" the other.   14:264-265; 20:95-96.

9.140   Gib Morgan accidently drops his watch into an oil well. It enters a stream of oil. Fourteen years later Gib "bails out" a well on another lease, finds the watch.   20:92-93.

9.141   In Russia, bears chase Gib Morgan's horse-drawn sleigh. They leap over the sleigh, eat the horses, become lodged in the harness and pull Gib to town.   20:97-98.

9.142   Cowboy sees bandits dividing loot. They discover him, put him in a hogshead, nail on the lid, and abandon him on the prairie. A buffalo herd comes along. The cowboy grabs the tail of a buffalo through the bung hole. In the buffalo's mad scramble the barrel breaks, releasing the cowboy.   9:34-37.

9.143   When Jim Baker, "Pie Biter," is captured by Indians, he avoids torture by playing his fiddle. When the E-string breaks and hits the chief in the eye, Jim escapes.   14:187-189.

9.144   In escaping Indians by sliding down a giant icicle hanging from a cliff, a cowboy sets his pants afire. His horse saves himself by sliding down an even larger icicle.   14:265.

9.145   Gib Morgan's sister-in-law keeps trim by walking five miles on a barbed-wire fence with a wildcat under each arm.   18:61.

9.146   Backwoods beauty can perform prodigious athletic feats; is a fierce gazer, screamer; has long toenails; is scratched so thoroughly by a wildcat that she never itches again; has feet so long that she appears to be walking on her knees; has feet so tough that she does not know when she is standing on a live coal; wears grotesque clothes and adornments; is aided in a fight with Indians by panthers, who admire her pluck; manhandles Yankee peddlers.   18:61-78.

9.147   In a petrified forest even the law of gravity is petrified. Man sees a petrified bird in mid-air.   18:84.

9.148   Cowboys tell "nesters" to catch toad frogs, a delicacy, by "roping" them. Toads will not jump over the loop.   6:87.

9.149   Pipeliners say that Paul Bunyan has only one arm, in the middle of his chest.   7:53.

9.150   Paul Bunyan descends to hell through an oil drilling. He meets Satan, who shows him his harem. Paul tries to steal a girl; Satan chases him back up the hole. Before leaving, Paul asks about the leg he has lost down an oil well (he now has a wooden leg). Satan assures him that his leg is already roasting; he cannot have it back. 7:52.

9.151   While drilling an oil well in the islands, Gib Morgan runs out of firewood for his boilers; he uses coconuts as fuel. The coconuts burn well but unnerve Gib's crew when they explode. Gib has to move the boiler a mile into the jungle.   20:70.

The Healer of Los Olmos cures a shepherd.

PART THREE
Alphabetical Index

PART III: ALPHABETICAL INDEX

Note on Procedure

Kinds of entries. The Alphabetical Index aims at a generous coverage within reasonable limits. It includes:

1. Personal names and place names.

2. The names of ethnic groups, of foods, of plants and animals (mammals, birds, reptiles, insects, etc.), of diseases and disabilities and the methods and substances used in their folk treatment.

3. Titles or first lines of songs, games, rhymes, refrains.

4. Proverbs and proverbial expressions, folk diction.

5. Subjects of a folkloristic, cultural, or historical bearing—for example, "Acculturation," "Ballad," "Camp meetings," "Grateful Dead Man theme," "Heroes," "Jack tales," "Liberty pole," "Marriage," "Occupational heroes," "Pie suppers," "Runaway Scrape," " 'Stamping' white horses," "Water witching."

6. In some instances, the names of organizations and titles of books and periodicals that are referred to in the articles indexed.

Treatment of titles, lines, phrases. Customary alphabetizing procedure is observed, whereby titles are entered according to the first word except for *A, An, The,* but first lines and proverbs (or folk expressions) according to the first word, regardless of its grammatical status. Titles of articles do not appear in the index (see the concluding paragraph).

Abbreviations. With one exception, the abbreviations here used reflect common practice. The exception is "dic."—which functions more as an editorial sign than as an abbreviation. It stands for *diction* and follows, in parentheses, words or phrases that appear primarily as folk usages—as words instead of as subjects identified by words.

References to appendices. Occasionally a page reference will involve either of two appendices found in the reprint editions of numbers 4 and 5 of the Society's volumes, *Happy Hunting Ground* and *Rainbow in the Morning.* (Sample: "4:page 17 of appendix.") Neither appendix is found in the original editions of these books as issued, with no title other than a "Publication" number, in 1925 and 1926.

References to Volume 26. Number 26 of the Publications, a miscellany typifying *Texas Folk and Folklore,* draws its material from articles previously published in the series. Inasmuch as Volume 26 thus constitutes a reprint edition of sorts, references to it may be discounted by the researcher who has at his disposal all earlier (than 1954) numbers of the Publications.

Article titles. The index excludes the titles of articles, as such. While it records the names of contributors to the Society's volumes

(1-36) and shows where their contributions appear, it makes no attempt to rearrange the wording of article titles so as to render their entry into an alphabetical listing meaningful. Volume-and-page references to the article "Well Done, Liar," would occur rather under the author's last name, and more usefully under appropriate key-words such as—for the article mentioned—"Lying," "Munchausen."

A ‮

"A boatman loved a maiden," 3:146.
"*A boca cerrada no entra mosca*," 24:118.
A-Bone (dic.), 34:16.
"A brown-skinned woman," with music, 2:63-65.
"*A buen hambre no hay mal pan*," 24:118.
"A burly coon you know," 2:61.
"A from izzard [Adam's off ox]," 5:81.
A-gas (dic.), 34:21, 26.
"A. Ginger Blue," 5:170.
"A hoss and a flea an' a little mice," 2:49.
"A keerful tongue makes a happy heart," 5:137.
"A lady walked in yonder garden," with music, 10:155.
"*A las dos de la mañana*," with music, 4:27.
"A man whose name was Johnny Sands," 6:224.
"A melon spiled early won't grow no better with age," 13:241.
"*A mí de la gallina me gusta el ala*," 24:118.
"A nice young ma-wa-wan," 6:211.
"A nigger in de cane patch," 7:104.
"A nigger an' a white man," 7:104.
"A person without teeth can find gladness in a soup bowl," 5:137.
"A pretty fair maid all in a garden," with music, 23:91-92.
"A rich Irish lady from London she came," with music, 23:37-38.
"A rich man for luck and a poor man for children," 5:85.
"A rocky vineyard does not need a prayer but a pickaxe," 14:150.
"A rustic was seated," with music, 8:113.
"A spry tongue makes a doleful way," 5:137.
"*A todo él tira y nada le da*," 12:216.
"A-walkin' the streets of Laredo," 7:149.
"A whistling gal and a flock of sheep," 13:160.
"A whistling girl and a crowing hen," 13:160, 239; 26:239.
"A woman, a dog, and a walnut tree," 13:240.
"A yaller gal sleeps in a bed," 7:103.
Aarne, Antti, 24:72, 80 f.; 25:183; 27:124 ff.
Aaron (in folk drama), 11:87.
Aaron's Rod theme, 13: 69-70.
"*Abandonada, El*," with music, 4:41.
Abba Mingo, 21:70.
Abbot, Horace, 15:108.
Abbot, E.C., 35:56 ff.

"Abe Lincoln Freed the Nigger" (cited), 36:115.
Abela, Tomas, 19:116.
Abendglocken (evening bells), ringing of at Fredricksburg, Tex., 2:69.
Abernethy, Francis E.: articles, 31:3-7; 33:146-150; 35:3-10; mentioned, 31:165; 33:198; 35:165; 36:vii.
Abert, James W., 25:44.
Abilene, Tex., 19:200; 22:220; 35:78.
Abolitionists, 7:81 ff.; 35:23.
Abraham (in tale), 19:31 ff.
"Abraham," with music, 7:117.
"Abraham looked around," 7:118.
Abrahams, Roger: articles, 31:119-134; 32:168-175, 199-201; 34:125-153; mentioned, 31:165; 32:269; 34:vi, 11, 243.
Abrahams, William, 20:55.
"Abraham's Bosom, In," 7:140.
Abrigo, Polo, 18:109, 114.
Academe, folklore of, 36:123.
Accordian, 5:98, 104.
Acculturation, 12:122ff.; Child ballads in U.S., 27:25-27; European lore in U.S., 6:26; 28:18-44; European tales among N. A. Indians, 11:5 ff.; 14:104 ff.; 28:33-34; 29:190-200; in Negro tales, 5:71-72; 29:172-173.
Acerbi, Guiseppe, 34:121.
Aceves, Jesús Silva, 29:120.
"Ach-ghuuooh" (refrain), 5:40.
Acsabuche Hills (Tex.), 27:166.
Achan (in song), 7:93.
Achilles, 1:70; 33:189.
Acknowledge the corn (dic.), 13:247.
Acorn Man, 1:39-40; 6:109-110; see Blood (clot of).
Acorns as human food, 9:93.
Across the peach orchard (dic.), 13:247.
Acuña, Manuel, 30:52.
Adam and Eve, 1:92; 31:5; 32:176 ff.; see Adam's; Rib, Adam's.
"Adam and Eve of the Mustangs" (poem), 16:153-154.
Adamic, Louis, 28:45.
Adams, Andy: article, 33:33-38; mentioned, 6:161; 30:285; 33:31, 100, 107, 198.
Adams, Andy T., 33:v, 38.
Adams, Billy, 30:168.
Adams, "Bull," 30:102.
Adams, Cal, 32:155.
Adams, Charlie, 34:15, 21, 35.
Adams, E.C.L., 7:140.
Adams, Ephraim Douglass, 3:141.
Adams, Harry Lee, 19:126.
Adams, Mrs. Helen, 35:100.
Adams, James Burton, 33:81.
Adams, Capt. John, 34:184.

Adams, Ramon F., 12:252; 16:291; 33: 75; 35:60.
Adams, T. B., 19:103.
Adams, W. A., 34:45 f.
Adam's: off ox (dic.), 5:84; 13:246; housecat (dic.), 13:246.
Adams Diggings, 22:153; 27:103.
Adcock, Joe, 19:151.
Add, Nig, 12:v; 33:94.
Addison, Joseph, his appreciation of ballads, 30:35.
"Adelita," 1:55-57; 22:177-178; with music 4:28.
"¡Adentro los escuadrones!," 28:98.
"Adieu to old El-lum" (cited), 6:198.
"Adiós, adiós, compañeros," 29:89.
"¡Adiós! mi Patria Querida," 12:222-224.
Adkins, Ben, 3:30, 37; 26:86, 93.
Adobe Walls (Tex.), 18:3; 22:133.
Adolfito, Don (in song), 4:40 f.
Adventure, tales of; see Part II, Section 5, of Analytical Index.
Adventures of a Ballad Hunter, 33:5 ff.
Adventures with a Texas Naturalist, 33: 10.
Aesop, 1:62; 18:49; 25:9; in Negro folklore, 7:141-142.
Aeteological myths; see Explanatory tales.
Afanasyev (Russian folklorist), 25:191-192.
Africa(n), 4:61; folklore in, 5:70, 72; folktales in relation to Southern Negro tables, 5:71-72; influence on blues and jazz, 36:117; song in U.S., 7:17; tale in Texas, 11:95; use of glass as grave decoration, 18:130.
Afterbirth: cattle, 8:30; human, 19:24.
Agarita root as remedy, 8:67, 69.
Agiabampo, Mex., 6:6, 8.
Agosto, flor de, in folk cure, 24:59.
Agreda, María de Jesús, 3:132-135; 14:197-198.
Agrícola, Father Michael, 34:118.
Agrito used as dye, 10:87.
Agriculture, beliefs relating to; see Fertility charm; Planting lore; Shan.
Aguacate, 9:93.
Agua Corriente (Tex.) as place name, 6:74-75.
Agua Dulce (Tex.), 18:137; 26:124; as place name, 6:75 f.
Agua Dulce Creek, 16:23 f., 26.
Agua Fría: Brewster County, Tex., 1:97; 2:21 ff.; 4:89, 96; 28:117-118; N.M., 10:64.
Agua Fría Canyon (Tex.) as place name, 6:75.
"Agua que va río abajo," 31:135.
Agua-Squash (Indian), 18:103.
Aguayo Expedition, 3:210, 216.
Ague, 8:20, 49, 52; see Chills.

Aguero, Francisco, 32:23.
Aguilar y Marocho, 30:50.
Aguirre, María Enriquez, 27:143.
"Ah got de blues," 2:60.
Ahearn, Michael J.: article, 29:147-152; mentioned, 29:vi, 231.
Ahimelech (in folk drama), 11:62 f.
"Ahora es cuando, yerbabuena, le has de dar sabor al caldo," 24:118.
Aijados, seven hills of, 3:8.
Aiken, Dave, 28:123.
Aiken, Perry, 25:173.
Aiken, Riley: articles, 12:1-87; 16:351-355; 26:24-39 (reprint); 27:78-95; 28:123-127; 31:135-140; 32:3-56; mentioned, 10:ii, 253; 12:vi, 1; 14:82; 15:172; 16:419; 17:34; 24:128; 27:201; 28:vii, 167; 31:165; 32:269.
Ainsworth, Roy, 3:iii.
Ainu of Japan, 35:8.
Aire en el corazón, a cause of death, 8:66.
Akins, Corbett, 34:45.
"Al haber gallinas hay gallos," 24:118.
"Al mal paso, darle prisa," 24:119.
"Al pescado que se duerme se lo lleva la corriente," 12:218.
"Al que le apriete el zapato, que se lo afloje," 24:119.
"Al que Dios le ha de dar por la trasera ha de entrar," 12:218.
"Al que le duela la muela, que se la saque," 24:119.
"Al que no le guste, que lo tire y monte en pelo," 24:119.
Alabama, 6:129, 227 f.; 36:108; the "tournament" in, 5:95.
"Alabama Boun'," 5:177.
Alabama-Coushatta Indians: burial customs of, 18:136; 36:40; how they came south, 13:298-299; music and folktales of, 13:270-299; 21:65-80; 26:12-18 (reprint).
Alabama Village (Tex.), 13:28.
Alamito Creek, 35:83.
Alamo, 3:19, 172-173, 237; 6:139; 14:185; 15:9-58; 18:67; 20:2; 30:59; see Rose; Bowie, James; Santa Anna (casa del).
Alamo de Cesaria Ranch, 28:123.
Alamo Heights in San Antonio, Tex., haunted house in, 29:227-229.
Alamo Plaza in San Antonio, Tex., 13:1; 25:119.
Alamocitos, Los, as place name, 6:75.
Alamogordo Creek as place name, 6:75-76.
Alarcón (explorer), 13:5; 30:283.
Alarcón, Pedro Antonio de (novelist), 9:124, 129.
Alarcón, Ruiz, 28:63.
Alarm Creek as place name, 32:126.

Amarillo, Tex., 6:76; 7:41, 9:3; 18:218; 19:161; 22:216; 36:62, 66.
Amarillos as place name, 6:75.
Amazons, mythical wealth of, 3:8.
Amber beads for asthma, 14:267.
Ambriz boys (King Ranch cowboys), 18: 106.
Ameca, Mex., 24:132.
Amelia Court House, battle of, 33:122.
America, European folklore in, 28:18-44; see Acculturation.
American: comic legend, 20:3; folk heroes, 28:43; folklore compared with European, 28:18-44; immigrants, attitude toward their traditional lore, 28: 23-25.
American Antiquarian Society, 18:63.
American Ballads and Folk Songs, 18:22.
American Folklore Society, 1:6.
American Songbag, 18:1.
Americans: creation of in Navajo myth, 14:132-133; their belief in Mexican weather signs, 2:87.
Ames, Nathaniel, 28:83.
Amicable Building (Waco, Tex.), 1:50.
Ammerman, Claude Tom, 33:172.
Amonderain, Juan Martin de, 19:176.
"*Amor Que Tenia, El*," with music, 9: 122.
"Amos and Andy, sugar and candy," 18: 198; 26:206 (reprint).
Amsterdam, 4:61.
Amulets, N.A. Indian, 7:29.
"An old ground hog," 1:28.
"An old man came home one night," with music, 23:65-66.
"An old white hen with yellow legs," 6: 65-66.
Anacahuita (wild olive), 9:93.
Anadarko, Okla., 22:11, 15.
Anadarko Creek as place name, 32:131.
Anahuac: legend of, 12:159; as place name, 13:27; valley, 4:10.
Anaya, E.V., 15:163; 26:289.
Anchors (dic.), 34:16.
"And de crepe keep a-hangin," with music, 7:114.
"And dere wus a day," 7:90; 26:170 (reprint).
"And grabbed Miss Mousie by the back," 5:48.
"And see not ye that bonnie road," 25: 104.
Andalucia, 36:27.
Andamarca, Peru, 3:6.
"*Andar en el charco seco*," 21:30.
Anderson, Albert Slayton, 30:164.
Anderson, "Bronco Billy," 34:69.
Anderson County, Tex., 18:134; place names, 31:75 f., 87, 94.
Anderson, G.M., 33:51 ff.
Anderson, J.W. (cowboy), 14:157.
Anderson, Joe (Central Texas), 19:173.

Anderson, John (Tyler, Tex.), 18:143.
Anderson, John Q.: articles, 25:152-159; 27:180-186; 29:3-13; 30:156-164; 31: 73-98; 32:112-147; 33:118-127; 34: 163-174; 35:73-81; mentioned, 25:254; 27:201; 29:v, 158, 231; 30:291; 31: 165; 32:199, 269; 33:198; 34:vi, 243; 35:165.
Anderson, Loraine Epps, 30:164.
Anderson, Nels, 36:118.
Anderson, Pat, 8:20.
Anderson, William A., 6:174.
Anderson, Tex., 7:139.
Anderwald, Pete, 8:17, 69.
"*Ando en busca*," 30:54.
Andrew; see St. Andrew.
Andrews, Roy Chapman, 25:35; 26:311-312.
Andrews County, Tex., 5:64; 21:43; 26: 280.
Anecdotes: backwoods, 18:11-78 passim; of character, 15:65; Crockett, 18: 147 ff.; about fiddlers, 18:45-46; historical value of, 15:59 ff.; about lawyers, 18:205-217; migratory nature of, 15:59-74; 25:1-17; preachers' use of, 14:158 ff.; relationship to physical and cultural environment in which they occur, 15:75-84; use of in Humphrey's novel *The Ordways*, 35:133 ff.; see Preachers; Preaching; see Part II, Section 6, of *Analytical Index*.
Anemia, cure for, 8:49.
Angel in Blue; see Agreda, María de Jesús de.
Angeles, Gen. Felipe, 21:23.
Angelina (Indian maiden), 13:29.
Angelina, Father, 14:198.
Angelina, Tex., 30:178.
Angelina County, Tex., 13:30; 27:27.
"*Angelitos hemos; del cielo venimos*," 9:76.
Angermiller, Florence, 15:95, 103.
Angling Lake (Tex.) as place name, 6: 85-86.
Anhinga (water turkey), 7:37; 26:286.
Anigstein, Ludwick, 25:39.
Animal(s): folk beliefs concerning sometimes have basis in fact, 25:18 ff.; heart sacrificed, 2:8; imaginary species in tall tales, 7:39 ff.; 8:125 ff.; 20:41-42; language understood by human, 15:128-129; personification of in Mexican *relación*, 29:108-121; pioneers' attitude toward, 2:49; tails in fact and folklore, 27:105-112; tales among Mexicans, 14:8-35; 18:188 ff.; tales among Negroes, 25:220 ff.; tales among Waco Indians, 1:54; as weather indicators, 2:87 ff.; Western wild, names of, 25:40-46; see Reptile myths; see Part II, Section 2, of *Analytical Index* (Animal Tales); see names of

animals.
Animal helpers; see Part II, Section 5, of *Analytical Index*.
"*Animalitos, Los*," 12:v-vi.
Animas (Las) River, 9:27, 69-84 passim.
Animas, Rancho de Las, 13:10.
Animism, origin of, 1:66.
Animosa, Iowa, 23:145.
Annanias (in folk drama), 11:88.
"Annie Breen from Old Kaintuck," with music, 6:207.
"*Año de mil novecientos*," with music, 21:24-26.
"*Año de noventa y cuatro*," with music, 4:13-15.
Ansley, John A., 33:119.
Anson, Tex., 18:115.
Ant lions, boys teasing, 36:49.
Antelope, 18:98, 101.
Antelope Creek as place name, 32:121.
Antelope Draw as place name, 13:2.
Ant(s), 2:93; 5:64-65; 12:81 ff., 131 ff.; 18:188 ff. (formula tale involving); 19:136; 22:25 f.; 26:77-79; bites, remedy for, 8:49; 26:259; as remedy for rheumatism, 8:10; see Red ants.
Anthem (anecdote about pronunciation of the word), 25:9-10.
Anthony; see St. Anthony.
Anthony, Reed, 33:96.
Anthony, New Mex., 10:71.
Anthrax, remedy for, 8:30.
"Anti-Over" (game), 17:148-149.
Antipodal Petroleum Company, 20:53; 30:79.
Anti-Slavery Society, 7:83-84.
Antonette's Leap, legend of, 3:171-176.
Antwerp, 36:58.
Anvil, man breaks horn of in anger, 19:54.
Apache, Okla., 22:1, 3, 15.
Apache Creek as place name, 32:131.
Apache Indians, 2:19, 24; 3:67-68, 70, 93, 165; 8:72; 9:90 ff.; 10:72-76 passim; 12:109; 13:24, 26, 29, 121; 19:44 ff.; 22:51, 110-120, 142 ff., 150; in Chisos Mtns., 28:106 ff.; 35:84 ff.; as cowboys, 7:173; see Kiowa-Apache.
Apache Gold and Yaqui Silver, 22:153.
Apache John, 22:51, 137.
Apatzingan (Mayo Indian hero), 11:27.
Ape hangers (dic.), 34:27.
Aphrodisiacs, 24:116; 34:176 ff.
Aphrodite, 33:189; 36:41.
Apis worship, 1:67.
Aplastaceras (a giant), 12:78-79.
Apodaca (viceroy), 30:47.
Apollo, 33:191.
Apostolic succession, 1:65; 14:166.
Apparitions; see Part II, Section 7, of *Analytical Index*.
Appendicitis, remedy for, 8:78.

Appetite, exaggerated; see Part II, Section 9, of *Analytical Index*.
Apple-counting tale, 21:95-96.
Appleby, Tex., 7:123.
Applegate, Frank, 24:2.
Appleseed, Johnny, 28:43; 33:118.
"*Aquí me siento a cantar*," 9:60-62; 26:147 (reprint).
Arab, consecration of tent-ground by, 2:9.
Arabian horses, Nefdee strain, 16:94.
Arabic romance in Austin, Tex., 34:187-202.
Arango, Doroteo; see Villa, Pancho.
Aransas County, Tex., place name, 31:94.
Arapahoe Indians, 3:165; 18:4; 19:89; see Cheyenne.
Arbor, brush, 25:244.
Arbuckle, Gen., 19:180.
Arbuckle Mtns., 3:64; 4:9.
Arcadia, La., 35:36.
Arcadian; see Cajun.
Archer, Branch Tanner, 15:73.
Archer City, Tex., 8:121-122; 18:123.
Archetypes, mythic, in *The Winter of Our Discontent*, 36:93-102.
Architecture: early Texas, 15:175; see Houses.
Arctic Ocean, 4:60.
Ardmore, Okla., 7:46; 26:315.
Argot; see Diction.
Argumedo, Benjamin, 28:98.
Aristophanes, 36:123.
Aristotle, 30:72; his comments on the relative merits of poetry and history applied to folklore, 15:5; and snake lore, 21:63.
Arizona, 2:87; 3:96, 239; 4:87, 89; 6:193-194; 9:97, 180 f.; 10:79-81; 19:94, 98; cowboys of, 7:172 ff.; Paul Bunyan in, 7:58.
"Arizona," 9:181.
"Arizona Boys and Girls" (cited), 6:236.
Arizpe, Josefa Carrasco de, 22:166.
Arkansas, 5:57, 65; 19:70; 18:11 ff.; 19:177 ff.; 22:202 ff.; 23:236-238; apple peddlers in early Texas, 25:124; reputation of, 6:101, 207; 23:226; in songs, 7:5; 23:236-238; see "Arkansas Traveler."
Arkansas legal tender (dic.), 22:202 ff.
"Arkansas Overlap" (East Texas), 17:3.
Arkansas River, 22:129; 28:74.
"Arkansas Traveler, The," 5:108; 14:162, 187; 33:104; history of the song and skit, 18:11-60.
Arlington, Tex., 18:147.
Armadillo as food, 23:24; 31:54.
Armageddon (name of horse), 16:294.
Armán, Don José, 5:51.
"*Armas blancas*" (knives), 22:143.
Armstrong, A.B., 18:147, 222.

Aughinbaugh, W. E., 27:110.
Augustine; see St. Augustine.
Auner, A. W., 23:286.
"Aunt Jamima, do go home," 17:106-107.
Aury, Louis de, 3:92.
Austin, Mrs. C. F., 7:161.
Austin, Gene, 34:12.
Austin, Mary, 14:53, 55, 84, 90-92, 104;
 15:86, 101, 162; 26:289; 28:47.
Austin, Moses, 4:page 7 of appendix; 7:
 42; 10:118.
Austin, Stephen F., 3:5, 119, 121, 123,
 211, 236; 4:page 7 of appendix; 7:42,
 157-159; 8:131; 13:35, 55, 59; 15:
 61 ff.; 19:75; 26:213; 29:45; 32:114;
 see Austin's Colony.
Austin, Tex., 3:37, 167, 174, 231, 239;
 11:102; 15:60; 18:4, 34, 36, 52, 54,
 92, 135, 218; 19:71, 149, 200 f.; 26:
 128, 223-229; 29:45-51; 36:34, 40, 48,
 82, 87; beliefs and superstitions of
 Mexican-Americans in, 24:114-118;
 culture of hill folk near, 17:40-48.
Austin's Colony and colonists, 7:42, 155-
 159; 8:129-151; religion and, 14:159.
Auto, the, and Mexican folk plays, 9:77;
 11:50.
Autobiographies of Methodist frontier
 preachers, 35:19-33.
Automobile; see Car(s); Drag racing;

Ford epigrams; Truck drivers.
Autry, Gene, 28:102; 34:67-70.
Auz, Miguel Díaz de, 16:215.
Avery, William, 20:49.
Avila, Alonzo de, 16:200.
Avila, Hernando López de, 16:200.
Avocado: in riddle, 18:181; see Aguacate.
"A-walkin' the streets of Laredo," 7:149.
"Away down youndah on Cedar Creek,"
 7:86.
"Away he went trittety trot," 6:27.
"Away here in Texas," 6:140.
Axe: foils the Devil, 7:131; newly-rich
 farm woman's wish for new, 25:75-
 85; 26:336-346 (reprint); riddle
 about, 24:127; superstition about, 10:
 55.
Axle-grease, 8:45, 49, 54.
Axson, Stockton, 33:101.
"Ay, mi querida Nicolosa," 6:21.
Aydais Indians, 9:167.
Ayish Bayou as place name, 13:28.
Aymar, Gordon C., 25:38; 26:302.
Aynesworth, Anne, 27:164.
Azara, Medina, 29:99.
Azcapotzalco, 11:30, 32.
Aztec(s), 3:17, 197, 231, 233; 9:94, 98,
 101; 11:8-47 passim; 12:156, 159 ff.,
 246 ff.; articles of trade, 14:227; my-
 thology and legend of Weeping Wom-
 an (La Llorona), 24:73.

B

"B from bull's foot," 5:81.
Baal, sacrifices to, 1:67.
"B-A ba, B-E be, B-I bi, Ba-be-bi," with
 music, 6:228.
Babb, Arthur: article, 16:390-395; men-
 tioned, 16:419.
Babb, Stanley E.: poem, 3:179; men-
 tioned, 3:261.
Babington, Mirna, 32:71.
"Baby, I Can't Sleep," with music, 2:60,
 65.
"Baby, Take a Look at Me," 5:172; 5:
 page 12 of appendix.
Baby-switching prank, 22:229-230; 33:
 110-117.
Babyhead Creek as place name, 13:29-30.
Babyhead Mtn. as place name, 13:29-30,
 71.
"Babylon; or, the Bonnie Banks of For-
 die," 25:92.
Babylonian: burial customs, 36:41; civili-
 zation, 1:71; curses, 1:94.
Baca, Felipe, 9:69.
Baca, María, 10:66.
Baca, Prospero, 36:25.
Baca tribe of Africa, 36:149.
Bacatetes Mtns., 11:10.

"Bachelor's Lament" (cited), 6:234.
Bachue, 4:70, 72 ff.
Back door (in jump-rope terminology),
 18:198.
"Back from Holy Land, the pilgrim don-
 key's ears are just as long as ever,"
 14:152.
Back-up man (dic.), 18:203.
Backache, cure for, 8:50.
Backbone Stream as place name, 32:126.
Backslide (dic.), 7:12.
"Backward, Turn Backward," 6:203-204.
Backwoods belle, the, 18:61-78.
Backwoods humor, 15:80; 18:11 ff.; 19:
 63-81; see Backwoods belle; Preach-
 ing, frontier.
Backwoodsman, frontier preacher as, 35:
 27-28.
"Bacon in the pan," 6:136.
Bacon in remedies, 8:20 f., 36, 41, 45, 48,
 51, 76-77; 14:267; 30:248.
Bacon, James C., 20:56.
"Bad Companions"; see "Young Com-
 panions."
Bad luck, signs of, 13:155-160; 30:254.
"Bad Man from Bodie," 7:74.
Bad news (dic.), 34:26.

Bad news, breaking (tales), 25:10-13; see Climax of Horrors.
Bad scene (dic.), 34:26.
Badger fight, 13:231; 30:112-114.
Badgett, Jesse B., 21:122.
Badlands: "lost," 3:239; of N.D., surveying in, 21:46.
Badmen, 9:5-14, 27-33; as heroes, 31:123-125, 128-130; see Outlaws.
Baean (dic.), 22:91.
Baerg, J. W., 31:45, 47, 50.
"Baffled Knight, The" (cited), 25:55; 27:24 (foldout), 75.
Baffle Point (Tex.), 3:146.
Bailey, "Boots," 35:41 f.
Bailey, Brit (James B.), 13:55; 30:277-278.
Bailey, Joseph Weldon, 36:85 f.
Bailey, Vernon, 25:44.
Bailey's Light, 18:144-145.
Bailey's Prairie as place name, 13:55.
"Bailiff's Daughter of Islington" (cited), 27:24 (foldout), 75.
Baille, Father Nicholas, 13:60.
Baillie-Grohman (naturalist), 25:41.
Baily, Lyman J., 35:108.
Baird, A. J., 35:75 f.
Baird, Bessie, 23:54.
Baird, Dan O., 11:106.
Baird, James, 6:140; 8:134.
Baird, Joseph Armstrong, 36:43.
Baker (member of Chisom's gang), 33:74 f.
Baker, A. Y., 4:32; 26:144.
Baker, D.W.C., 3:16; 7:161; 15:59, 62, 73; 18:90.
Baker, Jim, 9:16-24; as "Pie Biter," 14:186.
Baker, Louis, 7:166.
Baker, Oby, 33:172.
Baker, Zillah, 11:97.
Bakersfield, Calif., 7:50; 26:318.
Bakwena tribe of Africa, 36:149.
Balaam as name of mule, 6:152-153.
Balaam's ass, 2:92; theme in tale, 24:87-88.
Balagia, Mrs. Charles G., 24:72.
"Balance all, Celie," 17:105-106.
"Balance, all you saddle warmers," 18:123.
Balboa, 3:7.
Baldness associated with handling swallows, 24:117.
Baldwin, James, 32:109.
Baldwin, Stanley, 25:5.
Balerio, Don Cecilio, 16:30-31.
Bales, Mary Virginia: article, 7:85-112; 26:167-174 (reprint); mentioned, 7:5, 183; 10:149.
Balkan ballads, human sacrifice reflected in, 2:10-13.
Ball, magic, 25:217-219.
Ballad(s): in American tradition as seen by a European folklorist, 28:34-37; about animals, 29:109-111; Arkansas variants of Texas, 30:212-217; Balkan, 2:8-13; British and American compared, 23:95-96; British in Texas, 10:131-168; Child in U.S., 10:131-168; 23:31-94; 27:23-77; collecting, 19:9-20; 21:1-3; communal origin of, 8:166-169; composition, Mexican, 4:30, 38-39; of doubtful value as sociohistorical evidence, 30:31-35; European kept alive in New World, 28:27-28; and funeral verse, 32:202-208; interplay between print and oral tradition, 28:34-35; making of a ("The Buffalo Skinners"), 18:1-10; Mexican, 4:10-43; 12:221 ff.; 21:1-34; 25:110-114; 26:143-158 (reprint); 28:91-105; 29:108-111, 132-135; 30:62-68; migration of "Texas Rangers" to Scotland, 32:190-198; names for types of in Mexico, 21:4; from Northeast Texas, 23:13 ff.; plea for intrinsic study of as works of art, 30:35-45; as protest songs, 21:6; rare in West Texas, 23:23; recited because singing sinful, 6:234; Robinhood type not popular in American West, 27:29; signature in, 25:97 ff.; style in East Texas, 23:27 f.; supernaturalism in rationalized, 27:43-51; an early Texas French, 5:49-55; use of the terms "version" and "variant," 32:226; see Balladry; Canción; Corrido; Cowboy; Songs; Tragedias; see titles and first lines of ballads; see Part I, Section 3, of Analytical Index for Child and Laws listings.
Ballad vendor, 21:5.
"Ballad of Leeper and Powell," origin of, 35:73-81.
Ballada, the Russian, its relation to the romance and occidental balladry, 25:86-96.
Balladry: occidental, may owe something to Russian ballada, 25:86-96; scholarship in, 8:160-169 (through 1930); 30:30-45; 32:199-268 (contemporary).
Ballard, Mrs. M. L., 30:114.
Balled up (dic.), 2:36.
"Ballet" book, 23:14.
Ballew, Bud, song about, 6:146-147.
Ballin, Mabel, 34:65.
Balling (dic.), 35:47.
Ballinger County, Mo., 27:49.
Ballowe, Hewitt L., 31:109, 117.
Balm-gentle as remedy, 8:90.
Balmonia as laxative, 13:234.
Balsam, caustic, in remedies, 8:37 f., 48.
Balsas, Río, 11:27.
"Baltimore," 1:19, 35; 7:23.
Baltimore, Ohio, 20:30.
Bambalón, Father, 28:62-63.

Bat: as folk remedy, 10:89; vampire, 25:28-31; 26:306-307; see Nighthawks.
Bates, B. A., 25:178.
Bates, Henry Walter, 25:29.
Bates, Jack, 35:75 ff.
Bates, Melverda, 25:182.
Bates, Monie, 19:24.
Bates, R. T., 34:45.
Bates, W. K., 35:75 ff.
Bath as remedy, 24:13-59 passim.
Batopilas, Mex., 32:12.
Batterson, Isaac, 21:120.
Battle, Kemp P., 5:41.
Battle, W. J., 4:page 19 of appendix; 5:48; 26:80; 33:10.
Battle of Mag Rath, 34:74 ff.
"Battle of Shiloh, The," 6:143-144.
"Battle of Shiloh Hills, The," 6:143-144.
Battle Stream as place name, 32:126.
Bauer, George, 31:79.
Baughman, Ernest W., 28:21; see Part I, sections 1 and 2, of *Analytical Index*.
Baughn, Calvin, 23:20.
Baum, Karl, 30:136-139.
Baum, Paul F., 30:217.
Baum, Vicki, 34:207.
Bay Creek as place name, 32:120.
Bay Ridge, Tex., 3:186.
Bayliss, Clara Kern, 14:76, 78.
Baylor family (Wilson County, Tex.), 30:273.
Baylor, Henry W., 8:18, 23.
Baylor, John R., 13:202.
Bayou Din Creek as place name, 32:126.
Bayou Rouge, La., 9:46.
Baytown, Tex., 36:35.
Bayview Cemetery, 18:133.
Bazan, Countess Emilia Pardo, 9:124, 127.
Beaird family (Parker County, Tex.), 13:213.
Beale, R. L., 7:114.
Beall, Frank, 5:96.
Beall, John, 5:97.
Bean, Roy, 6:83; 13:111-119; 14:254-256; 30:93.
Bean, Sam, 13:117.
Bean hauler (dic.), 35:46.
Beans: anecdotes about folk names for, and superstitions concerning, 17:49-58; see *Frijol; Frijoles; Frijollito* (mountain laurel bean).
Bear Creek: in Penn., 20:26; in Wyo., 33:110; in Tex., 17:83 (Parker County); 25:139 ff.; 33:151 ff.; 34:3 ff.; 35:103 ff. (Travis County).
Bear grass used in fence, 6:23.
Bear Gulch (Tex.), 13:2.
Bears as folk characters and in folk tradition, 9:37-43, 153-156, 158; 10:35-38; 18:v, 68, 71, 74, 76, 172 ff.; 19:41; 21:92-93; 22:30 ff., 44, 125; 24:100; 25:220-224, 238-240; 26:50-55, 59; 30: 8, 10 ff.; 31:106.

Bearded men, race of in Mexico, 11:26.
Bearpen Creek as place name, 32:121.
Bearsfoot Creek as place name, 32:121.
Beasley, John, 21:50.
Beast (dic.), 34:15, 23.
Beast of burden eaten by lion (motif); see Mule.
Beaton, Mary, 23:63.
Beatte (mustanger), 16:149.
Beatty, Arthur, 27:55.
Beaumont, Tex., 3:183; 7:90, 107; 26:337; 28:10.
Beauregard, P.G.T., 33:121.
"Beautiful Home, Sweet Home," 10:172; with music, 10:180.
Beauty and the Beast theme in Indian tales, 8:99-101; 14:107-109.
Beauty bush (spice bush), 18:16; 26:276.
"Beauty's skin deep, but ugly's to the bone," 5:page 9 of appendix.
Beauvoir, Simone de, 32:182.
Beaver and coyote (tales), 22:57-60.
Beaver Creek as place name, 32:121.
Beaver Creek Valley (Tex.), 4:105, 107.
Beaver Lake (Tex.), 13:2.
Beaver-tail cactus, 11:93.
Beaver, Tony, 3:120; 7:46; 20:3.
Beazley, Julia: articles, 3:185-189; 6:205-206; 13:182-183; 14:252-254; mentioned, 3:261; 6:241; 13:337; 14:284.
Becerra: Creek, 17:59, 61; Ranch, 17:60.
"*Becerrero, El*," with music, 9:120.
Beck, "Grandma" (Killeen, Tex.), 31:37.
Beck, Earl C., 27:33 f., 65.
Becker, Hanna Teubner, 30:264.
Beckett, Tom, 29:48.
Beckham County, Okla., 18:4; 27:181.
Beckwith, Martha W., 8:168; 34:145.
Bed wetting: remedies for, 8:23; 19:24; 26:260; 30:251; preventative of, 13:147; 26:231; superstition about, 13:159; 26:238.
Bedbugs, 30:5 f.
Bedias Creek as place name, 13:28; 32:131.
Bedichek, Roy: articles, 25:18-39; 26:295-314 (reprint); 27:105-112; mentioned, 15:148; 23:9; 25:254; 27:201; 30:6, 28; 33:7, 10 f.
Bedichek, Mrs. Roy, 25:134.
Bee(s), 5:10, 21, 26, 48; 10:128-130; 18:151; 19:154; tree, 5:107-108; 18:98-102; 26:200; wax, 7:63; 10:83; and Strap Buckner (tale), 10:128-129.
Bee Caves, Tex., 36:45.
Bee County, Tex., 7:27; 21:52; place name, 31:76.
Bee Dee Stream as place name, 32:126.
Bee martin, 7:37.
Bee Stream as place name, 32:121.
Beebe, William, 25:29.
Beech Stream as place name, 32:116.
Beecher, Dr. (Hamilton, Tex.), 30:250.

Beecher, Henry Ward, 23:286.
Beechey, F. W., 14:39-40.
Beef Hollow Stream as place name, 32:126.
Beef Stream as place name, 32:126.
"Been in the Pen So Long," with music, 5:161.
"Been on the Cholly So Long" (cited), 36:106.
"Been to de Gypsy to get mah fortune tole," 2:57.
Beer in folk curing, 8:28; 24:35.
Beeville, Tex., 3:37; 5:98; 7:176; 26:86.
"Before my face, honey and sugar," 13:244.
Begall (dic.), 23:25.
"Beggars of Ratcliffe Fair, The," 6:68.
Beggar's whine, Mexican, 9:114-115.
Begochidi (giant), 14:133-134.
"Behold a Stranger at the Door" (cited), 10:172.
Belafonte, Harry, 30:36 f.
Belario, Cecilio, 19:116.
Belching in folk belief, 30:258.
Belden, H. M., 4:page 12 of appendix; 6:205, 223, 232; 8:164 f.; 9:183; 10:150; 14:277; 25:48, 70, 72; 27:25 ff., 46-76 passim; 30:216; 36:118.
Belden, Lt., 9:10.
Beldin, F., 19:98.
Beliefs, folk; see Superstitions.
Bell (judge), 35:77.
Bell, George, 10:50-51.
Bell, Horace, 13:112.
Bell, Dr. John, 34:180, 182.
Bell, Josiah H., 8:132 f.
Bell, Peter, 23:23, 92, 136, 196.
"Bell, book, and candle"; see Bowl(s).
Bell County, Tex., 3:91, 208; 6:21 f., 225; 11:104; 13:178; 18:145; 23:50; 26:222; place names, 13:41; 31:88, 92 ff.
Bell Creek as place name, 32:115.
Bellamy, Edward, 33:144.
Bellamy, Tolstoy, 33:144.
Bellar, George, 25:177.
Belle, René, 36:133.
Bellini, 30:50.
Bells: evening, custom of ringing, 2:69; mysterious tolling of, 3:141-142; 28:124-125.
Bells, Tex., 23:128.
"Belly full, heart easy," 5:91.
Belly tank (dic.), 34:19.
Bellyache in horses, cure for, 8:31; 26:256.
Belmont, Ala., 19:21, 25.
Belton, Tex., 3:95, 229; 25:126; 31:34.
Beltran, José, 24:3.
Benalcazar, Sebastián de, 3:7.
Benavides, Fray Alonso de, 3:132 ff.
Benavides, Florencia, 19:116.
Benavides, Juan, 19:102.

Benavides, Margarito, 21:20, 22.
Benavides, Ysidore, 10:111.
Benavidez, Cesario, 17:66.
Benavidez, Paz, 17:73.
Benavido, Placido, 21:118.
Bench race (dic.), 34:25.
Bender, Tex., 17:82.
Benditas Animas, Arroyo de las, 3:210.
Bene (surveyor), 36:52.
Benedict, H. Y., 9:182.
Benedict, Ruth, 14:72.
Benefiel, Carl, 36:64.
Benham, P. D., 18:55.
Benito (Indian captive), 3:60-61.
Bennett, A. L.: articles, 31:34-40; 33:136-145; mentioned, 31:165; 33:198.
Bennett, Joseph L., 15:43; 21:119.
Bennett, Richard Dyer, 30:36.
Bennett, W. C., 14:207 ff.
Bennett Creek (Tex.), 14:200; 26:190.
Bennett Springs (Tex.), 28:161.
Bent, Col. (fur trader), 32:114.
Bent, A. C., 25:24, 38; 26:302.
Bent About Stream as place name, 32:126.
Bent Creek as place name, 32:114.
Bent eight (dic.), 34:21.
Benton, Thomas Hart, 23:100.
Benton, Wilbourne, 29:9, 13.
Bent's Fort, 6:131.
Beowulf, 21:7.
Beramendi family (early San Antonio, Tex.), 19:175 f., 184, 195.
Berceo (Spanish poet), 25:100, 102.
Berclair, Tex., 19:200.
Berg, N., 25:93.
Berkely, Mrs. B. F., 25:215.
"Berkshire Tragedy, The," 23:81.
Berlin: N. Y., 23:125; see *Llanos de Berlin.*
Bernal, Heraclio, 4:12-17; 21:6, 33; 28:100.
Bernard, Mrs. N. E., 10:134, 144.
Bernardo Plantation, 13:61.
Berrero, Emilio, 19:116.
Berrey, Lester V., 21:132.
Berries, wild, as pioneer food, 25:150.
Berry (McMullin County, Tex., rancher), 3:41-43; 26:98-100.
Berry, A. M., 21:125.
Berry, Jim, 8:25.
Berry Stream as place name, 32:118.
Bertillion, L. D.: articles, 3:77-78, 91-95, 230-233; 13:79-85; 18:149-150; mentioned, 3:261; 13:337; 18:222; 23:50; 25:47.
Besarrubia, José, 21:18.
Best, Tex., 7:47; 26:315.
Best girl (dic.), 2:32.
Bethany, Tex., 9:162.
"Better be a nettle in the side," 25:157.
"Betsy Brown," with music, 6:229.
Beulah Land (dic.), 19:8.

"Beulah Railway, The" (cited), 36:114.
Beveridge, Albert, 28:15.
"Beware, all fair maidens," 7:171.
Bewitchment, folk curing of, 24:26-27; see Witches.
Bexar, siege of, 15:35 f.
Bexar County, Tex., 5:112 ff.; 19:67, 195; 35:87; 36:16; place name in, 31:92; buried treasure in, 9:133-141.
Bexar District, 18:99.
Bexar and Nacogdoches Archives, 19:100, 105.
Bezoar stone; see Madstone.
Biard, J. M., 6:140.
Bible: as blood stopper, 8:31, 79; 30:251; 34:166; 35:15; as charm against Satan, 7:130; left-handed man referred to in, 29:76 ff.; use of in screw worm cure, 34:168-171; as source of Negro songs, 7:85-112 passim; use of in wart removal, 14:268; 34:165; in water witching, 13:176-181; see Biblical.
Bible in Spain, The, 18:xi-xii.
Biblical influence on Indian tale of dividing of waters, 22:105.
Bickerstaff, Ben, 33:122.
Bickler, Phillip, 6:141.
Bickler, Pinky, 14:256-259.
Bidding, mock, in Jamaica, 34:145-153.
Biddle, F. D., 25:125.
Biddle, Russell Sidney, 32:203.
Biddulph, John, 9:144.
Biedermann, Walter, 36:118.
Bienville Parish, La., 35:36.
Bier, O. G., 25:30.
Biesele, Rudolph Leopold, 36:59.
Big bash (dic.), 34:27.
Big Bend of Texas, 3:3, 214; 6:102-106; 7:145; 10:76; 11:90-92; 13:37, 39, 55-56, 61; 21:51; 25:205-216; 27:171-179; 28:106-127; 35:83-102; cactus in, 11:90; human hand in pictographs of, 4:89 ff.; Indian drawings in, 2:18 ff.; lost canyon of preserves buffalo herd, 3:238-241; Nigger Gold Mine of, 3:64-67; sheep introduced to, 15:95.
Big bucks (dic.), 34:13.
Big Dipper: as "Great Wagon," 9:49; as "Drinkin' Gou'd," 7:81-84.
Big drunk bean; see Mountain laurel.
"Big enough to go to the mill," 13:247.
"Big Feet" as Mexican name for Americans, 12:239.
Big go (dic.), 34:12, 27.
Big gun (dic.), 35:48.
Big Head Creek as place name, 32:126.
Big Hole Jack; see Bradley, Jack.
Big house (dic.), 35:48.
Big House Stream as place name, 32:125.
Big iron (dic.), 34:17, 26.
Big Lake, Tex., 7:47; 26:315; 27:166.
Big Lake oil field, 25:80-84; 26:341 ff.
"Big like a barrel and red ripe!," with

music, 25:123.
Big Lobo Wolf (Indian), 22:4-138 passim.
Big Lump School, 13:47.
"Big Red" (dust storm), 36:65.
Big Rich Mtns. (Tenn.), 7:81; 26:159.
"Big Rock Candy Mountain" (cited), 36:116.
Big rumper (dic.), 34:20.
Big Sandy, Tex., 13:273 ff.
Big Sandy Creek, 3:84 f.
Big Satan as place name, 32:115.
Big Sister Creek as place name, 32:115.
Big Spring, Tex., 7:151; 29:155.
"Big talker, little doer," 13:244.
Big Thicket of Texas: balladry of, 23:24 ff.; Elizabethan English in, 23:25; historical sketch of, 23:24-25; predominance of English surnames in, 23:25.
Big Trestle Stream as place name, 32:126.
Big Wienie (dic.), 34:26.
Bigelow, George, 16:139.
Bigfoot Wallace; see Wallace, Bigfoot.
Bighorn sheep, 25:40-41.
Biggs, Henry, 28:139.
Biliousness, cure for, 8:50.
Billingsley, Ben, 16:239.
Billingsley, Walter, 10:120.
"Billy Gelef," 5:171.
Billy the Kid, 9:7, 27; 13:61; 22:142; 24:2; 25:7; 27:97 ff.; 32:232; 33:70-80; 35:60.
Bilocation, miracle of, 3:132 ff.
Biloxi Creek as place name, 32:131.
Biloxi Indians, 7:30.
Binders (dic.), 34:16.
Binkley, William Campbell, 3:95; 21:131.
Birch Stream as place name, 32:116.
Birchfield, John, 25:177.
Bird, Jackson, 32:155.
Bird Creek as place name, 32:121.
Birds: cries of as bad luck sign, 7:62; hibernation of, 25:24-25; 26:303-304 (reprint); in sailors' superstitions, 4:60-61; songs of, their true function, 25:21; superstitions relating to, 7:32, 34 f.; 13:155-175 passim; 26:235-253 passim (reprint); 30:255-266 passim; of Texas, beliefs and superstitions relating to, 7:25-37; 26:283-289 (reprint); as weather signs, 5:113; 7:28-29, 32-34; see White bird; see names of birds.
"Birds for Sale" (game), 22:231.
Birdsall, John, 21:122.
"Birmingham Jail," with music, 23:149.
Birth control: Mexican belief concerning, 24:144; practiced by Tehuana Indians of Mexico, 12:140.
Birthmarks, how to make vanish, 8:50; 26:260.
Biscoches, 9:69.

Bishop, Merrill: article, 15:119-121; memtioned, 15:175.
Bishop, Rufe, 33:39, 42.
Bishop, T. Brigham, 23:145.
Bishop, Tex., 2:88.
Bisklitchin, John, 22:14-140 passim.
Bites; see Rattlesnake(s); Snake(s); Stings.
Bitter Stream as place name, 32:128.
Biznaga cactus, 9:95; 11:90, 93.
Black, C. C., 28:15.
Black, George, 18:59.
Black, Gus, 35:59.
Black, Ike, 19:173.
Black, William G., 34:171.
Black Bess (horse), 6:157.
Black brush as remedy, 8:53.
Black calabash, 22:164.
Black cat (dic.), 35:48.
Black Creek as place name, 32:120.
"Black Dem Boots," 1:31-32; cited, 1:36; see "Liza Jane."
"Black Gal, A," 7:104.
Black gum sprig as toothbrush, 13:153.
Black Hawk, 1:52.
Black Hills, S.D., 22:110; 33:84; 36:110; expedition to explore (1875), 9:89.
Black House Canyon, 6:74.
"Black Jack Davy," with music, 23:47-48.
Black Kettle: Indian chief, 16:102; legended mustang, 16:102-142.
Black King in Balkan ballad, 2:11.
Black magic; see Magic.
Black Mesa (N.M.), 14:114 ff.
Black Prince (legended horse), 16:370.
Black Stephen, 3:78.
"Black 'em boots an' make 'em shine," 1:31.
Black Thief (tale), 34:103-116.
Black Water Draw (Tex.), 16:74 ff.
Black and white magic, 25:195-199.
Blackaller, George, 8:25.
"Blackbird" (play-party song), 1:10, 35.
Blackbirds, 5:122; 7:25, 33 ff.; 26:283.
Blackburn, Bob, 19:173.
Blackburn, La., 31:24.
Blackfoot Indians, 30:12; creation story of, 29:192-200.
Blackfriars Bridge, 2:8, 10.
Blackhaw Creek as place name, 32:132.
Blackjack, Tex., as place name, 13:44.
"Blackjack Grove" (cited), 13:44.
Blackjack trees, 13:44; bark of as remedy, 8:35, 54; 13:234; 26:256.
Blackland Stream as place name, 32:119.
Blackleg, cure for, 8:31.
Blackman, Learner, 14:159.
Blackmon, A., 25:173.
Blacksmith: for a giant, 12:197; as "tire shrinker," 34:3-9.
Blackstone, Sir William, 30:95.
Blackwell, G. W., 19:133.

Blackwell, J. H., 19:133.
Blackwell, John William: article, 17:118-119; mentioned, 17:152.
Blacky carbon (dic.), 34:20.
Bladder trouble, remedies for, 8:31, 50, 68; 26:260.
Blade, Jean-Francois, 25:193.
Blaffer, R. L., 12:viii.
Blair, Hugh, 25:158.
Blair, John, 15:32, 34.
Blair, Sam, 16:406.
Blair, W. Frank, 25:24; 26:302.
Blair, Walter, 18:42; 20:5; 36:80.
Blake, Charles H., 25:38; 26:302.
Blake, R. B.: articles, 14:195-199; 15:27-41; mentioned, 14:284; 15:175.
Blake, Sallie E., 5:99.
Blakely, A. B., 25:176.
Blakeny, Mary, 25:182.
Blanca Flor (Satan's daughter), 12:61-66.
Blanca Ranch, 31:141.
Blanco Canyon (Tex.), 3:111; 16:74, 88; as place name, 6:75.
Blanco County, Tex., 6:147; 9:132; 31:88, 90; 36:37 f.
Blanco Mine, 9:132.
Blanco River, 3:24, 231; 9:132; 26:107.
Bland, Jane Cooper, 18:59.
Blaney (frontier preacher), 34:58.
Blanton (lawyer at Gonzales, Tex.), 10:121-122.
Blasig, Anne, 30:258.
Blatchley, W. S., 5:76.
Blau, Abram, 29:71, 83 ff.
Bleam, Harry, 30:87-88.
Bleeding: as remedy, 8:22, 31, 33, 36 ff., 41, 43 ff., 47, 63, 72, 80; remedies for, 8:31, 51, 79, 83; 30:251; 34:166; see Charm(s).
Bleeker, Silas, 19:171.
Bleeker, Valdimar, 19:171.
Blemishes on horses, remedy for, 8:31.
Blessing, Tex., 13:38, 71.
Blevins, Tom, 33:72.
Blind (dic.), 36:116.
Blind Butler; see Butler, M. B.
"Blind cow, I will lead you" (game), 22:232-233.
"Blinde Kuh, Ich fuehre dich"; see "Blind cow."
"Blind Man's Bluff," 17:148.
Blind pear, 11:92.
Blindness: associated with birds, 13:158; 26:238; curing of, 24:33, 56.
Bliss, Mrs. Jim, 33:112.
Blisters, remedy for, 8:18-19.
Blittersdorf, Louise von: article, 3:99-103; mentioned, 3:96, 262; see Moses, Louise von B.
Blitz Öl as remedy, 30:248.
Blizzard, severe, 8:122; 16:122 ff.
Bloat, remedy for, 8:31.
Blocker, Ab, 8:10, 14, 29; 13:v; 26:255;

Brownsville, Tex., 4:37; 7:27, 33; 21:28; 24:15, 27; 26:284; 36:16, 34.
Brownsville *Galaxy*, 19:69.
Brownwood, Tex., 27:103; 33:110.
Bruce, Robert, anecdote about, 15:59.
Bruhl, Gustav, 9:94.
Bruises, remedies for, 8:20, 58.
Brujería (dic.), 10:66; 25:196.
Brujo(a), 9:53; 10:63; 11:26; 12:115-117, 119-120; 24:16, 31 f.; 25:195-199; 25:195 ff.; see *Curanderos*; Witch; Wizard.
Brunner, Rev. A., 9:80.
Brunner, Theodore B.: article, 31:8-22; mentioned, 31:166.
Bruno, martyrdom of, 1:70.
Brunvand, Jan H.: article, 33:100-109; mentioned, 33:199, 36:123.
Brushy Creek (Tex.), 10:128.
Brushy Stream as place name, 32:118.
Bryan, Frank: articles, 16:359-372; 17: 1-25; mentioned, 16:419; 17:152.
Bryan, William Jennings, 22:224; 31:34; 36:84.
Bryant, Billy, 31:61.
Bryant, Edwin, 25:44.
Bryant, Harold C., 15:150.
Bryant, W. H., 31:71.
Bryarly, Rowland T., 32:128.
Bryson City, N.C., 30:37.
Bubble skirts (dic.), 34:18.
Bucero, corruption of *vaquero* (in song), 6:160.
Buchan, Peter, 35:66.
Buchanan, Mr. (Marshall, Tex.), 25:128.
Buchanan, Annie, 29:14-31.
Buchanan, James (plantation owner), 10: 33.
Buchanan, John, 20:14, 48.
Buchanan Lake, 17:40.
Buck, Johnny, 16:117.
Buck: Creek as place name, 32:121; Den as place name, 13:52; Snort as place name, 13:52, 71; see Buckhorn.
Buckeroo (dic.); see *Bucero*.
Bucket (dic.), 34:18.
Buckeye as remedy, 8:61 f., 65, 81; 13: 138; 14:267; 18:158; 26:274; 35:15.
Buckheister (cocker), 30:102.
Buckhorn Creek as place name, 32:121.
Buckhorn Saloon, 19:135.
Bucking; see Pitching; Rodeo.
"Bucking Bronco, The," with music, 7: 170-172.
Buckle and tongue, to make meet, 9:153.
Buckley, Bruce, 32:230.
Buckley, Eleanor Claire, 3:210, 216.
Buckner, Strap (Capt. Aylett C.), 3: 118 ff.; 5:82; 8:129-151; 9:13; 10:127-130.
Buckner's Creek, 3:119 f., 130; 8:133.
Buckra (dic.), 4:44; 6:119.

Bucks up (dic.), 34:15, 25.
"Buckskin" (foam on cooking cane juice), 17:27.
Bucksnag Creek as place name, 32:121.
Buckthorn as remedy, 8:45, 69; 26:258.
Buckwheat, cultivation and use of, 33: 176-180.
"Bud Ballew's Last Draw," 6:145.
Buda, Tex., 36:46.
Budnick, J., 21:125.
Buena Sevi, Mex., 30:222.
Buena Vista: ranch, 17:59 ff.; song about battle of, 7:160.
Buffalo, 7:21, 35; 9:10-11; 10:116; 16: 80-81, 84, 88, 130; 22:18-132 passim; hunting, 6:72, 79-83 (in Texas Panhandle); 6:154 (in Oklahoma); 18: 1 ff. (diet of hunters, skinning); bones, 6:79-80; "chips," 6:78-80; hides, 25: 16-17; 20:10 (processed at Wilcox, Penn.); lore and importance of to Indians, 5:126-136; fat used in rites, 6: 111-112; place names derived from, 6:81-83; as food, 5:132-133; milk, 18: 78; white, 5:130; hide and mane become meat, 22:49-50; how Kiowa-Apaches acquired, 22:39, 52; see Big Bend; see following entries.
Buffalo Bayou (Tex.), 6:134; 36:3.
Buffalo Bill, 9:11; 16:106; 21:49; 25:7; 33:51, 62.
Buffalo bird (cowbird), 7:35; 26:284.
Buffalo-Child-Long-Lance, Chief: article, 16:155-170; mentioned, 16:422.
Buffalo clover, legend of, 1:99.
Buffalo Creek as place name, 32:121, 135.
"Buffalo Dance Song," music only, 13: 289.
"Buffalo Gals" (cited), 7:18.
Buffalo Gap (Tex.) as place name, 13:2; 32:125.
Buffalo gourd for snakebite, 8:84.
Buffalo Heights, Tenn., 20:37.
"Buffalo Hunters, The," 6:198-202.
Buffalo Jack, 33:88.
Buffalo Jones, 6:80.
"Buffalo Skinners, The," 32:172-173; with music, 18:1, 5; cited, 6:201; origin of the song, 18:1-10.
"Buffalo Song, The," 18:2, 4.
Buffalo Springs Creek as place name, 32: 125.
Buffon, 25:42 f.
Buford, J. C., 7:151.
Bug-catcher (dic.), 34:18.
Bug out (dic.), 34:16, 23.
"Bug under the chip," 5:81.
Bugbee, Thomas S., 6:84.
Bugbee Canyon (Tex.) as place name, 6:84.
Buggess, Lake, 3:91.
Bugler Stream as place name, 32:126.

Burt, Prof. (Cornell University), 15:76.
Burton, Pinkie, 30:19.
Burton, Sir Richard F., 14:149; 25:30.
Burton, West (Wes) and family, 3:16, 64, 96, 214, 239; 6:121 ff.; 30:19.
"Bury Me Beneath the Willow," with music, 23:144.
"Bury Me Not on the Lone Prairie," 7: 147; see "Oh Bury."
"Bury-me-not" theme in the Southwest, 29:88-92.
Bushland, R. C., 34:167.
Bustamante, Gen., 14:199.
Bustillo, Domingo, 19:192.
"But de axe am sharp," 5:140.
"But wages are going to start," 12:231-232.
Butcher Knife Creek as place name, 13: 36, 72.
"Butcher's Boy, The," with music, 23:89.
Butches (news), 25:133.
Butler, Bill, 29:214.
Butler, "Blind"; see Butler, M .B.
Butler, Kay, 36:13.
Butler, M. B., 7:89; 26:169.
Butler, P. B., 6:160.
Butler, Reece, 22:152.
Butler, W. G., 6:160.
Butler, Penn., 20:27, 90.
"Butt his brains out on a stooping post oak," 13:246.
Butter: imitation called "Charlie Taylor," 30:171; as remedy, 8:26, 28, 72; in proverbial expressions, 5:83; 14: 152; see "Perfect butter."
Butter Bowl Mtns., 13:3.
Buttercup as remedy, 8:50, 59, 72; 26: 260, 263.

Buttercup Stream as place name, 32:118.
Butterfield, Jack C., 15:57; 19:60.
Butterfield Stage Route (Line), 13:24, 39; 35:94.
Butterfly(ies): in superstitions, 5:121, 123; 13:164; 26:243; in tale (races with thundercloud), 12:87; as weather sign, 2:93.
Buttermilk as remedy for freckles, 8:56.
Butternut Stream as place name, 32:118.
Button Stream as place name, 32:126.
Button willow, 18:157; 26:273.
"Buying" warts, 35:14.
Buzzard(s), 5:78, 122; 7:33 f., 112; 13: 159-160, 163, 171; 17:115-117; 19:76; 21:65-66; 26:12, 239, 242, 250, 284; see Vulture.
Buzzard, Betsy, 18:64, 74.
Buzzard Creek as place name, 32:121.
Buzzard Roost as place name, 13:2.
"Buzzard" troupes on Nevis Island, 32: 168-169.
"Bye, Bye, My Darling," with music, 23: 164.
Byers, Tex., 14:200; 26:190.
Byington, Robert H.: article, 30:140-155; mentioned, 30:291.
Byler, Ella, 5:97.
Byler, Frank, 5:104; 8:14, 48.
Byler, Mrs. R. F., 12:viii.
Bylina, the, 25:86 ff.
Byrd, James W.: articles, 33:157-163; 36: 3-13; mentioned, 33:199; 36:v, 153.
Byrd, John Henry, 18:57.
Byrd, William, 18:62.
Byrd Mine, 4:89.
Byrom, Bill, 30:204.
Byron's *Mazeppa*, 16:47.

C

"C. C. Rider," 5:179.
Cab freight (dic.), 35:46.
Caballada (dic.), 8:133; 10:115.
Caballero, Fernán, 6:9.
"*Caballo Fragado*," 4:39.
Cabbage (dic.), 13:245.
Cabbage, 18:182; 19:66 f.; leaves as remedy, 8:16.
Cabestros, 10:115.
Cabeza de Vaca, Nuñez, 3:8; 13:21-22; 15:60; 17:50; 25:30.
Cabin Stream as place name, 32:126.
Cabins: frontier Texas, 15:175; see Houses.
Cabras (Las) Ranch, 24:11-22 passim.
Cacahuate, Don (folk character), 12:1; 32:53-56.
Cachao, 1:40.
Cache Creek (Okla.), 6:73.

Cackle crate (dic.), 35:46.
Cactus, 9:97-98; 19:135; folk names for, 11:90-93; giant in Arizona, 9:97; origin of bloom, 8:99-101; see Prickly pear; see specific names.
Cactus Creek as place name, 32:118.
"*Cada loco con su tema*," 24:119.
"*Cada oveja con su pareja*," 24:119.
"*Cada pobrete lo que tiene mete*," 24:119.
Caddi Ayo, 1:39.
Caddo, Lake, 13:28; 36:3; legend of, 13:68.
Caddo Creek as place name, 32:131.
Cade, Edward W., 33:119.
Cadena, Jesús, 25:112.
"*Cádiz salada claridad*," 29:106.
Cadodachos country, 6:110.
Caffelt, Joe, 22:224.
Cage, Corrine, 35:100.

Cain, 36:96; banishment of, 1:92; to raise (dic.), 9:153.

Cain, Hoyd, 6:190; 26:136.

Caiphas (in folk drama), 11:67.

Cajeme, Mex., 11:17.

Cajun: family on Texas Coast (house described), 7:62 ff.; songs, 23:20 f.; superstitions, 31:108-117.

Cake in Greek wedding ceremonies, 36:142, 145.

Cake bread (dic.), 13:248.

Calabash, black, 22:164.

Calabaza (pumpkin), 9:103.

Calabacear (dic.), 12:220.

Calabazar (dic.), 12:220.

Calamity Creek as place name, 13:39, 72.

Calanche, Chano, 12:57-60.

Calaveras Creek, treasure on, 9:134-138.

Calcasieu River, 34:38.

Calculated (dic.), 2:32.

Calder, Alexander, 25:167.

Calderón, Fernando, 30:50, 52.

Caldwell, Catherine, 18:132.

Caldwell, John, 21:119.

Caldwell, Mable, 7:170.

Caldwell, Mrs. Seb F., 10:50.

Caldwell, Kans., 7:168.

Caldwell County, Tex., 3:103; 10:52; 17:87; 22:227; place names, 13:43, 62; 31:78.

Calf(ves): failure to suck as weather sign, 2:91; Indian disguised as, 25:249-250.

Calf Creek as place name, 32:121.

Calf-wheel (dic.), 7:51.

Calhoun (Indian agent), 35:84.

Calhoun, John W., 5:21.

California, 3:10, 96, 98; 19:73, 94, 100; 35:109 ff.; 36:62; entered by Spanish party in 1542 (?), 35:109-111; Indian pictographs in 2:24; place names, 13:35.

California Creek as place name, 32:126.

California pants, 4:54.

"Californian's Lament, The," 6:131.

Call: to cattle, cowboys', 2:36; and response in religious service, origin and nature of, 7:89; see Calls.

Callaghan Ranch, 17:61.

Callan, Austin: article, 3:169-171; mentioned, 3:261.

Callaway, Luke, 3:77.

Callaway, Morgan, Jr., 4:page 8 of appendix; 33:5.

Calleja, Gen., 28:96.

Callensburg, Penn., 20:6.

Caller at cowboy dances, 2:33; 4:55-57; 18:116.

Callihan, W. C., 3:189.

Callison, John J., 33:72.

Calls: dance, 2:34-35; 4:55-57; 7:9, 12 f.; to food, 6:135-136, 185.

Calomel as remedy, 8:36 f.

Calva shipping pen (Ariz.), 7:176.

Calvin, John, 14:155.

Calvinism, 35:26; frontier attitude toward, 14:155.

Camara, Rolo, 29:38.

Camargo, Mex., 10:112, 114.

"Cambric Shirt, The," 27:42-43; with music, 10:137; cited, 10:132; 27:65, 74.

Camellia leaf tea as remedy, 30:250.

Camden: Ark., 23:14; S. C., 19:67.

Cameron (Sec. of War), 20:16.

Cameron, Kenneth W., 25:158.

Cameron County, Tex., 3:43, 51; 4:35; 12:1; 19:99, 102; 22:64.

Cameron Ranch, 13:7.

Camp Allen (Tex.), 21:128.

Camp Duffau Stream as place name, 32:126.

Camp McDowell (Ariz.), 9:97.

Camp Meeting Stream as place name, 32:126.

Camp meetings, 10:169-175; 13:61, 194; 25:143; 35:19-33 passim; 36:73-80.

Camp Necessity (Tex.), 13:39-40, 72.

Camp Rice Stream as place name, 32:126.

Camp Stream as place name, 32:125.

Camp tales (dic.), 1:99.

Camp Wilkins (Penn.), 20:16 f.

Camp Wright (Penn.), 20:17.

Campa, A. L.: article, 14:249-250; mentioned, 11:50; 14:285; 28:33, 93, 105; 30:70, 75.

Campamocha (insect), 19:44.

Campbell (minister on Little Llano River), 19:166.

Campbell, Alexander, 14:168.

Campbell, Charles, 8:72.

Campbell, Mrs. Hawes, 5:27.

Campbell, Isaac, 21:119.

Campbell, Jim, 3:189.

Campbell, Judge (Texan), 15:69 f.

Campbell, Killis, 4:page 12 of appendix; 5:27; 7:44.

Campbell, Lock, 3:64 ff.; 30:267.

Campbell, Mahlon, 9:185.

Campbell, Marie, 28:29, 38.

Campbell, Olive, 23:291; 32:238.

Campbell, Tom, 31:34.

Campbell and Sharp, 5:10.

Campbellism debated, 14:166; 35:25.

Campbell's Bayou, 3:190.

Campeachy, Tex., 3:181.

Camphor gum as remedy, 8:22, 42, 58.

Camping by roadside in early East Texas, 17:7 ff.

Campo de la Rueda as place name, 13:8, 72.

Campo de Santos (dic.), 2:82.

Campos (Tonkawa Indian), 21:118.

Campos, Candelaria, 33:134.

Camps (dic.), 7:166.

Cerezo, Sebastián, 29:104.
Cerf, Bennett, 24:1; 33:94.
Cerrito de la Santa Cruz (Ojinaga, Mex.),
25:206 ff., 210; 27:171 ff.; 35:87.
Cerritos watering place, 4:34.
Cerro de la Plata, legend of, 3:8, 12.
Cerro del Hechizo (in Chisos Mtns.),
28:115.
Cervantes, 12:2.
Chabela, La Guera, in ballads, 25:112.
Chachalacas (birds), cry of a sign of
rain, 7:33; 26:284.
Chain tales; see Part II, Section 4, of
Analytical Index.
Chalk Draw as place name, 13:3.
Chalk Stream as place name, 32:128.
Chambers, Bud, 16:406.
Chambers, C. W., 13:274 ff.
Chambers, Cornelia: article, 13:106-110;
mentioned, 12:252; 13:337.
Chambers, Hickman, 13:275 f.
Chambers, John C., 20:19, 42, 44 f.
Chambers, Robert, 6:28-69 passim, 235.
Chambers, Whittaker, 27:101.
Chambers County, Tex., place names,
13:46; 31:91.
Chamber's Hill (Ft. Worth, Tex.),
18:131.
Champagne, anecdote about, 15:78.
Chamusco (dic.), 11:7.
Chance, Benjah, 31:88.
Chancellor, Tex., 27:168.
Chandler, Dr. (Hamilton, Tex.), 30:250.
Chandler, M. W. T., 28:106.
Chaney (treasure hunter), 3:24-26.
Chaney, Jim, 29:40.
Chaney, María, 29:37; see Valadez,
María.
Chanfrau, F. S., 18:55.
"Changa," Manuel la, 9:61; 26:149.
Channel Stream as place name, 32:119.
Channing, Ellery, 14:158.
Channing, Tex., 22:226.
Chants: in children's games, 22:233 ff.;
as cures, 35:12; of food vendors,
22:171; see Charm(s).
Chanty, sailors', 7:21.
Chanute, Kans., 20:44.
Chapala, Lake, 11:23.
Chaparral, 18:95; 19:76, 136.
Chaparral cactus, 11:92.
Chaparral cock; see Roadrunner.
Chaparro Creek as place name, 13:35, 72.
Chaparro Prieto Ranch, 16:177 f.; 26:110-
112.
Chapel Hill, Tex., 28:133.
Chapeónes, 14:215.
Chapin, E. H., 9:183.
Chapman (sheepherder), 15:94.
Chapote, 9:92.
Chapped hands, remedy for, 8:52.
Chappell, Louis W., 36:105 ff.
Chappell, William, 25:52; 30:31.

"Chappies" (word for children), 23:281.
Chapultepec, Mex., 18:162; defense of,
30:59-60.
Charahuen, Lake, 11:29.
Charamusca, 9:103.
Charbon (anthrax), 7:64; 8:30.
Charco (dic.), 13:10.
Charco (Goliad County, Tex.), 24:55.
Charco Seco, El (in El Paso, Tex.), 21:29,
30.
Charcoal: Indians' use of in paint, 2:23;
making, 25:141; 33:151-156; as rem-
edy, 35:16; vendors, 25:134-135;
33:151 ff.
Chariot, golden (in Negro tale), 19:29-
35.
Charivaris; see Shivarees.
Charles I, 30:101.
Charles II, 30:101.
Charles IV, 30:47, 50.
Charles V, 4:11; 9:106.
"Charles Giteau," with music, 23:118.
Charleston, S.C., 7:102.
"Charleston Gals" (cited), 7:102.
"Charley on the Square" (cited), 1:36.
"Charley over the River" (cited), 1:36.
"Charlie," 13:315.
"Charlie Taylor" (imitation butter),
30:171.
"Charlottes" (meaning shallots), 7:137.
Charm, the quality of in folktales, 24:1-
8.
Charm(s): agricultural, 8:28; 28:81-90
passim; for asthma, 8:50; for bleeding,
8:51, 60-61; 30:251; 34:166; 35:15;
blue stone as safeguard against mari-
tal infidelity, 30:183-184; for burns,
34:171, 173; burying hummingbird at
midnight, 24:117; cat's bones as,
13:174; 17:113; 26:253; for damp-
ness, 2:32, 89; for evil eye, 2:82-83;
for fits, 8:80-82; for good luck, 36:138;
for insect bites, 8:58; for labor pains,
8:58; in Mexican belief, 24:116-117;
for nail in foot, 8:60; in Negro life,
13:137 ff.; 28:48 ff.; 30:183-184; for
nose bleed, 8:60-61; 35:15; for pain,
8:61; for protecting horses against
theft, 30:253; relationship of to literary satire, 1:89-90; as remedies,
30:251-252; 35:12, 14, 16; for rheumatism, 8:65; for rotten teeth, 8:66;
for screw worms in cattle, 8:14, 45;
26:258 (reprint); 34:163, 166-171; for
smallpox, 8:66; for sneezing, 2:84; for
sore eyes, 8:67; for sore throat, 8:67;
for stammering, 8:67; for stye, 8:68;
for *susto* (fright), 2:83-84; for tapeworm, 8:69; for tears while peeling
onions, 8:69; for teething babies, 8:69;
threadwinding, 24:117; for thrush,
8:69; "Twelve Truths" as, 30:220; for
warts, 5:124-125; 8:14, 21, 70-72;

34:164-165; wishing, 13:164-165; weather, 2:88-89; 17:73; 19:89-93; see Bible.
Charro (dic.), 12:152.
Charts indicating buried treasure, 3:10, 18, 23, 36, 49, 183; see Treasure.
Chas, chas (words imitative of working), 10:93.
Chase, Richard, 32:214.
"Chase The Buffalo," with music, 17:99-100; see "Shoot the Buffalo."
Chastain, Joe, 17:82.
Chata (dic.), 6:7; 12:219.
Chato (Mayo storyteller), 11:7 ff.
"Chatsworth Wreck, The" (cited), 36:107.
Chaucer: his birth date, 30:30; his *Nonne Preestes Tale*, analogues of, 6:65-66; 14:82-84.
Chaunticleer, 6:65-66; 14:82-84.
Chavarín, El (character in folktale), 24:132-136.
Chávez, Cecilio, 12:224.
Chávez, Chico, 30:102.
Chávez, José Carlos, 28:109, 120 f.
Chávez, Luisa, 24:72.
Cheater (dic.), 18:203.
Cheater slicks (dic.), 34:15.
Checkup, Tex., as place name, 13:66.
Cheese: Mexican way of making, 12:188-189; the moon as, 12:16, 214; 34:49-52.
Cheetwah (Indian), 3:131-132.
Cheney, M. G., 31:59, 71.
Chernyshev, V. I., 25:90, 95.
Cherokee County, Tex., 15:38; as place name, 13:28; place names in, 13:42, 66; 31:81, 87.
Cherokee Creek as place name, 32:131.
Cherokee Heights, Tenn., 20:37.
Cherokee Indians, 1:51, 54; 3:197 f.; 13: 42, 298; 30:156, 159.
Cherokee Strip, 6:154, 157, 169; 33:35, 36-37.
Cherry (dic.), 34:15.
Cherry Grove, Penn., 20:54.
Cherry Stream as place name, 32:116.
Cherry tree bark as remedy, 8:54.
"Cherry Tree Carol" (cited), 27:24 (fold-out), 74.
Cheshire, Joseph Blunt, 28:17.
Cheshire cat, 5:82.
Chesshir, Sam, 18:109-110.
Chesterfield, Lord, 29:73.
"Chevy Chase" (cited), 30:33, 35.
"Chew your tobacco and spit your snuff," 18:117.
Chewing gum, folk varieties, 10:87; 12:187.
Chewing tobacco; see Tobacco.
Cheyenne, Wyo., 7:154.

Cheyenne and Arapahoe Territory, place names in, 6:90-97.
Cheyenne Indians, 3:165; 6:90; 8:74; 18:4; see Southern Cheyenne.
Chiaizaque, 4:75.
Chibcha Indian folktales, 4:68-79.
Chibchacum, 4:70, 72 ff.
Chicago: Ill., 18:55-56; University of, 22:4.
Chicane (dic.), 34:20.
Chicharrones, 9:95.
Chichimec Indians, 12:144 ff.
"Chick nor child," 5:82.
Chichimecatecle, 14:230 ff.
Chickadees, 7:34.
Chicken(s): anecdotes involving, 7:74; 18:77; as bad luck sign, 5:122; in *Nonne Preestes Tale*, 6:65-66; 14:82-84; sacrifice of, 2:8; as Satan's help-ers, 7:128-130; tales involving, 19:30; 21:81-83, 93 (theft of); 21:99-100; 26:64-66 (preachers' fondness for); used in folk curing, 8:62, 81; as weather sign, 5:113; see Cockfighting; Owls; Rooster.
"Chicken Dance Song," music only, 13:291.
Chicken gizzard as cure, 14:267.
"Chicken on a hillside picking up gravel," 18:117.
Chicken-ladder (dic.), 12:90.
Chicken pox, remedy for, 24:106.
"Chicken Reel," 18:115.
Chicken snake, 5:66, 76.
Chickering, Geraldine J., 27:33, 40, 62 ff.
"Chickimee Craney Crow" (game), 17:141-142.
Chicot County, Ark., 18:51.
Chicotes, 18:114.
Chié as Mexican thirst-quencher and re-storative, 9:89-90.
Chihuahua, Mex., 12:1, 224 f.; 14:207; 15:134; 25:155; roadrunner in, 15:150-151.
Chihuahua City, Mex., 10:77; 12:194.
Chihuahua dog as remedy for rheuma-tism, 8:13, 65.
Chihuahua-El Paso Expedition, 35:90.
Chihuahua Trail, 6:102; 13:24, 85; 35:84 ff.
Chilchipin, 9:91; see *Chiltipiquin*.
Chilcoyote, 9:87.
Child: eaten by father, 22:65-67; 27:77-78; offspring of the Devil, 9:54; reared by coyotes, 14:120-121; un-wanted, starved by father, 8:103; see Infant.
Child, Francis James, 4:4; 8:169; 14:276; 23:20, 34, 291; 25:57, 66, 70 ff.; 27:23 ff.; 30:57; 32:217 f., 224, 233-234, 237, 252; 35:70-71.
Child ballads, 10:131-168; 23:31-94; 35:120-121; analytical study of their oc-

currence in Middle West and Lower Mississippi Valley, 27:23-77; see Part I, Section 3, of *Analytical Index*.

Child-bearing and avoidance thereof, Mexican beliefs concerning, 24:114.

Childbirth, superstitions and remedies relating to, 8:40, 58; 19:21-28; 24:114; see Miscarriage; Moon.

Childe Roland, 14:153.

"Childe Waters" (cited), 27:24 (foldout), 74.

"Children of the Heavenly King" (cited), 10:172.

Children captured by Indians, 6:51-53.

Children's games; see Games; see names of games.

Children's songs; see Games; Rhymes; Songs; see titles and first lines of songs.

Childress, John, 18:150.

Childress, Tex., 18:2.

Childress County, Tex., place names, 13:52; 31:80.

Chili con carne, 9:76, 107, 109; 22:161, 168 ff.

Chili peppers: as remedy, 8:49, 52; 26:260; varieties of, 9:90-91, 99; 22:169.

Chili relleno, 9:76, 107.

Chile Queen Plaza in San Antonio, Tex., 22:168.

"Chile queens," 22:171; 25:119.

Chills and folk remedies for, 8:20, 49, 52; 18:157; 26:247.

Chiltipin Creek as place name, 13:3.

Chiltipiquin, 13:3; see *Chilchipin*.

Chimayo Mesa (N. M.), 14:116 f.

Chimeneas Ranch, legend about, 6:14-17.

Chiminigagua, 4:70, 72 ff.

Chimney Stream as place name, 32:126.

China (dishes) dropped by winged horse, 7:127-128.

China tree (wild china), using seeds of as beads, 18:160; 26:276.

China Stream as place name, 32:116.

Chinaberry tree: tying sick horse to as cure, 24:39; see China tree.

Chinati (formerly San José), Tex., 32:56.

Chinati: Mtns., 6:102, 104; 35:89; Peak, 6:104; 25:206.

Chindi, 15:143.

"Chinquapin eater" as meaning of "Nacogdoches," 13:40.

Chinquapin (Yonker Pin) Stream as place name, 13:40; 32:116.

Chip-chap-tiqulk, 14:67.

"*Chiquita, si me muriera*," 29:90.

Chirimoya, 9:87.

Chirino, Antonio, 15:29, 32.

"Chirp rubber," to (dic.), 34:16.

Chirrionera (snake in tale), 12:88 ff.

Chisholm, Jesse, 35:59-60.

Chisholm Trail, 6:142, 149; 13:4, 259; 19:172; 21:10; 26:150-151; 33:3; 35:59-60.

Chisos, origin and meaning of the word, 28:106-122.

Chisos Indians, 28:111.

Chisos Mtns., 2:19; 3:240; 19:98; 28:106-127.

Chisos Spring (Tex.), 28:113.

Chisum, Jim, 6:83.

Chisum, John S., 6:83; 13:50; 16:84; 19:107; 33:71 ff.; 35:59-60.

Chisum Canyon (Tex.) as place name, 6:83-84.

Chitlings (*menudo*), 22:170.

Chittenden, Larry, 13:40; 33:12 f., 82.

"Chivalrous Man-Eating Shark," 30:92.

Chivaree; see Shivarees.

Chivarros, 10:95.

Chiz[z]ler (dic.), 34:21.

Chloe's house (dic.), 13:249.

Chloroform in folk remedies, 8:32 f., 41.

Choctaw: Indian as informant, 8:123; ponies, 16:367.

Choctaw Creek (Tex.) as place name, 13:28; 32:131.

Chochiti Indians, 14:72.

Chocolate Bayou, 3:189 f.

Chocolate Creek as place name, 32:120.

Choke (obstructed throat) in horses, remedy for, 8:34.

Cholera: epidemic in Texas, 36:52; in animals and fowl, remedy for, 8:35; 26:256.

Cholla cactus, 11:93; 15:164; 26:291-292, 293.

Chontli, 19:51-52.

"Choose your partner, form a ring," 2:34; 26:186.

Chores, farm, 25:146-149.

Chotilapacquen (Nueces) River, 13:6.

Chourro sheep, 15:85.

Chrisman, Pat, 34:64.

Christ, 2:97; 4:62; asks poor man for food, 9:70-71; and disciples see dead dog, 13:97; in Freud's theory, 32:78, 91; in Jung's theory, 33:193 ff.; in Kickapoo Indian tale, 32:29-31; life of in Negro folk play, 17:126-140; in lore of Big Bend region of Texas, 27:171-179; as lost child or infant in Mexican folk plays, 9:72; 11:48-89; 36:16 f.; and man's garden, 14:239-240; as "St. Joseph of Christ," 14:208; in Spanish pageant, 36:96, 102; see Jesus; "*Posadas*."

Christi, W., 25:58, 70 f.

Christian Science as superstition, 1:72.

Christiansen, Reidar Th.: article, 28:18-44; mentioned, 27:128; 28:167.

Christmas: ball at Anson, Tex., 18:115; among German-Americans of Texas,

"Come in town on an easy walk-a," with
music, 7:116.
"Come light, go light," 13:243.
"Come listen to my tragedy," with music,
23:126-127.
"Come, my love, and go with me,"
13:315-316, 322-323.
Come off (dic.), 2:31 f.
"Come on, Death, why is you so slow?,"
7:88; 26:168 (reprint).
"Come on an' take some Johnny cake,"
6:26.
"Come Out Dat Kitchen, Liza," 2:47.
"Come, Philanders" (cited), 7:17.
"Come, Sinners, to the Gospel Feast,"
10:178-179.
Come the soft soap over (dic.), 18:73.
"Come, Thou Fount of ev'ry blessing,"
with music, 10:182.
"Come through by Brister's," 13:247.
"Come ti yi yoopee," 15:94.
"Come ye that Love the Lord" (cited),
10:176.
Comfort, Tex., 36:34, 37.
Coming West, The, 14:268.
"¿Comiste gallo?," 12:213.
Commerce, Tex., 36:11.
Commercials, radio singing, 25:115.
Common law marriage, folk designations
for, 13:248.
Communal theory of ballad origin, 8:166-
169.
Communion service in prison, 19:10-12.
"Como agua para chocolate," 12:213.
Como Creek as place name, 32:127.
"Como Dios quiere," 12:220.
"Como moscas a la miel," 24:119.
"Como quiera nace el maiz estando la
tierra en punto," 12:218.
"Como Los Rayos del Sol" (cited), 6:198.
"Como la romana de Tacho," 12:212.
Compañia de Manufacturas de Coahuila,
19:183.
Companions: tale of rich and poor, 12:29-
44; 21:35-42; 24:128-132; 26:46-49
(reprint); see Lying partnership.
"Company" (visitors), superstitions about,
5:116-117; 13:162-164; 26:242-243 (re-
print).
Comstock, John H., 31:46, 50.
Concan, Tex., 3:57; 13:46.
Concatana Creek as place name, 32:132.
Concepción, Tex. (Duval County), 24:49.
Concepción Mission, battle of, 19:193.
Conception by sunlight, 1:91.
Concho River, 3:8; 6:74; 13:2, 39; 14:174-
184; 15:119; 18:3, 98 ff.; 19:110, 161;
22:217.
Conclin, George, 21:132.
Concrete; see Cement.
Cone family (Wilson County, Tex.),
30:273.
Coneflower as remedy, 8:84-85.

Confederate songs, 6:141-144; 7:167; see
Civil War.
Confidence man, 35:140.
Confusion, folk similes denoting, 5:82 f.
Congal Claen (Caech), 34:74-101 passim.
Congaree River (S.C.), 7:140 ff.
Conger, W. E., 35:40 ff.
Congo snake (amphibian), 4:50.
Conjuring, 9:151-152; 13:139-141, 144;
17:113-114; 19:21 ff.; 31:108-113, 117;
see Brujos; Witchcraft; Wizards; Voo-
doo.
Connelly, Henry, 35:84.
Connolly, Charles, 36:109.
Connor, Seymour V., 35:56.
Conquistadors, 3:7, 223; 4:10, 68-71;
12:175 ff.; 19:97; horses of, 16:197-
226.
Conrad, H. L., 15:102.
Conservation, concern for in Gib Mor-
gan's tales, 20:4.
"Consolation Flowing Free," 7:23.
Constellations: as imagined and named by
Texas Mexicans, 8:91-92; 9:49-50; in
Navajo myth, 14:72-73; see Astron-
omy; Pleiades; Stars.
Constrictors (snakes), 5:68.
Contour (as musical term applied to folk
music), 32:251.
"Contrabando del Paso, El," 21:30;
26:152-155 (reprint).
Contrabandos (smugglers), 21:29-30.
Contreras, Calixto, 21:25.
Convict Creek as place name, 32:127.
Conway, Ellride, 19:169.
Conway County, Ark., 18:51.
Cook, David, 25:176.
Cook, E. V., 19:134.
Cook, Frederick A., 30:83.
Cook, Jack, 31:93-94.
Cook, James, 8:49; 25:42; 34:182.
Cook, Katherine, 7:161.
Cook, Lorene, 3:138.
Cook, Thomas, 5:10.
Cooke, Lewis P., 21:119.
Cooke County, Tex., 3:81 ff.; 18:216.
Cooking: campfire, 17:81; without recipe,
30:184.
Cooksey, Mr. (Sweetwater, Tex.), 33:123.
Cooled off (dic.), 2:35.
Coolidge, Calvin, 29:9; 30:90; anecdote
of the wasted eggs, 9:11.
Coon (dic.), 10:25; 13:245.
Coon (raccoon) in tales, 5:158; 9:165-
166; 10:25; 22:30.
Coon, Judy, 18:67-68, 70.
Coon, Tom, his courtship, 18:75.
"Coon-Can Game, The"; see "Po' Boy."
Coon Creek as place name, 32:121.
Cooper, Courtney Riley, 9:12.
Cooper, James (Alpine, Tex.), 28:117.
Cooper, James Fenimore, 28:19.
Cooper, Tom, 36:64.

Cooper Creek Cemetery, 18:130, 132.
Cooperation among pioneers, 17:26-32, 44 ff.; 26:195-202.
Cooter (dic.), 6:119.
Copano as place name, 13:27.
Coplas, 21:4; 28:96; 35:149 ff.
"Coplas del Payo," with music, 8:113.
Copper mines in Texas, lost, 3:72 ff., 77.
Copper as thirst alleviator, 8:18.
Copperas Grove as place name, 13:46, 72.
Copperas pants, 13:46.
Copperas Stream as place name, 32:128.
Copperhead, 4:50; 5:75; as rattlesnake's "pilot," 4:49.
Corazon (horse), 16:253-268.
Cordova, Gabriel: article, 25:195-199; mentioned, 25:254; 27:143.
Cordova, Vicente, 15:32 f., 35.
Cordova Rebellion, 15:35.
Cordova's Island (El Paso, Tex.), 21:29-30; 26:153.
Corelli, Marie, 34:175.
Coreopsi, 12:201.
Corley, Viola Fountaine, 5:79.
Corn, 19:36, 44, 66 f.; 22:115 ff.; 26:275; face powder made from, 18:160; 26:275-276; first crop in Texas, 3:236-237; in folk expressions, 13:247; as remedy, 8:40, 72; superstition about planting, 13:172.
Corn binder (dic.), 35:47.
Corn cob, 8:33, 47; 12:88.
Corn dance, 13:280-283, 289; 14:106.
"Corn Dance Song," music only, 13:289.
Corn dodger, to have the (dic.), 1:45.
Corn dodgers, 1:45; 18:21.
Corn Hill as place name, 13:4.
Corn maiden, 14:106, 114.
Corn meal as remedy, 8:12, 55, 61.
Corn-sheller, 13:224.
Corn shucks as weather sign, 2:94.
Corn starch, 13:223.
Corn Stream as place name, 32:118.
Corn thief (man's neighbor caught stealing from his crib), 7:78.
"Corn whiskey" (cited), 7:153; see "Rye Whiskey."
Cornbread; see "Yaller bread."
Corner, William, 15:10.
Corominas, Juan, 30:284.
Coronado Expedition, 3:8 f., 78, 98; 9:132; 13:18 f.; 15:60.
Coronado's Children, 15:6; 22:150; 30:12, 18-19, 23.
Corpse sits upright in coffin, 12:114; 24:95.
Corpus Christi, Tex., 3:14, 184, 210; 4:31; 5:96-97, 104; 6:23; 10:95, 112, 114-115, 118; 16:27; 18:133, 137 ff., 200; 19:57, 98, 126, 201; 22:157, 162; 24:13, 20 f., 25; 26:124 ff., 322; 27:138; 29:223; 36:35.
Corpus Christi *Caller*, 19:127.

"Corpus Christi Carol," 30:32.
Corral (village in Mexico), 6:5.
Corral de aventura (trap for mustangs), 16:39.
Corral Stream as place name, 32:123.
Corrales de espiar (spy pens for catching mustangs), 16:41.
Corrals, kinds of and requirements for good, 33:34-35.
Corre camino (roadrunner), 15:146; as guide for lost travelers, 15:169-170; see Roadrunner.
Correas, Maestro, 30:283.
Correr-el-gallo (horseback sport), 16:288-290.
Correr del paisano (roadrunner), 10:5.
Corri, Henry, 21:117, 124.
Corrida (crew of *vaqueros*), 9:49; 18:105 ff.
Corrido(s), 9:59; 21:1-34; 22:176; 25:87, 100, 113; 26:143-158; bury-me-not theme in, 29:88-92; concerning railroads, 29:132-135; contrasted with the *romance*, 21:3-4; 29:108-111; contrasted with *sones*, 35:154; dealing with Mexican immigrants, 12:221 ff.; as folksong form, 21:3-5; method of delivery, 21:32-33; origin of along lower Rio Grande Valley, 28:103-104; in relation to history, 30:62-68; rise and decline of in Mexico, 28:91-105; significance of Mexican Revolution in popularizing, 28:101-102; see the following titles.
"Corrido del Capitan Jol [Hall]," with music, 21:16, 19-22.
"Corrido de la Emigración," 12:234.
"Corrido de Gregorio Cortez," 27:22.
"Corrido de heraclio Bernal," with music, 21:7-9.
"Corrido de Kansas," with music, 21:10-12; 26:150-152 (reprint); cited, 28:103 f.; 29:92.
"Corrido Norteño, El," 28:99.
"Corrido de los Pronunciados," with music, 21:16, 17-19.
"Corrido de Rosita Alvirez," 25:113-114.
"Corrido de Texas," 12:227-228; 26:157-158 (reprint).
Corsicana, Tex., 13:22, 42; 29:14 ff.; 31:64.
Cortes, Cecelia, 24:132.
Cortez, Señor (South Texas), 24:17.
Cortez, Gregorio, 16:342; 28:98; 30:26; life, legend, and song of, 27:3-22.
Cortez, Hernán, 1:58; 3:6 f., 234; 9:75, 91; 11:47; 12:248; 16:197 ff.; 19:60 f., 71, 97; 25:216; 28:91, 96.
Cortez, Mary, 25:176.
Cortez, Román, 27:4 ff.
Cortez, Santos, 4:39; 30:3-4.
Cortina, Juan N., 6:22; 28:104; 30:67, 101.

Cory, V. L., 8:63.
Coryell, Mr. (surveyor), 13:37.
Coryell County, Tex., 3:209; 6:216;
13:37, 57; 14:192; 29:157; 30:194 ff.;
Fox and Coon Hunter's Assn. of,
30:197-198, 201; murder ballad ori-
ginating in, 35:73-81; place names,
31:82; 88, 95.
Coryell Creek, 13:37, 72.
Cos, Gen., 3:16; 15:45 ff.; 26:87.
Cosby, Flint, 6:203.
Cosijoeza (Zapotec chief), 12:248.
Cosmetics, folk, 8:88; 10:87 f.; 12:184-
185; 18:160; see names of substances.
Costaleros (dic.), 36:29.
Cotera, Augustus C., 13:56.
Cotera Wells as place name, 13:55-57, 72.
Cotterill, R. S., 14:159.
Cotton, 19:67; 25:140-141; 26:276; chop-
ping, 10:45, 52; gins, 13:230; 36:45-
50; hauling to Mexico, 16:58-59;
picking, 36:46-47; as remedy, 8:50,
18:23-24; in sayings, 11:103; 13:244;
seed, uses of, 36:48; superstitions con-
cerning, 19:145-152; worm, 36:46.
Cotton, John, 7:7.
Cotton Mouth Creek as place name,
32:121.
Cotton Palace at Waco, Tex., 1:50.
Cotton patch license (dic.), 13:248.
Cotton Stream as place name, 13:3;
32:118.
Cottondale, Tex., 13:4.
Cottonwood: bark as dye, 18:161; 26:276;
leaf as headache remedy, 8:57; 26:262.
Cottonwood Stream as place name,
32:116.
Cottrell, Fred W., 36:107 ff.
Cotulla, Tex., 15:155; 21:52.
Cougar: names for and origin of name,
25:41-42; see Panther.
Coughs, remedies for, 8:53; 10:88; 26:247.
Coulter, J. M., 8:64.
Council Stream as place name, 32:126.
Counsels, three wise (tale), 11:9-47; 12:7-
10; 26:24-27 (reprint); 30:173-175.
Counting, tales involving, 21:83-84, 95-96.
Counting rhymes (jump-rope), 18:195-
197; 26:203-204 (reprint).
Counting souls (tale), 22:207-214; 25:245-
247.
Coup, counting, 22:85-89.
Couper, Fred, 10:134 ff., 149, 158, 166-
168.
Courtship, 32:154-155; among Mexicans,
2:79; 12:185, 219; superstitions con-
cerning, 5:117-119; 13:148-155; see
Marriage.
Courtwright, Jim, 27:99.
Cousey, George, 16:75.
Coushatta Indians: burial customs of,
18:136; see Alabama-Coushatta.
Coutant, C. W., 19:58.

Cove Stream as place name, 32:119.
Cow(s): gives bloody milk, 5:66-75; see
Cattle.
Cow Bayou as place name, 13:23, 72.
"Cow Cañon Quadrille" (cited), 9:33.
Cow-critter (dic.), 4:53.
Cow-crowd (dic.), 9:59.
Cow Head Road as place name, 13:22, 72.
Cow-horn: blowing a, 15:179; as hunting
horn, 35:6; as remedy, 8:21.
Cow horses: in branding cattle, 18:105 ff.;
colors of, 16:234-249; names of and
terms for, 16:234-249; 33:13 ff.; cures
for, 8:12 ff.; 16:234-249; tall tales
about, 19:45-56; see Cutting horse;
Rodeo.
Cow Puncher's Assn. of the Cherokee
Strip, 6:169.
Cow sucker (milk snake), 4:45.
Cowan, Jewell, 6:227.
Cowbird, 7:35; 15:150; 17:108; 26:284.
Cowboy(s): activities of at branding
roundup, 18:105-114; the American,
characteristics of, 33:26-38; of Arizona, 7:172 ff.; Cajun, on Bolivar's
Peninsula, Tex., 7:62-68; character of
compared with sheepmen's, 15:94;
code, 33:27-31, 39-50; dances, 2:31-
37; 4:53-58; 5:104-106, 110-111; 9:33;
18:115; 22:215-230; 26:183-189 (reprint); 33:110 ff.; dance calls, 18:115-
125; 26:186-189 (reprint); dress, 7:166
(once wore red ducking pants); 33:46
(hat); 33:46-47 (boots); fiction about,
33:31-33, 37; folk beliefs and lore of,
5:64-68; 6:90-97 passim; 8:121-123;
9:27-34, 48-62; 35:55-63; "graces"
spoken by, 33:23; humor and humor-
ists, 31:99-107; lingo, 33:12-25; love
letter, 19:71-73; the Mexican, 2:87,
91; 4:30 ff.; 6:7-22, 160; 8:86 ff.;
9:48-62; 21:9-10; as motion-picture or
television hero, 33:32, 51-69; 34:68-
69; 35:127-132; as non-hero, 33:60-62;
the Northwestern, his songs and
dances influenced by Texans, 4:53-58;
an old-time representative of the,
7:164-171; poets, 33:81-88; saddle,
33:15-16; songs, 1:3 ff.; 2:43-45; 4:53-
58; 6:154-204; 7:145-154; 9:118, 183;
26:131, 136; 33:3-9, 81-88; songs,
some characteristics of, 7:145-154;
split by barbed wire (jest), 30:176;
the Texas, 1:59; 4:41, 53; 6:72, 83-
86; tales told by, 35:55-63; at "Tournament" in Texas, 5:98; truck driver
an extension of the, 35:47-48; the
word, original meaning of in Texas,
10:109-111; work of, 33:12-50 passim;
see Horses; Sennitt, Georgie ("The
Lad"); Rodeo.
*Cowboy Songs and Other Frontier Bal-
lads*, 18:1; 33:6.

world, 14:68-69; as representative animal of the Southwest, 14:38-66; revises creation, 14:69-70; and the rock that grew, 22:71-72; as a scavenger, 14:55-56; sense of humor of, 14:50 ff.; Seton's eulogy of, 14:65-66; significance of, 14:6; slays meteors, 14:71; slays nine moons, 14:71; song of, 14:57-59, 85-92; span of life, 14:62; spelling of the word, 14:39-40; spread of the, 14:60; steals chickens, 14:54; steals *maguey* juice, 14:18-21; 26:39-42; stories about, charm in, 24:6; stories about, when told, 22:136 f., 140; tames the horse, 14:70-71; ties down the rays of the sun, 14:128; traps crow, 22:53-55; 26:4-5; tries to steal the sun, 22:73-74; as umpire in hand game, 22:19-22; as ventriloquist, 14:57; as a weather sign, 2:90, 99; weeps the first tears, 14:68; whips cactus spines with tail, 11:4, 92; why he has a black nose and black streaks on jaws, 14:120; why he has yellow patches behind his ears, 14:44; why his eyes are slanted, 14:41; and wildcat make each other ugly, 22:56; and yellowhammer, 22:60-61.

Coyote Creek as place name, 32:121, 124.
Coyote giving (dic.), 14:91.
Coyote prickly pear, 11:93.
Coyote Ranch (Texas-Mexican border), 12:201.
Coyote Ridge as place name, 13:2.
Coyote's candles (a cactus), 11:93.
"Coyote's Song, The" (poem), 14:58.
Coyotillo as poison, 9:91.
Cozzens, Samuel W., 9:180.
Crabapple, Tex., 4:104, 107.
Crabapple Stream as place name, 32:116.
Crabb, V. C., 6:84.
Cracker (poor farmer), 4:44; 7:32.
Craddock, John R.: articles, 2:31-37; 3:111-115, 135-137, 167-168; 6:184-191; 7:78; 26:100-105 (reprint); mentioned, 2:4; 3:261; 4:53, 55; 5:104; 6:174, 241; 7:183; 18:115 f.; 22:221; 26:131 ff.
Craigie, William A., 21:132.
Cramer (Illinois oilman), 20:51.
Cramps, folk cures for, 8:31 f., 53; 24:40; 35:15.
Cranberries (said to be found in Texas), 18:100.
Crane, Ichabod, 30:75.
Crane, Mrs. R. O., 13:48, 232.
Crane, T. F., 25:193.
Crane Canyon as place name, 13:2.
Crane and Fox tale, 25:8-9.
Cranes: sandhill, migration of as weather sign, 2:94; 7:33; screeching of, 19:72.
Cranfill, J. B., 17:80; 22:222.

Crank, Velma, 3:164.
Crate o' sand (dic.), 35:46.
Cravens, William, 34:53.
Crawfish lore, 21:65; 26:12.
Crawford, Mrs. W. W., 30:268.
Crayfish; see Crawfish.
"Crazy as a bat," 2:15.
Cream Level Stream as place name, 32:126.
Cream of tartar as remedy, 8:36.
Creasing mustangs, 16:16, 44-46.
Creasy, "Aunt," 19:21.
Creation: of Alabama-Coushatta Indians, 21:66; 26:14; of birds, 12:19; 26:36; of Blackfeet Indians, 29:192-200; of Grand Canyon, 14:128; of the horse, 14:131; of men, 22:18-20; of Mexican, 14:134; of Milky Way, 14:128; of Miwok Indians, 14:67; of Navajo Indians, 14:131 ff.; of night and day, 14:127-128; of oceans, 29:196; of Pueblo Indians, 14:132; of rivers and streams, 29:196-197; of seasons, 14:73; of sheep, 14:131; of stars, 14:72; of the sun, 14:72, 132; of white man's God, 14:133; of white men, 14:132; 29:198; of the world, 4:75-77; 6:109; 14:127-134; 21:65-66; 22:18-20; 26:12; 29:194-200.
Creaton, Mrs. John, 6:141.
Creek Indians, 19:86.

Creel, Dana, 23:179.
Creeper (dic.), 2:60.
Creeps (cattle disease), remedy for, 8:20, 36; 26:256.
Crego (man in song), 18:1-2, 5.
Cremony, John C., 22:150-152.
Creole folktales a blending of foreign and native elements, 4:68.
Creosote bush, 6:102; 26:258; as remedy, 8:30, 45, 68.
Crib (dic.), 6:26.
Crick in the neck, remedy for, 14:267.
Cricket, 5:123; 6:47-48; 12:vii; 13:155; 18:109; 26:76-77.

Crier (early South Texas settler), 3:38; 26:94.
Cries; see Cry.
Crimmins, Martin L.: article, 9:165-166; mentioned, 4:89; 8:65; 9:189; 11:107; 17:155.
Cripple, folk curing of a, 24:51-52.
Cripple Creek, Colo., 33:14.
Crispin (ballad hero), 25:114.
Cristiano (legended horse), 16:316-319.
Cristo: in church in Ojinaga, Mex., 27:172 ff.; see Part II, Section 8, of *Analytical Index*.
Crittenden, Robert, 19:180.
Crockery Stream as place name, 32:126.
Crocket, George, 11:107.
Crockett, David, 6:205; 13:52; 15:13, 16, 22 f., 43, 46, 49, 54 f., 58; 18:45, 63, 147-148; 19:134; 20:2 ff.; 21:49; 23: 243; 24:2; 25:156; 28:86; 30:59, 72 f.; 32:114, 165; 34:29; emulated by backwoods preachers, 35:28; National Forest, 31:8.
Crockett, "Sally Ann Thunder," 18:78.
Crockett, "Sister," 25:128.
Crockett, Rev. Tenny, 13:274.
Crockett, Tex., 28:134, 188.
Crockett Almanacs, listed, 18:63-64.
Crockett County, Tex., 8:157.
Crocodile attacks Sappina Wing, 18:69.
Crompton, John, 31:50 f.
Cromwell (oilman), 25:83-84; 26:345.
Crook, Alice M.: article, 12:184-189; mentioned, 12:253.
Crook, Gen. George, 9:96.
Crooked Stream as place name, 32:119.
Crosby, Bing, 32:173.
Crosby County, Tex., 3:111; 6:88 f.; 22:194, 199 f., 220; 26:100.
Crosbyton, Tex., 6:88 f.
Cross: in Indian pictographs, 2:22; in Mexican superstition, 24:114; sign of as charm, 8:103-106; 10:63-64; 12:24; 13:187; 14:237; 17:73; 30:252; see Crossroads.
Cross, Judge S. C., 32:117.
Cross-Bar Hotel (dic.), 30:97.
Cross-eyedness, folk simile about, 5:81.
Cross-fertilization jokes; see Part II, Section 9, of *Analytical Index*.
Cross Timbers, 18:150; 19:89.
Cross Timber Stream as place name, 32:116.
Crossell (Cross L) Ranch, 9:32 f.
"Crossell Waltz" (cited), 9:33.
Crossing over (dic.), 10:57, 59.
Crossroads, Tex., 28:139.
Crossroads in cure for fistula, 8:11.
Croton Creek, 3:78; as place name, 32:128.
Croton oil as remedy, 8:22, 37, 43.
Crouch (a water-witch), 13:179.

Croup, remedies for, 8:26, 52 f., 59; 14:267-268; 26:261; 35:15.
Crow(s), 6:69; 7:26, 30, 34, 110; 19:68; 22:22, 52 ff.; 26:4-5; build nest of barbed wire scraps, 36:62; as familiar spirit, 1:53-54; in Mexican superstition, 24:114; mysteriously gather when Seventh Book of Moses read, 30:255-256; reveal treasure, 15:128-129.
Crow Creek as place name, 32:121.
Crow Flat as place name, 13:2.
Crow Indians, 28:10.
Crowell, Thomas Y., 34:35.
Crowing hen, an epithet, 25:145.
Crowley, Daniel J., 34:126.
Crowsnest Creek as place name, 32:121.
Crucifixion, the, Negro sermon on, 19:11-18; 26:177-178 (reprint).
"Cruel Miller, The" (cited), 6:213.
"Cruel Mother, The" (cited), 25:55, 93; 27:24 (foldout), 74.
"Cruel War, The," with music, 23:271.
Crumb (dic.), 1:45.
Crumbed (oil-field dic.), 18:202.
Crumble-in (cornbread in sweet milk), 13:215.
Crumes, Molly, 16:394.
Crush, David P., 31:91.
Crush, Tex., as place name, 31:91.
Cruz, Mrs. P. O., 18:181.
Cruz, Ramon de la, 29:103.
Cruz, Santa Ana, 16:175; 26:109.
Cry: of mule driver ("Hi-lo !"), 24:8; see Street vendors.
Crystal Stream as place name, 32:128.
"*Cuando Dios lo quiera*," 2:99.
"*Cuando salimos pa' Kansas*," 21:11; 26:151.
"*Cuando uno quiere a una*," with music, 4:25-26.
"*Cuando ven el palo caído todos quieren hacer leña*," 24:119.
"*Cuando vino el alambre, vino el hambre*," 6:8.
"*Cuatro Palomitas Blancas*," with music, 9:121.
Cuba, 3:8; 7:176 f.
Cubanacan, palace of in Cuba, 3:8.
Cubbison, George, 20:27.
"*Cucaracha, La*," 4:20; 12:13; with music, 4:25-26; as song of marihuana smokers, 14:225-227; 26:30.
Cuchulainn, 34:79.
Cuckoo family of birds, 7:28-29; 26:286.
Cucumbers: as cosmetic, 8:56; planting, superstition about, 13:172; tales involving, 18:83-84; 20:87; 26:262.
Cuenca, Spain, 27:139.
Cuenta, Zapata, 9:72.
Cuernavaca, Mex., 1:99.
Cuero, Tex., 2:38, 43; 5:156; 13:23, 72, 148.

"Cynically smile the scoffers and say,"
6:146.
Cypress: trees, 18:126, 162; 26:277; wood
used in making drum, 13:277-278.

Cypress Bayou, 36:3.
Cypress Creek, 7:42; 28:7; as place name,
32:116 f.
Cypress Swamp (Del.), 14:160.

D 〜

"*Da y ten, y harás bien*," 24:119.
Daché, Lilly, 29:10.
"Daemon Lover, The," with music,
10:159-162; 23:56-58; cited, 10:135;
27:24 (foldout), 28 f., 61, 63 f., 75.
Daffan, Katie, 4:page 19 of appendix.
Dagger Flats as place name, 13:3.
Dagger Hollow (Tex.), 6:5.
Daggett, Mary, 8:156.
Dahlia cactus, 11:92.
Daily Texan, 25:81.
Dairs, Arthur Kyle, 10:138.
"Daisy" (song), 13:317.
Dakota Winter Counts, 2:23.
Dale, Edward Everett, 33:172.
Daley, Luke, 25:79; see Staley.
Dalhart, Tex., 36:62.
Dalhart, Vernon; see Slaughter, Marion
T.
Dallas, Tex., 13:22; 18:2, 146, 214-215;
19:160, 220 f.; 25:118; 28:52-68 pas-
sim; 35:11, 43; newspapers, 3:14 f.,
56; 17:120; 22:231.
Dallas County, Tex., 8:157; place name
in, 31:88.
Dalmatia, 36:40.
Dalrymple, James, 25:176.
Dalrymple, W. C., 3:98.
Dalton, Cornelius, 9:144.
Dalton, Emmett, 27:99, 101.
Dalton, Frank, 27:99, 102; 30:162.
Daly, Henry, 35:85, 96-97.
Daly, Richard C., 35:96-97.
"Dan Tucker"; see "Old Dan Tucker."
"Danced himself out of the church," 2:35.
Dancer, riddle about, 24:126.
Dances and dancing: calls, 9:228; 18:24,
115-125; 22:228, 230; 32:23-25; cowboy, 2:31-37; 4:53-58; 5:104-106, 109-
111; 7:9-12, 14, 18; 9:33; 17:78 ff.;
18:115-125; 19:33; 22:215-230; 26:183-
189 (reprint); 30:168-169; 33:110 ff.;
Gypsy and European Spanish, 29:93-
107; Indian, 5:128-129; 9:169, 172;
13:270-293; 14:106; 19:82-93; Mexican, 2:35, 77-78; 9:71, 73-75; 25:110-
112; 35:147-156; of mine workers at
Johannesburg, South Africa, 36:147-
152; Negro, 7:105; 17:16 ff.; pioneer,
13:43-44, 235-238; 17:45; 19:80; 25:
144-145; regarded as sinful, 23:110;
25:111, 207; square, 5:104-106, 109-

110; 7:9-12, 14, 18; 17:93; see Devil;
Fiddlers; Play-parties; see names of
dances.
"Dander riz up," 5:87; 18:69.
Dandridge, Tenn., 18:148-149.
Daniel (biblical) in folk drama, 11:84 ff.
"Daniel in the lion's den," 5:page 7 of
appendix.
Daniels, E. M., 29:83.
Daniels, Elijah, 25:177.
Daniels, Joseph, 21:123.
Dante's heaven and hell, 1:76.
Danville: Ill., 20:37; Ind., 36:9.
"*Dar atole con el dedo*," 24:120.
"*Dar gato por liebre*," 24:120.
Darby ram; see "Ram of Darby."
Darden, Mrs. F. A. D., 3:202.
Dark Canyon as place name, 32:120.
Dark Creek as place name, 32:120.
"Dark and gloomy there was a town,"
with music, 10:147.
Dark Valley Creek as place name, 32:120.
Darkness, primordial (in tales), 22:17-18,
20, 22, 25.
"Darling, I am growing bold [*sic*],"
7:147.
"Darling Nelly Gray" (cited), 7:18.
"Darling Russell, he has left us," 32:203.
Darnell, Col., 13:57.
Darnell, W. L., 8:133.
Darnley, Lord, 30:33.
Darrington Prison Farm, 19:9; 26:175.
Darter, W. A., 3:207.
Darwin, Charles, 25:29; 32:14.
Datil (a cactus), 9:92-93.
Daugherty, J. G., 25:173.
Daugherty, James R., 12:viii.
Daveko (Indian), 22:109 f., 141.
Davenport, Beulah, 6:199.
Davenport, John, 25:177; 28:107; 30:269.
David (biblical in folk drama), 11:63, 86.
David of Sassoun, 34:200-201.
Davidson, Bill, 6:81.
Davidson, Doctor (proper name), 3:83.
Davidson, Pete, 3:83.
Davidson Draw (Tex.) as place name,
6:81.
Davie, Maurice R., 32:103-105.
Davies, W. H., 25:115.
Davis, Anna Landrum, 5:93.
Davis, Arthur Kyle, 8:161; 10:138-168
passim; 25:48-73 passim; 32:64, 243 f.,
268.

Davis, Billie, 7:170.
Davis, C. T., 18:29.
Davis, Champ, 27:181, 186.
Davis, "Cyclone," 33:47.
Davis, Dee, 15:4.
Davis, Ed (rancher), 27:181.
Davis, Edgar B., 31:66 ff.
Davis, Gussie L., 33:167.
Davis, Hassie, 6:229.
Davis, I. J. , 9:153, 160-162.
Davis, James B., 18:147.
Davis, Jefferson, 6:143; 10:174.
Davis, Leita Reeder, 29:155.
Davis, Lydia, 29:161.
Davis, M. L., 30:102.
Davis, Mollie E. Moore, 2:3; 3:211 f.;
  13:16.
Davis, Oscar, 31:67.
Davis, Mrs. W. T., 23:241.
Davis Mtns., 2:19; 3:232, 238; 6:199; see
  Big Bend.
Davis Ranch (Texas-Mexican border),
  24:52.
Davis Ranch (Wheeler County, Tex.),
  27:181; 32:119.
"Davy Crockett," with music, 6:205-206;
  23:243-246.
Davy Crockett: Memorial (Crockett,
  Tex.), 23:243; National Forest, 31:8.
Dawn, Navajo prayer to, 15:143.
Dawson, Robert, 34:41.
Dawson, Thomas, 34:176.
Dawson County, Tex., place names,
  13:62; 31:80.
Day, Mr. (in anecdote), 15:75.
Day, Donald: articles, 18:89-104; 19:63-
  81; mentioned, 18:xii, 221; 19:vii,
  201 f.
Day, F. H. K., 15:32, 34.
Day, James M.: article, 34:37-49; men-
  tioned, 34:v, 243.
Day-counting by making notches, 22:126.
Day of the Dead, 24:18; 32:211 ff.
"Day oh, Day oh," 30:38.
Dayatt Ranch (Kans.), 16:118.
Daylight, creation of; see Darkness.
"Days of Forty-nine, The" (cited), 6:171.
"De blood come twinklin' down,"5:151.
"De cuatro pares de pantalones," 27:82.
"¿De donde vienes y para donde vas?"
  24:120.
"De la Sierra Morena," with music, 4:27-
  28.
"De las Tres Que Vienen Ai," with music,
  12:229.
"De old River Jurdan was so deep," 19:8.
"De one dat drap de crutch de bes' gits
  de mos' biscuits," 11:102-103.
"De pequeña centella grande hoguera,"
  12:218.
"De quickah death, de quickah heaben,"
  11:102.

"De spirit can sing," 5:137.
"De tal palo tal astilla," 24:120.
Dead resurrected; see Death; Ghosts;
  Resuscitation.
Dead Creek as place name, 32:120.
Dead Horse Canyon, 3:209; as place
  name, 13:26 f.
Dead Horse Stream as place name,
  32:126.
Dead Indian Creek (Okla.) as place
  name, 6:93-94.
Dead Man's: Canyon, 13:46; Crossing,
  13:45, 72; Hole, 13:46; Hollow, 13:44;
  Island, 13:46; Ranch, 13:45, 72.
Dead Nigger Creek as place name, 13:46.
Deadman Creek as place name, 32:115,
  126.
Deadwood, Dakota Territory, 30:74.
Deaf Smith County, Tex., place name,
  31:88.
Dean family (Texas Panhandle), 22:219-
  220.
Dean, Bob, 15:108.
Dean, Ira, 34:168.
"Dear Honey," with music, 23:168.
"Dearest one, do you remember," with
  music, 23:272-274.
Death: animals feign, 1:47-49; 17:115-
  117; 18:177-180; 25:230-235; -bed
  story, 14:168; bell, 3:141-142; flower
  of, 22:155-167; "Godmother," 12:76-
  77; 16:353-354; Mexican beliefs and
  customs pertaining to, 2:80-82; 18:129-
  136; 22:155-163; Negro attitude toward, 10:55 ff.; 13:130 ff.; omens of
  and superstitions concerning, 5:119-
  120; 7:26- 37 passim, 119-121; 10:55-
  57; 13:140, 160-162, 233; 17:118-119;
  22:155-167; 24:115; 26:240-242; the
  only friend of the poor (tale), 24:80-
  81; personified, 9:70-71; 12:76-77;
  16:353-354; sticks to a tree, 30:241-
  242; rising from, 12:2-4, 33, 60; 22:35,
  44, 94; see Day of the Dead; Funeral
  customs; Grave decoration; see Part
  II, Section 5, of Analytical Index.
"Death of Floyd Collins, The," 32:229-
  230.
"Death of Little Joe, The," with music,
  6:222.
De Aury; see Aury.
Deaver, J. M.: article, 7:42-44; mentioned, 7:5, 183.
De Avila; see Avila.
Debates concerning religion, 14:166; 28:
  139-140; 30:124-125; 35:24-26.
Debating societies, 32:162.
De Beauvoir, Simone, 32:182.
Decameron, The, 25:17.
DeCamp, David: article, 34:145-153;
  mentioned, 34:vi, 243.
Decatur, Tex., 14:259-260; 18:2; 28:13.

"Did you get justice or what you went after?," 30:95.
Didapper (pied-billed grebe), 7:36-37.
"Didn't He Ramble," with music, 5:157-158.
Diego, Juan, 12:221.
Dienst, Alex: articles, 3:208-209, 241-242; mentioned, 3:261.
Diesmero Ranch, 16:54.
Dietrich, Charles, 6:92.
Diez, J. A., 21:109.
"Diez Perritos, Los," 29:114.
Diez y seis; see Sixteenth of September.
Dignowity, Hartman: articles, 4:59-63; 6:98-101; mentioned, 4:115; 6:240 f.
Dillard, A. J., 25:175.
Dillard family (Uvalde County, Tex.) cattle brands, 25:180.
Dillingham, Dave, 17:81, 155; 18:34-35, 52; 25:136.
Dillingham, J. D., 23:238; 26:140.
Dillon, Myles: article, 34:103-116; mentioned, 34:vi, 74, 243-244.
Dilworth Spelling Book, 6:25, 71.
Dime for good luck, 35:14.
Dime Box, Tex., as place name, 13:53, 73; 31:94.
"Dime con quien andas y te diré quien eres," 24:120.
Dimmit County, Tex., 3:84.
Dimond, William, 9:184.
Dimple in chin as a sign, 13:172; 26:251 (reprint).
Dinero, Tex. (Live Oak County), 24:55.
Dinn, Albert, 3:34; 26:89 f.
Dinn, John, 13:26.
Dinner Stream as place name, 32:126.
Dinsmore, Silas, 21:130.
Diogenes, 36:130.
Dionne Quintuplets, 19:68.
Dionysus, 33:191.
"Dios los creó y ellos se juntan," 24:120.
"Dios te salve, valiente Zaragoza," 30:65.
"Dipped" (mixed-blooded), 13:248.
Dipper; see Big Dipper.
Diptheria, remedy for, 10:90.
Dirt-daubers in folk remedy, 8:54.
"Dirt show up de quickes' on de cleanes' cotton," 11:103.
Diseases, folk curing of; see Cures and curing; *Curanderos.*
Dishonesty, folk expressions concerning, 5:81-82.
Dishrag as cure for warts, 5:124; 8:21, 72; 14:193; 35:14.
Dismal Swamp (N. C.), 15:80.
Disney, Walt, 30:59.
Dissiway, Florence, 31:94.
"Distant stovewood am good stovewood," 11:103.
Distemper, remedies for, 8:21, 36; 26:248.
"Distressed Ship-carpenter, The" (cited), 10:159.

Ditmars, Raymond L., 8:126; 21:58 ff.; 25:30.
Dittmar, Otto, 4:103.
Dividing-the-dead folktale, 10:38-42; 22:207-214; 25:245-247; 29:169; 31:17-19.
Dividing waters theme, 3:211 ff., 217; 22:104-105; in Indian lore may pre-date contact with Europeans, 22:105.
Divination of husband by dream, 36:141-142.
Divining rod: for minerals and treasure, 3:45, 91, 100 f.; 6:5; 9:132; for oil, 9:45-46; for water, 13:176 ff., 233; 28:162.
Dix, Dorothy, 30:23.
Dix, John J., 16:26.
"Dixie" (cited), 10:122.
Dixie Creek as place name, 32:127.
Dixon, Billy, 6:82; 13:60-61; 18:3.
Dixon, Mo., 28:64.
Dixon Creek (Tex.) as place name, 6:82; 13:61.
Do-good-ativeness (dic.), 18:77.
Do it brown (dic.), 1:45.
"Do-si-do," origin of the phrase, 7:16.
"Do si do and around we go," 18:117-118.
Do a ton (dic.), 34:20.
Doak, C. C., 27:186.
Doak, John M., 8:21 f., 27, 38.
Doan, C. F., 13:58.
Doan's Crossing, store at, 13:58.
Dobbs, L. D., 25:175.
Dobell, Jack; see Duval, John C.
Dobie, Bertha McKee: articles, 3:137-141, 141-142, 143; 6:23-71; 7:135-136; 12:159-161, 162-174; 26:67-77, 117-118 (reprints); mentioned, 3:261; 4:9; 6:6, 24, 241; 7:6, 183; 12:253; 25:188; 30:5 f.; 31:15; 33:10 f.
Dobie, Ella Byler, 17:78.
Dobie, Elrich H., 4:30; 15:155; 33:9.
Dobie, J. Frank: articles (prefaces, head-notes), 1:v (reprint ed. of 1935); 2:1-2, 87-99; 3:iii-v, 3-12, 12-20, 24, 28-43, 43-49, 51-52, 52-57, 60-62, 64-67, 72, 78, 80-81, 84-85, 95-99, 99-100, 111, 118-120, 130-131, 137, 141-142, 153-154, 163-164, 171-176, 179-180, 197-198, 200, 202, 204, 209-217, 230-231, 233, 238-241, 242-243; 4:7-9, 30-43, 53, 64; 5:3-4, 93-103; 4:page 1 of appendix; 6:5-6, 121-183, 238; 7:5-6, 69-77, 155-180; 8:5-7; 9:v; 10:5-7, 109-123; 12:v-viii, 194-200; 13:[v], 1-78, 190-191; 14:5-7, 104; 15:146-174; 16:171-183, 234-249, 291-303, 403-413; 18:vii-xii, 1-10; 19:36-41; 21:43-64; 22:142-154; 24:1-8; 25:1-17; 26:83-87, 87-89, 89-90, 90-94, 95-96, 96-97, 98-100, 105-112, 143-147, 289-295 (reprints); 27:113-117; 28:3-17; 30:3-29;

Duval, John C., 4:46; 6:29, 47-48; 15:10; 26:76; 28:vii; 29:10, 13; 30:287-288, 289; 31:50.
Duval County, Tex., 4:8; 10:94; 13:6, 10, 45; 16:411.
Dwarfs, tribe of in Mexico, 11:16, 23-25.
Dwyer, Thomas A.: article, 16:47-60; mentioned, 16:420.
Dye, Caroline (Negro fortune-teller), 2:57.
Dye, Henry, 31:78.
Dye pot, 13:222.
Dyer, J. O., 3:92, 180.
Dyes, folk, 18:161; 26:276-277 (reprint); see names of dyeing substances.
Dying; see Death.

"Dying Cowboy, The," 6:173, 181-183; 7:147; 29:88-92; origins of, 6:173 ff.; 9:183-184.
"Dying Girl's Message," with music, 23:176.
"Dying Hobo at the Western Water Tank, The," 2:40-41; cited, 36:116.
"Dying Ranger, The" (cited), 6:150; 7:167.
Dykes, Carrie, 19:21-28.
Dykstra, W., 25:192.
Dysentery, remedies for, 8:54, 70; see Diarrhea.
Dyspepsia, remedies for, 8:83; 10:86; see Stomach.

E

"Each prophet comes presently," 25:157.
Eagle, 5:158; 6:40, 48; 7:112; 18:65; 22:22, 40, 47, 71; Aztec knights of the, 12:159.
Eagle Creek as place name, 32:121.
Eagle Lake (Tex.), 2:3; legend of, 3:201-204.
Eagle Lake Bayou, 3:202.
Eagle Mtns. (Tex.), 10:75 f.; 13:2.
Eagle Pass, Tex., 13:9, 22, 73.
Eagle Springs (Tex.), 3:98; 10:75 ff.
Ealy, Mrs. T. F., 33:70.
Ear wax as healing ointment, 8:55, 72.
Earache, remedies for, 8:54-55, 83.
Earmarking cattle, 17:60; 18:108; 19:106-116.
Earhart (cowman), 13:43.
"Earl Brand," 27:60; cited, 27:24 (fold-out), 29, 60, 74.
Earle, Thomas, 21:127.
"Early, Early in the Spring," with music, 14:271, 275 ff.
Early, Gen. Jubal, 25:3.
"Early to bed, early to rise," 13:243.
Earnest, D. C.: article, 16:414-416; mentioned, 16:420.
Earp, Wyatt, 9:13, 27.
Earth, creation of; see Creation.
Earthquake religion (dic.), 10:170.
Easley, V. O., 31:90.
Eason, Mrs. Dock, 23:86, 168, 170, 269.
East, Mattie Carter, 23:128; 26:141-142; 30:213.
East Bay (Texas Coast), 3:146.
East Mont Cemetery, 18:135.
East Texas, 3:3, 54; 7:80; 16:359 ff.; 23:13 ff.; 36:40; "blues" from, 2:64; colloquialisms in, 13:245-249; early folkways of, 17:1-39; horses in, 16:367 ff.; hunting in, 35:3-10; drawl or "whang," 23:27; silver ingots buried

in, 34:37-49; see Big Thicket.
Easter: "Black," 36:61 ff.; as celebrated by Texas German-Americans, 2:71-72; 36:57; origin of the word, 1:65; see Holy Week.
Easter Monday, 2:68, 71.
Easterling, Bill, 13:113.
Eastland, Tex., 7:47; 26:315; 29:8-10.
Eastland County, Tex., 22:220; 29:8; place names, 13:47; 31:85, 89.
"Eat the meat and leave the skin," 33:23.
"Eat When Yo're Hungry," 5:169; 26:165.
"Eating his way to the wool-sack," 30:96.
Eau Claire, Penn., 20:27, 32, 90.
Ebony tree of Mexico, 9:93.
Ecatepec, Mex., 30:48.
"Echó mano a la pistola," 25:114.
Echoaciously (dic.), 18:72.
Eckert, Flora: article, 3:163-167; mentioned, 3:261.
Eckhart, Meister, 33:192.
Ecks (revivalist), 30:82.
Eckstein, Gustav, 25:26; 26:305.
Eckstrom, Fannie H., 8:161.
Eclipse: the first, 14:128; Mexican beliefs connected with, 24:115.
Economic: determinism, relation of folk metaphor to a theory of, 2:14; interpretation of Negro songs, 5:pages 3-13 of appendix.
Ector County, Tex., place name, 31:91.
Eczema, remedy for, 24:107.
Edal (dic.), 4:36.
Eddins, A. W.: articles, 1:44-46, 47-49; 2:50-51; 3:236-237, 237-238; 9:153-164; 13:86-105, 239-244; 26:50-55, 218-219 (reprints); mentioned, 2:4; 3:261; 4:page 21 of appendix; 9:189;

10:10, 38 f.; 12:251; 13:338.
Eddy, Mary O., 5:5, 16; 6:29, 223 f.; 27:
51.
Eddy Stream as place name, 32:119.
Edgar, James, 13:39.
Edgar's Boneyard (Tex.), 13:39, 73.
Edison, Thomas, 34:13.
Edmonds, John E., 9:144.
Edmondson, John, 21:123.
"Edward": a Texas variant, 23:59-63;
26: 137-138 (reprint); cited, 25:63;
27:24 (foldout), 29, 35, 74; 30:31.
Edward, David B., 3:72.
Edwards, B. W., 8:141.
Edwards, Clarence E., 22:226.
Edwards, Hayden, 3:92; 13:40; 15:34.
Edwards, Jonathan, 14:158; 34:51; 36:73.
Edwards, Monroe, 18:93.
Edwards, W. S., 21:54.
Edwards County, Tex., place name, 31:
75.
Education in the Texas hill country, 17:
42-43.
Eel, lamprey, 4:51.
"Ef yore gal gits mad an' tries to bully
you-u-u," 2:61.
"Efectos de las Crisis," 12:232.
Effigies, 1:84 f.; 12:115-117; 24:88-89; 25:
196; see Santos.
Egbert (Pennsylvania oilman), 20:51.
Eger, C. W., 19:198.
Egg-Nog Branch as place name, 13:41,
73.
Eggnog from eagle eggs, 18:78.
Eggs in folk remedies and superstition,
2:83; 8:34, 48, 51, 54, 65, 76-77; 9:
58; 10:84-85; 13:148; 14:268; 24:55-
56, 107-109; 26:231; 35:12, 14.
Egypt, Tex., as place name, 13:51.
Egypt as place of origin of Tehuana In-
dians, 12:138-139.
Egyptian civilization, effect of climate on,
1:71.
Eifler, Gus K.: article, 34:215-217; men-
tioned, 34:vi, 244.
"Eight hands form a ring," 18:119-120.
Eightmile Coleto Creek as place name,
32:120.
Eire, Penn., 33:102.
Eisenhower, Dwight D., 33:162; 36:85.
Ekchuah (Maya god of peddlers), 22:164.
Ejemplos (songs), 21:4.
"El Año del '63," 8:110.
"El día diecinueve de Marzo," 4:39-41.
"El día diez de diciembre," 21:17-19.
"El diecisiete de Agosto," 21:30; 26:153.
"El diez y seis de diciembre," 21:21-22.
El Dorado, 3:6-11 passim.
"El es como el carrizo, no tiene corazón,"
12:218.
"El flojo y el mezquino dos veces andan
el camino," 24:120.
"El hábito no hace al monje," 24:120.

"El hombre pone y Dios dispone," 24:
120.
"El lunes me picó un piojo," 29:119.
"El muerto al poso," 22:155.
"El pan ajeno hace al hijo bueno," 24:
120.
"El pan para los muchachos," 12:27; 32:
31.
El Paso, Tex., 3:66, 68, 131, 231, 236;
4:89; 9:96; 10:71-81 passim; 13:3, 54,
112, 120-129; 18:4, 129; 21:29-30; 26:
118, 152-155; 30:28, 99, 114; 32:60 ff.;
33:76 f.; 35:83-102 passim; 36:16.
El Paso County, Tex., gold mine in, 2:3.
El Paso Del Norte, Mex., 7:117.
El Paso Road, 18:100.
El Paso School of Mines, 18:x.
"El Pecado se dice pero el pecador no,"
24:121.
"El piojo y la pulga se quieren casar,"
29:118.
"El primer pensamiento es el mejor," 24:
121.
"El que boca tiene a Roma va," 24:121.
"El que es buey hasta la correa lame,"
12:213.
"El que la hace la paga," 24:121.
"El que mucho abarca, poco aprieta," 12:
216.
"El que nace para guaje nunca llega a
ser jícara," 12:217.
"El que nace para tamal del cielo le caen
las hojas," 12:217.
"El que no habla nadie lo oye," 24:121.
"El que no quiere ruido que no críe co-
chinos," 24:121.
"El que no se arriesga no pasa la mar,"
24:121.
"El que para tonto nace hasta guaje no
para," 24:121.
"El que por su cuenta es buey hasta la
coyunda lame," 24:121.
"El que por su gusto es buey hasta la
coyunda lame," 12:213.
"El que se levanta tarde ni oye misa ni
compra carne," 12:217.
"El que solo vive solo muere," 24:121.
"El que tiene buen voto se hinca a cual-
quier santo," 24:121.
El Sauce Ranch; see Sauce.
Eladio, Col., 21:25.
Elam, Bessie, 31:40.
Elberta, Lake, 14:262.
Elbow Stream as place name, 32:126.
"Eldah Came To My House," 7:110.
Elder, Trip, 32:118.
Elderberry, 9:96; beads for teething, 18:
158; 26:274.
Eldorado, Tex., 21:55.
Eldridge, Eloise, 18:132.
Eleven Slash Eleven Ranch, song of, 7:
178.
Elfer, Maurice, 15:54.

"Elfin Knight, The," 27:42, 65; with music, 10:137; cited, 10:132; 27:24 (foldout), 29, 42 ff., 65, 74.
Elgin, Robert Morris, 31:78.
Elgin, Tex., 7:94; 13:65-66, 73; 26:172; 28:133.
Elguézabel, Juan Bautista, 28:120.
Eliade, Mircea, 36:41, 43, 94 f., 102; his contribution to the study of myth, 32: 80; 34:219-241.
Elijah, 19:14; 33:189.
Eliot, Lynn, 22:225.
Eliot, T. S., 32:214; 34:20.
Elisha, 24:70.
Elizabeth I, 34:158.
Elizabeth II, 34:141.
Elk, 22:18, 31, 54, 125.
Elk County, Penn., 20:10.
Elkhart Creek as place name, 32:132.
Elliot, Charles Loring, 18:57.
Elliott, Raymond, 29:156.
Ellis family (Menard, Tex.), 28:10.
Ellis, Mrs. A. C., 19:136-168 passim.
Ellis, Annie Laurie, 6:173.
Ellis, Frank, 3:91.
Ellis, Fred, Sr., 32:127.
Ellis, Mrs. H. J., 21:56.
Ellis, Havelock, 34:207.
Ellis, S. H., 16:44 f.
Ellis County, Tex., 8:157.
Ellsworth, Kans., 16:410.
Elm; see Slippery elm.
Elm Fork of Clear Fork of the Brazos, 18:99 ff.
Elm Pass (near Bandera, Tex.), 14:238.
Elm Stream as place name, 32:116.
Elysium, 1:68.
Embrujada (dic.), 10:85.
Emerick, Albert G., 7:160.
Emerson, Ralph Waldo, 4:64; 32:112; 33:5; and folk diction, 25:152-159.
Emerson, Tex., 13:54.
Emigrants; see Immigrants.
"Emigrant's Farewell, An," 12:222, 224.
Emlenton, Penn., 20:7.
Emma, "Aunt," old-time mammy, 6:119-134.
Emmons, Martha: articles, 7:119-134; 10:55-61; 11:94-100; 13:130-136; mentioned, 6:5; 7:183; 10:6, 186, 188; 11: 107 f.; 12:251; 13:338.
Emory, Grant, 20:31, 34.
Emory, W. H., 10:5; 28:120.
Emory, Mt. (Chisos Mtns.), 28:114 f.
Empalme, Mex., 11:5.
Emrich, Duncan, 30:194.
"*En boca cerrada no entran moscas*," 12: 215.
"*En el mil nueve cientos y diez*," with music, 4:36-38.
"*En este tiempo fatal*," 12:232-233.
"*En la tardanza está el peligro*," 24:121.
"*En martes ni te cases ni te embarques*,"

24:121.
Enchanted Rock (Llano County, Tex.), 1:99; 3:153-156.
Enchantment: of city, 3:8; 12:174, 246-248; 13:185-189; of person in sleep, 12:22-23.
Encinal Creek as place name, 13:23.
Encinal del Perdido, plain of as place name, 13:8-9, 73.
Enchiladas, 7:165; 9:76, 109; 22:161.
Encino Ranch, 9:48.
Enderle, B. L., 4:103.
Enfare (wedding meal); see Infare.
Engagements: among Mexicans, 2:79; see Courtship.
Engerrand, George C., 30:258.
"Engineer Riggs" (cited), 36:107.
English, use of by Kiowa Apaches, 22:12, 140.
English, John, 16:62.
English, Levi, 16:62.
English and Scottish folk tales in Texas, household collection of, 6:25 ff.
Ennis, James, 18:2-3, 5.
Ennis, Tex., 25:134.
"Enough of a good thing is enough," 13: 244.
Enree, J. L., 19:198.
Entertainers, Mexican in Haymarket Plaza, 22:173.
Entertainment on the frontier, 25:143-144.
"*Entiérrenme en campos rasos*," 29:90.
Entraaverlo Creek as place name, 13:5.
"*Entrada del Ferrocarril a Guadalajara*," 29:128.
"*Entre la espada y la pared*," 24:122.
"*Entre menos burros más elotes*," 24:122.
"*Entregar*" (cited), 12:186.
Entwistle, William J., 25:95; 27:27; 29: 109; 35:68.
Epacta (lunar reckoning), 2:95-96.
Epilepsy, folk curing of, 24:26-27, 37-38.
Epiphany, feast of, 14:208.
Epley Spring, 13:258 ff.; 19:172 f.
Erath, George B., 13:27, 37, 88; 15:71.
Erath County, Tex., 13:25, 37; 30:107; place name, 31:92 f.
"*Eres el gacho*," 12:218.
Erie County, N. Y., 33:103.
"Erlington" (cited), 27:24 (foldout), 74.
Eros in Freud's theory, 32:88.
Erskine, Gladys Shaw, 21:49.
Eruption, curing of, 24:53.
Erysipelas: power to cure, 30:251; remedy for, 8:55; 10:87.
"*Es José y María*," 8:91.
Escajeda, Josefina: article, 12:115-121; mentioned, 12:253; 13:120.
Escalante, Juan de, 16:200.
Escapes, narrow, from death by a bullet, 33:118-127.
Escobas Ranch, 6:18.

Escondido Creek, 29:214.
Escopeta, 10:115.
"Escuchen, señores, esta triste historia," 29:128.
"Ese tuerto de Salcedo," 28:99.
"Esel, lass dich hoeren" (game), 22:234.
Eskimos, their name for themselves, 1:87.
Eskridge (early Arkansas judge), 19:180.
Espada, Mission of, 3:172.
Espantosa, Lake, as place name, 13:11-12, 81.
Espego, Antonio de, 2:22.
Esperanza: Creek, 17:118 f.; 30:27; Ranch, 31:141.
Espinel, Vicente, 28:97.
Espinosa, Aurelio M., 4:11; 9:72; 14:104; 24:72; 25:184, 190; 27:139, 144; 28:91; 29:90, 92; 30:242 f.
Espinosa, Isidro de, 1:39, 43.
Espinosa, José Manuel, 27:140.
"Está cerrado de un tiro," 12:213.
"Esta es la bota," 29:113.
"Esta noche caballeros," 8:90.
"Estaba un payo sentado," with music, 8:113.
"Estaba la rana cantando debajo del agua," 29:112.
Estancia, New Mex., 33:85.
Estava, José María, 35:156.
"Este rancho de los Guerras," 8:111.
Esteban, "Tío," 10:103-104.
Estébanez Calderón, Serafin, 29:104 f., 109.
Estill, Julia: articles, 2:67-74; 3:24-27, 153-156; 4:103-114; 9:130-132; 22:231-236; 26:207-212 (reprint); mentioned, 2:5; 3:261; 4:115, 117; 9:189, 191; 10:187; 11:107; 22:231; 36:55 ff.
Estill, J. T., 3:36; 4:117.
Estill, William H., 3:155.
Estonian fable, 19:156.
"Eternal vigilance is the price of supremacy," 13:242.
Etiological tales; see Explanatory tales.
Eubank, Jesse T., 13:250.
Eubank, Ruth; see Page, Mrs. J. E.
Eumenides, 1:86.
Eureka Springs, Ark., 33:102; 35:113 ff.
European folklore contrasted with American, 28:18-44.
"Evah bell yuh heah ain't uh dinnah bell," 11:102.
"Evahbody say 'goodnight' ain't gone home," 11:104.
Evans, Anna, 20:13, 15.
Evans, Augusta Jane, 33:59, 120.
Evans, C. N. B., 14:169, 172 f.
Evans, Dub, 30:13.
Evans, Frank, 32:268.
Evans, George W., 33:88.
Evans, Mrs. J. L., 18:134.
Evans, James, 20:13.
Evans, Joe, 25:8.

Evans, Moses, 3:250; 18:89-104.
Evans, Sally, 18:91.
Evans' Creek (pass, valley) on Clear Fork of the Brazos, 18:101.
Evansville, Ind., 27:53.
Eve, 36:96, 140; see Adam and Eve.
Eve of St. Agnes, 28:49.
"Even in Paradise," 14:152.
Evening star in Negro tale, 10:43-44.
Eve's necklace (plant), 18:160; 26:276.
"Ever' time a fine, prancin' horse gits a shoe," 5:137.
Evergreen sumac, 18:162.
Everson, William, 33:64.
Evert, Mrs. L., 8:23.
Everton, E. M., 30:90.
[Every . . .; see also Evah; Ever' . . . .]
"Every Darkie Workin' on the Levee," 2:47.
"Every fellow to his own notion," 5:79.
"Every man has got to kill his own snakes," 13:242.
"Every sausage knows if it is mek outer cow or dorg," 13:241.
"Everybody invited and nobody slighted," 2:31.
"Ev'ybody talkin' 'bout heaben ain't goin' dar," 5:151.
Evil: origin of, 12:143 ff.; powers exerted through tangible, intangible means, 1:82-86 ff.; 25:195 ff.
Evil eye and remedies for, 1:86, 88; 2:82-83; 4:92; 8:59-60; 10:84-85; 13:162; 17:73; 18:69, 139; 24:107-109; 25:198; 26:242; 27:187-188; 35:11-12.
Evil One, 8:102-109, 145-149; see Devil.
Ewing, Alexander, 21:127.
Ewing Ranch, 30:169.
Exaggerations, humorous; see Part II, Section 9, of *Analytical Index.*
Exclamations: folk, 5:92; differ in meaning from one culture to another, 22:5.
Excreta, burying to guard against witchcraft, 1:84; 25:196.
Exempla, comic, in frontier preaching, 14:155-168.
Explanatory tales; see Part II, Section 1, of *Analytical Index.*
Expulsion-return formula in Arabic romance, 34:187-194.
External soul, 1:83-84; 12:82-83, 128-129, 133; 14:241-249; 22:27-28; 32:44-49.
Extraordinary companions, 11:30 ff.; 12:77-79; see Hearing ability.
Eye(s): animal can remove its own, 22:67-70; of ox as weather sign, 22:143; removal of foreign bodies from, 35:14; witches exchange with cats, 10:68-70; 30:221, 223-224; see Evil eye; Eye trouble.
"Eye that believeth on de Lord, gonna hab evahlastin' life," 2:48.
Eye trouble, remedies for, 8:19-20, 26, 42,

Fireworks, 14:213, 217-218; in early Texas, 5:107.
"Firolera, La," with music, 4:22.
First-born, sacrifice of, 1:69.
"First couple dance by right," 18:123.
"First couple down the center," 4:57.
"First couple out to the couple on the right," 18:121-122.
First Creek as place name, 32:120.
"First gent leads the hall," 1:24.
First-Man, 14:128.
"First old boy through the hall," 18:118-119.
"First young gent to the opposite lady," 1:28.
"First young man across the ring," 13:320-321.
Fischer's Store, Tex., 36:37.
Fish: enchanted, 12:127 ff.; helps youth find ring, 32:27; silver, that holds secret of enchanted city, 12:247; in tall tales, 9:157; 19:37; 20:61-62, 98-99; 22:200-202.
"Fish an' bread had a time," 7:111.
Fish Creek as place name, 32:121.
"Fish in the Mill Pond" (cited), 1:36.
Fishback, Lon, 6:161.
Fishback yarns, 7:42-44; 8:157; 13:43.
Fisher, King, 9:7.
Fisher, S. Rhoads, 13:55.
Fisher County, Tex., as place name, 13:55; place name in, 31:81.
Fisherman and snake (tale), 24:133-136.
Fishhook cactus, 11:91.
Fishin' job (oil-field dic.), 7:48.
Fishing forbidden (tale), 21:87-88.
Fisk, Greenleaf, 21:119.
Fiske, John, 31:48.
Fistula, cures for, 8:11-12, 22, 37-38.
Fits in humans and dogs, cures for, 8:38, 45, 80, 81-82; 13:246; 26:258.
Fitzgerald, F. Scott, 9:175.
Fitzhugh, Tex., 36:45.
Five Civilized Tribes, 19:89.
Five-window (dic.), 34:18.
Fivemile Stream as place name, 32:120.
Fix up (dic.), 2:36.
Flag of Freedom newspaper, 7:162.
Flag Stream as place name, 32:126.
Flagg, Ray, 10:181.
Flaig, Eleanore, 31:42, 50.
Flamades, 36:136.
Flamenco, 29:93-107; 35:147 ff; origin of term, 29:98-99.
"Flanking" calves, 18:105 ff.
Flannel rag as cure, 14:267 f.
Flapjack cactus, 11:92.
Flatonia, Tex., 5:156; 13:167; 21:35; 26:163, 230.
"Flat River Girl," 7:176.
Flat Rock Stream as place name, 32:128.
Flat Stream as place name, 32:119.
Flat Top Mtn. (West Texas), 16:414 f.

Flatterations (dic.), 18:6.
Flaxseed: meal as cure, 8:76-77, 83; 14:267; for removal of foreign objects from eye, 35:14.
Flea(s), 5:18, 21, 23, 28, 30, 34, 37 ff.; 8:88; 12:vi; 19:135; 27:109.
Fleming, Dick, 33:3, 8.
Fleming, Mary, 22:63.
Fletcher, Curley, 33:82.
Fletcher, Henry T., 8:10.
Fletcher, Monroe, 19:167.
"Flies in the buttermilk," 1:15.
Flies as weather sign, 2:93; 5:113.
Flight; see Obstacle flights.
Flint, origin of, 22:18-22, 30-44.
Flint, Timothy, 14:159.
Flint Creek, 3:72; as place name, 32:128.
Flintlock rifle and equipment described, 6:49-50.
"Flirtation," with music, 23:166.
Flitters (fritters), 13:216.
Floersheim, Sol, 15:108.
Flood(s): coyote causes, 14:128; in Texas, 17:40-41, 62 ff.
Flor de Agosto for stomach trouble, 24:59.
Flor de la vida, 32:14; see Flower(s).
Flora: of deep South Texas, 17:59; see Plants.
"Flora Ella"; see "Florella."
Floral decoration of graves, 22:156 ff.
"Florella," 23:100.
Florence, Tex., 22:186.
Flores, Francisco G., 19:114; 30:279-281.
Flores, Gen. Emilio, 11:5.
Flores, José María, 19:186.
Flores, Josefa, 17:60.
Flores, Juan Joseph, 19:105.
Flores, Manuel, 3:93.
Flores, Tomás, 24:24.
Flores, Victor, 17:73.
Flores St., San Antonio, Tex., 13:1.
Floresville, Tex., 17:98.
Florida, account of the "tournament" in, 5:99-103.
Flour as remedy, 8:54.
Flourney, Bob, 18:143.
Flower(s): in cattle brands, 22:163-167; flaming or red, of evil, 12:143-151; gods, Mexican, 22:155 ff.; of life, 12:32 ff.; 32:14; yellow, symbol of death in Mexican culture, 22:155 ff.; see names of flowers.
Flower, Robin, 30:58.
"Floyd Collins" (cited), 32:229-230.
Flu, remedy for, 14:268.
Flugians (dic.), 5:90.
Flux, remedy for, 8:55.
Flycatcher, 7:33, 35; 26:284.
"Flying Dutchman" (game), 17:34.
Flying Dutchman legend, 4:61-62.
Flying saucers; see UFO's.
Fodder (dic.), 18:76.
Fogel, E. N., 11:94.

with music, 13:323-324.
"Get off the Tracks" (cited), 36:115.
"Get yo' little wagon, roll the baby out,"
    5:170.
Getaway Stream as place name, 32:112,
    126.
"Getting Upstairs" (cited), 1:36; 7:18.
Ghost: cactus, 11:93; dance, 22:80; Creek
    as place name, 32:127; horse, 16:155-
    170.
Ghost tales; see Part II, Section 7, of
    Analytical Index.
Ghost towns: Cold Springs, 30:123-131;
    San Patricio, 30:115-122; Seattle, 30:
    123; Thurber, 30:107-114.
"Ghostly Visitant, The" (cited), 25:93.
Ghosts, 9:50-58 passim, 151; 18:82, 131-
    147 passim; Cajun, 31:113-117; Mex-
    ican, 10:77-78, 100; 28:164-165; Negro
    10:31-32, 38-42, 57-59; 19:25-26; 31:
    113-117; see Ghost tales; Spirits.
Giant(s), 6:109-110; 10:79-81, 127-130;
    11:17-47 passim; 12:52-54, 78-79,
    126 ff., 133-134, 194-200; 14:114-118;
    34:112-115; race of in Mexico, 11:17;
    named Catorce, 12:194 ff.
Giant-killer twins, 14:114-118.
Gibbon, Edward, 30:58-61.
Gibsland, La., 35:36.
Gibtown, Tex., as place name, 13:54, 73.
Giddings, Tex., 5:156; 26:163.
"Giddy-ap, giddy-ap (cluck, cluck, cluck)
    giddy-ap," with gestures, 5:43.
Gift of healing, 24:12 ff.
Gila River, 7:173, 175 f.; 30:13.
Gilbert, Lanvil: article, 28:69-80; men-
    tioned, 28:vi, 168.
Gilbert, M., 8:120.
Gilbert, W. E., 25:48, 70.
Gilbert, W. S., 33:117.
Gilbert farm, treasure on, 8:120-121.
Gilchrist, A. G., 25:193; 30:31.
Gilcrease, J. W., 25:177.
Gilded Cacique, 4:68, 71.
Gilderoy's kite (in folk simile), 5:90.
Giles, Val C., 33:124.
Gilfillan, Archer B., 15:94, 104, 114.
Gillespie, Minnie, 19:21.
Gillespie, T. H., 21:60-61, 63.
Gillespie County, Tex., 2:67 ff.; 3:154;
    4:103 ff.; 22:234; as place name, 31:
    80, 91; German-American culture in,
    2:67-74; 36:52 ff.; Fair, 28:50.
Gillett, James B., 25:8.
Gillette, Mrs. George R., 8:10.
Gilliland, Henry, 13:235.
Gilliland, Joe, 13:235.
Gillis, Everett A.: articles, 25:200-204;
    28:81-90; 29:153-160; 33:81-88; men-
    tioned, 25:255; 28:vi, 168; 29:vi, 232;
    33:v, 199.
Gilmore, Frances, 32:199.
Gilpin, H. A., 19:98.

Gilson, Bill (marshall), 33:123.
Ginger (dic.), 1:45.
Gingerbread Boy, 6:30 ff.
Ginned (dic.), 3:112.
Ginseng, 18:33.
Gipson, Fred, 29:12 f.
Giraffe, 27:108.
Girardeau, Claude M., 3:211.
"Girl I Left Behind Me," 1:25, 28 f., 36;
    13:320-321.
Girón, Tomasa, 13:129; 26:123-124.
"Git Along, Little Dogies," with music,
    7:148.
"Git on Board, Little Chillen" (cited),
    36:113.
"Git your partner if you want'er dance
    Josey," 1:12.
"Give the Fiddler a Dram" (cited), 17:82.
Givens, Ripley, 32:160.
Gizzard: of chicken as remedy, 8:13, 26,
    57, 60; 14:267; of hawk as mock
    remedy, 8:26.
Gjerset (historian), 35:66, 68.
Glade devil, 5:65.
Glade Stream as place name, 32:119.
Glanders, no remedy for, 8:39; 26:257.
Glanton, John, 35:89.
Glascock, Clyde C.: article, 9:124-129;
    mentioned, 1:4; 9:190; 11:106; 18:x.
Glasgow, University of, 15:75.
Glass: ground, for tapeworm, 8:69; brok-
    en, as grave decoration, 18:130-131.
Glass, Bell, 30:125.
Glass, Dick, 30:125.
Glass wrapped (dic.), 34:17.
Glassburn, Robert P., 21:57.
Glaze Creek as place name, 32:120.
Glenwood Stream as place name, 32:119.
Glimp, Ardelia Woods, 28:149.
Glimp, Sarah Jones Caroline, 28:149.
Globe, Ariz., 12:232.
"Glory, glory, hallelujah," with music,
    13:136.
Glover's Gap, W. Va., 20:102.
Glyptodont (as fabulous beast), 7:41.
Gnats, 2:93.
"Go bring me back my blue-eyed boy,"
    with music, 23:151-152.
"Go bring me some of your father's
    gold," with music, 23:34-36.
"Go hom-a, baby, cry," 25:131.
"Go on, Mule, You Better Stop Saddlin',"
    5:167.
Go round (dic.), 2:32.
"Go to Sleepy," with music, 23:267-268.
"Go and tell Aunt Rody," with music,
    23:262-263.
"Go through the forest, and take a crook-
    ed stick after all," 2:15.
Goacher's Trace, 13:58.
Goard Stream as place name, 32:118.
Goat bean; see Mountain laurel.
Goat butter as mock remedy, 8:26.

Goat Creek as place name, 32:121, 123.
Goat-herders, 8:86 ff.; 12:87; see *Pastores*.
Goats: control of kidding of, 2:96; and
  ecology, 18:161; lead, 15:107 ff.; lech-
  ery of, 21:33-34; for milking, 2:76;
  remedies for, 8:42; 26:257; weather
  signs associated with, 2:90; 9:63.
Goatsuckers, 7:26 f.
Gobbler Creek as place name, 32:121.
God, Freud's theory of origin of, 32:87,
  90.
"God does not pay wages every Satur-
  day," 14:152.
"God made de nigger," 7:104.
"God-Men, The" (poem), 32:217.
"God told Norah for to sketch his plan,"
  19:17.
Goddard, P. E., 2:25, 27-28; 3:231.
Godfather, in Mexican culture, 6:12.
Godmother Death, 12:76-77; 16:353-355.
Gods, flowers as symbols of in Mexican
  culture, 22:155-167.
"God's water" (rainwater) as cosmetic,
  8:88.
Goethe, 24:2; 25:95.
"Going to Boston," 1:16-17; cited, 1:35;
  7:7.
"Going Down Town" (cited), 1:36.
"Going to Leave the I. and G.," 2:41.
"Going to the Mill" (game), 17:150.
Goiter, remedy for, 35:13.
Gold, buried, and mines of; see Part II,
  Section 8, of *Analytical Index*.
Gold and silver, combing out, 6:44; 26:75.
Gold Stream as place name, 32:128.
Golden Arm tale, 6:41-42, 54; 25:183-
  194; 31:12-13, 15-16, 163.
Golden Bough, The; see Frazer, Sir James
  G.
Golden Fleece (tavern), 18:18.
Golden hoof, symbol of sheep industry,
  15:86, 117.
Golden log (tale), 31:3-7.
Golden tooth, man with (the Devil),
  12:66-72.
"Golden Vanity, The" (cited), 27:24
  (foldout), 29, 75.
Goldenrod, 18:161; 26:276.
Goldenrod Stream as place name, 32:118.
Goldfish, Samuel; see Goldwyn.
Goldman, Mrs. W. W. (Lois), 17:92.
Goldsmith, Oliver, 25:47, 95; 30:35.
Goldstein, Kenneth S.: article, 32:188-
  198; mentioned, 32:201, 215, 270.
Goldthwaite, Tex., 14:200; 19:168; 26:
  190, 193.
Goldwyn, Samuel, 33:53.
Goliad, Tex., 3:3, 33; 6:23-29 passim;
  10:118-119, 120; 13:8; 15:10, 64; 18:
  138; 26:89, 125; 28:54.
Goliad County, Tex., 6:48; 10:25, 31;
  place name in, 31:90.
Golondrina as remedy, 10:89.

Gomara, Francisco López de, 16:203 ff.
Gomez (Indian), 35:88.
Gomez, Elizario, 28:131-132.
Gomez, Eugenia Camara de, 29:38.
Gomez, Gertrudis, 11:13.
Gomez, José, 21:10 ff., 33; 23:212; 26:151.
Gomez, Pedro (or Urbano), 25:206.
Gomorrah, curse on, 1:92.
Gongora (poet), 30:47, 283.
"Gonna Hab Everlastin Life," 2:48.
Gonzales, A. E., 7:141-142.
Gonzales, Genaro, 31:157.
Gonzales, José, 24:72, 116-117.
Gonzales, Jovita: articles, 6:7-22; 8:86-
  116; 10:99-108; 12:107-114; 26:19-24
  (reprint); mentioned; 6:241; 8:174;
  10:188-189; 12:250, 253; 15:173.
Gonzales, "Lone Wolf," 35:142.
Gonzales, María, 31:156.
Gonzales, Melchiades, 21:20, 22.
Gonzales, Solito, 30:270.
Gonzales, Tex., 19:195.
Gonzalez, Alejandro, 19:116.
Gonzalez, Doroteo, 24:18.
Gonzalez, Rosalinda: article, 31:141-155;
  mentioned, 31:161.
Goober (dic.), 6:120; 9:18.
Gooch, Ben H., 3:20.
Good Friday, 4:61; 36:28.
Good Gal and Bad Gal tale, 6:42-45; 26:
  74-76 (reprint); 27:89-91.
Good Hope, Cape of, 4:61 f.
Good luck, signs of, 5:123-124; 13:155;
  30:254.
Good Stream as place name, 32:126.
Good time (prison dic.), 1:45.
Goodall, Walter, 32:165.
"Goodbye, Little Birdie [Bonnie Blue
  Eyes], Goodbye," with music, 23:193-
  195.
"Goodbye, my beloved country," 12:222-
  224.
"Goodbye, Old Paint," 22:230.
Goodgrit, Katy (folk character), 18:68,
  70.
Gooding, Cynthia, 30:36.
Goodland, Kans., 16:102.
Goodnight, Charles, 6:73 ff., 82, 92;
  8:18 f., 29 f., 34, 41 f., 51, 68 f.; 13:60;
  22:227; 25:4; 26:255; 35:57.
Goodnight-Loving Trail, 6:198, 201; 13:
  24, 60; 35:57.
Goodrich, Chauncey, 21:114, 118, 129.
Goodwin, Bud, 5:96.
Goodwin, Harold, 34:65.
Goodwyn, Frank: articles, 9:48-62; 16:
  304-306; 18:105-114; 26:147-150 (re-
  print); mentioned; 9:190; 16:420; 17:
  156; 18:221; 23:212; 29:36.
Goolscap (Indian culture hero), 29:174.
Goose, 2:50-51; 5:41, 48, 113, 116; see
  Geese.
Goose Creek: Kans., 16:118; Tex., 13:47;

H

H O Canyon Stream as place name, 32: 123.
"Ha!" as Kiowa-Apache indication of approval, 22:5.
Haakerson, James A., 30:90.
Haase, Nando, 34:30.
Habitch (dic.), 30:97.
"*Hablando del diablo pronto la cabeza asoma*," 24:122.
"*Hablen del rey de Roma y pronto la cabeza asoma*," 24:122.
"*Hacer de uno cera y pabilo*," 24:122.
Hackamore, 10:117; origin of the word, 16:272.
Hackberry Stream as place name, 32:116.
Hackett, Charles Wilson, 28:120 f.
Hackett, Dave, 32:152.
Hackney, V. H., 36:12.
"Had it in me as big as a horse," 13:246.
Haeckel's Law, 32:74, 97.
Hagerman, Mrs. (Ranger, Tex.), 25:76; 26:337.
Hague, Katherine, 29:230.
Haigood, Penelope, 23:37.
Hail Center, Tex., 16:93.
Hair: of dog as remedy for its bite, 8:54; 30:250; grower, folk, 8:57; 26:262; horse, used in cement, 25:139; as remedy, 8:61; in witchcraft and superstition, 1:83; 7:121; 13:152-153, 158, 175; 24:117; 25:196; 26:233, 238, 253; see Gray hair.
Hairy (dic.), 34:13, 20.
Hairy cactus, 11:91.
Hakac, John, 36:122.
Hakluyt, Richard, 25:41.
Halbouty, Michel T., 30:91.
Halderman, C. H., 20:34.
Hale, Duff, 17:78.
Hale, "Grandpa" (Mills County, Tex.), 19:171.
Hale, Harve, 30:202, 204.
Hale, Meredith: article, 29:136-141; mentioned, 29:232.
Hale County, Tex., place name, 31:94.
Haley, Bessie, 23:138.
Haley, J. Evetts: articles, 6:72-89, 198-204; mentioned, 6:5, 241; 16:241; 30:29.
Haley, Lawrence, 13:61.
Haley Peak as place name, 13:61.
Half Stream as place name, 32:120.
Halff, M., 33:48.
Hall, David: articles, 11:90-93; 13:176-181; mentioned, 11:106, 108; 13:338.
Hall, Ed (La Salle County, Tex.), 21:52.
Hall, Ed (West Texas freighter), 35:85 f., 92 ff.

Hall, Ida B.: article, 17:141-151; mentioned, 17:153.
Hall, James, 32:68.
Hall, Jim (Almena, Kans.), 16:107.
Hall, Capt. Lee, 21:19 ff., 33; 32:148.
Hall, Mita H., 30:217.
Hall, Warren D., 3:189.
Hall, William C., 36:78.
Hall Cemetery, 18:130.
Hall County, Tex., 6:84; place name in, 31:91.
Hall tree, ghostly, 18:141.
"Hallelujah [I'm a] Bum Again," 2:39.
Hallettsville, Tex., 24:95-96.
Halliwell, S. O., 5:9, 11; 6:38, 55 ff., 66, 68, 71, 235.
Halpert, Herbert, 28:30; 30:57 f., 68; 32:236.
Haltom, Iantha Carr, 7:125.
Ham, J. S., 19:67.
Ham Stream as place name, 32:126.
Haman, the name in a proverb, 5:85.
Hamburger, Texas style, 25:130.
"Hamburger Bill" (Ft. Worth, Tex.), 25:129.
Hamer, Capt. Frank, 30:28; 35:44.
Hamer, Marcelle L.: article, 15:59-74; mentioned, 12:251; 14:5; 15:175; 17:vi, 155 f.
Hamill, Allen, 31:71.
Hamilton, Alexander, 32:105.
Hamilton County, Tex., 16:410.
Hamilton's Valley (Tex.), 3:21.
Hammack, J. W., 35:77.
"Hammah Keep-Ringin', De," with music, 7:114.
Hammer, Cornelius, 25:177.
Hammershaimb, V. U., 35:68.
Hammett, Ann, 18:132.
Hamner, Laura V., 22:226.
Hampton, Gen. Wade, 16:367; 30:198.
Hampton, Will, 31:38 ff.
Hanaii Indians, 1:41.
Hand, human, in primitive art, 4:80-102.
Hand game between animals and stone monster, 22:18-21.
Hand of Glory motif, 17:113.
Handkerchief, red (in tale), 18:142.
Handman, Max Sylvius: article, 2:8-13; mentioned, 2:4.
Handy (oil-field dic.), 18:204.
Handy, W. C., 2:52 ff.
Hanged man sends rain, 12:120-121.
"Hangerman," 23:46.
Hangin' Day (dic.), 35:79.
Hanging tree, 18:146; 29:207.
"Hanging was good enough for my fathers" (anecdote), 18:214 ff.

Hat-in-mud tale, 7:75-76; 33:100-109.
Hat in superstition, 13:158; 26:238 (reprint).
Hatch, Davis B., 10:112.
Hatch, James, 7:157, 161, 170 f.; 10:122.
Hatch, Sylvanus, 7:157.
Hatcher, Mattie Austin: articles, 5:49-55; 6:107-118; mentioned, 3:4, 197; 5:183; 6:241; 7:161; 9:134, 167.
Hatcher, Peter, 18:166.
Hatcher Ranch (Colo.), 9:77.
Hatfield, Sadie: articles, 18:157-162; 26: 273-278 (reprint); mentioned, 18:222.
Haunted Hollow (Nacogdoches, Tex.), 7:124-125.
Haunted houses; see Part II, Section 7, of *Analytical Index.*
"Haunted Wood, The," 6:129-130.
"Have you heard the lates'," 5:173; 26: 165 (reprint).
Havernick, Walter, 36:42.
Havie (buffalo hunter), 16:79.
Haw Stream as place name, 32:116.
Hawk(s), 18:97; in Kiowa-Apache tales, 22:18, 23 f., 26; 26:1-2 (reprint).
Hawk Run (near San Antonio, Tex.), 18:97.
Hawking (vendors') cries, 25:115-138.
Hawkins, Isaac Newton, 17:84.
Hawkins, J. F., 31:75.
Hawkins, Sir John, 34:175.
Hawkins, Martha, 30:215 ff.
Hawkins, S. J., 31:75.
Hawks, W. E., 6:161.
Hay fever, remedy for, 8:13.
Hay Hollow as place name, 13:4.
"*Hay muchachos viejos y viejos muchachos,*" 24:122.
"*Hay muertos que no hacen ruido y son sus penas mayores,*" 24:122.
Hay Stream as place name, 32:118.
Hayes, C. Willard, 31:65.
Hayes, Rutherford B., 9:10 f.; 36:3.
Hayes, Mrs. Rutherford B., 9:10 f.
Hayhook Ranch, 36:62 f.
Hayles, the (a musical group), 18:55.
Haymarket Plaza (San Antonio, Tex.), 21:5; 22:168-178; 25:119.
Haynes, A. K., 31:89.
Hayrick Stream as place name, 32:119.
Hays, Jack, 3:10, 154; 10:113; 13:53, 112; 19:74; 32:115, 122; 35:90.
Hays, Will, 23:241.
Hays County, Tex., 5:7; 19:132; 22:152; 36:34, 46.
Hayshaker (dic.), 35:47.
Haystack Mtn. as place name, 13:3.
"*Haz bien y no mires a quien,*" 24:122.
Hazlegrove, A. F., 18:37.
Hazlitt, W. C., 22:210.
"He came from his palace grand," with music, 23:202-203.
"He followed her up, he followed her

down," with music, 10:138-140.
"He has teeth as white as pearls," with music, 23:164-165.
"He howls as a leper howls," 14:58.
"He is like the Pope's mule," 13:242.
"He's a man at the table," 2:16.
"He rode up to the mill house door,' 5:19.
"He should tear the cat," 36:144.
"He walked up and down the street," 2:40.
"He who would great things have done," 11:14.
"He who would please the fair," 11:14.
"He would plant it in pears and thorns," 9:182.
"He would skin a flea for the hide and tallow," 13:242.
Head: -hunting, 1:67; significance of soft spot on infant's, 2:84; see Headless; Heads.
Headache, remedies for, 8:57, 82; 24:36, 109-110; 26:247, 262 (reprints).
Headache post (oil-field dic.), 4:65; 7:51.
Headless ghosts, 3:135-137; 9:51-52; 10: 100-101; 18:140-141; 28:164-165.
Headrick, Okla., 7:11.
Headright grants, 15:31-32.
Heads, severing (Indian tale), 22:130-133.
Healdton, Okla., 6:145-146.
Healers, folk, 12:70-72, 76-77; 24:9-68; 26:264-273 (reprint); 29:14-44; see Cures; Curanderos; Screw worms; Warts.
Healer of Los Olmos; see Jaramillo, Pedro.
Healing, folk; see *Curanderos;* Cures.
Heard (treasure hunter), 9:31.
Heard, Elma: article, 13:294-297; mentioned, 11:106; 13:338.
Heard, John J., 9:175 f.
Hearing ability exaggerated (tale), 32: 54-55.
Hearn, Lafcadio, 14:153.
Hearne, Tex., 7:85, 89, 95 f.; 19:200 f.; 26:168, 173.
Heart: animal's sacrificed, 2:8; trouble, remedy for, 10:90; 24:27; that jumps (tale), 22:27-29; witch's, 25:219.
Heatley, R. D., 35:77.
Heaton, Ada, 29:61.
Heaton, Ed, 29:61.
Heaven, jests about entering or being ejected from; see Part II, Section 6, of *Analytical Index.*
Heavener, E. G., 27:111.
Heaven's Gate Church, 19:19.
Hebbronville, Tex., 10:102; 12:211; 13: 26.
Hebe-jebes (dic.), 5:85.
Heberard, John, 19:179.
Hebert, Rachel Bluntzer, 19:108; 30:117-119, 122.

Hebrew superstitions, 1:88.
Hecate, 33:189.
Hedenberg, Charles J., 21:123.
Hedgehog cactus, 11:91.
Hedionde ("stinking place," South Texas), 16:25-26.
"Heel and Toe" (cited), 1:36.
"Heel and Toe Polka," 13:333.
Heel-flies, 2:93; 13:228-229.
Heffington, Jim, 17:84.
Heffington, Steve, 25:134.
Hefflebauer, Hugo, 2:73.
Hegel, 14:145.
Hegner, Robert, 25:39.
Heifer branded (dic.), 18:115; 22:226.
Heifer Creek as place name, 13:73.
"Heigho crowdie!," 5:12.
Heil Öl as remedy, 30:249.
Heilman, Mollie, 10:187.
Heimsath, Charles H.: article, 3:132-135; mentioned, 3:261.
"Heintzelmaenchen" (game), 22:235; 26:211.
"Heirat in Januar wenn's eisig und kalt," 30:254.
Helen of Troy, 33:189.
Helena, Tex., 6:25, 28.
Hell: in anecdotes of frontier religion, 14:160-161; 34:51-62; associated with steam locomotive, 25:245; Paul Bunyan in, 7:52; see "Hell in Texas"; see Part II, Section 6, of *Analytical Index*.
"Hell to breakfast," 19:vii.
Hell chickens (obstacle flight tale), 7:128-130.
Hell diver (pied-bill grebe), 7:36-37.
Hell hounds, 1:75-77.
Hell Roaring Hollow as place name, 6:82; 13:48, 74.
"Hell in Texas" (poem and tradition relating to), 9:175-182; 19:134-138.
Hellbender (salamander), 5:63; 7:42.
"He'll be thinking where the summer wages go," 7:174.
"Hello, cowboy," 32:170.
Helm, Boone, 6:143.
Helms, Jack, 10:121.
Hemi (dic.), 34:21.
Hemingway, Ernest, 28:66.
Hemisphere cactus, 11:91.
Hemley, Myron R., 10:71.
Hemorrhage, folk treatment of, 8:57; 24:38-39; 26:266-267 (reprint); see Bleeding.
Hemorrhoids; see Piles.
Hemphill family (Veal Station, Tex.), 13:227.
Hemphill County, Tex., place name, 31:87.
Hempstead, Tex., 13:38.
Hempstead County, Ark., 19:182.
Hen(s), 5:10, 113, 119, 159, 166; 6:65-66; 7:129-130; 18:182; 19:66.

"Hen with chickens" (game), 22:235.
Henderson, Alice Corbin, 33:81, 85.
Henderson, B. B., 18:119.
Henderson, Carl, 31:37.
Henderson, Hamish, 32:194, 198.
Henderson, J. G., 4:90 f.
Henderson, John, 15:151.
Henderson, Monte, 13:259, 265 ff.
Henderson, Gen. Pinckney, 15:68.
Henderson, Sue: article, 18:144; mentioned, 18:222.
Henderson, T. F., 32:228; 35:67, 70-71.
Henderson, William, 25:192.
Henderson County, Tex., 3:241; place name in, 31:91.
Hendren, Joseph W.: articles, 14:270-279; 25:47-74; poem, 27:151-161; mentioned, 14:286; 25:255; 27:202.
Hendricks, David, 34:34.
Hendricks, Evarts, 19:129.
Hendricks, George D.: articles, 25:40-46; 29:69-87; 30:69-75; 32:176-187; 35:127-131; mentioned, 25:255; 29:v, 232; 30:292; 32:270; 35:165-166.
Hendricks, H. G., 19:129.
Hendricks, Peggy: article, 25:217-219; mentioned, 25:255.
Hendricks Lake (East Texas), treasure in, 34:37-49.
Hendrix, John M., 22:222.
Hendrix, W. S.: article, 1:75-77.
Henneman, John Bell, 6:57.
Hennepin, R. P. Louis, 21:106, 111.
Hennersdorf, Ida, 22:234 f.; 26:209 f.
Hennessey, Pat, 6:91.
"Henny Penny," 18:188.
Henriquez, Cecilia G.; see Hernandez, Cecilia.
Henriquez Rosa; see Hernandez, Lily.
Henry VIII, 30:101; 34:158.
Henry, Mr. (Belton, Tex.), 33:139 f.
Henry, David, 12:252.
Henry, G. W., 35:32.
Henry, John; see "John Henry."
Henry, Mrs. John (Dallas, Tex.), 12:252.
Henry, Mary Malvina, 21:127.
Henry, O.: 8:152-153; 9:32; 13:43; 14:169, 172-179; 17:78, 124; 25:17; 29:46; his Texas stories as reflection of social customs, 32:148-167; politics in his stories, 36:81-91.
Henry, Patrick, 16:179; 26:112; 32:105.
Henry, Thomas, 18:206-207.
"Henry Green," with music, 23:125-126.
"Henry Martyn" (cited), 27:24 (foldout), 29, 75.
Heptameron, The, 25:17.
"Heraclio Bernál, decía en su caballo alazán," with music, 4:13.
Herbals, 8:18, 25-26, 75-76; 9:85-117 passim; see names of plants.
Herbs: pacifying effect of on horses, 19:50; long life attributed to, 33:134; see

Plants; see names of herbs.
Hercules, 1:70; 9:13.
Herd, David, 25:71.
"Here, Sambo! And Ringo!," 14:253 f.
"Here sits an old man going down to
sleep," 1:27.
"Here for twenty-five cents," 17:52.
"Here we go to Baltimore," 7:23.
Hereford, E. H., 10:183.
Hereford, Tex., 18:129.
"Here's luck to all you homesteaders,"
with music, 7:175.
"Here's one lash for the cow I stole,"
9:79.
Herff, Dr. (San Antonio, Tex.), 24:31-32.
Hermit of Las Vegas, N. M., 10:124-126.
Herms, Chris, 8:63; 26:263.
Hernandez, Cecilia G., 24:72, 74, 86-87,
94, 100 ff., 110-112; 26:271-272.
Hernandez, Chita de, 24:108.
Hernandez, Darío, 21:16-19, 20, 22, 34.
Hernandez, Eduwiges, 24:43.
Hernandez, Estevan, 19:116.
Hernandez, José, 30:227 ff.
Hernandez, Lily, 24:72, 111; 26:271-272.
Hernandez, Petra Rocha de, 24:62.
Hernandez, Rodolfo, 24:74.
Hernandez, Gen. Rosalío, 21:25.
Hernando (with Cortez), 16:210, 212 f.
Herndon, Dallas T., 18:51.
Herndon, W. H., 28:15.
Herne, Peregrine, 25:40 f.
Herod, 1:90; in folk drama, 11:54, 85.
Herodotus, 9:145; 30:29, 58.
Heroes: American, 28:43; 35:140; Amer-
ican occupational, 20:20; frontier, 30:
140-155; in Mexican balladry, 21:6-7;
Negro, 29:170-189; 31:119-134; rail-
road, 36:105-108; see Cowboy; Culture
heroes; Occupational heroes; Outlaws;
Western hero.
Heron, 7:34; and coyote (tale), 25:8-9;
see Cranes.
Herrera, Martin, 22:142-149.
Herrick, Robert, 25:115.
Herskovits, Melville, 31:122 f.; 34:145.
Hessen, 36:57.
Hester, Dr. (Belmont, Tex.), 19:25.
Hester, Aunt Ruthie, 19:23.
Hester, W. B., 6:136.
Hewett, J. E., 25:180.
Hexes; see Bewitchment; Evil eye; Magic
(black).
Heydon, John, 33:118.
Heyward, Dubose, 7:142.
Hibbs, Ethel, 4:page 19 of appendix.
Hibernia, San Patricio de, 30:115.
Hiccoughs, cure for, 8:57.
"Hickey, pickey, zickey, zan," 6:68.
Hickman, Edward, 32:232.
Hickok, Wild Bill, 9:6, 12 ff.; 30:74.
Hickory nuts, 17:30; 26:200.
Hickory Stream as place name, 32:116.

Hicks, A. W., 31:77.
Hicks, Mary A.: article, 17:108-112; men-
tioned, 17:152.
Hicks, Milly, 11:102; 26:221.
Hico, Tex., 27:103.
Hidalgo, Father Miguel, 2:79; 9:87.
Hidalgo County, Tex., 9:91; 19:100 ff.
"Hide-and-Go-Seek," 17:147-148.
Hideous (dic.), 18:164.
Hides (dic.), 34:15.
Hidetown, Tex.: Scurry County, as place
name, 13:48, 74; Wheeler County,
18:4.
Hiester, Miriam W.: article, 30:226-242;
mentioned, 30:292.
Higgins, Patillo, 31:61, 64 f.
Higgins, W., 3:205.
High-Five (dic.), 30:97.
High Hunting Eagle (Indian), 16:164.
High lonesome (dic.), 2:35.
"High-Lonesome Waltz," 9:33.
High-powers (dic.), 7:50.
High sheriff (dic.), 16:359 ff.
Highbank Stream as place name, 32:119.
Highlanders, curses among, 1:88.
Highsmith, Samuel, 3:155; 32:114.
Highsmith Creek as place name, 32:114.
Hightower, Annie, 17:154.
Hightower, Bob, 16:96.
Hightower, Tom, 16:96.
"Hijo Desobediente, El," 29:91.
Hildebrand, Ira P., 34:206.
Hildesmueller, Peter, 2:73.
Hill, Charlie, 6:199.
Hill, Ethel Osborne, 23:24.
Hill, George A., 12:viii.
Hill, George Washington, 21:119.
Hill, J. L., 33:72; 35:56, 60.
Hill, Jerome J., 6:122.
Hill, Joe, 36:80, 110.
Hill, Quinus, 31:37.
Hill, Robert T., 28:107, 120.
Hill, W. H., 25:176.
Hill folk near Austin, Tex., folkways of,
17:40-48.
Hill Oil Company, 28:131-132.
Hill Stream as place name, 32:119.
Hillman, Arwed, 36:59.
Hillo, Pepe, 29:103.
"Hills of Mexico, The," 6:201.
Hillsboro, Tex., 7:95.
Hilly land, tall tales about; see Part II,
Section 9, of Analytical Index.
"Hi-lo!" (cry of mule driver and va-
quero), 24:8.
Hindsville, Ark., 30:212.
Hindus, curses of, 1:93.
Hines, J. R., 19:81.
Hines, William "Missou," 33:113.
Hinguanza, Monico, 24:49; 26:267-269.
Hinkle, H. W., 5:18.
Hinojosa (deputy sheriff of Brownwood,
Tex.), 4:37 f.

Home Ranch Stream as place name, 32:123.

Home remedies; see Cures; see names of remedies and of ailments.

Home Stream as place name, 32:126.

"Home Sweet Home" (cowboy lyric), 6:165.

Homesteaders (in song), 7:175.

Hominy, how made, 25:126-127.

Homo sapiens, periods of development, 1:68.

Honchos (dic.), 34:26, 32.

Honda on ropes, 18:111-112.

Hondo River, 6:198.

"Honest Tramp, The," with music, 6:124-125.

Honesty in the early West, 33:49-50.

Honey, 7:50, 76; gathering wild, 10:128-129; 17:30; 18:98, 102; as remedy, 8:76; 14:268; see Metheglin.

Honey Creek (Tex.), 4:103; 15:151; 18:98; 19:132; treasure on, 3:13, 19.

Honey Stream as place name, 32:125.

"Honor your partner and the lady on the side," 18:120-121.

"Honors right and honors left," 18:117.

Hood (oil driller), 20:43.

Hood, James L., 19:186, 198.

Hood County, Tex., place names, 13:28; 31:80, 90.

Hoof, injured, remedies for, 8:40, 43.

Hoof and mouth disease; see Mouth disease.

"Hook, line, and sinker," 5:81.

Hook men (dic.), 18:203.

Hooked up (dic.), 2:36.

Hooker, Gen., 20:19.

Hooks, remedy for, 8:36-37, 40.

Hoop snake, 4:46 f.; 5:76-77; 7:42; 8:124-128.

Hoop-and-pole game, 14:129.

Hooper, John M., 21:123.

Hooper, Johnson Jay, 20:46; 36:75-78.

"Hooting" a girl, 22:221.

Hoover, Herbert, 30:90; 34:44.

Hoover, J. Edgar, 18:164; 19:156.

Hoovercrats (dic.), 36:85.

Hoovervilles (dic.), 36:61.

Hope out, to (dic.), 17:26; 26:195.

Hopi Indians: 4:9; 19:82; snake dance of, 2:89.

Hopkins, B., 6:93.

Hopkins, Vivian C., 25:158 f.

Hopkins County, Tex., 17:87; 29:9; place name, 31:75.

Hopper, Hedda, 33:94.

Horace as satirist, 1:95.

Horace, Mrs. L. B. Jones, 9:145.

Hord, Wirt, 30:91.

Horehound as remedy, 8:52 ff.; 10:88; 14:268; 26:260 f.

Horn: hunting, 35:6; "sons of a," 21:18, 33; worshipers, 3:230-233.

Horn, the (Africa), 4:59; 8:21, 39-40.

Horn, Charles Edward, 5:10.

Horn, Elder, 14:168; 33:121, 125.

Horn, Robert C., 14:168.

Horn, Tom, 27:99.

Horn-swoggled (dic.), 5:92.

Hornaday, W. T., 14:53.

Horned snake lore, 21:68.

Horned toad, 5:64, 75; 13:139; 19:135; 26:281; 29:3-13.

Hornedo, Consuelo, 10:77.

Hornets in tales, 10:24; 12:18; 26:34-35, 57 (reprints).

Horns, Eliza, 19:81.

Hornsby, Callie, 29:161.

Hornsby, Reuben, 8:11.

Horse(s): American Indians and, 2:20-22; 15:3-4; 16:143-170; anti-Indian, 16:335; behavior of as weather sign, 2:91-92; 5:113; 13:171; beliefs about, relating to color, markings, etc., 2:58; 13:242; 16:195, 228, 245, 247-248; borrowed, dies (tale), 21:88-89;

W. R. L.

bought in Texas for use in Georgia, 3:77; a boy's first, 16:390-395; breeding and raising, 16:53 ff.; that can run backward, 16:342; colors of, 2:58; 16:13-14, 32-33, 52, 69, 87-88, 104, 145, 190, 195, 228-232, 244-247, 271, 274, 339; of the conquest, 16:197-226; cowboys and, 16:373-383, 403-416; 33:13-15, 39 ff.; cures for, 8:9-49 passim; 16:248-249; 24:39, 46-47; 26:256-259 passim, 267; cutting, 16:403-408; of Dick Turpin, 6:157; that drinks tequila, 16:396-402; in drought, dwindle to colts, 19:66; dupes ox (tale), 18:190 ff.; in East Texas, 16:367 ff.; feet of, Indians burned when sore, 22:127; in folk sayings, 5:86; gaits of an influence on rhythm of cowboy songs,

7:145-146; of Gregorio Cortez, 16:342; 27:6, 10 ff.; how Apaches got, 22:39, 51-52; 26:3 (reprint); in Kiowa-Apache tales, 22:20, 44 f., 51 f., 79 f., 83, 87 ff., 104, 111, 117, 121-142 passim; language of, 15:131-137; last

ᴨᴿ ᴌ

wild herds in Texas, 16:19-21; legended individuals, 16:83-95, 102-142, 153-185, 309-416; meat, 22:145; in the movies, 34:69-70; names for and naming of, 16:232-244, 300-301, 378, 386; 33:13, 15; Nefdee strain of Arabia, 16:94; Old Fanny, 9:130; pacing (tall tale), 32:55; pacing white, 3:223-226; 16:11-12, 171-183, 245; 26:105-112 (reprint), of the Pampas, 16:187-196; pitching, 16:17-18, 253-304; 19:152, 154; race, 16:373-383; 18:101-102; 30: 169-170; reining, 16:283-287; rhyme concerning the quality of, 13:242; ridden into saloon, up flight of stairs, 10:118; saves party from Indian ambush, 31:38-40; selling, 5:104; sense of smell of, 16:342-350; smart (tales), 16:406-407; 19:54-56; Spanish-American, 16:187-233; "stamping" white, 13:165; 26:244; stealing, 13:114; stolen (anecdote), 17:70-71; in superstitions and cures, 5:116; 13:162, 167, 169, 171; 19:50; 13:151, 163-164; in Texas place names, 13:25, 26, 31, 38-39, 44, 56; as theme of songs, 6:20 ff., 123; "thumbing" to make pitch, 16: 352, 376; white, as good luck sign, 5:123; winged, 7:127-128; woman

married to, 22:97-100; see Cow horses; Horse-breaking; Mustangs; Stallion.
Horse-breaker cured of hemorrhage, 24: 38-39; 26:266-267 (reprint).
Horse-breaking, 8:14; 16:58, 144-148, 165-168, 194, 242; Texas-Mexican, 16: 269-290.
Horse car (dic.), 34:19.
Horse Cave, Ky., 32:229.
Horse Creek (Tex.) as place name, 13:27.
Horse-crippler cactus, 11:90.
"Horse Dance Song," music only, 13:292.
Horse-fly, 10:23.
Horse Thief Canyon as place name, 32: 127.
Horse Thief Creek as place name, 32:121.
"Horseback Men" (poem), 16:417-418.
Horseback opinion (dic.), 30:96.
Horseback riding as early amusement, 32:155.
Horsehair: used in cement, 25:139; as cure, 14:268.
Horsehead Canyon as place name, 13:25.
Horsehead Creek as place name, 32:121.
Horsehead Crossing on the Pecos, 13:24-25, 74.
Horsemanship: use of Spanish bit in early Texas, 16:51; see Horse-breaking; Indians.
Horsepen Creek as place name, 32:121.
Horseshoe(s): as magical cure, 14:268; pitching, 25:145; in superstitions, 5: 121, 123; 13:150, 173; 26:232, 251; 30:252.
Hosack, D. M., 20:37, 44.
Hosmer, Edmund, 25:153.
Hospitality, frontier, 32:150.
"Hot as blue blazes," 2:15.
Hot dog (dic.), 34:26.
"Hot pepper" (jump rope term), 18:198.
Hot rod racing, terminology of, 34:11-35.
Hot Springs: N. C., 7:81; 26:159; Tex., 10:76.
Hough, Emerson, 3:226.
Hounds: hunting with, 30:194-204; 35:5; see Dogs.
House, Boyce, 17:154 f.; 25:85; 29:8-9, 13; 30: 88, 90.
House broken (dic.), 35:46.
"House Carpenter, The," with music, 10: 159-160; 23:56-57; cited, 10:135; see "Daemon Lover."
"House that Jack Built," 1:26; 18:188.
House Stream as place name, 32:125.
House-raisings, pioneer, 17:26, 30-31; 26: 200-201 (reprint).
Houses: pioneer in Texas, 13:203-205; 15:175; Texas ranch, 32:148-149.
Houses, haunted; see Part II, Section 7, of *Analytical Index.*
Houston, Sam, 3:87; 6:107 f.; 10:113; 13: 59, 64, 273; 14:158; 15:43, 54, 61 ff.; 19:13; 21:113, 115-116, 117; 25:1 ff.;

30:25; 32:114.
Houston, William S., 9:175 f.
Houston, Tex., 2:61; 5:107; 6:38; 13:22; 15:68; 18:138; 21:113 f., 117 f.; 25: 124, 126; 26:125; 33:8; newspapers, 3:44, 182, 200 f.; 15:52; 36:3, 34.
Houston County, Tex.: place name, 31: 85, 88; 28:146; as setting for razorback yarns, 9:16-24; tales from, 31:8-22.
Houston Stable (early Texas livery stable), 21:118.
Houx, John F., 21:54.
Hovey, Tex., 27:165.
"How Come That Blood on Your Shirt Sleeve," with music, 23:59-63; 26:137-138 (reprint); cited, 25:63; 27:35, 74; 30:31.
"How Firm a Foundation" (cited), 10: 172.
"How Happy Every Child of Grace," with music, 10:179.
Howard, Henry, 16:141.
Howard, James: article, 25:160-170; mentioned, 25:255.
Howard, Roy, 6:88.
Howard Canyon, 15:97.
Howard County, Tex., place name, 31:79, 93.
Howe, Tex., 18:130.
Howell, Ben: article, 22:200-206; mentioned, 22:200.
Howell, James, 34:180.
Howells, Joe A., 31:89.
Hoxie, Jane, 6:39.
"Hoy se casa el Huiltacoche," 29:117.
Hoyt, Homer: article, 16:96-101; mentioned, 16:421.
Huaco as cure for snakebite, 15:168; 26: 295 (reprint).
Huamuxtitlan, 11:27.
Huapango, the Mexican, 35:147-156.
Huastic Indian tale, 32:52.
Huatebampo, valley of, 11:9.
Hubbard, Freeman, 36:105 ff.
Hubbard, H. H., 17:87.
Hubbard, Hugh, 17:79, 83, 84-85.
Hubbard, Louis H., 4:page 19 of appendix; 17:156.
Hubbell, Jay B., 6:221; 14:172.
Hubert, Ernest E., 21:46.
Huckstering on the frontier, 17:35.
Huckvale, Fred, 19:136.
Huddleston, Aldon C., 29:208.
Hudgins, Charles D., 3:141.
Hudson, A. P., 8:61; 18:163; 25:49, 70; 27:33-76 passim.
Hudson, H. C., 21:121.
Hudson, W. H.; article, 16:316-319; mentioned, 4:7 f.; 15:157; 16:421; 24:7; 25:29; 31:46, 48, 51.
Hudson, Wilson M.: articles and prefaces, 21:35-42; 22:179-184; 24:v, 128-132,

132-136; 25:183-194; 26:46-49 (reprint); 27:vi, 138-150; 29:vii; 32:72-100; 33:v-vi, 181-197, 34:v-vi, 219-239; 35:vii-ix; 36:v-vii; mentioned, 21:35; 22:179; 24:128, 132; 25:256; 27:161, 202; 30:225; 31:12; 32:270; 33:181-197, 199; 34:244; 35:61; 36: 102.
Huerta, Solís de la, 16:216.
Huerta, Victoriano, 15:159.
Huffer (dic.), 34:23.
Huffington, Steve, 28:7.
Huffman family (South Carolina), 6:51-53.
Huggins, Jim, 13:160, 169; 26:239, 248.
Hughes, Alex, 33:148.
Hughes, H. H., 4:7.
Hughes, Jim, 33:148 f.
Hughes, Luke, 33:149.
Hughes Springs, Tex., 29:155.
Hugo (legended bullfrog), 14:262-263.
Huguenot proper names, 1:5.
Huichol Indians, 14:208, 215.
Huisache tree, tale involving, 28:158-159.
Huitaca, 4:70, 72 ff.
Huitzil, 11:22, 24 f., 29.
Huitzilopochtli, 11:25, 42.
Huizar, Bruno, 19:192.
"Hull-Gull" (game), 17:150-151.
Human sacrifice, 1:67; 2:8-13; 3:155-156, 197; 22:156.
"Humble Yourself" (cited), 10:173.
Humboldt (naturalist), 25:29.
Hummingbird, 7:30, 40; 25:24 f.; 26: 302 f.
Humor, folk: backwoods, 19:63-81; of the cowboy, 31:99-107; 35:48-59; relating to frontier preachers and preaching, 14:155-168; 30:185-193; 34:51-62; 36: 73-80; Joe Sapp as a typical community wit, 31:34-40; see Anecdotes; Journalism; Jokes; Politics; Pranks.
Humphreys, Col. (oilman), 29:23; 31:69.
Humphreys, Henry, 21:126.
Humphreys, Imogene, 14:53.
Humphreys, W. J., 2:97.
Hundred mile coffee (dic.), 35:48.
"Hungry as a wolf," 2:15.
Hunnicutt, Ruth: article, 22:185-193; mentioned, 22:185.
Hunnington, "Colonel," 3:191 f.
Hunt, the communal in East Texas, 35: 3-10.
Hunt, Flournoy, 21:114, 126.
Hunt, Capt. John C., 21:116.
Hunt County, Tex., place names, 31:78, 88, 91.
Hunter, C. M., 30:267.
Hunter, Dave, 19:152.
Hunter, J. Marvin: articles, 3:67-72; 14: 254-256; 18:126-128; mentioned, 3: 116, 261; 35:56; his Frontier Times magazine, 2:3; 3:67, 97; 4:8; 8:17,

23; 11:107; 14:286; 15:100; 17:156; 18:222; 19:98, 111; 26:260; 27:103; 33:25.
Hunter, John, 22:11.
Hunter, John Warren, 3:11, 13 ff., 19-20, 98.
Hunter, Robert Hancock, 15:65.
Hunter, W. D., 7:161.
Hunting; see Hounds; Hunt; see the following entry.
Hunting, tall tales about; see Munchausen; see Part II, Section 9, of *Analytical Index*.
Hunting Bayou Stream as place name, 32:126.
"Hunting of The Cheviot" (cited), 27:29.
Hunting Shirt Stream as place name, 32: 112, 126.
"Hunting Song," 6:225.
"Hunting the Wren," 6:69; with music, 23:252-253.
Huntington, Collis, 28:47.
Huntsman, Adam, 18:147-148.
Huntsville, Tex., 13:59; 34:57.
Huntsville Penitentiary, 18:214; see "Huntsville-Boun'."
"Huntsville-Boun'," 5:161; 5:page 11 of appendix; 26:163 (reprint).
Hurd, Peter, 22:142.
Hurlbert, James R., 21:132.
Hurley, Elizabeth: article, 25:115-138; mentioned, 25:256.
Hurley, Tom, 33:103.

"Hurrah for Arkansas," with music, 23: 236-237.
Hurricane Stream as place name, 32:126.
"Hurrikin decks of their ponies," 8:118.
Husband, divination of by dream, 36:141-142.
"Husband's Dream, The" (cited), 6:126.
"Hush up, hush up, pretty Polly-o," 10: 140.
Huson, Hobart, 32:118.
Huston, Gen. Almanzon, 21:116.
Hutcheson, William T., 29:208.
Hutchin, John Nathan, 28:84.
Hutchinson, C. E., 31:51.
Hutchinson, W. H.: article, 35:109-111; mentioned, 33:v, 32; 35:166.
Hutchinson County, Tex., place names, 13:61.
Hutto, A. B., 27:181.
Hutto Ranch, 27:180-186.
Huxley, Tex., 17:34.
Hyacinth, origin of, 3:197.
Hyatt, Bill, 33:12.
Hyde (Pennsylvania oilman), 20:51.
Hyde, Imogene, 23:266, 268.
Hyde Park Fairgrounds (Austin, Tex.), 25:135.
Hydetown, Penn., 20:51.
Hydrophobia, 8:24, 43, 66; see Madstone.
Hynes Ranch, 16:373.
"Hypopalorum" as remedy, 8:79-80.
Hysteria, folk curing of, 24:30-31.

I ~

I. W. W., 2:38.
[I . . . ; see also Ah . . . .]
"I Ain't Bothered," 5:166.
"I'm A. Ginger Blue and I tell you mighty true," 5:170.
"I'm Afloat" (cited), 7:161.
"I'm Alone in This World," with music, 10:181-182.
"I Am Bound for the Promised Land" (cited), 10:172.
"I'm Goin' Back to Arkansas Tomorrow," 2:47.
"I am going far away, Nora darling," 23:158.
"I'm Goin' Home," with music, 7:107-108.
"I am going to sing to you, señores," 12: 225-227.
"I'm Gonna Have Me a Red Ball All My Own" (cited), 36:112.
"I'm a Good Old Rebel," 6:143.
"I'm New Bawn," with music, 7:93; 26: 171-172 (reprint).

"I am an old bachelor," 23:249.
"I am an old miser," 23:247.
"I'm off to Philadelphia in the mornin'" (cited), 12:221.
"I'm a poor old bachelor a-settin' around," 6:234.
"I'm the rompedor Romperón," 11:18.
"I'm a roving gambler," 23:184.
"I'm Seventeen Come Sunday," 7:23.
"I'm a steer with blunt horns," with music, 9:118.
"I'm so glad the hogs all dead," with music, 5:162-163.
"I'm tired of workin', but can't fly," 2:64.
"I am a wandering cowboy," 6:190; 26: 136 (reprint).
"I came in by Laredo," 12:200.
"I don't know—living like a wild cat—don't catch nothing, don't eat nothing," 2:16.
"I Don't Like to See Boys," with music, 23:232.
"I dreamt last night I wuz walkin'

("Mr. Lo"), 16:335; trickster motif among, 29:174-175; see Medicine bundle; Medicine men; Pictographs.
Indigo, false *(baptisia)*, 18:161; 26:277.
Indio Creek as place name, 32:131.
Indio Ranch, 13:30.
Indios Junction, Los, 13:30.
Indigestion, remedies for, 8:13, 26, 57.
Indle, S. W., 20:54; 30:79.
Infant(s): sacrifice, 1:67; superstition prohibiting measuring the length of, 13:161; 26:241; see Child; Infanticide; Head.
Infante, Pedro, 28:102.
Infanticide: in folktale, 8:103; see Child; Innocents.
Infare (wedding meal), 7:69; 13:233; 23:25.
"Influenza Train, The" (cited), 36:114.
Ingersoll, Ernest, 7:36; 14:38, 46.
Ingraham, J. H., 14:159.
Ingram, Seth, 8:136.
Initiation, 1:81, 87; 32:152; 35:6 f.; hoaxing a form of on the American frontier, 35:135.
Inmortal as cosmetic and remedy, 12:184, 187.
Innocents, slaughter of as Hebrew prophecy, 1:90.
Innuit (Eskimos), the name of, 1:87.
Inocencio (storyteller), 24:7.
"*Inocente palomita*," 31:150.
Inquest (in anecdote), 14:255-256.
Insall, Clarence, 30:13.
Insanity, folk curing of, 24:39, 110.
Inscriptions: Indian on rock, 2:20, 28; on vehicles, 17:120-125; 35:49.
Insect bite or sting; see Stings.
Insects; see specific names.
Institutions of modern man, primitive folklore bases of, 1:62 ff.
Intangible things, injury through, 1:86 ff.
Interjections: differ in meaning from one culture to another, 22:5; see Exclamations.
Ioni Creek as place name, 32:131.
Iowa, 19:134.
Iowa Indians, 19:82, 89.
Iowa Park, Tex., 8:158.
"*Ir por lana y volver trasquilado*," 24:122.
Ireland, 18:9; satirists in, 1:79; see Irish.
Irion County, Tex., place name, 13:28.
Irish: fairies in Texas, 13:185-189; immigrants and the railroad, 36:109; immigrants, songs about, 36:109-110; immigrants in Texas, 30:115; storytelling style, early, 34:73-116; superstitions, 1:93; tales, 34:73-116.
Irish Creek as place name, 32:127.
"Irish Girl, The," with music, 23:159-160.
Irish Lad, the; see Sennitt, Georgie.

"Irish Potatoes" (game), 13:322-323.
"Irish Trot," 1:10-11; cited, 1:35.
"Irish Washer Woman," 23:232.
Iron as charm against witchcraft, 10:63-64; 14:194.
Iron Head (folk singer), 18:168; 33:8.
Iron(s) Stream as place name, 32:114, 126, 128.
"Iron wedge" bread, 18:1.
Irons, John, 32:114.
Irving, Washington, 3:iv, 9, 119; 4:7; 5:134; 9:124; 10:6; 16:148, 171; 26:106; 33:97.
Irwin, Howard, 33:158.
Isaac (biblical), 19:12.
Isaacs, John, 31:87.
Isaiah, 19:13; as character in folk drama, 11:83 f.
Isbell, Branch: article, 5:104-106; mentioned, 5:93 ff., 183; 22:225.
Ishi (Indian), 1:87.
Ishtar, 31:33; 36:41.
Isidore; see St. Isidore.
Isinglass: Canyon as place name, 13:3; Stream as place name, 32:128.
Isis, 36:41.
Island Stream as place name, 32:119.
Isle du Bois Stream as place name, 13:52; 32:116.
Ismael (Mexican Indian storyteller), 30:9-10.
Israel, "Uncle," 7:103; 11:101.
"It's a-hailin'," 7:107.
"It is for cake that we run in debt," 25:157.
"It's Death to Bonnie and Clyde," 23:95.
"It is not enough to say, 'Our Father',", 14:151.
"It's not what you want that makes you fat," 13:244.
"It's round in your cavy, and it's rope out your hack," 7:179.
"It's whether ye will be a rank robber's wife," 30:40.
"It Just Suit Me," with music, 7:94-95.
"It rains an' it hails an' it's cold stormy weather," 1:13.
"It was in and about the Martinmas time," 25:51.
"It was in a city," with music, 9:185-186.
"It was early in the month of May," 10:148-149.
"It was just before George Custer's last fight," 6:133-134; 23:120.
"It was late one Sunday evening," 23:83.
"It was on last Monday morning, all troubled in mind," with music, 6:123-124.
"It was way down in lower Texas," 6:169.
Italian immigrants: customs of, 30:110-112; superstitions of, 1:86.

J

Jewett, Sarah Orne, 23:286.
Jewish music, influence of on Gypsy music, 29:99-100.
"Jew's Daughter, The" (cited), 27:24 (foldout), 75.
Jibbonancy (dic.), 20:67, 70, 104.
Jicarilla Apaches, 22:133.
"Jig was up," 8:118, 125.
Jiggle juice (dic.), 34:23.
Jim Crow load (dic.), 35:47.
Jim Hogg County, Tex., 13:9.
Jim Nail Branch as place name, 13:58.
Jim Ned Creek, 16:181-182; as place name, 13:58; 32:132.
"Jim Oxford and His Salt Creek Girl," 7:176-178.
Jim Wells County, Tex., 3:47.
Jiménez, Baldemar A.: article, 31:156-164; mentioned, 31:166.
Jimmy (dic.), 34:29.
Jimson weed: poultice or salve of, 8:45; 26:258; tea, 8:50; 26:260.
Jingle-bob earmark, 6:83.
"Jo, jo; carne y hueso huelo aquí," 32:48 f.
Joan of Arc, 25:5; 33:95.
Joan of Arc, Sister, 17:157.
Job (biblical), 19:66.
"Job's Goin' to Heaben," with music, 7:90-91; 26:170 (reprint).
Joe, Peg Leg, 7:84; 26:161.
"Joe Clark, Old," 7:12, 19.
"Joe Bowers," with music, 23:107-109; cited, 6:143.
"Joe Turner," 2:53.
"Joe Turner Blues" (cited), 2:53.
Johannesburg, South Africa, folk dancing in, 36:147-151.
Johannson, Hans, 30:201.
John; see St. John.
John (Negro culture hero); see John tales.
John, "French," 13:48.
John the Baptist, controversy about what he ate in the wilderness, 28:139-140.
John the Bear; see Jack the Bear; Juan Oso.
"John Barleycorn," 20:33.
"John Brown Had a Little Indian," 7:21-22.
"John Brown's Body" (cited), 7:18; 10:122.
John-The-Conqueror-Root chewed for luck, 13:137.
"John Dobber," with music, 23:67-69.
"John Grumlie," 23:228.
"John Hardy," with music, 7:115; cited, 34; 36:104 ff.; see "John Henry."
"John Henry" (cited), 29:173 f.; 30:31, 34; 36:104 ff.; see "John Hardy."
John Law (dic.), 30:79.
John tales, 10:9-54 passim; 21:81-104; 26:55-56 (reprint); 29:178-182.

"Johnnie Brown"; see "Little Johnny Brown."
"Johnnie Cox," 6:145.
"Johnny Germany" (cited), 10:155.
Johnny cake: how made and story of, 6:30-33; story of, 26:69-71 (reprint).
"Johnny Mee-Kee-Mee-Coy," 7:110.
"Johnny Sands," with music, 6:223-225.
Johnson, Judge (Little Rock, Ark.), 19:180.
Johnson, Allen, 30:186.
Johnson, Alvey R., 21:119.
Johnson, Charles H., 36:80.
Johnson, Dr. Charles S., 32:105, 108.
Johnson, Charlie, 7:164-171; 33:84, 86 f.
Johnson, Elmira, 10:59; 13:132.
Johnson, Emma, 7:90, 107; 26:170.
Johnson, Frederick, 28:120-121.
Johnson, George, 28:7.
Johnson, Guy B., 5:147, 155 ff.; 8:161, 164-165; 10:173; 29:174, 187; 32:236; 36:105 ff.
Johnson, Jack, 18:130.
Johnson, James, 25:71.
Johnson, James Weldon, 5:145, 149-153; 7:85-112 passim; 26:169 f; 36:113 ff.
Johnson, Joe, 17:9.
Johnson, Rosamond, 25:116; 36:113 ff.
Johnson, Samuel, 30:28.
Johnson, W. (anthropologist), 29:70, 85.
Johnson, "Wild Horse," 16:118.
Johnson County: Tex., place names, 31:77, 91 f.; Wyo., 33:112.
Johnson rod (dic.), 34:21.
Johnston, Gen., 20:19.
Johnston, Elizabeth Settle, 6:145 f.
Johnston, Hugh Blair, 21:119.
Johnston, Joe B., 33:44.
"Johnny Cock" (cited), 30:34.
"Joh-woh-wonny," with music, 23:257-258.
Joiner, C. M. ("Dad"), 30:78, 81; 31:68, 70.
Joint snake, 4:46; 8:124-128.
Joints, stiff, remedy for, 30:249.
Jokes: moron, 13:106-110; 19:155-161; practical, 9:65; 13:91; 17:10 ff., 71-72; 19:149-154; 32:152-153; see Pranks; see Part II, Section 6, of *Analytical Index.*
"Jol," Capt.; see Hall, Lee.
"Jolly Beggar, The" (cited), 27:24 (foldout), 75.
"Jolly Cowboy, The" (cited), 6:188.
Jonah (dic.), 13:157; 26:237.
Jonah-like experience, 18:44-49.
Jones, Allah, 7:119.
Jones, Asa, 7:174; 16:237, 408; 21:52 ff.
Jones, Buck, 34:70.
Jones, "Buffalo," 6:80.
Jones, Casey, 28:47; 32:207; 34:29; 36:105 f., 115.
Jones, E. O., 28:131-132.

K

L

loma," 12:213.
Le Noir, Phil: article, 10:124-126; mentioned, 10:189; 33:81.
Lea, J. C., 33:78.
Lea, Lida, 3:192.
Leach, MacEdward: article, 30:30-45; mentioned, 27:25 f., 31, 76; 30:293; 32:201; 34:145.
Leacock, Stephen, 30:72, 75.
Lead: for boils, 8:77-78; for sick dogs (jest), 8:28; for nose-bleed, 8:19, 60-61; for poison oak, 8:62; for teething babies, 8:69; for thirst, 8:18; see Lead mine.
Lead Belly, 18:165; 33:8.
"Lead 'em up," 1:9; cited, 1:35.
Lead goats, 15:107 ff.
"Lead this lady to Baltimore, Susie Anna Jane," 1:19.
Lead mine, lost, 3:77 ff.
Lead-pencil cactus, 11:92 f.
Leakey, John, 25:175.
Leakey, T. F., 25:175.
Leakey, Tex., 3:57.
"Leaks like a riddle," 5:87.
Leal, Joaquin, 9:134 f., 138.
Leal, Juan, 19:110, 114.
Learight, Willela, 32:158.
Lease, W. B., 25:175.
Lease-hound (dic.), 15:79.
Leather Stream as place name, 32:126.
Leather-winged bats, 7:28.
Leaton, Ben, 35:83-102 passim.
Leaton, Ed, 35:92.
Leaton, Isabella, 35:92 f.
Leaton, Joseph, 35:93, 95.
Leaton, Juana, 35:84, 86 f., 92 f., 95.
Leaton, William, 35:92 f., 95 f., 97-100.
"Leave it. Ah No! The Land Is Our Own," with music, 6:141-142.
Leazar, Beta, 17:157.
LeBauve, Mrs. Courtney, 31:118.
Lebenswecker, 30:249.
Lechuguilla, 6:102.
Lechuguilla Mtns., 10:73.
LeClercq, Jaques, 36:133.
"Lecture on riding bad horses," by London Brown, 16:273.
Leddy, Betty, 24:73; 26:127.
Lee, J., 15:34.
Lee, Jack H., 15:161.
Lee, James Ward: articles, 30:212-217; 33:164-170; 34:155-161; mentioned, 30:293; 33:199; 34:vi, 244.
Lee, Robert E., 13:40; 16:245; 30:83; 32:114, 164.
Lee, Wilson, 14:163.
Lee Avenue Academy of Music, 18:55.
Lee County, Tex., place name, 13:53.
Leeper, Jim, 35:73 ff.
Leesville, Tex., 33:114.
Left-handedness; see Sinistrality.
"Left hind swing," 8:118.

Leg rattles, 19:85.
Legends; see Part II, Sections 7 and 8, of *Analytical Index*; see names of individuals, places, etc., that figure in legends.
Legends of Texas, 18:vii; 30:5, 8.
Legs: bowed, straightened in folk healing, 24:51; cramps in, remedy for, 35:15; of soldiers continue to pain after amputation, 1:84.
Lehmann, Herman, 18:126; 22:11.
Lehmann, Ruth P. M.: article, 34:73-102; mentioned, 34:vi, 244.
Leisy, Earnest E.: articles, 8:152-154; 9:183-184; mentioned, 8:6, 174; 9:190; 14:169, 172 f.; 23:18.
Leitco, Alma, 30:249.
Lelia, Lake, 6:82.
Lelio (character in folk drama), 11:61.
Lemmons, Theodore G., 4:pages 14, 19 of appendix.
Lemon as remedy, 8:55, 59; 26:261, 263 (reprint).
Lemonade, 25:131-132.
Lemons, Bob (Negro mustanger), 16:61 ff.
Lemons, Bob (ranch foreman), 16:302-303.
Lemons, Duncan, 16:63.
Lemos, Eufemia P. de, 24:63-65.
Lenderman, Mrs. Washie, 31:18 f.
Lent, 36:57, 141.
Leon County, Tex., 3:89; place names, 31:79, 86, 88, 91 f.
Leon Creek, 9:133; as place name, 32:121.
Leon River, 3:95; 18:145; 30:196 ff.
Leon Springs (near San Antonio, Tex.), 18:97.
Leoncita Creek as place name, 32:121.
Leopard; see Jaguar.
Leopard Creek as place name, 32:121, 124.
L'Epinay, M. de, 13:272.
Lerma, Felipe, 24:42.
Lerma, Mex., 11:30.
"*Les cantaré un corrido*," with music, 12:236-237.
Leser family of Austin, Tex., 35:107-108.
Leslie, Warren, 25:161.
"Let every man skin his own eel," 13:242.
"Let Me Sleep in Your Barn," with music, 6:124-125; 23:116.
"Let's all go down to see Rowzer," 17:94.
"Let's go down to Jurdan," 19:1, 6, 8.
"'Let's go huntin', says Robbin to Bobbin," 6:70; 23:253.
Letona (Governor of Coahuila and Texas), 19:187.
Letras, 11:49 ff.
Letters: riddle about, 24:126; superstitions about, 5:116-117; 13:162; 26:242-

121; 9:146-149; 13:137 ff., 155-160; 24:114 ff.; 26:235-239 (reprint); 35: 14; 36:138 f.; see Destiny.
"Luck of Edenhall," 1:92.
Lucket, Dr., 16:32.
Lucky accidents, tales involving; see Brave Tailor; Doctor Know-All; see Part II, Section 9, of *Analytical Index.*
Lucky Boy, 22:30-32, 44.
Lucky Woman, 22:4.
Lucrezia Borgia (Buffalo Bill's rifle), 9:11.
"Lucy Long" (cited), 7:18.
Lucy Stream as place name, 32:115.
Lueg, Maurita Russell: article, 28:160-166; mentioned, 28:168.
Lufkin, Tex., 7:96; 18:144; 25:117, 119; 30:184; 36:12.
Luján, Eliseo, 4:21.
Luján, Mauro, 13:128; 26:123-124.
Luján, Natividad, 28:116.
Luke, Bill, 17:85.
Luling, Tex., 31:66; as place name, 13: 62, 74.
Lullabies, 23:267-268.
"Luluh," 5:164-166; 5: page 10 of appendix.
Lumbering, tales about, 30:178-184.
Lumberjack songs, 8:160.
Lumholtz, Carl, 14:207, 223.
Luminarias, 9:76.

Lumm, L. M., 29:151.
Lummis, Charles F., 3:8, 132; 4:22; 9:77; 14:38, 42, 48 f., 54, 57, 78, 81; 25:42.
Lump jaw, remedies for, 8:28-29, 41-42.
Lumpkin, Ben Gray, 25:71.
Luna (Spanish poet), 29:95.
Lunacy, remedy for, 8:59; 26:263 (reprint).
Lunched (dic.), 34:20.
Lung trouble, remedy for, 8:59; 26:263 (reprint).
Lupe, Dona (folk healer), 10:83 ff.
"Lupita," with music, 4:24.
"Lurella," 23:100; see "Jealous Lover."
Luz del llano, 9:53.
Luz Bel: as original name of Lucifer, 30:231; in folk drama, 36:16, 20.
Lye: as remedy, 8:12, 22, 70, 77; soap, 8:55; 35:106-108.
Lyford, Tex., 4:36.
Lying; see Tall tales; see Part II, Section 6, of *Analytical Index.*
Lying partnership (tales), 10:25-26; 12: 55-57; 18:79-80; 19:36-41.
Lyman, J. H., 15:114.
Lynn County, Tex., 6:73.
Lyons, Billy, 31:129.
Lyons, Charley, 31:101; 33:42.
Lytle, James T., 7:161 f.; 10:122.
Lytle, Luther, 13:228.
Lytton Springs, Tex., 13:43.

M

"Mable, Mable, set the table," 18:198; 26:205.
[Mac-; see also Mc-.]
MacAllan, Mr. (from Hidalgo County, Tex.), 9:91.
MacGillivray, James, 33:103, 105.
Macedonia, 36:35 ff.
Machines, folk attitude toward, 36:104-105.
Macht, Rabbi Wolff, 11:106.
Maciel, Antonio, 13:128; 26:123.
Maciel, Bonifacia, 13:128-129; 26:123 f.
MacKenzie, Ray, 8:161; 28:27.
Mackin, Ethel, 8:21.
Macksburg, Ohio, 18:61; 20:28 f.
Mac Veenglish; see Veenglish.
"Mad as a biting sow," 18:211.
"Mad as a setting hen," 2:15.
Mad dog, child escapes from, 24:46; see Madstone.
"Madam, will you make me a cambric shirt," with music, 10:137-138.
Maddox, Allen, 6:152.
Maddrey, Etta, 3:175.
Madeira vine as remedy for sore eyes,

18:159; 26:275 (reprint).
Madero, Francisco, 24:87; 30:60.
Madero, Raul, 21:25.
Madison, James, 34:38.
Madison County: Ark., 30:215; Tex., 14: 267-268; 31:91.
Madison Square Garden, 18:105.
Madisonville, Tex., 23:188.
"Madre mia, lléveme uste al baño," 30:49.
Madrid, 36:30.
Madrid, Margarita, 35:101.
Madrona tree, its bark and roots as dye, 18:161; 26:276 (reprint).
Madstone, 8:24, 66; 28:3-17; 29:147-152; 31:37.
Märchen; see Part II, Section 5, of *Analytical Index.*
Maggies (dic.), 34:16.
Make out a meal (dic.), 13:248.
Mag Rath, battle of, 34:74.
Magdalena, N. M., 27:103.
Mage (foreman of SMS Ranch), 16:373-383.
Magee, Augustus, 14:198.

Magellan, Straits of, 4:59.
Magic: in connection with the human hand, 4:91-97; contagious, 35:7; in Indian tales, 22:21, 29, 31, 33, 35, 45-46, 48 ff., 57, 80, 97-100, 104-105, 107, 112-113; of Negro conjurers, 9:151-152; 13:139 ff.; 17:113-114; in primitive art, 4:86; among Tejas Indians, 9:168-170; sympathetic, 1:82 ff.; 13:137 ff., 174-175; 25:196; 26:253; 36:139; white and black along Texas-Mexican border, 25:195-199; see Charms; Conjurers; Voodoo; Witch(es); Witchcraft; see Part II, Section 5, of *Analytical Index*.
Magic Creek as place name, 32:115.
Magical objects in folktales; see Part II, Section 5, of *Analytical Index*.
Magician; see *Brujo*; "Twa Magicians"; Wizard.
Magnolia Stream as place name, 32:116.
Magpie, 7:26; 8:87; 22:19.
"Magpie, The," 8:87.
Magues (Indian), 22:142-148.
Maguey plant, 9:94-95, 98; tale involving, 14:18 ff.
Maguire, Mrs. Pat, 33:vi.
Magus, Simon, 33:189.
Magyars, their ballads, 2:11.
Mahone, Gen., 32:165.
"Maid Freed from the Gallows" (cited), 27:24 (foldout), 29, 60 f., 75; see "Hangman's Rope" for late version.
"Maid of Monterrey," with music, 7:160-163; cited, 10:122.
Maidu Indians, 14:68.
Maiville, Phillip, 33:124.
Major, Mabel: article, 10:131-168; mentioned, 10:186 f., 189; 12:251; 17:154, 156; 18:ix; 27:33, 56, 77.
Major Stream as place name, 32:126.
"*Mal de Amor, El,*" 29:89.
Mal de ojo, 17:73; 27:187 ff.; see Evil eye.
"*Mala la hubisteis, franceses,*" 25:89.
Malaria, remedy for, 8:59; 26:263 (reprint).
Malchus (character in folk drama), 11:65.
Malden, Mass., 29:82.
Maley, Albert, 5:97.
Malinchi (princess), 9:74-75; 25:216.
Malinowski, Bronislaw, 29:185, 189; 32:84-86, 95, 97, 210.
Malke, Robert, 30:258.
Mallery, Garrick, 19:100 ff.
Mallihua (marihuana), 14:227 ff .
Malo, "Tío" Pancho, 8:111; 10:105-108.
Malo in goats, remedy for, 8:42.
"Malograda" (tale), 14:249-250.
Malone, Dumas, 30:186.
Malone, John, 32:118.
Malone Creek as place name, 32:118.

Malta, Mont., 6:193.
Malthy, Jeff, 13:39.
Maltsberger, Jack, 16:405.
Maltsberger, W. J., 8:22, 38.
"Mama, Have You Heard the News?" (cited), 36:106.
"Mama told me to open the door," 23:217.
Mame (fruit), 9:92.
Man, stages in his development, 1:68.
"Man from the Gallows, The," 25:188-189.
Man in the moon; see Moon.
Man on the pot (oil-field dic.), 4:65.
Manadas of range horses, 16:33, 38, 55-58, 71-73, 79, 96-97, 173-175.
Manahuilla (Indian girl), 32:132.
Manahuilla Stream as place name, 32:132.
Mañanitas (dic.), 21:4.
"*Mañanitas de San Juan, Las,*" 6:20.
Manceras, Valentin, 21:6.
"*Mancornadora, La,*" 12:219.
Mandan Indians, 14:69; burial customs of, 18:131.
Maney, Mason, 19:134; see Manney.
Mangana (rope throw), 18:113-114.
Manganador, 18:113.
Mango, 9:89, 93, 98.
Mangostins, 9:98.
Mankin, Carolyn: article, 30:260-265; mentioned, 30:293.
Manley, Walter, 21:52 ff.
Mann, Marshall, 21:114, 126.
Mann, Pamela (Pamelia), 15:65; 21:113-135.
Mann, William, 21:114, 130.
Manney, Mason, 8:25-26; see Maney.
Mannington, W. A., 20:44.
Mano for tortilla making, 15:137.
Manoa family (Brownsville, Tex.), 4:37.
Manole the Masterbuilder, 2:11 f.
Mansfield, Richard, 13:235.
Mansfield, La., battle of, 33:123.
Mansfield, Tex., 7:126.
Mansfield Cemetery, 18:132.
Manship, Andrew, 35:32.
Mansion House (early Houston, Tex., hostelry), 21:117-119.
Manta, Justo, 17:66.
Mantle, Mickey, 29:81.
Mantrams, 1:93.
Manuel la Changa, 9:61; 26:149.
Manure: buffalo, 6:79-80; 8:44; cow, 8:44, 49, 77; sheep, 8:57, 59.
Manzanet, Damian, 3:133-134; 13:6.
Maoris of New Zealand, foundation sacrifices among, 2:8.
Map, Walter, 36:132.
Mapes vs. the State, 16:19-20.
Mapimi, mines of, 4:15.
Maple, Ed, 16:118.
Maple sap, 18:75.

McCarty, Henry, 33:76.
McCarty, Joe, 35:109 ff.
McCauley, J. E., 18:xi, 1; 33:4, 88.
McClain, T. J., 17:87.
McClellan Creek as place name, 6:75-76.
McClellan saddle, 33:16.
McClesky, Cordie, 25:75-85; 26:336-338, 346.
McClesky, George, 13:203.
McClosky (member of Chisom's gang), 33:74 f.
McClure, S. S., 36:90.
McCord, May Kennedy, 23:92, 193, 196, 202.
McCormick, Edna, 25:35; 26:310.
McCormick, Jim, 20:21, 28.
McCormick, W. L., 25:35; 26:311.
McCullen, J. T., Jr.: articles, 30:132-139; 33:128-135; 34:175-185; 36:125-134; mentioned, 30:293; 33:199; 34:244; 36:vi, 154.
McCulloch, Ben, 3:20 f.; 18:94.
McCulloch, W. P., 13:268.
McCulloch County, Tex., 3:18; 6:175; 21:46; place name, 31:81, 92.
McCullough, Dan, 10:50-51.
McCullough-Williams, Martha, 15:56.
McCumber, Kate, 30:121.
McCutcheon, Roger P.: article, 33:176-180; mentioned, 33:200.
McDaniel, E. T., 31:87.
McDaniel, H. F., 3:118-119; 10:127.
McDavid, Raven I., Jr., 32:64, 71.
McDonald, Bill, 33:123.
McDonald, Edward, 36:12.
McDonald, J. M., 34:156.
McDonald County, Mo., 27:184.
McDowell, Gen., 20:19.
McDowell (Camp), Ariz., 9:97.
McDowell County, W. Va., 18:32.
McDuff, Marihelen, 25:165, 168.
McFaddin family (Victoria County, Tex.), 13:300.
McFarland, Jack, 34:35.
McGary, A., 17:86.
McGee, James M., 21:120, 132.
McGillivray, Duncan, 25:41.
McGinnes, Jim, 16:141.
McGinnis, John, 4:page 17 of appendix; 25:11.
McGloin, James, 30:115, 118.
McGloin, Pat, 30:115, 118.
McGrew, J. C., 25:177.
McGruder (Negro folk character), 21:90ff.
McGuffey First Reader, 33:17.
McGuire, Harriet, 10:71.
McIlhenny, Edward A.: article, 14:135-144; mentioned, 14:286.
McKay, Mrs. Arch, 36:11.
McKay, George, 11:103; 26:221.
McKean County, Penn., 20:42.
McKee, Fred, 17:156.

McKee, William, 17:79.
McKeithan, D. M., 17:vi.
McKellar, Sarah S.: article, 12:101-106; mentioned, 12:vi, 254.
McKenna, James A., 15:165; 26:293.
McKenzie: Expedition, 16:80; Trail, 6:82.
McKenzie, E. C., 36:70.
McKinley, William, 36:114.
McKinney, Collin, 28:11-13.
McKinney, Eliza C., 25:176.
McKinney Falls (Tex.), 16:173; 26:107f.
McLain, Mrs. C. B., 10:157.
McLaughlin, Guy, 33:44.
McLaurin, J. J., 20:9, 12, 49.
McLean, Angus, 7:168.
McLean, Eunice, 7:169.
McLean, Katie, 7:169.
McLean, Norman, 7:169.
McLean, W. P., 3:105, 107.
McLennan County, Tex., 1:52; 13:23, 37.
McManus, Seumas, 1:4; 4:page 14 of appendix.
McMillan, John M., 15:76.
McMullen, Mrs. B. H., 20:28.
McMullen, John, 30:115, 118.
McMullen County, Tex., 3:3, 28-43, 60, 84; 13:45, 49; 16:19; 17:118; 26:83-100; place name, 31:76.
McNeil, Angus, 19:185.
McNeil, Irving, 25:22; 26:300-301.
McNeil, Norman L. (Brownie): articles, 21:1-34; 22:168-178; 26:150-155 (reprint); 27:23-77; 29:32-44; 35:65-72; mentioned, 17:155; 21:1; 22:168; 23:8; 25:119, 136; 27:v, 202; 29:233; 35:166.
McNeil, Tex., 3:229; 26:115.
McNeil Branch (Crosby County, Tex.), 3:111.
McNeill, Hampton, 15:166; 26:293.
McNeill, Leslie, 5:97.
McNeill, P. E., 5:97.
McNeill, Pate, 3:30; 26:85, 89; see the next entry.
McNeill, Pete, 24:55-56; see the preceding entry.
McNeill, Tol, 3:46.
McNeill, W. E., 5:97.
McNeill, Wallace, 3:38; 26:94.
McNelly, L. H., 6:150.
McPherson, C. R., 25:177.
McQuay (oil-field foreman), 20:54.
McSween, Alexander, 33:70 ff.
McTee, A. R.: articles, 4:64-67; 34:202-213; mentioned, 4:115, 117; 34:vi, 244.
McWhirter, Mrs. George M., 33:137 ff.
"Me abandonastes, Mujer," with music, 4:42-43.
"Me dió las calabazas," 12:219.
Meacham, W. C., 25:177.

Meter in folk music, 32:248.
Metfessel, Milton, 8:163.
Metheglin Creek, 3:208; as place name,
13:41-42, 75.
Methodist(s): in anecdotes, 13:100-101;
30:127-128; in baptizing chant, 19:2;
ministers on the frontier, 35:19-33.
Methvin, Henry, 35:37 f., 44.
Methvin, Ivan, 35:37 f., 44.
Methvine, J. J., 22:11.
Metzger, John, 36:56.
Meusebach, John L., 36:51 f.
Mexia (Tex.) Prisoner of War Camp,
30:200.
"Mexican," meaning of to certain Mexi-
can Indians, 12:136; see Mexicanos.
Mexican hairless dog as cure for rheu-
matism, 8:13, 65.
"Mexican hog," 13:23.
Mexican overdrive (dic.), 35:47.
Mexican Springs (in Texas Big Bend),
13:56.
Mexican strawberry (cactus fruit), 6:12.
Mexican Stream as place name, 32:115.
Mexican superstitions, 1:65; 2:75-84;
4:15; 5:115 ff.; 9:63-68 passim; 10:77-
78, 100; 13:120-129; 19:50, 94-105;
22:164 ff.; 24:114-118; 28:164-165;
29:214-225.
Mexican War, 3:24, 84, 97; 10:112-123
passim; 19:74, 130; 23:197.
Mexican Water Hole (near Refugio,
Tex.), 24:3 ff.
Mexicanos (dic.), 12:142; see "Mexican."
Mexico City, 3:36, 97, 234; 18:52; 26:
289.
Meyer, Dean, 10:171 ff.
Meyer, Edward W., Jr., 25:39; 26:303.
Meyer, Friedrich Wilhelm, 25:91.
Meyer, Henry E.: article, 10:169-185;
mentioned, 10:189.
Meyer, Julius, 25:137.
"Mi Caballo Bayo," 6:21.
"Mi casa es pequeña," 8:91.
"Mi chinita me decía," 12:228; 26:157.
"Mi marido está en la cama," with mu-
sic, 4:22.
"Mi novia, mi maguey," 14:18.
"Mi Querida Nicholasa," 6:21.
Miami: Fla., 12:234; 33:134; Tex., 6:73;
36:62.
Miami es la población," 12:234-235.
Mica, Joseph, 36:106.
Mice: how to catch (tall tale), 19:68; as
remedy, 30:251; vomited by bewitched
girl, 10:66; see Mouse.
Michael, the archangel, fights Lucifer,
30:231; 32:178; 36:16 f.
Michael, Dorothy Jean: article, 18:129-
136; mentioned, 18:222; 36:42.
Michaelis, Helen: article, 16:339-342;
mentioned, 16:422.
Michel, Concha, 12:229.

Michiel, John, 33:131.
Michis Indians, 12:162 ff.
Michoacan, 11:22, 27.
Micks, Don W., 25:39.
Mictlancihuatl, 22:158, 163.
Mictlanteceutli, 12:143 ff.
Mictlantecuhtli, 22:156, 158, 163.
Midas, Mexican legend of, 15:134-136;
30:239.
Middlebrook, G. F., 30:184.
Middleton, John, 30:165.
Midland, Tex., 6:86 f.; 13:51; 21:43.
Midland County, Tex., 6:85.
Midnight Auto Supply (dic.), 34:21.
"Midnight Special, The," 23:183; cited,
36:115.
Midwifery, Negro, 19:21-28; see Labor
pains.
Miel (juice of mescal), 9:94, 98.
Mier, Mex., 24:20; 10:110, 113.
Mier Expedition, 10:110, 113.
"Mighty pretty motion," with music, 17:
96-97.
Milam, Ben, 7:42; 28:11-12.
Milam County, Tex., 3:96, 99-102; 10:
127; 13:27; 26:106; place name, 31:
79, 86, 88, 91, 93.
Milam Square, San Antonio, Tex., 13:1;
22:172.
"Milamo" bird, 7:40 f.
Milburn, George, 36:108 ff.
Milburn, W. H., 14:156 f.
Mildren, Jacob, 20:52.
Mile and a Half Stream as place name,
32:120.
Miles (gang-leader), 13:65.
Miles, A. L.: article, 30:194-204; men-
tioned, 29:157; 30:293.
Miles, Elton R.: articles, 25:205-216;
27:171-179; 28:106-122; 35:83-102;
mentioned, 25:256; 27:202; 28:vii,
168; 35:166.
Miles, Mrs. Elton R., 27:164.
Miles, Eva, 7:85, 95; 26:173.
Milk: ghostly stealing of, 7:127; of mare
as remedy for whooping cough, 8:17;
in various remedies, 8:54, 63, 66,
76 f., 84; see Buttermilk.
Milk-fed bass (tale), 22:200-202.
Milk purslane; see Purslane.
Milk snake, 4:45; 7:26.
Milkweed: for rattlesnake bite, 8:63;
26:263 (reprint); as other remedy,
8:53, 70; 10:89.
Milky Way, 2:98; 8:91; 9:50; creation
of, 14:128; see Stars.
"Mill Pond, " 1:21, 35.
Mill Stream as place name, 32:125.
Millar (assayer), 32:62.
Millar, Pete, 34:35.
Miller (Live Oak County, Tex., treasure
hunter), 3:55.
Miller, Alexander, 30:155.

Miller, Betty, 8:65; 26:264.
Miller, Billy, 13:113 ff.
Miller, Ernest, 5:97.
Miller, Gabe, 14:258-259.
Miller, Hazel, 30:107, 114.
Miller, James, 16:23 f.
Miller, Joaquin, 27:97.
Miller, Joe, 28:87.
Miller, Roy, 12:viii.
Miller, S. G., 5:97.
Miller, Samuel, 16:23.
Miller, Seymour, 30:105.
Miller, Thomas B., 27:113.
Miller, V. G., 5:97.
"Miller Boy," 1:13; 13:306, 325-326; cited, 1:35; 7:17.
Miller and the Devil (tale), 14:251-252.
Millerites, 35:25.
Mills, Enos A., 14:46 ff.
Mills, Roger Q., 36:87.
Mills brothers of South Texas, 3:38-39; 26:95-96.
Mills County, Tex., 13:258 ff; 14:200 ff.; 19:167 ff.; 26:189 ff.
Milne, Alexander, Jr., 9:176.
Milne, Lorus J., 29:13.
Milne, Margery J., 29:13.
Milstead family (Bandera County, Tex.), 13:35-36.
Milton, John, 28:66; 34:13.
Milton (N. C.) *Chronicle*, 8:152; 14:169 ff.
Mindietta, Tex., 10:94.
Mine Stream as place name, 32:128.
Mineral or gold-finding rod, 3:45, 91, 100 f.; see Divining rod; Minometer.
Mineral Stream as place name, 32:128.
Mineral Wells, Tex., 13:3; 21:52.
Mines, lost, 3:3-108 passim; 9:133 ff.; 10:71-77; 12:173-174; 22:149 ff.; 28:114; 30:12-14, 19, 266-272; 32:57-63; see Part II, Section 8, of *Analytical Index*; see names of mines.
Mines, tales of from Germany (mine spirits), 30:262-265.
Ministers; see Preachers; Preaching; Religion.
Minnesingers, 32:246, 248.
Minometer for finding treasure, 6:5; see Divining rod.
Minor, J. P., 31:89.
Minstrels, 22:173.
Minter, Billy, 3:174.
Miracles, 1:70; 10:53-54; 24:102-106; see Tornadoes; see Part II, sections 1 and 8, of *Analytical Index*.
Mirage, 16:131.
Miranda, Bernardo de, 3:5, 13, 15.
Miration (dic.), 5:82.
Miraval, Jesús, 15:122 ff.
Mired Mule Ranch, 32:149.
Mireles, Jovita Gonzales de: article, 16:396-402; mentioned, 16:420; 19:111.

Miro, Gov. (of La.), 19:177-193 passim.
Mirrick (or Merrick), Timothy, 6:210; 32:202.
Mirrors in superstition, 13:148, 153, 160 f.; 26:231, 234, 240 f. (reprint); 30:255.
Miscarriage in Mexican folk belief, 24:114 ff.
Misfortune, omens of, 5:120-122; see Luck; Omens; Superstitions.
Mishaps in tall tales; see Part II, Section 9, of *Analytical Index*.
"Miss Susan Jane," with music, 23:241.
Mission cactus, 11:92.
Mission Creek as place name, 32:127.
Mission River, 13:4.
Missionaries in Texas-Mexican border country, 17:67-68.
"Missionary Baptist," 19:6.
Mississippi, 4:48; "blues" from, 2:64.
Mississippi River, 18:19, 45, 52, 60, 74; 20:98.
Mississippi screamer (dic.), 18:69.
Mississippi Valley, 21:106; Child ballads in, 27:23 ff.
Missoula, Mont., 21:46.
Missouri, 4:45; 5:65; 9:9; 19:89; 36:40.
Missouri River, 28:73.
Missouri Volunteers, 35:85.
"Mr. Chinnery, then an M. A. of great parts," 5:11.
"Mr. Frog he would a-wooing ride," with music, 5:24.
Mister-ladies (dic.), 18:93.
"Mr. Lo" as pioneers' name for Indians, 16:335.
"Misther [sic] frog lived in a well," 5:9.
Mistletoe: as remedy, 8:40, 57, 70; 10:86; 19:57; 26:262 (reprint); superstition involving, 13:148; 26:231 (reprint).
"Mrs. Williams' Lamentation," with music, 7:156-159.
Mitchell, Charley, 20:40 f.
Mitchell, Clara, 20:40 f.
Mitchell, Dave, 20:40 f.
Mitchell, Frank, 6:83; 16:409.
Mitchell, Grover C., 30:167.
Mitchell, Helen, 19:21.
Mitchell, J. D., 21:47, 49.
Mitchell, John E., 19:108.
Mitchell, Ind., 3:229; 26:115.
Mitla, 12:249.
Miwok Indians, 14:67.
Mix, Oliver Stokes, 34:63.
Mix, Tom, his portrayal of the cowboy, 34:63-71.
Mixtlancihuatl, 22:156.
"Moaning" dove, 7:31-32.
Mobeetie, Tex., 6:76; 9:32; 18:4; 27:182.
Mobile, Ala., 7:84.
Moccasin (footgear) speaks, saves man, 22:106.

Moccasin (snake): stump tail, 5:58 f.;
water, 5:59; 26:279; water, swallows
its young, 21:50.
Moccasin Creek as place name, 32:121.
Mochis, Los, Mex., 11:6.
Mock bidding in Jamaica, 34:145-153.
Mockingbird: its mocking qualities, 6:10-
11; 21:109; 26:19 ff.; in tale (roped),
19:51-52; and woodpecker believed
related, 7:32.
"Mocking birds sang in the sixty trees,"
3:147.
Moctezuma, 12:249; see Montezuma.
Model T Ford epigrams, 17:120-125.
Moebus, Arthur, 30:258 f.
Moerbe, Mrs. E. F., 30:258.
Moerbe, Martin, 30:258.
Mohammed, 4:94.
Mohammedans, 1:58, 71.
Mohawk Valley (N. Y.), 23:190.
Moira, 33:190.
Moki Indians, 1:5, 67.
Molasses: as remedy, 8:33, 35; 14:268;
see Syrup.
Mole, 5:18, 48; as coyote's wife, 14:66;
captures horse, 22:51-52; 26:3.
"Molly, Molly Bride" (game), 17:142-
143; cited, 1:36.
Molpe (character in folk drama), 11:61.
Monarco (chief of dancers), 14:215.
Monardes, Nicholás, 33:129.
Moncayo, José Pablo, 35:156.
Monclova, Mex., 9:86; 24:87-88.
Moncrieff, Hugh, 25:24; 26:302.
Monday, superstitions concerning, 7:120;
13:154, 173.
"Monday for h e a l t h, T u e s d a y for
wealth," 13:154.
Money: mysteriously provided, 24:47;
superstitions about, 5:123-124; 13:165-
166; 26:245 (reprint).
Money, John A., 31:88.
Monitor (newspaper), 19:68.
Monkey(s): form tail-to-tail chain, 20:
69-70; "signifying," 21:125.
"Monkey" (mineral rod), 3:45.
"Monkey and the Baboon, The," 31:128,
133.
Monkey motion (dic.), 34:25.
Monkey Stream as place name, 32:112,
126.
Monroe, Marshall, 3:44.
Monroe, Zack, 33:48.
Monroe, W. Va., 36:107.
Monster B r i d e g r o o m ; see Cupid and
Psyche.
Montague, Margaret Prescott, 3:120.
Montague County, Tex., 3:83, 97, 229;
26:115; place name, 31:89.
Montaigne, 25:156.
Montalgo (deputy sheriff), 4:35 ff.
Monte Albán (Mex.), 12:246 ff.
Monte Redondo (South Texas), 16:33.

Montejo, Francisco de, 16:200.
Montemayor, Juan de la Garza, 29:223,
225.
Monterrey, Mex., 3:52, 66, 93; 10:113,
118, 120, 122 f.; 12:208 f.; battle of,
in song, 7:160-163; flood of, 12:152 ff.;
robbery at, 8:119-120; 18:181.
Montes Claros, Don Muño, 24:73; 26:
127.
Montezuma, 3:6, 234; capital of, 3:7;
cave of, 3:231, 233-236; legend of in
New Mexico, 14:174; and Monte
Albán, 12:249; in New Mexican folk
festival, 9:72-76; in hero tale, 11:9-
47 passim.
Montgomery, Ellen, 13:233.
Montgomery: Ala., 19:25; Tex., 10:93-
94.
Montgomery County, Tex., 5:93; 17:81;
place name, 31:82, 93.
Montigny, Dumont de, 21:106 ff.
Montpelier, Ind., 20:42.
Mooar, J. Wright, 13:61.
Mooar's Draw (Creek) as place name,
6:82; 13:61.
Mooch (dic.), 1:45.
Moon: affects size of scar cattle brand
makes, 30:257; as archetype, 36:98-
99; and birth, 2:96; 19:23; as cheese,
12:13-19, 214; 22:62-64; 32:49-52;
man or woman in the, 4:76-77; 7:80;
22:26; 29:197 ff.; superstitions involv-
ing, 13:157, 166, 172; 26:237, 245,
250-251 (reprint); 30:257; tying
horse to tip of, 12:72-75; 30:238-239;
as w e a t h e r sign (lunar reckoning:
"*Epacta*"), 2:95-97.
Moon, Joe, 20:25.
Mooney, James, 22:111, 131, 133.
Mooney, Lump, 16:414.
Moonlighter (dic.), 35:46.
Moonshine: in the Big Thicket of Texas,
23:24; in Texas Hill Country, 17:47-
48.
Moor, Charles Paul, 18:4.
Moore, A. W., 18:44.
Moore, Arbie: article, 6:196-197; men-
tioned, 6:242.
Moore, Bessie, 36:3 ff.
Moore, "Uncle" Billy, 6:48-51.
Moore, Byron, 23:212, 232, 234.
Moore, Dorothy: article, 18:141; men-
tioned, 18:222.
Moore, E. T., 25:177.
Moore, Eunice, 7:119.
Moore, Francis, Jr., 21:120.
Moore, Gabe, 8:15.
Moore, Helen Ashworth: article, 13:300-
336; mentioned, 13:338.
Moore, Jack, 8:25.
Moore, John M., 35:58-59, 62.
Moore, John W., 21:120, 124, 132.
Moore, Julia A., 33:165.

13:185-189; mentioned, 13:338; see Blittersdorf, Louise von.
Mosley, Tom, 4:33; 21:26 ff.; 26:145.
Mosqueda, José, 30:287.
Mosquitos, 18:6; 19:136; tales about, 18:80; 20:74-75.
Moss, Tate, 13:36.
Moss (tree) used in cement, 25:139.
Moss Creek as place name, 32:120.
Moss Hill, Tex., 29:209.
Moss Stream as place name, 32:118.
"Mother, Mother, I am sick," 18:195; 26:203 (reprint).
Mother Goose rhymes, 23:207.
"Motherless Child" (cited), 10:173.
Motherwell manuscript, 25:59; 35:66.
Motifs; see Part I of *Analytical Index*.
Motley County, Tex., 16:84; place name, 31:77, 92.
Motor-mouth (dic.), 34:27.
Mott Stream as place name, 32:116.
Mound Prairie as place name, 13:28.
Mound Stream as place name, 32:119.
"Mount, mount for the chase!" (poem), 3:225.
Mt. Bonnell, legend of, 3:171 ff.
Mt. Emory, 28:114.
Mt. Franklin, 3:131.
Mt. Morris Theatre, 18:55.
Mt. Scott, 22:130.
Mt. Tolima, 4:71.
Mt. Zion, 7:112.
Mountain opens, 22:33.
Mountain boomer, 5:65.
Mountain Elk (Indian), 16:161.
Mountain goat, 22:125; 25:40-41.
Mountain Home, Tenn., 20:37.
Mountain laurel, beans of used as intoxicant by Indians, 18:162; 26: 277.
Mountain lion, 22:18, 31 f., 125; see Cougar; Panther.
Mountain oyster (dic.), 13:217.
Mountain pink as cure, 8:55; 26:261.
Mountain Spirit, 30:265.
Mountain stem-winder (fabulous beast), 7:39.
Mountain Stream as place name, 32:119.
Mourning customs, Mexican, 2:81-82; 22:155 ff.
Mourning dove, 7:31-32; 26:285.
Mourning Dove (Indian), 14:40, 66 ff.
Mouse, 5:5 ff.; 6:39-41; 22:44; 26:68, 71-73, 77-79, 80-81, 81-82; see Mice.
Mouth disease in animals, remedy for, 8:46.
Movies and the cowboy, 33:51-68; 34:63-71; see Western hero.
Moxie-mead, 25:132-133.
Mozambique, 36:150.
Mud: tales involving, 8:44, 49, 53, 58; 25:7-8; 33:100-109; as place name, 13:47; 32:119.
Mud Forest, "King bear of," 18:76.

Mud puppies, 4:51-52; see Salamander; Water dog.
Muddy Creek as place name, 32:119.
"Muddy roads call de mile-post a liah," 11:103.
Mueller, Esther L.: article, 36:51-59; mentioned, 36:v, 154.
Mueller, Willie F., 30:260.
Muerto Creek as place name, 13:46.
Mugging cattle, 18:105 ff.
"Muh fathah died w'en Ah wus sebben years ole," 29:163.
Muir, Andrew Forest: article, 21:113-135; mentioned, 21:113.
Muir, Edwin, 27:129 ff.
Muisca Indians, 3:7; 4:68.
Mukewater Creek as place name, 32:127.
Mulberry Canyon as place name, 13:25.
Mulberry: leaf tea as remedy, 8:67; roots as dye, 13:222.
Mulberry Stream as place name, 32:116.
Mule(s), 5:167; 10:52; in tales, 13:68; 16:348-350; 19:29-35; 20:64, 86; 22: 202-204; 25:240-241; 28:59, 135-138; 29:51; 30:175; raising, 16:56-59.
Mule cactus, 11:91.
Mule Creek as place name, 13:26-27; 32:121.
Mule-tail weed tea as remedy, 8:83.
Muleshoe, Tex., 13:47.
Muley (dic.), 16:367; 18:106.
"Muley" saddle, 16:367.
Mullein as remedy, 8:52 ff.; 13:169; 18:159; 26:261, 275.
Mullen, Patrick B.: article, 35:133-145; mentioned, 35:166.
Mullenhoff, Karl, 25:193.
Mullens, James W. ("Honey Jim"), 6:198, 201.
Mullins (horse-breaker), 16:257-258.
Mullin's Prairie, 7:101.
Mumblety-peg, 25:145; 36:49.
Mumme, S. B., 8:9.
Mumps, remedies for, 8:78-79, 82.
Munchausen, Baron, and his tales, 12:1; 18:84-85; 19:42-56; 20:4-5, 54; see the following entry.
"Munchausen Philosopher's Stone," 20:53-54; 30:79.
Mundine, Hank, 28:147.
Muñecos (dolls) in witchcraft, 25:196.
Munn, M. J., 31:70.
Munn, S. W., 20:44 ff.
Munro, Jack, 10:135.
Murchison, A. H., 19:102; 32:127.
Murderer's Creek as place name, 13:46.
Murdock, Henry, 23:286.
Murieta, Joaquín, 27:97.
Murillo, Angela, 24:72, 117.
Muroc shift (dic.), 34:22.
Murphy, Jesse, 30:276.
Murphy, Jim, 3:112 ff.; 23:122; 26:112-114, 138-140; 27:102.

Murphy, John, 3:38 ff.; 26:94, 96.
Murphy, John Mortimer, 25:42.
Murphy, "King," 35:41 f.
Murphy, Mittie P., 35:73.
Murphy, R. C., 27:111 f.
Murphy, Thomas, 33:70 ff.
Murphy, Winifred, 18:136.
Murray, Sir James, 33:180.
Murray, Lindley, 23:14.
Murrey, William Henry ("Alfalfa Bill"), 13:195.
Murry, Sam, 31:105.
Muscadine Stream as place name, 32:118.
"Muscatine Waltz," 9:33.
Muscle Stream as place name, 32:126.
Muscles, sore, remedy for, 30:249.
Muse, Kindred H., 21:119.
Mush men (dic.), 18:108.
"Mush-Pot" (game), 22:228.
Mush Stream as place name, 32:126.
Mushroom as remedy for bleeding, 8:31.
Music: of Alabama Indians, 13:270-293; in the cattle country, 32:158; dance, 5:109; folk, transcription and analysis of, 32:237-268; German, 2:72; guitar, 22:176; Mexican, 2:78; 5:98; 35:147-156; mysterious, 3:137 ff., 141 ff.; pioneer, 5:108; at play-parties, 7:12, 16; see Fiddling.
Music Bend in the San Bernard River, 3:137-141.
Música (rustic Spanish musical instrument), 9:74; 15:123 ff.
Musical chants, 25:115-138.
Musical instruments: of Alabama Indians, 13:277-278; in early East Texas, 23:27, 28; Mexican, 5:98; 15:123; of Mexican vaquero, 6:20; of pioneer Texas, 5:108; 7:156; 25:145; shepherds' música, 9:74; 15:123; of Tejas Indians, 6:112, 117; see Pito.
Musique, Clara, 19:2, 5.
Muskingum, Great Liar of the, 18:84 ff.
Muskingum River, 18:85.
Muskogee, Okla., 7:176.
Músquiz, Mex., 19:89; 32:31.
Mussel Creek as place name, 32:121.
"Muss i denn" (song), 23:157.
Mustang Bayou as place name, 13:25.
Mustang cattle (dic.), 13:23.
Mustang Creek, 28:136; as place name, 32:121.
Mustang grape, 6:29; 13:70, 214; root as remedy, 35:16.
"Mustang Gray," with music, 10:121-123; cited, 7:161 f.
Mustang Gray loop, 10:114.
Mustang Pens as place name, 13:4, 25.
Mustangers, 16:61-66 (Bob Lemons); Mexican, 10:110; 16:4-52 passim, 69-95 passim, 96-101; outfitting party of, 16:48-49; in Texas, Mexican and Anglo laws concerning, 16:4-5.

Mustangs: capturing, methods of, 1:60-61; 10:110-114, 117-118; 16:5-11, 39-42, 48 ff., 62-66, 69 ff., 73 ff., 77 ff., 98 ff., 144, 145-146, 148-150, 159 ff.; characteristics and habits of, 1:59-60; 16:11 ff., 38, 52, 71-73, 96-97, 104-105, 110, 141-142, 148, 155 ff., 159 ff.; colors of, 1:58; 16:13-14, 32-33, 52, 69, 87-88, 97, 104, 145; creasing, 1:60-61; 16:16, 44-46, 75-76, 110, 145-146, 150, 176-180; disappearance of, 16:19-21, 76-77, 142; foundered after being chased, 8:15; legended individuals, 3:223-226; 12:190-193; 16:102-142, 155-186; origin of, 1:58-59; 16:3-5, 14, 94-95, 153-154; origin of the word, 16:3; pen or traps for, 13:10, 21, 25; 16:5-6, 7, 25-26, 27-29, 39-43, 50-52, 69-70; price of, 6:23, 35; selling, 16:5, 35, 53, 76, 141; stallions, fierceness of, 16:72, 79, 83; see Mustangers.
Mustangs, The, 30:26 f.
Mustangs and Cow Horses, 18:xi; 33:3 f.
Mustard: as a cure, 8:57; tale involving, 7:72-75.
Mutton, bones and fat of as remedy, 8:21, 25.
[My . . . ; see also Muh . . . .]
"My beautiful brown maid, my heart is sad," with music, 8:116.
"My Blue-Eyed Boy," with music, 23:151-152.
"My Father says he'll meet me," with music, 10:184-185.
"My Father's Gone to Glory," with music, 10:172, 181-182.
"My foot's in the stirrup," 22:230.
"My granddad viewing earth's worn cogs," 30:172.
"My hands is black," 25:135.
"My Heart's Tonight in Texas"; see "Tonight."
"My house is very small," 8:91.
"My Juanita, I Must Leave You," with music, 13:255-257.
"My Lawd's a Battle Ax," with music, 7:95; 26:173.
"My little dove, come to my hearth," with music, 8:115.
"My love is a vaquero," with music, 7:171.
"My lover is a cowboy," 6:189; 26:135.
"My Luluh," 5:165-166; 26:164-165 (reprint).
"My minny me slew," 6:53; see Juniper tree tale.
"My Mother Chose My Husband," 30:92.
"My mother and father were Irish," 13:327.
"My mother is a butcher," 18:197; 26:204.
"My Mother Was a Lady," 33:169.
"My name is Charles Giteau," 23:118.

"My name is Kindlin Willie," 25:135.
"My name's Ran, I wuks in de san'," 32:107.
"My name is Sanford Barnes," 23:226.
"My name it is Joe Bowers," 23:108.
"My Old Hammah" (cited), 36:112.
"My Ole Man's a Railroad Man," 5:169.
"My Parents Reared Me Tenderly," 6: 185; 26:133.
"My Pretty Little Miss," with music, 23:210-211.
"My Pretty Little Pink," with music, 23:197-198.
"My woman used to tell me," 12:228.
Myers, John C.: article, 31:53-57; men-

tioned, 31:166.
Myrick, Asa, 21:124.
Myrick, Timothy; see Mirrick.
Myrtle Stream as place name, 32:116.
Myth(s): interpretation of, 34:219-241; Jung on, 33:181-197; Navajo creation, 14:127-134; of the primal horde, 32: 72-100; reflected in Indian pictographs, 2:28; of the American South vs. the West, 35:136, 139, 140-145; of the Tejas Indians, 6:107-118; 9:167-174; of the western hero, 35:141-142; in *The Winter of Our Discontent*, 36: 93-102; see Part II, Section 1 of *Analytical Index*.

N ⌒

N A Ranch, 6:86.
Nabors, Drucilla, 4:105.
Nabors, Frances, 4:105.
Nacimento, Mex., 32:31.
Nacimientos, 9:77.
Nacogdoches (Indian), 14:195-196.
Nacogdoches, Tex., 1:41; 3:3, 33, 85 f., 88, 93, 204 f.; 7:119 ff., 157; 11:98; 13:40-41, 68 f., 75; 14:195-199; 18: 148; 25:117; 26:190; 28:65; 30:178; 34:39; see Holy Spring.
Nacogdoches Archives, 15:32 ff.
Nacogdoches *Chronicle*, 19:67.
Nacogdoches County, Tex.: early records in, 15:28 ff.; place names, 31:87, 91.
Nacogdoches Indians, 1:41; 9:167; 14: 195-196.
Naconiche Creek as place name, 32:132.
"*Nadar, nadar y a la orilla ahogar*," 12:216.
"*Nadie sabe el bien que tiene hasta que lo ha perdido*," 24:124.
"*Nadie sabe para quien trabaja*," 12:216; 24:124.
Nagual, El, 30:229-231.
Nahua Indians, 14:67.
Nail, Edith, 25:215.
Nails: carpentry, used in cures, 8:22, 30, 41, 61; see Fingernails.
Names: in ballads a sign of early stage in their development, 25:99; folk, of cacti, 9:90-93; given to guns, 35:5; taboo concerning, 1:86; of wild animals of the western U. S., 25:40-61; see Diction; Colors; Ford epigrams; Horses (names); Nicknames; Place names.
Nana (La) Creek, 3:204 f.; 14:196; as place name, 13:69.
Napkin, magic, 6:45-47.
Napoleon, 15:34, 40; 19:138; 25:5.
Naranjal, El (lost goldmine), 12:173-

174.
Naranjo, Pedro, 24:72, 89-90.
Narayana, 33:191.
Narcissus, 3:197.
Narrow escapes; see Part II, Section 9, of *Analytical Index*.
Narvaez, Pánfilo, 16:208.
Narvaez, Rodrigo de, 12:107.
Nashville, Tenn., 2:53.
Nason, Charles, 20:44.
Nason, Ed, 20:44.
Nasuit (storyteller), 14:127, 131, 134.
"Natchett" (Natchez), 7:102.
Natchez, Miss., 19:2 f., 184, 186; 28:54; frontier religion in, 14:159.
Natchez Creek (Tex.) as place name, 32:131.
Natchitoches (Indian), 14:195-196.
Natchitoches, La., 5:49 ff.; 15:40; as place name, 13:40; 14:195.
"Nateka Dance Song," music only, 13: 293.
Nation, Carrie, 33:167.
National Geographic, 1:85; 22:16; 26: 304.
Natividad, Jesusita, 29:144.
Natli (Hermaphrodite), 14:129.
Natto, Ibrahim, 36:127, 130.
Natural (dic.), 35:48.
Natural history in folklore, 25:18-39.
Natural Wells Creek as place name, 32: 120.
Naulach (Indian), 11:21-25.
Nausea, remedy for, 8:13, 60.
Navajo Indians, 6:78; 9:94; 14:72, 74, 76, 127-134; 15:96, 107, 142-145; 19: 88; 32:134, 142; creation of, 14:131-134.
Navarre, Margaret of, 25:17.
Navarro, Eugenio, 19:195.
Navarro, Don Hesu, 3:155.
Navarro, José Angel, 3:155; 19:198.

swecker, 30:249; linseed, 8:31, 34 f.;
olive, 8:58; 24:26; panther, 8:67-68;
rattlesnake, 8:65, 68, 84; see names
of substances.
Oilum, E. Pluribus, 30:78.
Ojía root as remedy, 12:187.
Ojibwa Indians, 19:100, 105.
Ojinaga, Mex., 21:23; 25:205-216; 27:
171 ff.; 32:44; 35:83 ff.
Ojo; see Evil eye.
Ojo de Manta (Indian), 22:144.
"Ojos que no ven, corazón que no siente,"
12:218; 24:124.
Okanogan Indians, 14:40, 66.
O'Keeffe, J. G., 34:75.
Okies, 36:61, 70.
Oklahoma, 3:64, 83, 174, 205; 36:61; folk
medicine in, 8:74-85; Indians in, 19:
88 ff.; outlaws of, their shooting abili-
ty, 9:9; place names of western, 6:90-
98.
Oklahoma Folklore Society, 8:7.
Oland, Warner, 34:65.
[Old . . . ; see also Ole . . . .]
Old (dic.), 1:44.
Old Adam (dic.), 5:82.
"Old Bachelor, The," with music, 23:248-
249.
"Old Brass Wagon, The," 1:17; 7:19;
cited, 1:35.
"Old Brien-O-Lin," 6:235; cited, 10:168.
"Old Chisolm Trail, The," 6:155, 201;
7:179; with music, 7:149-150.
"Old Cowboy, The," 7:164; 33:86.
Old Cox (fiddler); see Cox, "Old."
"Old Crummy [Crumpy]," 6:229.
"Old Dad Done Come Again," 7:100.
"Old Dan Tucker," 1:14; 18:62; cited,
1:35; 7:18; dance call, 4:57; play-
party song, 13:318.
"Old Doc Collins" (cited), 1:36.
"Old Dunny was a rocky outlaw," 16:
295.
"Old Fodder," with music, 23:269.
"Old Gray Goose, The," with music, 23:
262-263.
"Old Gray Horse, The," (cited), 6:189.
"Old Gray Mare" (cited), 7:18.
"Old Grey," with music, 6:123-124.
"Old Hen Cackle, The," 5:159; 26:163
(reprint).
Old Hickory Cemetery, 18:134.
"Old Jay Bird," with music, 23:266.
"Old Jean Lafitte once passed along these
sands," 3:179.
"Old Joe Clark," 1:32-34; 7:12, 19; 30:
181; cited, 1:36.
"Old Limpin' Joe and Jumpin' Joe,"
6:68.
"Old Maid, The," with music, 23:218.
"Old Man Under the Hill," with music,
10:164-165; cited, 10:136; see "Farm-
er's Curst Wife."

"Old Man Who Came Over the Moor,"
23:217.
Old Maud (dic.), 4:65.
"Old Mill, The," with music, 6:213-214.
"Old Mother Hubbard" (game), 17:149.
"Old Obadiah," 13:250-251.
"Old Paint" (cited), 7:153.
Old Rip (horned toad), 29:8-10.
"Old Rover" (cited), 6:230.
Old Scratch (dic.), 5:92.
"Old Scout's Lament, The" (cited),
6:131.
"Old Shawnee, The," 6:213.
"Old Shoe Boots and Leggins," with mu-
sic, 23:217.
"Old shoe sole is about wore out," 22:
228.
"Old shoes are easy to the feet," 25:157.
"Old Smoky"; see "On Top of Old
Smoky."
Old States (dic.), 23:24.
Old Testament, 19:12.
"Old Texas Trail" (dance song), 4:58.
"Old-Time Cowboy," 6:171-173; 22:215.
"Old Time Religion Is Good Enough for
Me," 18:217; cited, 7:97.
"Old Uncle Ned" (cited), 7:151.
"Old Uncle Tom" (game), 17:145.
Old Wolf (Indian), 30:270.
"Old Woman from Ireland, The," with
music, 23:207-208; see "Old Woman's
Story."
"Old Woman of Slapsadam" (cited),
6:223.
"Old Woman's Story," with music, 10:
165-166; see "Old Woman from Ire-
land."
Old Zip Coon (minstrel-show character),
23:243.
Oldham, Albert E., 31:69.
Oldham, Williamson S., 15:69 f.
Olds, Fred A., 8:154.
"Ole Aunt Dinah," 5:171.
"Ole Bull" (fiddler), 17:80-81.
"Ole Bull and Ole Dan Tucker," 17:81.
"Ole Dad Done Come Again," 7:100-101.
"Ole J. Gould owns the Katy Line," 2:41.
"Ole Joe Clark makin' ties," 30:181.
"Ole Joe! Ole Joe kickin' up behind and
befo'," with music, 5:141.
"Ol' Massa take keer o' himself," 11:102.
"Ole Tom Palmer come down South," 7:
102.
Olea, Cristobal de, 16:216; see Olid.
Olid, Cristoval de, 16:200; see Olea.
Olive: wild, 9:93; oil in folk curing, 8:58;
24:26.
Oliver, Charles, 29:45.
Oliver, Harry, 25:13.
Oliver Creek, 28:13.
Ollinger, Bob, 27:96.
Olmos Creek; see Los Olmos Creek.
Olmos Ranch; see Los Olmos Ranch.

Olmstead, Frank, 32:57-59.
Olrik, Axel, 27:126; 29:110.
O'Mara (Illinois oilman), 20:51 f.
Omens: birds as, 7:26-37; 26:283-289 (reprint); of death, 5:119-120; 7:26-37 passim, 119-121; 10:55-57; 13:160-162; 17:118-119; 24:115; among Mexicans, 2:82-84; of misfortune, 5:120-122; 36:138; among Negroes, 7:119-121; see Luck; Superstitions; Weather.
O'Mike, Mrs. (Texarkana, Tex.), 25:125.
"Omne tulit punctum, qui miscuit utile dulci," 9:129.
"On the Banks of the Old Pedee," 6:213.
"On the first of May as we set sail," with music, 10:162-163.
"On golden platters, rancid butter," 14:152.
"On the Greenbriar Shore," 30:217.
On the outside (dic.), 1:45.
"On Red River Shore," with music, 6:158-159.
"On Springfield mountain there did dwell," 6:210; 32:202.
"On Top of Old Smokey," with music, 23:178.
O'naga as place name, 13:50, 75.
Oñate, Cristobal de, 12:165, 183.
Oñate, Juan de, 12:175-179, 181 f.
Oñate, María de, 12:165 f.
"Once dere wuz er frog lived in er mill," 5:46.
"Once I courted a fair beauty bride," 23:87.
"Once I had a little sweetheart," 23:162.
"Once There Was a Man, He Came from the West," with music, 13:251-252.
"Once there was a poor widow woman," 23:33.
"Once upon a day," 9:182.
"Once you've loved with fond affection," 23:142.
One Arm Stream as place name, 32:132.
"One-ery, two-ery," 6:69.
"One Evening as I Sat Courting," with music, 2:6-7.
"One evening, one evening, one evening in May," with music, 7:167.
One Eye (Indian), 13:42; see One Eyed.
One Eye Creek as place name, 13:42; 32:112, 132.
One Eyed Chief (Indian), 16:143; see One Eye.
One-Leg Nimshilling campground, 35:20.
"One more chance!," 2:60.
"One Mornin'" (Negro song), 5:160-161; 26:163 (reprint).
"One morning alone, in silence reclined," with music, 7:159.
"One Morning in May" (cited), 7:167.
"One for sorrow, two for joy" (rhyme), 13:160; 26:239 (reprint).

"One wheel off the old brass wagon," 7:19.
"One white foot, buy him [catch him]," 13:242; 16:246.
O'Neale (cocker), 30:102.
O'Neale, Carlos Feliz, 33:132.
Oneida, Ohio, 19:102, 104.
O'Neill, Rose, 19:82.
Onion: as cure, 14:267; 24:55, 61, 82, 84; 26:263; 35:13; as answer to riddle, 18:183; wild, 9:96; 13:3; wild as remedy, 10:88; see Tears.
Onion Creek, Tex., 4:103 ff.; 16:173 ff.; 26:107, 109, 111; 29:50; as place name, 13:3; 32:118.
"Only a Bum" (cited), 36:108.
Onomatopoeia in folktale; see "Pot Song."
"Oor Mae Had an Ee till a Man," with music, 10:166-167; cited, 10:136, 158.
Ópata Indians, 12:164; 26:291.
O'Phaller (friend of Billy The Kid), 33:75.
Opium for distemper, 8:36.
Opossum, 7:42, 106; 9:165-166; 10:11-12; 18:98, 177 ff.; 22:20; 25:28, 31-32, 42-44, 251-252; 26:307-308; manner of giving birth, 21:51.
O'Pry, Floyd, 31:13, 15 ff.
Oquin (Tonkawa Indian), 21:118.
O'Quinn, Trueman E.: article, 13:245-249; mentioned, 13:339.
"Or if thou hast uphoarded in thy life," 3:185.
Oracle; see Counsels, three wise; Seer.
Oral history, 28:37-38.
Orbita, Juan de, 16:220.
Orcabessa, Jamaica, 30:38.
Orchard Stream as place name, 32:116.
Orcoquiza Indians, 3:99.
Ordas, Diego de, 16:200, 204.
Ordways, The, myth and folklore in, 35:133-145.
Orégano, 12:188.
O'Reilly, Edward, 3:120.
O'Reilly, "Tex," 3:64.
Orejanos (dic.), 17:60; 18:110.
Órgano cactus, 11:92.
Orient Railroad (K. C. M & O), 31:101.
Origin myths; see Part II, Section 1, of *Analytical Index.*
Original sin, Freud's theory of, 32:92.
Orion, 8:92.
Ornelas, Señora (Camargo, Mex.), 9:100.
Orner, Frank, 6:157.
Ornithryncodiplodicus (fabulous beast), 7:38-39.
Oroville, Calif., 35:109.
Orphan Boy gets wife (Indian tale), 22:85-90.
"Orphan Girl, The," with music, 23:281-283; cited, 6:133.
Orpheus, 33:189.

P ⏦

Pantagruel, 36:125 ff.
Panther(s): as cause of pitching in west-
ern horses, 16:18, 293-294; as demon
or ghost, 29:136-141; hunting, 16:30-
31; names for, 25:41-42; roping, 16:
31; tales, 19:126-133; 25:16; 28:151-
153; 29:166-168; 30:3; white, 10:94.
Panther Canyon as place name, 13:2.
Panther Creek as place name, 32:121.
Pantomime in folktale narration, 6:27-
28.
Panurge, 36:125.
"Panza llena, corazon contento," 12:216;
24:124.
"Pap Runnels," 2:44.
Papago Indians, burial customs of, 15:
164; 26:292 (reprint).
Papalotiando (dic.), 18:111.
Paper (writing) as remedy, 8:54; 35:14.
"Para eso son los bienes," 24:125.
Paradise Stream as place name, 32:116.
Paradise lost, East Texas tale of, 31:3-7.
Paralysis, folk curing of, 24:30-31.
Paramount Singers, 17:154.
Paraque (goatsucker), 7:27 f.
Parasites, external, remedy for, 8:61.
Pardner of the Wind, 30:27.
"Parece que no quiebra un plato," 24:
125.
Paredes, Américo: articles, 25:110-114;
27:3-22; 28:91-105; 29:88-92; 30:56-
68, 285-289; mentioned, 25:256;
27:v, 202; 28:vii, 169; 29:233; 30:
294; 36:4, 12.
Paredes, Felipe, Jr., 14:241.
Parham, Chub, 36:117.
Parida Creek, 17:59, 76.
Paris, Tex., 6:140; 13:51; 23:138, 152.
Parker, Bernice, 7:119, 122.
Parker, Bonnie, 23:95-98; 35:35-44.
Parker, Cynthia Ann, 6:73; 13:29, 199-
200, 203; 22:11.
Parker, Isaac ("hanging judge"), 30:159.
Parker, Isaac (of Houston, Tex.), 21:
119.
Parker, Isaac D., 13:199-200, 203.
Parker, Joshua, 8:135.
Parker, Laura Bryan, 3:211.
Parker, Marian, 32:232.
Parker, Marsh, 16:125.
Parker, Quanah, 6:73; 13:29.
Parker, Silas, 13:199.
Parker County, Tex., 13:191-238 passim;
16:179, 337; 17:83; 19:120; 29:
201 ff.; place name in, 31:76, 94.
Parkman, Francis, 25:44.
Parks, Etta: article, 19:29-35; mentioned,
19:200, 202.
Parks, H. B.: articles, 7:81-84; 9:15-26,
133-141; 26:159-162 (reprint); men-
tioned, 7:5, 184; 9:190 f.; 10:5, 127,
187; 12:106, 250; 18:162; 26:277.
Parks, Joe, 6:158.

Parmer, Allen, 9:9-10.
Parmer County, Tex., place name, 31:
92.
Paroxysm, religious; see "Jerks."
Parr, Archie, 30:5.
"Parra ha pasado a la historia," 28:101.
Parral, Mex., 21:23.
Parraleña tea as remedy, 10:90.
Parras, Mex., as grape-growing region,
9:96.
Parrett, Mrs. J. W., 18:117.
Parrett, Vanita: article, 18:115-125; men-
tioned, 18:222.
Parricide, primal, 32:72-100.
Parrilla (Mexican officer), 3:81.
Parillas (Las) Ranch, 24:18.
Parrot, Ursula, 34:207.
Parrot tales, 12:21-26; 27:82-86; 28:157-
158.
Parry, Milman, 32:255.
Parry-Lord hypothesis, 32:222.
Parsons, Elsie Clews, 29:175, 187 ff.
Partearroyo, Cecilia Gil de, 27:143.
Parter, Mrs. J. R., 12:viii.
Participation, Levy-Bruhl's law of, 1:80-
82.
Parties; see Play-parties; "Toodala."
Partnership in raising crops (tales), 9:
153-156; 14:118-120; 25:220-233.
Partridge Creek as place name, 32:121.
Partridges, 7:43.
Pasadena, Calif., 29:11; 31:44.
Pasaño, Anasete, 4:33; see Pizana.
Pascal, Billie, 6:199.
Paschal, F. L., 19:198.
Paseo (dic.), 9:40.
Paso Piedra on the Nueces River, 10:
120.
Paso Santa Margarita, 16:23.
Passel (dic.), 9:17.
Passenger pigeons, 20:95.
Pastel, 9:72.
Pasternak, Boris, 33:120.
Pasteur, Louis, 28:6.
Pastimes: pioneer, 13:230-232, 235-238;
25:145-146; see Games.
Pastorela, 36:17.
"Pastores, Los," 1:100; 9:77; 11:48; 36:
v, 15-25.
Pastores, Mexican: occupation and char-
acter of, 9:63-68; superstitions of, 9:
66-68; 15:119, 121; tales and songs
of, 8:86-116; 9:66 ff.; 15:122-133;
weather signs of, 2:87-99 passim; see
Goat-herders; Sheep herder.
Pasture Draw as place name, 32:123.
Pat (Irish folk character), 18:83.
Pater, Walter, anecdote about, 36:122-
123.
Patience, proverbial expressions advising,
5:84.
Patino, Ramon, 36:25.
Pato (El) Creek, 17:59.

Pence, Jack, 14:5.
Pencil cactus, 11:92 f.
Pendergast, David M., 30:61, 68.
Pendleton, George C., 3:241.
Penitas Creek, 29:223.
Penitentes, 10:125; 11:48 f.; their practices and tenets, 9:77-81; satirical rhyme concerning, 9:79; in Seville, 36:28 f.
Penn, A. W.: article, 7:38-44; mentioned, 7:184; 8:25.
Penninger, Robert, 36:59.
Pennington, Nancy, 10:137.
Pennsylvania: folklore in early western, 20:10-11; oil industry in, 20:2-56 passim; the tall tale in early, 20:11-12.
Penny, to remove warts or thorns, 35:14.
Penny dreadful: as folksong, 33:164-170; in magazines for men, 34:155-161.
Pennybacker, Anna J. Hardwicke, 15: 11 f., 17, 42.
Pennyroyal, 18:160; 26:276.
Pension (dic.), 35:48.
Pentecost Monday, 2:68, 71.
Peoria, Ill., 32:57.
"Pepa no quiere coser," with music, 8: 112-113.
Pepper, 8:108; 10:88; in remedies, 8:19, 39, 49 f., 52, 54; in sayings, 13:174 f.; too much (tale), 30:128.
Pepper-box gun, 6:81.
Pepper Creek Camp as place name, 13: 2-3.
Peppermint in remedy, 8:56.
Pepys, Samuel, 25:47, 58, 71.
Perancejo, Pepe (prospector), 32:5 ff.
Percy, Bishop, 10:149; 25:55, 62, 65, 70, 72; 32:212, 228; 35:65.
"Perennial Lover, The," 10:104.
Peres, Paulo, 19:115.
Pérez, Antonio, 24:62-63.
Pérez, Blas, 30:116 ff.
Pérez, Gil, 16:351 f.
Pérez, Manuel, 29:44.
Pérez, María, 29:41-44.
Pérez, Soledad: articles, 24:71-127; 26: 77-79, 127-130, 223-229, 270-272 (reprints); mentioned, 24:71; 25:189; 27:143; 28:121.
Pérez Martínez, Héctor, 28:92, 105.
"Perfect butter, packed in a dog's skin," 14:152.
Performance (dic.), 34:21.
Pericanos (dic.), 22:144.
Perkins, Cap, 16:289.
Perkins, Ed, 16:289.
Perkins, J. G., 29:150.
Perkins, Mrs. S. S., 29:148.
Pernety, Antoine de, 21:107 ff.
"Pero ya se va a llegar el pago," 12:231-232.
Perrault, 6:42, 45, 55.
Perrin (cowboy), 28:9-10.

"Perro que come huevos sigue aunque le quema el pico," 12:215.
"Perro que ladra no muerde," 24:125.
Perrow, E. C., 6:189, 221, 223, 227.
Perry, Bliss, 1:3; 4:page 14 of appendix.
Perry, E. L., 12:viii.
Perry, F. C., 36:133.
Perry, George Sessions, 25:76, 119, 130, 166; 26:337.
Perry, Troup D., 7:31; 26:285.
Perryman, Judge (Coryell County, Tex.), 13:57.
Perryman Thicket as place name, 13:57, 75.
Persephone, 33:189.
Perseus, 1:88, 91.
Persimmon: beer, 18:27, 39; Mexican, bark tea as remedy, 8:52; in saying, 13:243.
Persimmon Stream as place name, 32: 116.
Personification of animals in the Mexican *relacion*, 29:108-121.
Pert (dic.), 9:17.
Pertul, Mollie, 13:79 ff.
Peru, 3:6; 4:68; 36:146; Indians of, 30: 73.
Peru, Kans., 20:43.
Pescador, Juan, 12:79-87.
Peshlikai (Indian), 14:74-76.
Pesky (dic.), 18:64.
Peter; see St. Peter.
Peter Parley (dic.), 4:49.
Peterkin, Julia, 7:142; her *Green Thursday*, 4:7.
Peters, Fred J., 18:59.
Peters, Jeff, 32:160.
Peters Creek, 33:178.
Petigo (Indian), 13:275.
Petrie, Flinders, 32:211.
Petrified: forest in Arizona (tale), 18: 84; wood, origin of, 10:79-81.
Petroglyphs; see Pictographs.
Petroleum geologist, his folk image, 31: 58-72.
Petroleum Producers Association, 30:83.
Petronita, Tex., 3:43.
Petrunkevitch, Alexander I., 31:52, 55.
Petruschichev, Sozont Kuzmich, 25:108.
Petterson, James, 21:123.
Pettus, Tom, 10:24-25.
Pettus, William, 21:121.
Pewee flycatcher; see Phoebe.
Peyote, Tex., 29:142; as place name, 13: 3.
Peyote cactus, 11:90-91; 22:3, 80, 108 ff.
Peyton, Green, 25:168.
Peza, Juan de Dios, 24:73; 26:127.
Pflugerville, Tex., 10:128; 30:185.
Phanourios ceremony, 36:142.
"Phantom Drag, The" (cited), 36:115.
Phantom Hill (Tex.), 18:101.
Pharaoh, 7:159.

Q

Q-ship (dic.), 34:20.
Quachita River; see Washita.
Quadrilles, names of western, 9:33.
Quail, 7:36; call of, 2:93; frightens coyote (tale), 22:61-62; migration of, 2:92; not destroyed by roadrunner, 15:149 ff.; shooting, 9:2 f.; tall tale involving, 18:85-88.
"Qualee, qualee, bulum-bulumba, cullumba," with music, 7:117.
Qualia, Charles B., 3:215.
Quanah, Tex., 3:207; 9:3; 22:222; as place name, 6:73; 13:29.
Quantrell, 9:9-10; 27:98.
"Quantrell's Call" (cited), 6:198.
Quapaw Creek as place name, 32:131.
Quarry, Tex., as place name, 13:4.
Quarry Stream as place name, 32:126.
Quarternight, Fox, 30:286.
"Que bonitas mañanitas," 6:20.
"Que bonito era Bernál," 4:16.
"¡Que frío, que frío!," 6:8.
"¿Qué quieres, pastor?," 6:8.
Quebracho trees, 11:15.
Queen, Capt., 22:190.
"Queen of Elfan's Nourice" (cited), 25:99; 27:44.
Queen's Delight as remedy, 14:268.
Quesada, Gonzalo Jimenez, 3:6 f.; 4:69.
Queso de tuna, 9:88, 103.
Quetzal, 11:15, 17.
Quetzalcoahuatl, 1:64; 11:15, 25 ff., 46; 16:207.
Quevedo (Spanish poet), 30:57 f.

Quick Killer (Indian), 22:150-162.
Quicksand Stream as place name, 32:128.
"Quién les da posadas, a estos peregrinos," 9:76.
¿Quién sabe? (dic.), 2:91; 9:33; 12:220.
Quién Sabe Ranch, 33:48.
"Quién Sabe Waltz," 9:33.
"Quien todo lo quiere, todo lo pierde," 24:125.
"¿Quiéres que te lo cuente otra vez?," 12:29.
Quihi Creek as place name, 32:132.
Quihi Prairie, 21:69.
Quillin, Ellen Schulz, 15:148, 160.
Quilling (remedy for labor pains), 8:58.
Quilting, 17:30; 26:199-200.
Quinine: bark as remedy, 35:13; used by pioneers, 13:233.
Quinine plant; see Mountain pink.
Quinn, Dolph, 10:115.
Quinn, Jesse P., 31:86.
Quinn, Pat, 10:112, 115, 118.
Quiñones, Jesús Jaime, 12:152.
Quintana, Carlota, 10:62.
Quintana, Tex., 3:142.
Quintillas, 28:96-97.
Quirk, Tom, 33:100.
Quiroga, Mex., 11:26 f.
Quitaque: Canyon, 13:27; 16:85; Creek as place name, 32:132.
"Quítese de aquí mi padre," 29:91.
Quixote, Don, 30:25.
Quizando, Mariano, 12:89-99.

R

Rabb, William, 8:132.
Rabbit: as bad luck sign, 5:121; foot of as charm, 5:123; jack, 7:111, 120; as remedy, 8:24, 64; tales involving, 7:131-138; 9:153-156; 14:24 ff., 36; 18:81, 172, 177 ff.; 21:73 ff.; 25:220-230, 233-238, 241-242; 26:15-17, 42-45, 50-53 (reprints); 27:114-117; 29:178-180; 32:49, 52; 33:95.
Rabbit, to (dic.), 2:17.
"Rabbit" (play-party song), 1:12-13.
Rabbit Creek as place name, 32:121.
"Rabbit Dance Song," music only, 13:291.
"Rabbit jumped the garden gate," 1:13.
Rabbit Shoulders (Indian), 22:124-130.
Rabb's Creek, 8:132.
Rabelais, 36:125 f.

Rabies, treatment for, 8:24, 43, 66; 17:73; 26:257; see Madstone.
Raby, J. R., 30:197-198.
Raccoon; see Coon.
Race: coyote and dogs, 14:13-17; coyote and frog, 14:81-82; coyote and rabbit, 14:78; coyote and turtle, 14:76-78; fat and thin sheep, 14:22-24; man, horseback, and Indians, 14:188-189, 265; 28:137-138.
Racial discrimination in folklore, 32:101-111.
Racing, drag, 34:11-35.
Radcliffe-Brown, 32:210.
Radeleff, R. D., 34:168-169.
Radin, Paul, 32:214.
Radio: its influence on folktales, 23:23, 25; 24:1-2; its introduction to the Big

Rhodes, Eugene Manlove: article, 33:26-32; mentioned, 16:243; 27:101; 33:200.

Rhus virens (kinnikinnik), 18:162; 26:277.

Rhymes: children's, 22:234-236; 24:120; 25:119; counting out, 7:21; folk, in early Texas manuscript collection, 6:23 ff.; Mexican folk, 8:93, 102; rope-jumping, 18:195-199; 26:202-207 (reprint); street vendors', 9:111-112; 22:171; 25:115-138; used at conclusion of cowboy dances, 22:230.

Rhyming rats to death, 1:79.

Rhythm as musical term, 32:250.

Rib, Adam's, 32:178-180; in jocular tale, 32:4-5.

Rice: growing, 35:158-160; as symbol of fertility and longevity, 36:138 f.

Rice Springs (Tex.), 16:375.

Rich, Carrol Y.: article, 35:35-44; mentioned, 35:167.

"Rich Irish Lady," with music, 23:37-38; cited, 27:75.

"Rich man, poor man, beggar-man, thief," 13:150; 18:196; 26:203 (reprint).

"Rich Merchant, The" (cited), 10:157.

Rich person: folk expressions concerning, 5:85; see Companions, tale of rich and poor.

Rich yo-yo (dic.), 34:25.

Richards, Abe, 23:50-51.

Richards, Billy, 10:112, 120-121.

Richardson, Albert D., 13:39.

Richardson, Daniel, 18:134.

Richardson, Levy, 9:12, 13.

Richardson, Mark, 17:98.

Richardson, Rick, 34:45.

Richardson, Rosa, 10:178-179.

Richardson, Samuel, 29:75; 33:169.

Richardson, Tom, 33:45.

Richardson, Vivian, 17:120.

Richland Stream as place name, 32:119.

Richmond, W. E.: article, 32:217-227; mentioned, 28:35; 32:201, 271.

Richmond, Va., 8:152.

Richmond (Tex.) *Telescope*, 3:201.

Rickaby, Franz, 7:176; 8:161.

Rickard, J. A.: article, 18:181-187; mentioned, 17:156; 18:223.

Riddle (meaning "tell"), 23:45.

Riddle, Dee, 6:216, 220.

Riddles, 23:251; Mexican, 18:181-187; 24:126-127; 31:151-153; see Neck riddle.

Ride, legended distance-covering, 16:221-225.

Ride it up (dic.), 2:31.

"Ride on, King Jesus" (cited), 7:92.

Rider, John, 30:130-131.

Ridge Stream as place name, 32:119.

Riding herd on (dic.), 35:48.

Ridings, Mrs. Grace Du Pre, 6:222, 224.

Riesberg, Harry E., 34:44.

Rifera, 27:189-191; see Fortune-teller.

Rig (dic.), 2:36.

Rigby, John, 6:155; 30:27.

Rigdou, Fred, 32:173.

"Rigdum bullydimy kymy," 5:12.

Riggs, Lynn, 7:10, 13.

"Right hands crossed, shu-dah," with music, 13:330-331.

"Rigtum butty middy kimo," 5:26.

Riker, Thad, 5:32.

Rile (dic.), 9:41.

Riley, James Whitcomb, 16:123.

Riley, Mrs. Lawton, 36:10-11.

Riley, Mary, 23:22.

Riley, Ralph, 28:131-132.

Rimbault, E. (C.?) F., 25:54, 70.

Rincón, Pedro, 24:72, 88-89, 96-100, 103-104.

Rincón, de Las Piedras (N. M.), 6:78.

Ring(s): as medicinal charms, 8:58, 65, 68, 70, 80 f.; princess's lost, 22:179 ff.; 32:27; talking, 34:114-115; wedding, 36:145.

Ring off (dic.), 18:203.

"Ring up four, Celia," with music, 17:102-103.

Ringworm, remedies for, 8:65 f.; 10:87; 35:14.

Río Balsas, 11:27.

Río Blanco, 19:132.

Río Bravo, 12:109; 26:143; see Río Grande.

Río Bravo Oil Company, 31:60.

Río Grande, 2:19, 22 f., 88, 94; 3:4, 21, 36 ff., 48, 50 ff., 60, 64 ff., 74, 79, 97 f., 132, 168, 209, 238 f.; 4:31, 34, 87, 7:27, 32; 9:85-117 passim; 10:72, 99, 110 f., 114 ff.; 12:109, 135, 206; 13:26, 56, 111-119 passim, 120-129 passim; 17:59; 18:98; 19:36, 94, 98, 126, 133, 135, 176; 21:29-30; 24:12, 21, 52; 25:206; 26:93, 95, 109 ff., 143; 35:83 ff.; 36:46; see Río Grande Valley.

Río Grande, Republic of the, 10:110.

Río Grande, silvery (dic.), 6:187-188.

Río Grande Valley, 16:400; 18:137; 27:187; folk foods of, 9:85-117; Mexican population in, 2:76, 88; place names in 31:85; settlement and history of, 2:75-76.

Río Grande City, Tex., 10:120.

Río Ruidoso, 15:125; 22:142.

Ríos, Raphael, 31:67.

Ríos Amarillos as place name, 6:75.

Ripas Indians, 3:218-219.

Rippy Stream as place name, 32:126.

"Rise you up, my dearest dear," 1:30; with music, 17:99-100.

"Rise you up, my true love," 1:29.

Rissmann, E. J.: articles, 25:139-151; 33:

S

S. A. U. and G. Railroad, 19:57.
S M S Ranch, 6:190; 16:373-383 passim;
26:136; 33:12-13.
Sabinal, Tex., 3:52, 62 f., 80; 9:65; 13:22.
Sabinal River, 3:62.
Sabinas, Río de, 16:344.
Sabine, Tex., 30:178.
Sabine County, Tex., place name, 31:94.
Sabine River, 5:49, 56; 13:245; 14:158,
198; 17:34; 30:178; 34:57.
Sacahuiste, 13:7, 27.
"Sacar dinero hasta de las piedras,"
24:125.
Sack (dic.), 1:45.
Sacred mushroom, 11:91; see Peyote cac-
tus.
Sacredness of kings, 1:87.
Sacrifice, human: of first-born infants,
1:67-69; foundation, 2:8-13; on
mountains, 12:162-164; 22:155-156.
Saddle, cowboy's, 33:15-16.
Saddle-broke (dic.), 6:23.
Saddle Horse Stream as place name,
32:123.
Saddle sores on horses, remedies for,
8:19, 45; 26:258.
Saddle Stream as place name, 32:123.
Saddle tank (dic.), 35:48.
Sadler, Margaret Rose, 36:102.
Saengerfests, 2:72.
Saenz, Marcelino, 24:56.
Saenz, María, 24:65.
Saeta, 36:30.
Saga; see Family; Fort Leaton.
Sage, 19:72; tea as remedy, 8:33, 56, 82;
26:256 (reprint).
Sage Stream as place name, 32:118.
Sahagún, Bernardino de, 24:73.
Sahaurita, Ariz., 30:102.
"Said the ole rooster to the hen," 5:166.
Sailes, La., 35:36.
Sailor: peg-legged, 7:82-84; see Sailors'.
"Sailor Boy, The," with music, 23:134.
"Sailor Boy's Dream, The," 9:184.
"Sailor's Return, The," 23:90; as cowboy
song, 6:194-195; with music, 10:155-
156.
Sailors': chanty mentioned, 7:21; super-
stitions, 13:174; 14:59 ff.; 26:253.
St. Agnes, Eve of, 28:49.
St. Andrew, 34:118.
St. Anthony, 24:104.
St. Augustine, 25:195.
St. Charles, Mo., frontier religion in,
14:159.
St. Charles Hotel, 18:50.
St. Christopher, 27:190.

St. Denis, 14:198.
St. Francis, 9:80; 25:108.
St. George, 21:7.
St. Isidore; see San Isidro.
St. James, 8:91; 16:204-205.
St. Jerome, 25:195.
St. John, 8:91; see next entry.
St. John's Day; see San Juan.
St. Joseph; see Joseph.
"St. Joseph of Christ" as name for
Christ, 14:208.
St. Lorenzo, 24:102-103.
St. Louis, Mo., 3:23, 79, 93, 97; 28:54;
34:40; World's Fair, 17:36.
"St. Louis Blues," 2:57.
St. Nicholas, 2:71.
St. Paul, 8:91; 11:52; 32:91-92.
St. Peter, 8:91; 11:52, 65; tales involv-
ing, 9:160-162; 12:10, 13, 155-158;
19:29-35; 26:27-30 (reprint); 29:63;
see next entry.
"St. Peter's tears" (rocks), 22:143.
St. Phanourios's Day, 36:141 ff.
St. Ronan, 34:79.
St. Simeon Stylites, 15:3.
St. Stephen's Day, 23:252.
St. Theodore's Day, 36:141 ff.
Saints: lives of, 15:3; stars as, 8:91; see
names of; see Part II, Section 8, of
Analytical Index for miracles of.
Sais, Flo, 29:145.
Sal de Rey Creek as place name, 13:3.
Salado Stream as place name, 32:128.
Salamanders, 4:51; 5:61-65; tiger, 5:72-
73; 26:280 (reprint).
Saldigna, Apolinario, 15:48 ff.
Saleas (pelts), 10:63.
Salem, Ohio, 18:18, 22.
Sales pitch for yogi oil, 17:35 ff.
Salgado, Isidoro, 28:117-118.
Saligny, M. de, 15:72 f.
Salinas, Barbara, 24:72, 76, 108.
Salinas, José María, 19:185.
Salinas, Placido, 4:39.
Saline Stream as place name, 32:128.
Saliva, control over in witchcraft, 1:84.
Sallet; see Poke salad.
Sallie Keaton Slough as place name,
13:58.
"Sallie's Red Dress," with music, 5:142.
"Sally Gooden," 18:118-119.
Sally hoot (dic.), 22:221.
Salpointe, J. P., 9:80 ff.
Salsipuedes Creek as place name, 13:5.
Salt, 13:3; as remedy, 8:19, 32 ff., 61 ff.,
76-77; in superstitions, 7:120; 13:148,
157; 24:116; 26:231, 236 (reprint).

Sawyer (cowman), 3:112; 26:101.
Sawyer, Tom, 36:77.
"Say nothing and saw wood," 5:91.
Sayings; see *Dichos;* Diction; Proverbs.
Sayre, Okla., 18:4.
Say-sos (dic.), 25:130.
Scabs (dic.), 36:110.
Scalawag (dic.), 6:160.
Scales, musical, 32:251.
Scalp Creek as place name, 13:28; 32:127.
Scalp-hunting, 35:89.
Scandinavian: sailors, 4:59; superstitions, 1:93; tale, 19:155.
Scantling (dic.), 22:228.
Scarborough, Dorothy: articles, 1:50-54; 2:52-66; mentioned, 1:5; 2:4-5; 4:154 ff.; 4:page 21 of appendix; 6:6; 7:8, 85-113 passim; 8:161; 23:8; 25:71; 27:27, 118; 36:106 ff.
"Scares," a type of folk narrative, 29:214-217.
Scary Lane (Lampasas County, Tex.) as place name, 13:44-45.
Scatter Stream as place name, 32:119.
Scavengers (dic.), 34:28.
Scepticism; see Skepticism.
Schaefer, Jack, 30:142.
Scharff, A. F.: article, 14:225-233; mentioned, 14:287.
Schedler, Paul W.: article, 35:11-17; mentioned, 35:167.
Scheffer, T. H., 25:46.
Scheherazade, 25:108.
Scheide, William, 20:xi.
Schendel, August, 31:87.
Schimerhorn, John, 6:81.
Schimerhorn Mtn., 6:81.
Schinhan, Jan Philip, 32:246-251, 256, 262.
Schlaudecker, Maj., 20:17.
Schlotter, Dorothy, 13:275.
Schmidt, Henry: article, 35:147-156; mentioned, 35:167.
Schmidt, W., 34:234.
Schneider, Eleanore, 30:258.
Schneider, Otto, 30:259.
Schnively; see Snively.
Schofner, Evelyn, 7:154.
Schoharie Hills, N. Y., 28:30.
Schomburgk, Richard, 25:29.
Schools: pioneer, 13:195; 19:117-125, 136-138; 25:142; 30:128-129; see Singing.
Schram, Wilbur, 23:9, 21.
Schreck Krauter, 30:250.
Schreiner, "Junior," 8:26.
Schreiner, Scott, 8:25.
Schrier, Noah, 33:40 f.
Schriewer, Mrs. Val, 36:37 f.
Schuetze, Louis, 36:53.
Schuetzen Fest, 2:72; 9:2.
Schultz, James E., 22:221.
Schulz, Ellen D., 8:10, 15, 63; 26:275.

Schuyler, George S., 32:103.
Schwettman, Martin, 25:82 ff.; 26:342 ff.
Scientific American, 29:11.
Scipio, Nolan, 17:110.
Scissors, superstitions involving, 13:157; 26:236; 35:14.
Scissortails, 7:33.
Scobee, Barry, 32:123, 128.
Scorpions, 19:136; lizards called, 4:51; 5:61.
Scotch-Irish: humor, 18:82; lore predominates in European lore in America, 28:29-30.
Scotland: ballad of "The Texas Rangers" in, 32:188-198; see Scottish.
Scott (cowboy in New Mexico), 9:177.
Scott, Florence J.: article, 2:75-84; mentioned, 2:5.
Scott, H. L., 22:111, 117, 138.
Scott, John (Indian), 13:273, 275.
Scott, Mrs. L. A., 6:224.
Scott, Lawson, 18:123.
Scott, Michael, 34:145.
Scott, Mt. (Okla.), 22:130.
Scott, Roy S.: article, 4:53-58; mentioned, 4:115; 6:155; 29:165.
Scott, Sir Walter, 5:93; 6:121; 23:32, 56; 25:71, 95, 116, 145; 28:3, 35; 30:216; 35:69 f.
Scottish tunes in Texas, 23:23.
Scours, remedy for, 8:45.
Scouton, Antonio, 21:117.
Scow (dic.), 35:47.
Scratch (dic.), 18:70.
Screwbean Stream as place name, 32:118.
Screw worms: as cure, 8:42; cures for, 8:45; 30:252; to "talk out," 8:14; 26:258; 30:252; 34:167-171.
Scripture, misapplication of on frontier, 14:163-164.
Scruggs, Arthur, 10:148.
Scudday, Roy: article, 19:162-164; mentioned, 19:200 ff.
Scuffle Hollow Stream as place name, 32:126.
Scurry County, Tex., 6:81; 14:268-269; place name, 31:77.
"Se fué y abandonó la muy ingrata," 30:51.
Sea: birds as weather sign, 5:113; gulls as good omen, 4:60; snakes, giant, 4:60; Northern, superstitions of the, 4:59-63.
Seabrook, William, 31:110, 117.
Seagull (dic.), 34:27.
"Sealy," 13:305; with music, 13:328-329.
Searcy, Richard, 19:181.
Sears, Edward S.: article, 19:175-199; mentioned, 19:204.
Sears, Minnie Earl, 18:54.
Seashells; see Shells.
Seasonal ceremonies, 6:113-117.
Seasons: creation of, 14:73; old-timers be-

lieve becoming milder or severer, 2: 98; see Seasonal.
Seattle, Tex., 30:123.
Seaview Bend, Tex., 3:142.
Sebasco, Bill, 3:227; 26:113.
Second Christmas (Dec. 26th), 2:68, 71.
Second Creek as place name, 32:120.
Sedeño, Juan, 16:200 f.
"Sediciosos, Los," 30:287.
"See a pin and pick it up," 13:155.
"See Saw Margery Daw" (cited), 6:69.
"See, saw, saddle the old goose," 6:69.
See-a-boo (Pima deity), 14:69.
Seego, Wiley, 13:7.
Seeley, Howard, 22:227.
Seer, 1:82, 87; in "Dr. Know-All" folk-tale, 22:179-184; lost possessions recovered through, 29:17; Negro, 29:14-32; see Curanderos; Fortune-teller.
Segua, La (a demon), 30:229-231.
Seguin, Tex., 9:2; 36:37 f.
Seguín, Juan N. 19:198.
Segundo, Felipe, 12:178.
Segura, Grace, 25:215.
Seizures, religious; see "Jerks."
Selig, William, 33:53.
Seligman, C. G., 32:84.
Selkirk, Alexander, 25:139.
Selkirk, William, 8:134.
Sells (dic.), 7:46.
Semana Santa in Seville, 36:27.
Sématma (Indian), 22:131.
Semi (dic.), 4:65.
Seminole, Tex., 13:28.
Seminole Creek as place name, 32:131.
Seminole Indians, 19:86.
Semonides of Amorgos, 32:176-177.
Sempual as remedy, 8:55.
Sendero (dic.), 13:7.
Seneca, S. Car., 31:25.
Seneca Oil Company, 20:52.
Senna as remedy, 13:234.
Sennitt, Georgie, 30:166-172.
Señor de los Guerreros (an icon), 12:166-169.
"Señores, I wish to tell you," 12:vi.
"Sent my brown jug down to town," 1:9; 13:311, 314-315; 17:94.
Sergeant Major Creek (Okla.), 6:90.
Seria, Paschal, 33:132.
Sermon: Negro, 19:9-20; 26:175-182 (reprint); see Preaching.
Serpent: dragon, 12:199; 15:125-133; see Lizard; Snakes.
Serpent Head (Indian), 22:114-120.
Serra, Antonio, 17:67.
Served a term in college (dic.), 30:96.
Set-fasts, 8:45; see Saddle sores.
Seth, "Uncle" (Bell County, Tex., Negro), 11:104 f.
Seton, Ernest Thompson, 14:40, 50, 53, 58, 61, 65 f.
Seton, Mary, 23:63.

Seven as magic number, 1:94; 22:109; see Seven Sisters; Seventh son.
Seven Cities of Gold, 15:60-61; see Cibola.
Seven-D Ranch, 33:40-41, 48.
Seven-F Ranch, 33:42.
Seven Heart Gap as place name, 13:4.
"Seven Long Years," 10:157-158.
Seven Sages, 29:76.
Seven Sisters (a coven of witches), 13:144.
"Seven ways for Sunday," 5:83.
Seventh son, 8:69; of seventh son, 8:79-80; 27:4.
Sevier, A. H., 18:49; 19:180.
Sevillano de Parades, Fray Miguel, 17:50.
Seville, 36:27-32.
Sewell, Marcus, 15:34.
Sewing machine (dic.), 34:19.
Sex; see Pornographic; Vulgarity.
Seyffert, F. R., 21:44.
Seymour, Tex., 18:1.
Shack bully (dic.), 13:248.
Shackleford County, Tex., 25:78; 26:339; place name, 31:85.
Shadle, Jake, 13:195.
Shadows, superstitions concerning, 1:85; 9:51.
Shafter, Tex., 35:99.
Shagaans, Christian, 36:150.
Shake-down (dic.), 18:21.
Shakers, 35:25.
Shakespeare, William, 5:116; 15:94; 25:115; 28:66; 29:76; 30:30, 57 f., 70, 95; 33:91, 97; 34:175.
Shalian, Artin K., 34:200.
Shaman, Alvin, 22:8-140 passim.
Shamburger, Betty, 25:217.
Shan beliefs relating to agriculture, 35:157-163.
Shanghai as place name, 13:59.
Shank's pony (dic.), 5:82.
Shannon, Mrs. A. F., 3:142 f., 213.
Shannon, John M., 15:99 f.
Shanties, 8:161; see Chanty.
"Shanus maidschen, wans canst de mauken?," 18:17.
Sharp, Cecil J., 5:10; 14:276; 23:291; 25:49 f., 57, 64, 67, 70, 72 f.; 27:27, 43, 47, 77; 28:27; 30:35; 32:237-243, 249, 254-255.
Sharp instruments, superstitions concerning, 1:85; see Scissors.
Sharp shooter (dic.), 7:49; 18:202.
Sharpe, C. K., 25:66.
Sharps rifles, 6:72, 203.
Shaver, Lillie T., 4:pages 14, 19 of appdix.
Shaw, Barbara: article, 18:142; mentioned, 18:222.
Shaw, Doris, 7:86.
Shaw, Henry Wheeler, 28:87.
Shaw, James, 21:119.

Shaw, Lloyd, 18:115.
Shawnee Creek as place name, 13:28;
     32:131.
Shay, Frank, 8:161 f.
"She was standing by her window," 23:
     172.
"She'll Be Comin' Round the Mountain"
     (cited), 36:113.
"Sheath Knife, The" (cited), 27:35.
Sheed, Rosemary, 36:102.
Sheep, 9:44, 63-68, 70; 10:13, 45; cattle
     will not graze where bedded, 6:79;
     drive, 15:101 ff.; shearing, 17:76;
     shearing contest, 15:116 ff.; Spanish,
     15:85, 90; in Texas Panhandle, 6:78-
     79; in tales, 6:43-44; 10:19-20; 21:84-
     85; 25:242-243; see Mutton; Ram; see
     the following entries.
Sheep Creek as place name, 32:121, 123.
Sheep dog(s), 9:70; tales involving, 15:
     95, 109-114, 119 ff., 126 ff.
Sheep head dumplings (tale), 25:243-245.
Sheep herder, 9:63-69; 15:87 ff.; his char-
     acter compared with cowboy's, 15:94;
     costume of, 15:96-99; as folk char-
     acter, 15:85-100; sheep ranch fore-
     man, 15:101 ff; see Pastores.
Sheep industry: in England, 15:90; in
     New Mexico and Arizona, 15:88; in
     the Southwest, 15:87; in Spain, 15:
     85; in Texas, 15:85-118.
Sheep Ranch Hollow as place name,
     13:4.
Sheep sorrel: pie, 13:213; as remedy,
     10:88.
Sheepmen: hostility between cowboys
     and, 15:88; immigration of, 15:89; in
     Midland County, Tex., 6:86.
"Sheffield Apprentice, The," 18:9.
Shelby County, Tex., 17:33; place names,
     13:52; 31:75, 86.
Shell down the corn (dic.), 13:247.
Shells as grave decoration, 18:133-134;
     36:33-43.
Shelton, Dr. (Wise County, Tex.), 13:43.
Shely, William, 22:155.
Shepard, Leslie, 33:166.
Shephard, Esther, 4:8; 7:45; 20:5.
Shepherd; see Pastores; Sheep herder.
Shepherd, David, 33:150.
Shepherd, Tex., 7:29; 26:288.
Sheppard, Morris, 13:48.
"Sherfield," with music, 18:8; cited, 18:4.
Sheridan, Gen., 9:14; 35:139.
Sherman, Gen., 5:164; 7:21; 19:134; his
     statement about hell and Texas, 9:182.
Sherman, J. W., 20:49.
Sherman, Tex., 5:164; 6:222; 18:3; 23:
     128-131, 190; 28:12, 54.
"Sherman Cyclone, The," with music,
     23:128-131; words only, 26:141-142;
     cited, 28:66.
Sherrill, R. E.: article, 3:72-77; men-

tioned, 3:262.
Shettles, E. L., 10:11.
Shields, Emily, 19:108.
Shields, Nelson T., 19:108.
"Shiloh," 6:143-144.
Shindig (dic.), 6:171.
Shine (Negro folk hero), 31:131.
Shiner, Henry, 3:30; 26:85.
Shinikinnik (Kinnikkinnik), 18:162; 26:
     277.
Shinn, C. H., 7:74.
Shipman, Daniel, 3:72.
Shipman, J. D., 35:77.
Shipman, W. K., 16:181.
Shipp, Byron, 8:7; 10:187; 11:109.
"Ships in de oceans," 2:62.
"Shipwrecked Sailors, The," with music,
     10:135, 162-163; see "Mermaid."
Shirley, Glen, 30:158, 163 ff.
Shirley, Myra Belle (Belle Starr), 30:
     158.
"Shirley Temple went to France," 18:
     199; 26:206 (reprint).
Shirt-tail cutting as hunting rite, 35:6.
Shitepoke bird as folk classification and
     weather sign, 7:34.
Shivarees, 30:254-255; 32:64-71.
Shoal Stream as place name, 32:119.
Shoat Creek as place name, 32:121.
Shockley, Martin S.: article, 36:147-152;
     mentioned, 36:vi, 155.
Shoe(s): in marriage superstition, 13:151:
     26:232; O. K. style, 15:97; turning
     upside down as remedy or charm,
     7:31; 8:23, 53.
Shoemaker, Henry W., 8:161.
Shoemaker, Hyde T., 14:46, 52.
"Shoo Die" (cited), 1:36.
"Sho Fly," 13:329-330; cited, 7:18.
"Shoot the Buffalo," 1:29-31, 36; 7:21;
     25:144; with music, 17:99-100.
Shoot the moon (phrase in tale), 11:105.
"Shoot a punkin in a churn," to, 5:80.
Shoot the scales (dic.), 35:46.
Shooting: fests, 2:72; 9:2; legended
     marksmanship, 9:1-14; tales involv-
     ing, 7:143; 9:28 ff.; 19:40-41; see
     Munchausen.
Shooting a snipe (dic.), 1:45.
"Shooting" an oil well, 7:53.
Short, Jake, 19:71.
Short, Tom, 8:21, 27, 36, 53.
Short Creek as place name, 32:120.
Short time (dic.), 1:45.
Short varmint (dic.), 22:205.
"Short visits make long friends," 13:244.
Shoshone Indians, 14:68.
Shotgun herder (dic.), 35:48.
Shotgun house, 29:14.
Shots, lucky; see Munchausen.
Shouts, Negro, as remnant of barbaric
     dances, 7:85, 105.
Shreveport, La., 18:143; 36:3.

Shrewish woman: comes to life in coffin, 30:175-176; tamed, 22:90-93; 30:175; 31:21-22.
Shrike (butcher bird), 15:158.
Shrine of the Virgin of Guadalupe, 19: 96.
"Shrinking" steel tires, 34:3-9.
Shropshire, Milton, 15:37.
"Sh-Ta-Rah-Dah-Dey" (cited), 36:109.
"Shu-dah," with music, 13:310-311, 330-331.
Shuck cigarette, 12:220.
Shuck, to light a (origin of the phrase), 17:9-10.
Shultz (of Mills County, Tex.), 13:259.
Shumard, Malnor, Jr.: article, 14:234-240; mentioned, 14:287.
Shurlock, Ruth Garrison, 33:150.
Shut-In Stream as place name, 32:119.
"Si Dios quiere," 12:216.
"Si es mi suerte ¿ que le voy a hacer?," 6:7.
"Si quieres dichoso verte conformate con su suerte," 12:216.
"Si se descuidan las jovenes bellas," 8:102.
"Si tu mal tiene remedio . . . ," 12:216.
Sicamas, 9:99.
Siddall, Mrs. Robert P., 5:93 ff.
Side-ache, remedy for, 30:252.
Side door sleeper (hobo term), 22:202.
Sidney, Sir Philip, 30:35.
Siebert, T. Laurence, 36:106.
"Siempre la res busca al monte," 12:213.
Sierra Blanca, Tex., 10:76.
Sierra Mojada, Mex., 32:49.
Sierra Morena, Spain, 4:21, 27.
Sierra Osoria, Lope de, 28:110.
Sierra Potoú, Mex., 19:95.
Sierrita de la Cruz: as place name, 6:75, 78-79; see Cerrito.
Siever, A. D., 30:81-82.
Sigala, Ralph, 25:215.
Sign(s); see Death; Luck; Omens; Weather.
Sign of the Cross; see Cross.
Signature in ballads and tales, 25:97-109.
"Signifying Monkey and the Lion," 31:125.
Silence breaking (tales), 25:13-15.
Silistine, Harden (Indian), 13:275.
"Silk, satin, calico, rags," 18:196; 26:203 (reprint).
Silkies cactus, 11:92.
Silsbee, Tex., 23:13, 102.
Silva, Padre, 9:89.
Silvas, Martin, 29:220.
Silver: as charm, 8:62, 81; cures involving, 8:13-14, 47-48, 61; see Part II, Section 8, of Analytical Index.
Silver Blue Island, 14:229.
Silver City, N. M., 10:64.
Silver Slipper (nightclub), 18:143.

Silver Stream as place name, 32:128.
Silver Toe tale, 6:41-42; 25:187-188, 191; 26:73-74 (reprint); see Golden arm.
Silvermine Stream as place name, 32:128.
Silvestre, Gonzalo, 16:221.
Simadhi, 36:142.
Simeon: in folk drama, 11:54; see St. Simeon.
Similes, folk, 5:79, 87-90; see Diction; Metaphor; Proverbs.
Simmons, Dr. (South Texas), 16:20.
Simmons, Frank: article, 14:182-194; mentioned, 13:178-179; 14:287.
Simmons, J. P., 5:62.
Simmons, James R., 25:35, 39; 26:311-312.
Simmons, Merle, 29:111; 30:61, 68.
Simms (stepfather of James brothers), 27:98.
Simms Bayou, 28:144.
Simon, Pedro (friar), 4:69-70.
Simpkins, Tom, 10:44-45.
Simpson, D. O., 19:167, 174.
Simpson, Mrs. D. O., 19:171.
Simpson, George, 28:16; 30:102.
Simpson, Henry, 19:173.
Simpson, Roy, 19:171, 174.
Simpson, William, 16:111, 114, 133.
Sims, Dunny: article, 19:155-161; mentioned, 19:203.
Sims, E. R.: articles, 11:48-89; 12:246-249; mentioned, 11:108; 12:254.
Sims, Ed, 30:126.
Sims, O. L., 4:90; 27:166.
Sinaloa, Mex., 6:16, 33; in ballad, 21:6-7.
Sinatra, Frank, 28:102.
Sinclair, Harry, 30:96.
Sinebourne, Henry, 29:93.
"Sinful to Flirt"; see "They Say . . . "
"Sing Polly Wolly Doodle All Day," 6:189; 26:135 (reprint).
"Sing, sing, what shall we sing?," 6:71.
"Sing-song-Polly, won't you ki' me oh," 5:32.
"Sing songs over a dead horse," to, 5:79.
Singer, Sam, 19:166.
Singer must lie on his back to sing well, 23:50.
Singing: games, 17:44; schools, 13:194; 25:143; 28:153-160; 29:153-160; style in East Texas, 23:27 f.
Sinistrality in fact and tradition, 4:97-98; 13:174; 26:252 (reprint); 29:69-87.
Sin-ke-lip (coyote), 14:40, 66.
Sin-kit-zas-cow-ha (horse), 14:70.
Sinton, Tex., 18:139; 24:63; 26:126; 29:41.
Sioux Indians, 3:230, 239; burial customs of, 18:131.
"Sir Aldingar" (cited), 27:44; 30:31.
"Sir Hugh" (cited) 27:24 (foldout), 29, 38 f., 57 f., 63, 72, 74 f.
"Sir Lionel" (cited), 27:24 (foldout), 29,

22:48; people who have never seen, 11:10.
Snow, Bob, 19:36; 30:16-17.
Snow, Luther, 30:16-17.
Snowden (of McMullen County, Tex.), 3:40; 26:97.
Snuff: aids childbirth (tale), 30:183; for croup, 35:15; used to stop bleeding, 8:31.
Snyder, Capt. (follower of Lafitte), 3: 190 f.
Snyder, Charley, 36:106.
Snyder, Howard, 2:63.
Snyder, Marcus, 30:10.
Snyder, Pete, 6:81 f.; 13:48.
Snyder, Tex., 6:81; 14:268 f.; as place name, 13:48, 76.
Snyder and Boyce (cow buyers), 7:165.
"So hard is the fortune," 30:217.
"So Long," 36:69.
"So you've come back to me once more," 23:154.
Soap: as remedy, 8:68, 76-77; 35:14; -maker, 6:26, 32 f.; making of, 35: 105-108.
Soap Creek as place name, 13:4.
Sociable (dic.), 2:31; 23:138; 25:145; 32:162.
Social, a (dic.), 22:228.
Social: customs in early Texas, 32:148-167; life in early Parker County, Tex., 13:230-238.
Social democracy, 32:150-151.
Social science, value of, 1:74.
Society for the Protection of German Emigrants in Texas, 36:51.
Socorro: N. M., 10:125-126; 13:121-128; 26:41; Tex., 13:123-126; 26:120 ff.
Socoyonostre, 9:97, 103.
Socrates, 1:70; 36:123.
Soda as remedy, 8:35, 49, 58, 65; 30:248.
Soda community, Tex., 23:209.
Soda Stream as place name, 32:128.
Sodom, curse of, 1:92.
Sodville (school), 13:47.
Soft soap (dic.), 13:232; 18:73.
Sokolov, U. M., 25:108; 27:137.
Sold out to the Yankees (dic.), 35:47.
Soldadillo, Juan (folk character), 32:15-17.
"Soldier, Soldier," with music, 23:261.
"Soldier Child, The," 7:162.
Soldier herb in folk curing, 24:57.
"Soldier's Joy," 18:115.
Soledad St., San Antonio, Tex., 13:1.
Solian Indians, 14:44.
Solíz, Luis, 18:109-110.
Solíz, Rachel, 24:72, 78-86.
Solm, Prince, 8:15.
Solomon: tales about, 12:2-4; 32:42-44; his weather wisdom, 2:87.
Solomon, Jack: article, 33:171-175; mentioned, 33:200.

Solomon River, Kans., 16:112.
Solorzano, Ponciano Humberto, 30:99.
"Sombrero Ancho, El," with music, 8: 112.
"Some punkins," 5:80.
"Some say I drink whiskey," with music, 23:161-163.
Somersetski (dance), 19:80.
Somet, John de la, 33:132.
Something turrible (dic.), 8:118.
"Sometimes I feel like an eagle in de air," 5:152; 10:55.
"Sometimes I feel like a motherless child," 5:151.
Sone, Rosemary, 17:155.
Sone, Violet West: article, 18:195-199; 26:202-207 (reprint); mentioned, 17: 155; 18:223.
Sones (dances), 35:147 ff.
Song(s): collecting, 21:1-2; 23:7-9; at Ozark folk festival, 35:120-124; as part of the huapango, 35:147 ff.; penny dreadfuls as a source of, 33:164-170; of protest, 36:104; revivals, 32: 235-236; slavic, 15:8; about trucking, 35:49-52; see Ballads; Carriers; Hobo; Negro; Railroad; Singing schools; Style; see Part I, Section 3, of Analytical Index; see vol. 23 (entire) for Texas folksongs; see vol. 30 for symposium on folksong; see names of songs.
Song ballet (dic.), 23:26 f.
"Song of the Eleven Slash Slash Eleven," 7:178-179.
"Song of the Interior," 12:231-233.
"Song of Little Llano, The," 19:165-166.
"Song to Morelos," 30:48.
"Song of the Wheels" (cited), 36:116.
Sonnichsen, Charles L.: article, 13:120-129; 26:118-124 (reprint); mentioned, 13:339; 14:285; 17:156; 18:x; 27:186; 33:70, 78.
Sonora: Mex., 4:13; 15:140, 156, 164; Tex., 18:80.
Sonora Mtns., 3:235.
Sons of Hermit (religious organization), 10:125.
Soot as remedy, 8:31, 52, 84.
"Sophia and Vasily," 25:92.
Soplón (a giant), 11:17, 20.
Sore: mouth, remedy for, 8:46; throat, remedy for, 14:267; 24:110; 26:247.
Sores, remedies for, 8:30, 66; 10:82, 92; see Saddle sores.
Sorgum Flats as place name, 13:4.
"Sorghumseed!" (battle cry of Third Texas Cavalry), 17:7, 12.
Sorrel; see Sheep sorrel.
Sorrell, A. C., 34:44.
Sorrell, Henry, 34:44.
Soto, Abel, 30:99.
Soto, Ramon, 9:65.

Sotol cactus, 6:102; 9:92-93; hair tonic made from, 8:57; 26:262.

Soul, 1:69; external, 1:83-84; 12:82-83, 128-129, 133; 14:241-249; 22:27-28; 32:47-49; white bird as child's, 8:103.

Soulard *vs.* United States, 19:180 f., 188.

Sour Creek as place name, 32:120.

Sour-Dough Charlie, 9:37.

Sour Dough Stream as place name, 6:92-93; 32:126.

Sour Lake as place name, 13:68, 76.

Sousa, John Phillip, 19:163.

South America; see Chibcha Indians.

South Carolina, 6:25, 28, 51; 7:140-144.

South Dakota, 14:42.

South Elm Creek, 18:101.

South Side of the docket (dic.), 30:96.

South Texas: cultural bonds with Mexico, 21:15; early folk life in, 17:59-77; fairs, 28:50; see Rio Grande Valley.

Southerland Springs, legend of, 1:99.

Southern: stocker (dic.), 34:19; style (dic.), 34:19, 25; myth, the, 35:136.

Southern Cheyenne Indians, 19:89.

Southey, Robert, 3:145; 25:88, 94; 33:131.

Southwest: Moorish treasure legends in the, 9:124-129; Spanish influence on Americans of the, 3:6, 9, 69.

Southwest Review, 4:8, 18; 36:121.

Southworth, Mrs. E. D. E. N., 33:59.

Sow belly, 7:72.

Sowell, Andrew Jackson, 3:16; 6:149, 151; 10:116, 122; 15:52.

"*Soy Novillo Despuntado*," with music, 9:118.

"*Soy Zapata Cuenta, jefe de mi nación*," 9:72.

Spade Draw as place name, 32:123.

Spaeth, Sigmund, 33:169.

Spain, 2:89; 4:11; treasure legends in, 3:9; 9:124-129.

Spaniard(s): influence of on the plains country, 6:72-79; mysterious, seeks treasure in Texas, 8:103-106; 13:123-126; 26:121-123 (reprint); 28:143-145; skins of tanned for boots, 4:13; among Tejas Indians, 6:108-110; in Texas, 1:101; 3:1-70 passim; traditions connected with, 6:5, 7, 14-20; see Spanish.

Spaniard, Jack, 30:165.

Spanish: chroniclers, 4:69-71; conquerors, 4:10, 68-71; and French in Texas, 5:49 ff.; horses in Mexico, 16:197 ff.; influence on blues and jazz, 36:117; influence on the imagination of Texas pioneers, 3:9; influence on sheep industry in Texas, 15:85 ff.; language in South Texas, 2:76; literature in relation to Texas treasure legends, 9:124-129; missions a source of horses, 2:20; music, New Mexico a center of,

4:18; treasure and mines in Texas attributed to the, 3:12-20, 36, 45, 49 ff., 55, 58, 72-77, 79.

Spanish bayonet (dagger): as food, 9:92-93; as remedy, 8:18, 23, 43-45; 13:234; 19:59; see Yucca.

"Spanish Fandango" (cited), 23:238; 26:140.

Spanish oak, bark and sap as dye, 18:161; 26:276.

Sparerib Creek as place name, 13:47; 32:126.

Sparrow in rite, 6:69.

Spear Creek as place name, 32:132.

Spears, M., 2:180.

Speck, Ernest: articles, 19:165-166; 22:194-199; mentioned, 19:200 f., 203; 22:194.

Speck, Frank G., 21:63.

Speech, folk; see Diction; Language; Metaphor; Proverbs.

Speech masquerade, 34:125-144.

Speirs, John, 30:45.

Spell, Lota May, 4:36.

Spell off, to (dic.), 18:203.

Spelling rhymes, 23:251.

Spellings, Mrs. H. A., 36:11.

Spells (hexes): in Mexican belief, 24:116-117; witches cast, 10:66-67; 12:115-117; 31:19-20; see Evil eye; *Susto.*

Spence, J. Roy, 27:163.

Spence, Lewis, 3:231.

Spence, Lithenia, 19:23.

Spencer, Herbert, 5:page 4 of appendix.

Spencer, Tom, 10:33-34.

Spencer, W. Va., 36:107.

Spenser, Edmund, 21:63-64.

Spice bush, 18:160; 26:276.

Spider(s): bites, remedy for, 8:44; as signs of good or bad luck, 5:121; 24:117; in tales, 22:72, 83; 26:7-8; webs as weather sign, 2:95.

Spider Rock (Haskell County, Tex.), 3:75.

Spider Woman in Indian tales, 14:111 ff.; 22:55.

Spielert, "Mutter," 30:251.

Spillane, James, 3:218.

Spillman, Max, 36:45, 48.

"Spin the Pan" (game), 7:15.

Spindletop Creek as place name, 32:127.

Spinners (dic.), 34:16.

Spinning, F. G., 18:51-52.

Spinning wheel foils the devil, 7:131.

Spirit of the Times, 36:74.

Spirits: Shan, 35:158-163; see Part II, Section 7, of *Analytical Index.*

Spiritualism, 1:70.

Spiritualists; see Fortune-teller.

Spirituals: Negro, 2:52, 58; 10:55-57, 60-61; 13:130-136; 19:1-8; white camp-meeting, 10:169-185.

T ⌒

Wister's *The Virginian* (baby born with rattlesnake rattles), 28:15-16; see Munchausen; see Part II, Section 9, of *Analytical Index*.
Tallahone Creek as place name, 32:132.
Talley, J. D., 22:152.
Talley, Thomas W., 5:46, 156 f.
Tallow Face Mtn. as place name, 13:47.
"Tam Lin" (cited), 6:235; 27:44.
"Tam O' The Linn" (cited), 6:235.
Tamales, 9:76, 107, 109; 22:161; tale involving, 21:35-42.
Tamaulipas, Mex., 4:33; 12:1.
Tampico, Mex., 21:35.
Tancitara, Mex., 11:29.
Tandakee Creek as place name, 32:132.
Tanked up (dic.), 2:35.
Tanquin, Mex., 32:52.
Tansey (herb), 19:72.
Tantaboque Creek as place name, 32:132.
Tanyana, 29:94.
Tanyard Creek, 16:359; 17:1 ff.; as place name, 13:4; 32:126, 128.
Taos, N. M., 9:73; 11:48; 12:129; 19:200.
Taovayas Indians, 3:81; 9:167, 173-174.
Tape Stream as place name, 32:126.
Tapeworm: girl cured of, 30:250; remedies for, 8:69, 82; tall tale about, 20:94.
Tar as remedy, 8:21.
Tar-Baby motif, 14:118-120; 18:191; 26:31-32 (reprint).
Tar Box Creek as place name, 32:112, 126.
Tar and feather party, 7:156 f.
Tarahumara Indians, 14:207-224; 15:171.
Tarantula juice (dic.), 13:26.
Tarantulas, 19:135; 26:280; lore concerning, 31:41-52.
Tarasco Indians, 11:23-29.
Tarbell, Ida, 20:12.
Tardy Creek as place name, 32:126.
Taris, Telesforio, 25:177.
Tarnacious (dic.), 18:70.
Tarrant County, Tex., 5:107 ff.; 6:167; 7:126; 18:56.
Tartarus, 1:68.
Tartt, Ruby Pickens: article, 19:21-28; mentioned, 19:202.
Tarwater, Hope, 28:112; 35:100.
Tarwater, Mack, 28:112.
Tarwater, Rebecca, 25:71.
Tasajillo cactus, 11:93.
Tascosa, Tex., 6:78-79; 13:46, 53; 16:96; 22:216.
Tascosa Creek as place name, 32:130.
Tasker, Charles P., 6:81.
Tasks: impossible, 11:36 ff.; 12:61-66; 14:110-114; see Fools' tasks.
Tasso, José, 18:51-52.
Tate, Tom, 18:109-110, 114.
Tatema, a kind of treasure trove, 24:129.

Tattlers (birds), 7:37.
Tatum, Paul, 34:43.
Tawakony Indians, 3:218-219.
Taylor, Albert Rhett, 14:251.
Taylor, Archer, 8:165; 27:123-124; 30:31, 285, 289; 32:217-218.
Taylor, B. W., 25:175.
Taylor, Bill, 7:123.
Taylor, Bud, 13:197.
Taylor, Charlie; see "Charlie Taylor."
Taylor, George (Texas pioneer), 13:224.
Taylor, George C.: article, 14:251-252; mentioned, 14:287; 25:12; 36:133.
Taylor, Mrs. H. W. (formerly Annie Roy Kiefer), 6:230.
Taylor, Henry, 3:63.
Taylor, Hugh McGehee: articles, 11:5-47; 12:135-142, 201-210; mentioned, 11:108-109; 12:254.
Taylor, Mrs. J. M., 20:30.
Taylor, Jim, 13:191.
Taylor, Lon, 33:116.
Taylor, Lucy, 13:210.
Taylor, N. A.: article, 3:118-130; mentioned, 3:262; 8:142-143; 10:127.
Taylor, Nancy Beaird, 13:222.
Taylor, "Pappy" (freighter), 33:49.
Taylor, Paul S.: article, 12:221-245; 26:157-158 (reprint); mentioned, 12:254.
Taylor, Sue, 33:116.
Taylor, T. E., 25:175.
Taylor, T. U., 13:237; 17:83; 18:34, 52; 19:107; 34:206.
Taylor, Tex (role played by Tom Mix), 34:63.
Taylor, Tom, 13:210.
Taylor, Mrs. V. M., 3:211.
Taylor, W. T., 13:198; 16:337.
Taylor, Walter: article, 27:192-200; mentioned, 27:203.
Taylor, Zachary, 7:160; 10:112-113, 118; 19:130.
Taylor, Tex., 10:128; 28:136.
Taylor County, Tex., place name, 31:92.
Tayopa Mine, 7:178; 32:60.
"*¿Te acuerdas cuando pusiste?*," 30:48.
Tea baggers (dic.), 34:19, 22.
Tea-squall (dic.), 18:71, 76.
"Teach your grannie how to pick ducks [suck eggs]," 5:79.
Teague, George, 33:49.
Teague, H. H., 8:142.
Teague, Tex., 27:193.
Tears from peeling onions, preventative against, 8:69; 26:264 (reprint).
Teas as remedies, 8:9-73 passim, 82-83; 26:246-275 passim (reprint); 30:250; 35:13; see names of teas.
Teasing: as form of humor, 29:58-68; among Kiowa-Apaches, 22:12, 48, 122, 129.
Tebo Creek as place name, 32:127.

Teco, El (betrayer of Gregorio Cortez), 27:17 ff.
Tecolote Ranch, 13:2.
Tecovas, Las (a trading point), 6:75-76.
Tecumseh Peaks, 16:182.
"Teddy Bear" (jump-rope rhyme), 18: 199; 26:206-207.
"Teeny-Tiny," tale of, 25:188-191.
Teepee: Creek as place name, 32:132; see Tepee.
Teeth, cures for bad, 8:24, 28, 41-42, 59, 62, 65, 69; 24:56.
Teeth-pick (dic.), 18:69.
Teething remedies, 8:24, 69; 19:25; 26: 264.
Tegetmier (Englishman), 21:60.
Tehuacana: Creek as place name, 32:131; Hills, 13:28; Indians, 1:50; 13:28.
Tehuacana Jim (Indian), 1:50 f.
Tehuan (Indian), 3:156.
Tehuana Indians, 12:135 ff.; likened to ancient Egyptians, 12:138-139.
Tehuantepec, Isthmus of, 19:60.
Tehueco Indians, 11:8.
Tejano (dic.), 12:211.
Tejas (dic.), 14:196, 237.
Tejas Indians, 3:133 f.; 13:64; mythology, customs, ceremonies of, 1:39-46; 6:107 ff; 9:167-174; 14:197-198.
Tejocote, 9:96.
Telegraph and Texas Register, 19:133.
Telepio (character in folk drama), 11:61.
Television westerns, classical and literary motifs in, 35:127-130.
Tell, Tex., as place name, 13:52, 77.
Telltales (birds), 7:37.
Temperance: songs, 6:237; 18:86 ff.; 33: 167; Sons of, 13:199.
Temple, Sir William, 36:127.
Temple, Tex., 3:154.
"*Ten cuidado que no te den gato por liebre,*" 12:212.
"Ten Thousand Miles Away," 23:179; cited, 36:116.
Tenancingo, Mex., 14:227.
Tenant communities, children's games in, 1:7.
Tenderfeet, tales for, 7:38-41; see Part II, Section 6, of *Analytical Index.*
"Tenderfoot Quadrille," 9:33.
Teneha Creek as place name, 32:132.
"*Tener suerte de gato boca arriba,*" 24: 125.
Tenerías: ranch, 21:27 f.; watering place, 4:34.
"*Tengan, tengan sangre,*" 9:75.
Tengo frío bird, origin of its name, 19: 60-62.
"*Tengo un dolor no se donde,*" 29:93.
Tenmile Stream as place name, 32:120.
Tennessee, 2:53; 12:81; 18:2; 22:214; 36: 73 f., 133.
Tennessee River, 7:84.

"Tenn-o-see," 13:312; with music, 13: 324-325.
Tenochtitlan, 14:227.
Teocalli, 22:156.
Tepee: Butte as place name, 13:3; Draw as place name, 13:28; see Teepee.
Tepeyac (sacred hill), 19:96.
Tequendama Falls, 4:68, 71; legend of, 4:78-79.
Teran (explorer), 13:5.
Terlingua, Tex., 4:89.
Terrapin(s): as weather sign, 2:93; why coal of fire placed on backs of, 5:69; see Turtle(s).
"Terrapin Dance Song," music only, 13:292.
Terrazas, Luis, 16:95; 19:98.
Terre Haute, Ind., 28:15.
Terrell, Dr. (of Haskell, Tex.), 3:76.
Terrell, C. V., 28:13, 17.
Terrell County, Tex., 3:64.
Terreros, Pedro de, 3:5.
Terrill, Alex W., 15:59 f.
Terrill, Annie C., 13:250, 255.
Terrill, Ruby, 33:8 ff.; see Lomax, Ruby T.
Terrill (I. M.) High School, 7:98.
Terry, Mrs. W. S., 36:12.
Tescino (the Devil), 1:42; see Texino.
Tesnus as place name, 13:54.
Tessebolle, Sir Jens Due of, 29:110.
Test: of chastity, 32:42-44; of obedience, 9:57; 12:21-26; of truthfulness, 12: 27-29; see Tasks; see Part I, Section 2, of *Analytical Index.*
Testal (uncooked tortilla), 15:140.
Testimony meeting (dic.), 17:46.
Tetanus, remedy for, 30:248; see Lockjaw.
Tetpac El Viejo, Mex., 11:28.
Tetter, remedy for, 8:66.
Teufel's Dreck (asafetida) as remedy, 30:251.
Teutonic psychology, 1:65.
Texan(s): cruelty of to Mexicans during Mexican War, 10:111-114; East, typical, 17:14; and Kansans, attitude toward each other, 7:168; West, typical, 17:14; see Texian.
Texarkana, Tex., 25:129; 36:9.
Texas: Alien Land Law, 14:178, Arabic hero-tale in, 34:187-202; British ballads in, 10:131-168; 23:31-94; Centennial, 17:40; drawl, 6:27; English and Scottish folktales in early, 6:25 ff.; First Republic of, 14:198; Homestead Law, 17:60; hostility between Spanish and French in, as reflected in early ballad, 5:49 ff.; Irish weaving song in, 6:226; legends of (bibliography), 3: 255-260; legends of, Mexican contribution to, 3:275; likened to Hell, 8: 106-109; 9:175-182; 19:134-138; 35:

"The leader was a fellow that came from Swenson's ranch," 33:13.

"The live-oak trees grow here and thar," 19:64.

"The love I had for you, my dear," with music, 9:122.

"The man that butchered the ram," with music, 5:157-159.

"The man who dances," 13:244.

"The moon was shining brightly," with music, 7:163.

"The morning rain is like an old woman's dance," 13:244.

"The old hen she cackle," 5:159; 26:163 (reprint).

"The oven is burning," 36:142.

"The polecat can't tell the buzzard that he stinks," 13:244.

"The reason why I don't work so hard," 5:page 8 of appendix.

"The red that is in my love's cheek," 30:41.

"The Road-Runner runs in the road," 15:147.

"The room is dark, mine eyes are dim," 13:104.

"The sailor's trade is a dreary life," 23:134.

"The shaggy duck," 25:94.

"The song of Little Llano I now compose," 19:166.

"The Spanish camp lies sleeping," 16:153.

"The stallions stamp, the donkeys get kicks," 14:152.

"The sun had gone down o'er the hills of the west," with music, 18:7-8.

"The whole value of a dime is in knowing what to do with it," 25:157.

"The year '63 was an unhappy one for me," 8:110.

[Them . . . ; see Dem . . . .]

[There . . . ; see also Der . . . .]

"There are more ways to kill a dog," 13:244.

"There goes Tom Moore, a bummer shore," 25:101.

"There's corn in the field," with music, 7:118.

"There's 'Ketchum and Cheatum,' " 30:78.

"There's nothing running around my house but the fence," 2:17.

"There's a tree in father's garden," 23:93.

"There sat Rosemary sweet as a rose," 18:197; 26:204 (reprint).

"There was a frog in yonder well," with music, 5:17-18.

"There was a little old woman," with music, 10:165-166.

"There was never a persimmon," 13:243.

"There was a noble ranger," 10:122.

"There was an old man and he was bent with age," with music, 23:276.

"There was an old man lived under the hill," with music, 10:164-165.

"There was an old man who had a mind," 23:228.

"There was an old man who owned a farm," 23:54.

"There was an old woman in Ireland," 23:208.

"There was an old woman lived by the sea shore," 10:142-143.

"There was a Romish lady," 23:284.

"There was a wealthy merchant," 10:151, 153 f.

"There were two boys," 23:225.

"There Were Two [Three] Crows," 7:110; with music, 14:280-283; 23:42-44.

"These few lines to you, dear Honey," 23:168.

Theseus as demigod, 1:70.

[They . . . ; see also Dey . . . .]

"They danced until the break of day," 5:47.

"They fit and fit," 19:69.

"They had a little fight in Mexico," 1:14.

"They Killed Brother Roman," 25:94.

"They said that Gumman Gro had a great store" (poem), 3:148.

"They Say It Is Sinful to Flirt," with music, 23:155-156.

"They say there is a stream," 23:237.

"They stood on the shore at evening," 23:166.

Thickety Stream as place name, 32:116.

Thief: neighbor who is a, 7:78; who retrieves powderhorn under water, 7:43; see Black Thief.

Thieves; see Cattle thieves; Two Thieves.

Third Creek as place name, 32:120.

"Third Party" flies, 2:93.

Third Texas Cavalry, 17:3 ff.

Thirst and thirst quenchers, 8:18 (bullets, copper, silver coins, prickly pear); 8:82 (plum, cherry pit, pebble); see Chie.

Thirteen: coins presented to Mexican bride as custom, 9:116; as name of trickster who dupes ogre, 34:201; see Catorce.

"This Mo'in', This Evenin', Sometime," with music, 5:175-177.

"This ranch of Los Guerras," 8:111.

"This Train" (cited), 36:114.

Thistle (cardo santo), legend of, 6:12-13.

Thoburn, Joseph B., 3:81.

Thomas, Maj., 13:39.

Thomas, Mrs. (Hays County, Tex.), 19:133.

Thomas, Church, 31:24 ff.

Thomas, Eloise, 31:27 f.

Thomas, Ezekiel, 21:125, 127.

Thomas, Gates: articles, 5:154-180; 26: 163-166 (reprint); mentioned, 5:184, page 1 of appendix; 18:ix; 25:1.

Thomas, Lowell, 33:102, 105.

Thomas, Mason, 25:1.

Thomas, N. W., 1:63.

Thomas, Rebecca Jane, 21:128.

Thomas, Robert B., 28:85.

Thomas, Will H.: article, 2:14-17; 5: pages 1-13 of appendix; mentioned, 1:5; 2:63 f.; 4:page 20 of appendix; 5:155; 5:page 1 of appendix; 18:ix; 26:171.

Thomas, Wright, 3:119 f.

"Thomas Rymer" (cited), 27:135.

Thomason, John W., 33:7.

Thompson (supreme court judge), 19:188.

Thompson, Al (of early Springtown, Tex.), 29:207.

Thompson, Algernon P., 21:130.

Thompson, Arthur, 1:89.

Thompson, Ben, 9:6 ff., 14:180.

Thompson, Bessie Lee, 5:45.

Thompson, Charles M., 13:275 ff., 294.

Thompson, Clyde, 30:184.

Thompson, Fred, 34:70.

Thompson, Gideon, 25:176.

Thompson, Grace, 18:131.

Thompson, Harold W., 33:103.

Thompson, High, 3:63.

Thompson, Irvin, 23:59; 26:137.

Thompson, Mrs. Irvin, 23:166, 171, 176.

Thompson, J. N., 23:226.

Thompson, "Smoky Hill," 6:80.

Thompson, Stith: articles, 1:78-95; 27: 118-128 ("Recollections of an Itinerant Folklorist"); mentioned, 1:4; 2:1, 82; 4:pages 15, 20 of appendix; 18: vii, 48; 24:72; 25:183; 27:vi, 137, 203; 29:174, 187; 30:227, 243; 32:177, 178, 214; 33:11, 195; 34:vi, 103; 36: vii, 126.

Thompson, W. S., 25:180.

Thompson, Will (treasure hunter), 3:63.

Thompson, William (Englishman), 33: 131.

Thoms, W. J., 1:62.

Thomson, William (physicist), anecdote about, 15:75.

Thor, 1:68.

Thoreau, Henry David, 13:48; 33:5, 104.

Thorn, Frost, 15:17, 30, 33, 35, 37.

Thorndale, Tex., 3:99, 101 f.; 13:185.

Thorne, Ben, 6:168-169.

Thornfield (Texas estate), 14:178.

Thorns, remedies for, 8:40, 42; 35:14.

Thorp, N. Howard (Jack), 6:166, 175, 188, 192; 7:170 f.; 9:176, 183 f.; 10: 122; 16:295; 29:12; 30:27; 33:6 f., 81 ff.

Thorpe, Dr.(marksman), 9:9.

Thorpe Springs, Tex., 27:103.

"Thou wilt come no more, gentle Annie,"

25:144.

"Thought I Heard that K. C. Whistle Blow" (cited), 36:111.

Thousand-legs, 14:112; see Centipede; Millipede.

Thrall, Tex., 28:139.

Thread: black in prevention of croup, 35:15; in Mexican folk belief, 24:118; silk, as remedy, 30:251-252; -winding charm, 24:117.

Threadgill, Tex., 4:103, 106.

"Three Black Crows [Ravens]," 7:110; 25:91, 99 ff.; 27:24 (foldout), 29, 64, 69, 74; 30:34; with music, 14:280-283; 23:42-43.

Three Corrals Stream as place name, 32:123.

Three Forks (Bell County, Tex.), 3:91, 95.

"Three Gay Punchers," 6:184; 26:131-132 (reprint).

"Three L [3L] Buceros, The," 6:160.

"Three Little Babes, The," with music, 23:32-33.

"Three Old Maids at a Skating Rink," 7:22.

"Three Ravens, The," 27:64, 69; 30:34; see "Three Black Crows."

"Three Thousand Texas Steers," 6:168-170.

"Three years ago Jack and Joe," 23:199.

Threemile Coleto Creek as place name, 32:120.

Threshing crew, description of, 19:167-174.

Throckmorton, J. W., 32:118.

Throckmorton Ranch, 16:373.

Throop, Mrs. L. N., 4:117; 5:78; 7:76.

Throop, Palmer A.: article, 7:139; mentioned, 7:117.

Thrush (ailment), cure for, 8:69; 26:283 (reprint).

Thrush (bird), 7:25, 34.

Thruston, A. S., 21:125.

Thumbs, superstition about, 13:153; 26: 234 (reprint).

Thunder (personification), 22:26; see Thundercloud; Thunderman.

Thunder Struck Creek as place name, 32: 112, 126.

Thunderbird, 22:44.

Thundercloud: personification, 12:87; riddle about, 24:127.

Thunderman, 22:33-44, 140.

Thurber, Tex., 30:107-114.

Thut, Henry, 32:114.

Thut Creek as place name, 32:114.

"Ti Risslety Rosslety," with music, 23: 66-67; see "Wife Wrapt in Wether's Skin."

Tiawichi, John, 32:132.

Tiawichi Creek as place name, 32:132.

Tick: in song, 5:21, 36, 46, 48; blood of

as remedy, 25:33.
Tick Stream as place name, 32:126.
Tickle-tongue; see Prickly ash.
"Tie Tamping Chant," 36:117.
Tierra Blanca, Tex., 6:75; 26:85.
Tierra Blanca Creek, 16:96.
Tidioute, Penn., 20:7.
Tiger Creek as place name, 32:121, 124.
Tiger Knight (Aztec), 12:159.
"Tight as Dick's hatband," 2:15.
Tijjena (meaning "medicine man"), 22:
    113 f.
Tijerina, Fernando M., 24:65.
Tilden, Samuel, 13:49.
Tilden, Tex., 3:30, 40 f.; 13:49; 26:85,
    97 f.
Tiling, Moritz, 36:59.
Tillhagen, Carl-Hermann, 36:42.
Tillman, Ben, 36:85 f.
Timber Stream as place name, 32:116.
Timbuck (New Mexico handyman),
    15:108 f.
Time: as an element in weather signs,
    2:90; proverbs concerning, 5:91.
Timmons, Carolyn, 36:70.
Timmons, Herbert, 36:70.
Timon, Harry, 24:34-35.
Timon, John, 19:120.
Tin Lizzie era, 34:13.
Tin Pan Alley, 28:102; 33:164 ff.
Tin Rag, Tex., 13:54.
Tinaja (dic.), 13:56.
Tinguindin, Mex., 11:23, 28.
"Tinker's dam," 5:84.
Tinkle, Jon Richard, 33:vi.
Tío Geromino Creek as place name, 32:
    131.
"Tío Pancho Malo Song, The," 8:111.
Tionesta, Penn., 20:xi, 7.
Tippecanoe, battle of, 33:118.
Tipps, J. H., 3:197.
Tires, steel, "shrinking" of, 34:3-9.
Tisquesuxa, 4:72.
Tithonus, 24:80.
Titus County, Tex., 7:42.
Tlacoteotl, 22:156.
Tlaxcala, battle in, 14:229.
Tlaxcalans, 1:39; 14:229 ff.
"To London," 1:11; cited, 1:35.
"To Whom God Wishes to Give" (poem
    based on Mexican tale), 27:151-161.
"To work upon the railway, the rail-
    way," 12:221.
Toads, 5:19, 60, 70, 125; horned, 5:64,
    75; 13:139; 19:135; 26:281; 29:3-13;
    spadefoot, 5:64.
Toadloop Draw as place name, 6:86-87;
    13:51-52, 77.
"Toady took a thought to ride," 5:19.
Tobacco: "Indian," 18:161-162; 26:277;
    Indian rites involving, 6:111-112, 115;
    Kiowa-Apache use of, 22:115 ff., 119,
    129 f.; longevity and, 33:128-135; non-

use of a virtue, 6:124; Paul Bunyan
    spends fortune for, 7:50; perique
    raised in Texas, 7:63; plug of as ar-
    mor against bullet wound, 33:123;
    raised in Texas, 13:226; as remedy,
    8:12, 32 f., 41, 45, 54, 56, 58, 83-85;
    12:187; 26:256, 258; 30:248; slang
    terms for, 1:45; sumac mixed with,
    22:129; "tea," 8:33; 26:256; see Frost
    weed; *Punche.*
Tobacco Stream as place name, 32:126.
Tobago Island; see Speech masquerade.
Tochonkono (Brazos) River, 3:211; 13:
    16-17.
"Toddy, O" (cited), 1:36.
Toe(s): length of, superstition about, 13:
    153; 26:234 (reprint); wiggled (tale),
    14:256-259; see Silver Toe.
Toelken, J. Barre, 36:123.
Toewash Creek as place name, 13:47; see
    Towash.
Toepperwein, Adolph, 9:1-5, 11; 10:186.
Toepperwein, Mrs. Adolph, 9:1-2, 4.
Toepperwein, Alfred, 15:160.
Toepperwein, Emilie, 25:134.
Toepperwein, Fritz, 25:134.
Toepperwein, Max, 9:4.
Tohoka Lake as place name, 6:73.
Tolbert (McMullen County, Tex., ranch-
    er), 3:41; 26:98.
Tolbert, Frank X., 31:88-89; 34:34; 36:
    12.
Toledo, Ohio, 32:163.
Tolima, Mount, 4:71.
Tollings, Sudy, 17:108.
Tolliver, K., 33:87-88.
Tolman, Albert H., 5:5, 16; 6:29, 223 f.;
    27:27, 34, 38, 55, 61, 63, 67.
Tolman, H. H., 8:167.
Toluca, Juan de, 12:10.
Tom, William, 32:115.
Tom Green County, Tex., place name,
    31:20.
Tom Sawyer, 31:35.
"Tom Twiss," 5:170-171.
"Toma de Zacatecas, La," 28:101.
Tomasita, Doña (Jim Wells County,
    Tex.), 24:22-24.
Tomate de fresadilla as remedy, 10:90.
Tomatoes: as remedy, 8:67; used in folk
    healing, 24:39; wild, 9:95.
Tombigbee River, 7:84; 26:161.
"Tombstone Terror," the, 7:74.
Tomkins, Augustus M., 21:122, 132.
"Tommy Linn," 6:235.
"Tomorrow is our wedding day," 23:144.
Toms Creek as place name, 32:115.
"Tom-Tit-Tot," taboo in, 1:87 ff.
Tonantzin, 19:97; 24:73.
Tonatico Canyon, 14:227.
Tone the Bell Easy, 18:ix; 22:213; 24:10.
"Tongue put us here" (tale), 10:48-50.
Tongue River (Tex.), 16:84, 88, 98; as

Trask, Willard R., 36:102.
Trasquilas (sheep-shearers), 17:76.
Trasvina y Retis, Antonio, 28:110-111.
Travelsted, E. C., 18:95.
Travers, Rev. J. C., 17:126.
Travis, Tom, 10:43.
Travis, William B., 14:185; 15:9 ff.; 21:
122.
Travis County, Tex., 25:139-151; 26:107;
27:181; 28:7; 32:66; 36:45; place
names, 31:86, 91, 95; see Bear Creek.
Travis District, 18:99.
Trawick, Tex., 30:184.
Treasure (see names of persons and sites
associated with): buried, 2:2; 3:3-108;
6:14-20; 8:118-121, 157; 9:58-59, 124-
144 passim; 10:71-81, 120-121; 12:173-
174; 13:13-15, 258-269; 14:175-176,
259-261; 17:73-76; 24:96-102, 128-
132; 26:46, 83-100, 120, 122 f. (reprints); 28:165-166; 29:162, 163-164,
201-213 passim, 224-225; 32:57-59;
34:37-50; cannon stuffed with, 3:9, 84-
89; cart loads of, 3:51, 79, 98; caves
stored with, 3:9, 11, 35 f., 45, 79, 233-
235; chests of, 3:33, 50, 52, 55, 88,
186, 190, 193; 29:211-213; concealed
by various parties, 3:28, 56 (Texas
bandits); 3:32 f., 51 f., 85, 87-88; 26:
87, 89; 29:209-213 (detachment of
Mexican army); 3:35 f., 45, 48, 101;
26:91 f. (Mexican bandits); 3:36 ff.
(Mexican adventurers); 3:41, 46, 48,
(ranchmen or sheepmen); 3:49 f., 55,
58, 74, 79, 84, 100, 214 (Spaniards);
3:90 ("three men"); 3:93-94 (Stein-
heimer); 3:97 (Mexican wagon
train); 3:102 (murderer); 3:103,
233 f. (Indians); 3:182 ff.; 34:37 ff.
(pirates); 24:99-100 (Mexican smugglers); cowhides of, 3:37; dreams
connected with, 3:89-90, 188-191 passim; dugouts of, 3:214; that has been
found, 3:11, 33, 43, 46, 48 f., 53, 55 f.,
90, 101, 183, 190, 235; guarded by
various agencies, 3:35 (dragon); 3:36
(rattlesnake); 3:47 (white panther);
3:47 f., 101 (ghost of murdered man);
3:54, 102-103 (dog); 3:58 f. (spirits);
3:102 (bull); 3:56 (giant skeleton);
3:183 (unnamed horror); 24:99
(ghostly riders); hunters of, 3:5
("documentary evidence" furnished
to); 3:10 (charts supplied to by Mexicans); 3:11-12; 32: 57-59 (enthusiasm of); 3:15 (ruins of smelter in
Ilano County, Tex., reported by); 3:
19 (evidence furnished to by early
historians); 3:99 (as preservers of
historical sites); jack- or mule-loads
of, 3:9, 15, 17, 28, 36 f., 56, 91-92, 93,
101, 214-215; 13:259-269; legends, 3:
3-12 (of Texas, sources of); 9:124-129

(in the Southwest, Moorish influence
upon); location of indicated or marked
by various means, 3:10, 18, 23, 28-31,
34, 36, 49, 83, 88, 91, 183; 13:258-269;
26:84-87 (charts, maps, waybills); 3:
28-31, 48; 26:83-87 (rock pens); 3:33-
34 (chain); 3:33, 36, 94 (Knolls or
Knobs); 3:36, 39 f., 51, 59, 75 (rocks);
3:39 f., 74 (*"platas"*); 3:40, 45-46, 59,
182 (fortune-tellers); 3:45, 91; 13:
264; 24:97 (mineral-finding rod or
electronic instruments); 3:46 f., 57-
58, 101-102; 24:101 (lights); 3:47, 58
(white object); 3:51 f., 75, 83, 94, 97,
100, 106, 183, 185; 14:175, 260
(trees); 3:73 ("plat rock"); 3:82
(animals drawn on trees and stones);
3:97 (line of hills); 3:188-189 (Lafitte's ghost); 3:214 (account written
on parchment); 6:18 (ebony tablets);
24:100 (strange animal); 24:102
(stagecoach); 24:129 ("*El Gran
Señor*"); *maletas* filled with, 3:9, 53,
56; robber of, 6:37; sacks of, 3:184;
14:260; signs of, 9:58; sunken, 3:84;
34:37-49; superstitions relating to, 3:
31, 35, 45 ff., 54-59 passim, 101-103;
9:58-59, 124-144 passim; 24:99-100;
that turned to mud, 24:131; that
turned to bumblebees, 3:53-54; vault
of, 3:184-185; wagonloads of, 3:32,
97, 103; see Mines, lost; see Part II,
Section 8, of *Analytical Index.*
Treat, Asher E., 27:33, 63, 77.
Tree: bark on as weather sign, 2:94;
hangman's, 18:146; 29:207; helps man
or children escape danger, 22:107;
25:219; petrified, 18:84; squeezes coy-
ote, 22:29; superstitions about plant-
ing cedar or willow, 13:162; 26:241-
242 (reprint); see names of trees.
Tree cactus, 11:93.
Tree frogs as weather sign, 2:93.
"Trembletoe"; see "William Tremble-
toe."
Trementines, France, 33:125.
Tremiño, Antonio, 9:173-174.
Tres Castillos Mtns., 10:75.
Tresmanos (Indian), 3:16.
Treviño, José, 24:45.
Treviño, Juan J., 31:142.
Treviño, Lino, 24:57-61.
Treviño, Remigio, 8:110.
Treviño, Tomás, 24:52; 26:269.
Treviño, Señora Tomás, 24:52-53.
Treviño Ranch, 17:74.
Trial and court scene (tale), 21:100-101.
Triangle cactus, 11:92.
Trias, Gov., 35:88, 92.
Trick'em; see Trickham.
Trickham, Tex., as place name, 13:50-51,
77.
Trickster(s): with cards, 22:173-176; fig-

Tuttle, George W., 31:44, 51.
"Twa Corbies, The," 25:91, 99 f.; with
music, 14:280-283; see "Three Black
Crows."
"Twa Magicians, The" (cited), 27:44.
"Twa Sisters," with music, 10:133, 141-
144; cited, 25:93, 102; 27:24 (fold-
out), 29, 48, 54, 59, 66 f., 74; see
"Two Sisters."
Twain, Mark, 6:41; 19:64; 20:33, 54-56;
23:207; 25:11, 184, 201; 28:87; 31:35;
32:181; 33:95, 117; 36:75, 79; see
Ram.
" 'Twas a cold, stormy night in the win-
ter," 23:76.
" 'Twas the frogge in the well," with
music, 5:7-8.
" 'Twas a stormy night in winter," with
music, 6:215.
" 'Twas in the town of Oxford," 23:81.
"Twelve Truths of Our Lord," 27:138-
150; 30:220.
Twelvemile Coleto Creek as place name,
32:120.
Twin Creek as place name, 32:120.
Twin culture heroes, 14:114-118; 22:
30 ff.
Twin Mtn. (near Brazos River), 18:100.
Twin Sisters (cannon), 6:139.
"Twinkle, twinkle, said a little star,"
2:43.

Twisters; see Tornadoes.
"Twistification" (cited), 1:36.
"Two, two, and round up four," 1:10.
"Two Brothers, The" (cited), 27:24 (fold-
out), 29, 35 ff., 58-59, 74.
Two Companions (liars), tale of, 10:25-
26; 12:55-57; 18:79-80; 19:36-41.
"Two Little Children," with music, 23:
287-288.
"Two Little Sisters" (cited), 1:36.
"Two niggahs'll draw fo' niggahs," 11:
104.
"Two Orphans, The," with music, 23:
285-286.
"Two sharply pointed stones grind no
flour," 14:152.
"Two Sisters, The," 10:141; cited, 30:31;
see "Twa Sisters."
Two Thieves tale: analysis of its develop-
ment, 22:207-214; see Graveyard.
Two-time loser (dic.), 30:97.
Twomile Stream as place name, 32:120.
Tygart's Valley, 14:160.
Tying in (dic.), 18:203.
Tyler, Thomas H., 25:72.
Tyler, Tex., 18:51, 143.
Tyler County, Tex., 3:85.
Tylor, E. B., 1:80.
Tyman, Walter, 12:152.
Typographical Advertiser, 30:79.
Tzintzontli, 19:51-52.

U 〜

UFO's: their meaning according to Jung,
33:193-194; in Fredericksburg, Tex.,
22:125.
Ugarte, Jacobo, 28:120.
Ugliness, folk similes about, 5:81.
Ugly Boy, 14:108-109; see Poor Boy.
Uharrie Hills, 15:76.
Uhland, Tex., 36:37.
Uhls, Edison, 10:136-168 passim.
Ulloa, Antonio de, 21:109 ff.
Ulster Cycle, 34:73.
Ulysses, 11:61.
"Un bien con mal se paga," 8:191 ff.
"Un día tres de septiembre," with music,
21:13-15.
"Un garbanzo de la libra," 24:125.
*"Un pájaro en la mano vale cien vo-
lando,"* 12:217.
"Un peso vale más que cien consejos,"
24:125.
"Uncle Bud," 5:180.
Uncle Remus, 1:54; 4:44; 5:3; 7:137;
10:10; 11:6-8, 94; 12.101; 14:119,
135; 24:191; 36:80.
"Unconstant Lover," 23:178.
Underground Railroad, 7:82-84; 11:102.

Undergrove, Bets, 18:64.
Underwood, J. P., 3:211.
Underwood, John Curtis, 14:58.
"Uneasy Ghost of Lafitte, The" (poem),
3:185.
"Unfortunate Rake, The," 32:213, 215-
216.
Union County Leader (Clayton, N. M.),
15:108.
Union Creek as place name, 32:126.

United Nations, 22:139.
United States Museum, 18:18.

W ⟿

"What goes over the debbil's back buckles under his belly," 5:137; 13:241.
"What Is Dis," with music, 7:109.
"What the little boy shot at," 5:80.
"What Shall I Do?," 5:142.
"What will the birds do, Mother," with music, 6:222.
"What you gwain to do when the meat gives out, my Baby?," with music, 5:175-177.
Whatley, Tom, 17:23.
Whatley, W. A.: articles, 4:10-17; 15:134-136; 16:227-233; 19:42-56; mentioned, 4:10, 116; 15:176-177; 16:423; 19:202.
Wheat Stream as place name, 32:118.
"Wheel come off the old brass wagon," 1:17.
Wheel for horse-drawn vehicles, shrinking tire of, 34:5-6.
Wheeler, Homer W., 16:105.
Wheeler, Mortimer, 36:43.
Wheeler, Tex., 19:129.
Wheeler County, Tex., 18:4; 21:53; 27:180 f.; 29:155; 30:164; 31:77, 94.
"When battle round each warlike band," 23:77.
"When a boy falls in love," 6:235.
"When this Cruel War Is Over," 23:271.
"When the First Trumpet Sounds," with music, 10:183.
"When first I saw sweet Peggy," with music, 13:253-255.
"When I's Dead an' Gone," 10:61.
"When I Lay My Burden Down," with music, 13:136.
"When I think of the last great round-up," 6:167.
"When I was boun' in trouble," 7:95; 26:173.
"When I was but a girl sixteen," 7:111; 10:149.
"When I was down in Derby's town," 23:230.
"When I was single," 23:210.
"When I was a young man I used to wait," 23:213.
"When I wus boun' in trouble," with music, 7:95-96.
"When de saints of God shall lib," 7:89; 26:169.
"When spring time does come," 2:39.
"When the sun come back," with music, 7:83.
"When they nailed Jesus to the rugged cross," 19:11.
"When a woman's blue," 36:115.
"When Work Is Done this Fall," 6:143.
[Where . . . ; see also Whar . . . .]
"Where cobwebs grow," 13:240.
"Where He Leads Me I Will Follow," 10:155.
Whiffle-pooffle (fabulous beast), 7:40-41.

Whilden, I. P., 29:49.
Whilden, Joe, 29:45-57.
Whilden, Paul, 29:49-50.
Whilden, Zee, 29:53-54.
"While I'm a bold cowboy," 7:177-178.
"While wandering through the woodlands," 6:237.
"Whip Jack, Will, and Tom," 6:67.
Whipporwill lore, 7:26 ff.; 21:78-80; 26:17-18, 283, 287 (reprints).
Whippoween, Katy, 18:78.
Whirlwind(s), 2:97; associated with the Devil, 8:103 ff.; in Navajo tale, 15:142-143.
Whiskey: anecdotes involving, 8:85; 13:90-91; 25:15-16; 31:103; 35:24; cowboys' use of, 22:227; 32:159-160; in remedies, 8:10, 12, 32 f., 52 ff., 84-85; 14:267 f.; 24:33, 39, 43; 30:125-126; 35:16; see *Mataburros*; Moonshine.
Whiskey Creek as place name, 13:42; 32:126.
"Whiskey by the Gallon" (cited), 17:82.
Whiskey Insurrection, 20:10.
Whitaker, Frank, 16:108.
White (veteran of Texas War of Independence), 3:84-85.
White, Berta Mae, 7:122.
White, Gilbert, 2:95; 21:58-59; 25:24; 26:303.
White, I. C., 31:62.
White, J. E., 31:81.
White, Mary, 5:17.
White, Newman I., 7:113; 10:173; 30:217; 36:107 ff.
White, Owen P., 25:80; 26:342.
White, Stewart Edward, 7:44.
White bird as child's soul, 8:103.
White Calf, James, 29:190 ff.
"White Captive, The," 18:2, 4; with music, 18:7-8.
White Comanches (dic.), 19:117 ff.
White Creek (Tex.), 3:38; 26:94; as place name, 32:120.
White Deer, Tex., 36:62 ff.
"White folks are all the time bragging," 5:page 9 of appendix.
"White folks goes to college; niggers to the field," 5:page 9 of appendix.
White-horse case (dic.), 30:95.
White Horse Plains (Colo.), 16:172; 26:106.
"White House Blues, The" (cited), 36:114.
White man: the term as used by Indians, 22:137-138; tricked by coyote, 22:78-79; 26:5-6 (reprint); tricks Indians with whiskey (myth), 21:66; 26:13 (reprint); why he will never reach the sun, 29:190-200.
White Mtns. (N. M.), 12:190.
White Mule Creek as place name, 13:26.

110 ff.
Witchcraft, 1:82-95; 25:195-199, 217-
219; court cases concerning, 25:197;
crows and, 30:255-256; owl bewitchment and, 30:218-225; see Part II,
Section 7, of *Analytical Index*.
Witches, 5:120; 7:132-134; 8:59-60; 9:
52-53, 71; 10:62-70; 12:115-116; 13:
144; 21:70-72; 25:195-199, 217-219;
see Witchcraft; Wizards; see Part II,
Section 7, of *Analytical Index*.
Witching for water, 13:176-181, 233; 28:
162.
"With eager eyes an Indian peered,"
3:145.
"With a ten dollar horse and a forty
dollar saddle," with music, 7:150.
"With Three Thousand Texas Steers,"
6:168-170.
Witt, Leander, 30:215.
"Wittam Miller, The," 23:81.
Wittee Museum (San Antonio, Tex.), 15:
148, 160.
Wittliff, William D.: article, 33:89-99;
mentioned, 33:v, 200.
Witwatersrand, South Africa, 36:147.
Wizards, 9:53-54, 56; 17:113-114; see
Brujos; Conjurers; Witchcraft.
Woden, Tex., 7:124.
Wolcott, Bobby, 34:35.
Wolf(ves), 5:113; 6:32-33; 18:64, 68,
71 ff., 76, 98, 100; 22:30 ff., 76; 25:
220-242; 31:27; girl who ran with,
13:79-85; head, magical, directs In-
dians, 21:72-73; 26:14-16 (reprint);
hunting of, 15:115; 30:196-197; leg-
endary, 15:115; 30:12; as predator on
sheep, 15:114- 116; timber, habits of,
16:155-156; white, 7:62 ff.; see Lobo
wolf; *Loup garou.*
Wolf Creek: Okla., 6:155; Tex., as place
name, 32:121.
Wolf hounds, 15:115.
Wolf Ribs (Indian), 16:164.
Wolfe, Ella Kraus, 30:264.
Wolford, Leah Jackson, 7:8.
Wolford, Louis, 20:44.
Woll, Gen., 6:28.
Woman(en): backwoods, 18:61 ff.; characteristics of established (jest), 32:3-
5; chivalrous attitude toward in the
Southwest, 32:153-154; creation of
and folklore concerning inferiority to
man, 32:176-187; liberation of among
Tarahumara Indians, 14:223; liber-
ation of among Tehuana Indians, 12:
138; married to a stallion, 22:97-100;
presence of aboard ship brings bad
luck, 4:61-62.
Woman in Blue, legend of; see Agreda,
Maria de Jesus.
Womanity (dic.), 18:77.

"Woman's Dance Song," music only, 13:
293.
Womb: protracted cow's, remedy for,
8:49; hemorrhage of, remedy for, 8:
57.
Women folks (dic.), 4:55.
Wonder tales; see Part II, Section 5, of
Analytical Index.
Wonmuck, Mrs. M. G., 31:22.
Wood family (Victoria County, Tex.),
13:300.
Wood, Ben D.: article, 1:55-57.
Wood, Ernest, 29:8.
Wood, G. W., 3:68.
Wood, Grant, 23:145.
Wood, Will, 29:8-9.
Wood, William A., his ranch, 13:300.
Wood Community (Victoria County,
Tex.), 13:300-336 passim.
Wood County, Tex., place name, 31:94.
Wood Hollow Stream as place name, 32:
116.
Wood Island Stream as place name, 32:
119.
Wood rats, their nests, 2:94.
Woodard, Horace, 15:161.
Woodard, Stacy, 15:161.
Woodhull, Frost: articles, 8:9-73; 9:1-14;
12:152-158; 26:254-264 (reprint);
mentioned, 8:6, 175; 9:191; 10:186 f.;
11:107; 12:255; 16:248; 28:17.
Woodpecker: lore concerning, 5:119; 7:
29, 32, 34 ff.; 26:287-288, 300 (re-
prints); pileated, 25:22-23; tales in-
volving, 8:93-95; 9:24.
"Woodpecker, The" (rhyme), 8:93, 95.
Woods (prospector), 13:268.
Woods, "Baldy," 32:151, 160.
Woods, Dee: article, 19:126-133; men-
tioned, 19:204.
Woods, Dever, 19:126.
Woods, James, 9:12.
Woods, M. L., 5:108.
Woodson, "Shorty," 6:80.
Woodson, W. D., 31:49.
Woodville, Tex., 31:3.
Woodward, Cavin, 8:12.
Woodward, Clyde J., 30:184.
Wool, Gen., 35:85.
Woolsey, Verne, 31:67.
Wooten, "Little Dick," 9:34.
Worcester, Mass., 18:63; 28:66.
Words; see Diction.
Work: folk expression about, 13:244;
-swapping on the frontier, 17:29 ff.
Work, John W., 36:108 ff.
Work songs, 6:209-212; 30:180-181; Ne-
gro, 5:154-180; 5: page 12 of appen-
dix; 7:101-102; 11:101-102; 36:117.
"Workingman's Train, The" (cited), 36:
115.
World, holding up the (tale), 12:13-19;
14:32-34; 26:33-34 (reprint).

X ✑

Y ✑

Photo by DAVID LEIBSON

Z

The
FOLKLORE
of
The Southwest
and Northern Mexico

J. CISNEROS

Navajo

Geronimo

Kachina Doll

Turkey Girl

Penitentes

Rattler

Los Pastores

Doña Tules

Llano Estaca

Yucca

Agua Matachines

Billy the Kid

Coronado

Wyatt Earp

Pancho Villa

Judas Hanging

El Paso Salt War

Pecos Bill

Piñata

Lost Canyon

Lost Nigger Gold Mine

The Devil Dancing

Headless Vaquero

Our Lady of Guadalupe